Multi-Asset Investing

A practical guide to modern portfolio management

by Yoram Lustig

HARRIMAN HOUSE LTD

3A Penns Road
Petersfield
Hampshire
GU32 2EW
GREAT BRITAIN

Tel: +44 (0)1730 233870
Email: enquiries@harriman-house.com
Website: www.harriman-house.com

First published in Great Britain in 2013

ISBN: 9780857192516

British Library Cataloguing in Publication Data
A CIP catalogue record for this book can be obtained from the British Library.

 Harriman House

To Mika

eBook edition

As a buyer of the print edition of *Multi-Asset Investing* you can now download the eBook edition free of charge to read on an eBook reader, your smartphone or your computer. Simply go to:

http://ebooks.harriman-house.com/multiassetinvesting

or point your smartphone at the QRC below.

You can then register and download your eBook copy of the book.

www.harriman-house.com

Contents

About the Author

Yoram joined AXA Investment Managers in 2013 as Head of Multi-Asset Investments UK and Deputy Global Head of Multi-Asset Investments. From 2009 to 2012, Yoram was Head of Multi-Asset Funds at Aviva Investors, leading the multi-asset team and managing a range of multi-billion, multi-asset portfolios. From 2002 to 2009 he was head of portfolio construction at Merrill Lynch, responsible for managing multi-asset discretionary portfolios.

Yoram began his career in 1998 as a lawyer, specialising in corporate, financial and commercial law. Yoram was awarded the Chartered Advisor in Philanthropy (CAP) designation in 2007; the Professional Risk Manager (PRM) certification in 2005; the Charted Financial Analyst (CFA) designation in 2004; an MBA from London Business School in 2002; and a law degree from Tel Aviv University in 1997. He is admitted to both the Israel and New York State Bars. He had studied Electrical Engineering for two years in the Technion – Israel Institute of Technology prior to his military service. Yoram is the author of the book Multi-Asset Investing: A practical guide to modern portfolio management (Harriman House, 2013).

Disclaimer

The views and opinions expressed in this book are those of the author in his private capacity and do not necessarily reflect those of any organisation or other person.

Acknowledgements

I have been fortunate to learn from many wise people over the years and I wish to thank them. Peter Stanyer, my first boss at Merrill Lynch, introduced me to investment management. Ben Guyatt and Andrew Keegan, my team members at Merrill. Steve Fedor with whom I have taken the Global Selects journey. My partners in the global philanthropic consulting group Ricardo Ferreira and Roger Matloff. My phenomenal multi-asset fund (MAF) team at Aviva Investors: Justin Onuekwusi, Nick Samouilhan, Gavin Counsell and Andrew Ridgers. Other colleagues at Aviva Investors, including Jonathan Abrahams, Mirko Cardinale, Adrian Jarvis and Jason Josefs. My family, my children Yoav and Yael, and my wife Mika. Whatever you read in this book, the bottom line is that the real objective of everything, including investments, is the welfare of the family and loved ones.

Preface

The objectives of this book

Multi-asset investing is relevant to almost all investors, whether they are private individuals or institutions. This book is intended for private investors, financial advisors, people with investment roles at institutional investment firms, investment managers and anyone who wishes to learn more about multi-asset investing.

The book aims to offer a better understanding of the different aspects of managing multi-asset portfolios. The objectives are to educate, share experiences and knowledge, and encourage investors to look beyond the numbers and investment marketing materials. It is not claimed that this book is comprehensive, as it would require multiple books to definitively cover the topic. Instead, we will move slowly from defining investment objectives, through formulating an investment strategy and the steps of selecting investments, to constructing and managing multi-asset portfolios.

There are plenty of risks along the way, as we do not know what is going to happen in the future. Had I been able to predict the future, I would not have written this book, but rather managed a multibillion hedge fund; I would now be sitting on the beach in Bermuda, drinking a margarita under a coconut tree. But as I cannot predict the future, I have shared with you what I have been learning over more than a decade. While there are many uncertainties, unknowns and risks in investment management, there are ways to properly manage investments, reduce risks and follow guidelines, rooted in common sense and practicality, to increase the probability of meeting clearly defined investment objectives. This is the knowledge that I have included in this book.

Investment management is a science, but not a very scientific one. Economists, economic theories and financial theories explain markets and provide insights into understanding them, but they usually fail in predicting market movements. So mathematical formulas and financial theories are necessary but insufficient – behavioural finance, market psychology, sentiment and emotions also play key roles in investment management. Therefore, it is commonly said that investment management is an *art and a science*. This book uses economic and financial theories as its basis, but takes a practical approach to investment management. Intuition, experience and grey hair all lead to common sense and judgment, which are so critical for success.

This book does include mathematics, technicalities and financial theories. However, I have tried to keep this fairly straightforward, with references to additional materials for readers who wish to learn more. As Leonardo da Vinci elegantly said "simplicity is the ultimate sophistication."[1]

The book's focus is not on multi-asset portfolios whose objective is generating returns to beat a benchmark through selecting securities and financial instruments across different asset classes. The book does not provide insights on *security selection* to beat the market. Such portfolios can be components within a multi-asset portfolio that is linked to the investor objectives. This book does provide insights on *investment selection*. Multi-asset portfolios utilise different investments, some of which include active security selection.

While the book includes original ideas, processes and methodologies, it is based on the work and research of the giants of investing from both academia and practice. As Sir Isaac Newton said, "if I have seen a little further it is by standing on the shoulders of giants". The bottom line is that I have been looking for this book for a long time and since I could not find it, I wrote it myself. I hope that you will find it useful and enjoyable.

Book structure

This book is in four parts that follow the four stages of the multi-asset investment management process:

1. Establishing objectives

2. Setting an investment strategy

3. Implementing a solution

4. Reviewing

At the end of each of these four parts there is a summary of the main points covered, or the bottom line.

All charts, diagrams, tables and analytics were created by the author unless otherwise stated. Where external data was used the sources for this have been given. Most charts, tables and analytics are based on the financial markets in the United States since they offer the most readily available history. However, the book covers global multi-asset investing and is applicable to investors in any country.

Introduction

Multi-asset investing demands a book. A multi-asset approach can provide diversification benefits, enhance risk-adjusted returns and link portfolios[2] with a wide range of investment objectives. The objectives vary, from generating returns or income, through matching liabilities or saving for retirement, to providing for the family. Multi-asset investing can be a solution for all these diverse investment objectives.

When using a multi-asset approach, investors need to consider their assets, liabilities, return objectives, risk appetite, specific circumstances, geographic location and, in the case of individuals, their investor psychology. These factors, together with the current economic and capital market conditions, allow investors to construct multi-asset portfolios to meet their specific investment objectives. This is what this book is all about.

Multi-asset investing has gained popularity in recent years and some have questioned whether it is here to stay or just a passing fad. The fact is that both individual and institutional investors invest in multi-asset portfolios to preserve and/or grow wealth or assets. Multi-asset portfolios are everywhere, they always have been and they are here to stay. Multi-asset portfolios are the past, present and future of investment management and they are certainly not a passing fad, as much as investing itself is not.

What is multi-asset investing?

Multi-asset investing is managing portfolios that include investments in more than a single asset class. There is no definitive definition of an asset class, but broadly it is a group of investments that share similar risk and return characteristics, perform similarly in certain market environments, respond similarly to financial events, and are subject to similar legal and regulatory definitions. Equities, bonds and cash are examples of traditional asset classes.

A relatively simple multi-asset portfolio may invest in equities and bonds in a fixed target allocation; for example, 60% domestic equities and 40% government bonds. Such portfolios are commonly referred to as a *balanced fund*. A complex multi-asset portfolio may invest in a range of globally diversified asset classes, use multiple investment vehicles, managed by different portfolio managers, include strategic and tactical asset allocations, and utilise derivatives, with all activities dynamically managed. This is commonly called a *multi-asset fund*.

A proper multi-asset portfolio is truly diversified across a range of asset classes, asset allocation is dynamically managed to position the portfolio to current market conditions and investment selection covers the full spectrum of investment choices. Multi-asset investing has moved a long way from the traditional, now old fashioned, equity-bond mix. Investors now expect investment solutions tailored to their financial needs, not just portfolios aiming to outperform a market index, such as the S&P 500 or FTSE 100. Beating an index is not part of any investor's real investment needs. Multi-asset investing should be linked to the real investment needs or objectives.

The activities of managing multi-asset portfolios include top-down asset allocation, bottom-up investment selection, portfolio construction to put everything together, and implementation, as well as risk management and performance reporting. These activities are typically more complicated for a multi-asset portfolio than they are for a single asset class, long-only portfolio.

Multi-asset portfolios tend to invest globally rather than solely domestically, as do many single asset class portfolios. Equity portfolios whose investment universe is the S&P 500, FTSE 100 or DAX 30 Index invest in stocks of companies registered in a single country[3] with a single currency. Multi-asset portfolios typically invest across multiple countries and multiple currencies, while they normally have a single base currency. This introduces additional complexities of cross-border investing, across different time zones and currencies.

Multi-asset investing covers many investment disciplines. It is markedly different to managing an active, single asset class portfolio, the objective of which is outperforming an index or a peer group sector. When an equity portfolio manager aims to outperform an index, the main activities are selecting favourable securities, ensuring that the portfolio is different from the benchmark and trying to outperform it within the risk parameters and investment constraints. A multi-asset portfolio manager, however, often focuses on asset allocation and selecting the managers who select securities, rather than the securities themselves.

The benchmark is sometimes a fuzzy composite of a few indices and is not as clearly defined as a published equity index, such as the S&P 500 Index. The risk objectives can combine various parameters and the return objective can be more than outperforming a benchmark. Multi-asset investing is clarifying and stipulating the investment objectives and combining different activities with the aim of meeting these objectives.

Multi-asset portfolios can be large, complex and can cover many asset classes. A single person, as skilled and talented as they may be, normally does not have all the necessary skills to manage such portfolios. Managing multi-asset portfolios often requires a multidisciplinary team approach. It requires a joint effort from portfolio managers, strategists, asset allocators, implementers, risk managers and performance analysts.

An equity portfolio manager directly controls the security selection decisions. While a multi-asset portfolio management team must have the ultimate responsibly and accountability for the entire portfolio, the team may not have direct control over all the investment decisions. Some decisions, such as security selection, may be delegated to other portfolio managers or outsourced to external managers. The multi-asset portfolio manager must have the flexibility to hire and fire underlying portfolio managers. However, the success or failure of a multi-asset portfolio depends on the joint efforts of all parties involved in managing the portfolio.

The list of activities for managing multi-asset portfolios is long and multi-asset investors must prioritise based on the importance of the different elements (judged by contribution to risk and return to the overall portfolio) and the available resources. Asset allocation is one of the most important investment decisions and should be given the appropriate attention since it links portfolios with investors' long-term investment objectives. Security selection, while critical to the overall success of multi-asset portfolios, can be delegated to other portfolio managers, outsourced to external managers and/or accessed through passive investments where and when appropriate. Multi-asset investors must have a robust manager and investment selection process. Success depends on successful investments.

Multi-asset investor types

Most private and institutional investors invest in multi-asset portfolios. An individual's pension plan is probably diversified across a few asset classes, such as equities, bonds and cash (if not, the individual may consider seeking a better financial advisor[4]). Including a residential house, whether it is considered an investment or a home, the individual has exposure to real estate as well. Human capital (future income) is another asset class, which may be considered as part of a portfolio (although it is tricky to do so). Most individuals are, therefore, multi-asset investors.

Private investors are different from institutional investors in many aspects, such as different investment objectives, constraints and psychologies. Emotions play an important role with private investors, in particular since their portfolios are typically their personal wealth and savings, which have been accumulated through hard work or inheritance and will determine their future and that of their families. When the family's welfare is involved, individuals get emotional; and rightly so.

Most institutional investors, such as pension plans, insurance companies, banks, endowments and foundations, are multi-asset investors. They invest money on behalf of their investors or customers. Most institutions have liabilities and a portion of their assets should be managed with the objective of meeting those liabilities:

- A *defined benefit pension plan*[5] needs to pay current and future pension benefits to its beneficiaries.

- An *insurance company* needs to hold sufficient assets to pay insurance claims when they arise and maintain its solvency.

- A *bank* holds a diversified portfolio, including deposits, loans and a messy capital structure, and one of its primary objectives is maintaining adequate capitalisation to weather financial stress.

- An *endowment* manages assets to meet its spending needs in line with its mission.

All these institutional investors typically hold a portfolio consisting of different asset classes with the objective of generating sufficient cash flows to meet current liabilities, while aiming to grow the value of assets (above the rate of inflation) to be able to meet future liabilities. The process of managing assets in line with liabilities is different to managing assets without considering liabilities and requires a different investment strategy. This will be covered later in the book.

Multi-asset investment management process

The multi-asset investment management process has four main stages:

1. Establishing objectives

2. Setting an investment strategy

3. Implementing a solution

4. Reviewing

The process is a never-ending, circular process. After the reviewing stage is completed, the process goes back to the investment objectives as they need to be regularly evaluated and updated, depending on market conditions and investor circumstances.

The multi-asset investment management process

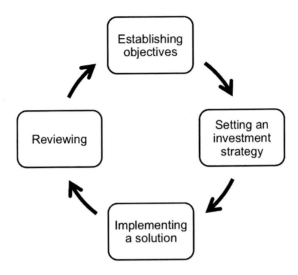

Establishing objectives

We start with the *establishing objectives* stage. The investment objectives define the starting point for planning and setting a portfolio's investment strategy. The objectives describe what the investor wants to achieve (return); what the investor should realistically expect to achieve given the distribution of potential outcomes (risk); and under what constraints the portfolio should be managed.

Portfolios should have a *benchmark*. It can be a *composite benchmark*[6], which sets the portfolio's neutral asset allocations across different asset classes. It is normally determined by a *strategic asset allocation* so the benchmark is aligned with the long-term investment objectives or policy; a *peer group* benchmark if the aim is beating competitors; the cash or inflation rate; an absolute percentage return; or the investment objectives expressed in some other form. Helping investors to formulate and articulate their investment objectives is one of the roles of financial advisors.

The benchmark anchors the portfolio to the investment objectives and constraints and should be aligned with them. The benchmark is used to evaluate the portfolio's performance; decide whether the portfolio is a success or failure; and monitor how it performs relative to the stated investment objectives.

Setting an investment strategy

Once the investment objectives and benchmark are set, the next stage in the multi-asset investment management process is *setting an investment strategy*. Multi-asset portfolios use three primary sources of return and risk:

1. *Strategic asset allocation (SAA)*

2. *Tactical asset allocation (TAA)*

3. *Investment selection*

SAA focuses on the long term (5 to 10 years) while TAA focuses on the short term (3 to 12 months). Investment strategy is the plan for achieving the investment objectives, combining long-term SAA with appropriate TAA short-term adjustments.

Implementing a solution

With the strategy formulated, the next stage is *implementing a solution*. Investment selection focuses on accessing asset classes and generating outperformance (or *alpha*) through security selection. Asset allocation defines how the portfolio is divided across different asset classes. Investment selection fills each asset class with appropriate investments. *Portfolio construction* puts everything together, considering interactions across asset classes. *Risk budgeting* allocates the portfolio's total risk to the three sources of risk and return.

The investment management process provides a framework to guide decisions. The multi-asset investor needs to set an appropriate investment management process for both the overall multi-asset portfolio and each one of the sources of return and risk. For example, the multi-asset investor decides on the universe of asset classes, the frequency of SAA reviews, and the rules for when and how SAA changes are implemented. Decisions under TAA include the way to get exposure to TAA, as well as TAA methodology, investment horizon and implementation (e.g. a derivative overlay, standalone TAA vehicle, trading exchange traded funds (ETFs), trading underlying physical investments, or a combination of all four). For investment selection the multi-asset investor needs to decide on the portfolio construction across all asset classes (e.g. number of investments, split between active and passive management, single-manager or multi-manager, investment styles, and so on).

The *implementing a solution* stage of the investment management process concludes with implementation of all the investment decisions. This step includes portfolio rebalancing, which is critical to keep the risk level of the portfolio in line with its target; cash management; and turning the theoretical target portfolio into a reality.

Reviewing

Once all the decisions are made and implemented the next and final stage of the investment management process is *reviewing*. *Performance attribution* explains how each activity contributed to the overall performance. All investment decisions and their implementation need to be regularly monitored and reviewed. As investor objectives, market conditions and investment performance are dynamic, the entire process must be dynamic as well and adjusted to changes. Simple examples include the need to rebalance asset allocation, manage cash flows, review SAA as *capital market assumptions* (expected return, risk and correlations across asset classes) change, and monitor and potentially change underlying investments as opportunities arise or managers fall out of favour.

This book covers all these stages, activities and elements of managing multi-asset portfolios.

Advantages of multi-asset investing

The advantages of multi-asset investing are numerous. A well-diversified, dynamically managed multi-asset portfolio offers the risk reduction benefits of diversification. Controlled risk taking, holistic *risk management* and disciplined rebalancing help preserve capital over time and link the portfolio to the investor's *risk tolerance*. A multi-asset portfolio can combine different *alpha* sources, such as tactical asset allocation and investment selection, to enhance returns.

Importantly, a multi-asset portfolio can aim to deliver on the comprehensive investment objectives of investors. Only by combining different investments across different asset classes can investors exploit the full investment opportunity set[7].

Professional standards

Asset managers, trustees overseeing portfolios or financial advisors advising customers are likely to have some level of responsibility for multi-asset portfolios and are subject to a set of professional standards and duties. This book aims to provide helpful insights on how to professionally fulfil the duties of a fiduciary.

Prudent Investor Rule

The Prudent Man Rule is based on the 1830 Harvard College v. Amory Massachusetts court decision[8]. The rule directs trustees "to observe how men of prudence, discretion and intelligence manage their own affairs, not in regard to speculation, but in regard to the permanent disposition of their funds, considering the probable income, as well as the probable safety of the capital to be invested".

The Prudent Investor Rule, which was adopted in 1992 in the US Uniform Prudent Investor Act (UPIA), adds to the Prudent Man Rule and sets out guidelines for trustees to follow when investing trust assets. The UPIA made five fundamental alternations in the former criteria for prudent investing[9]:

1. The standard of prudence was applied to any investment as part of the total portfolio, rather than to individual investments.

2. The tradeoff in all investing between risk and return was identified as the fiduciary's central consideration.

3. All categoric restrictions on types of investments were abrogated; the trustee can invest in anything that plays an appropriate role in achieving the risk/return objectives of the trust and that meets the other requirements of prudent investing.

4. The long-familiar requirement that fiduciaries diversify their investments was integrated into the definition of prudent investing.

5. The much criticised former rule of trust law forbidding the trustee to delegate investment and management functions was reversed. Delegation is now permitted, subject to safeguards.

According to the Prudent Investor Rule the total portfolio is considered when determining the prudence of each individual investment (portfolio context). A fiduciary is not held liable for individual investment losses, so long as the investment, at the time of investment, is consistent with the overall portfolio objectives and the risk/return trade-off was considered.

No category or type of investment is deemed inherently imprudent. Instead, suitability to the portfolio's purposes and beneficiaries' needs is considered the determinant. As a result, derivatives, for example, are not considered imprudent per se. However, while the fiduciary is now permitted, even encouraged, to develop greater flexibility in overall portfolio management, speculation and outright risk taking are not sanctioned by the rule either, and they remain subject to criticism and possible liability. Diversification is explicitly required as a duty for prudent fiduciary investing. A fiduciary is permitted to delegate investment management and other functions to third parties.

The requirements and guidance of the Prudent Investor Rule are completely in line with the principles of multi-asset investing. Evaluating investments in portfolio context, considering the risk/return trade-off of investments, diversifying, and selecting professional investment managers are all part of the multi-asset investing principles and process. If a trustee follows these principles, adherence to the Prudent Investor Rule's requirements is likely.

The Retail Distribution Review (RDR)

In June 2006 the UK FSA (Financial Services Authority) created its Retail Distribution Review (RDR) programme with the aim of ensuring that[10]:

1. Consumers are offered a transparent and fair charging system for the advice they receive;

2. Consumers are clear about the service they receive; and

3. Consumers receive advice from highly respected professionals.

If you are an IFA (Independent Financial Advisor) your customers probably invest in multi-asset portfolios or they should do so. Their portfolios should be well diversified, properly managed and match their investment objectives, in particular their risk profile. They need to be clear about the service that they receive and understand the rationale behind each investment decision in their portfolios if so they wish.

Asset allocation, investment selection, risk management and performance reporting are all important components of the service that you need to deliver. Your customers entrust you with their wealth, savings and family's future. One objective of this book is to help you fulfil your responsibility to your customers in a professional way.

The most important trait of any financial advisor or professional investment manager is being a *mensch*. Mensch, a word in Yiddish, means *a person of integrity and honour*[11]. If you take good care of your customers, think about their interests above anything else, and apply professionalism and prudence to managing their investments, you are fulfilling your obligation and you are a person of integrity[12].

PART 1

ESTABLISHING OBJECTIVES

Part 1 starts with the first step in multi-asset investing: establishing objectives.

The goals of Part 1 are to cover investment objectives and also to introduce the topics that will serve as the basis for the rest of the book.

INTRODUCTION

Investment objectives are the starting point. Before formulating and executing an investment strategy the investment objectives must be established. The objectives define the required results, the desired outcomes and the accepted risks. All the following stages of the investment management process and all the investment decisions are guided by the investment objectives and the ultimate goal of meeting them. For example, if the objective is generating current income, choosing an illiquid investment that does not pay income, attractive as it may be, does not fit the objective.

Only when the objectives are clearly defined can an investment strategy be developed to plan how the objectives can be achieved, what risks are permitted and within what constraints the portfolio is to be managed.

The investment strategy for a multi-asset portfolio typically includes:

1. Strategic asset allocation (defining the universe of asset classes and deciding how investments are allocated across them over the long-term).

2. Tactical asset allocation (adjusting the strategic asset allocation to short-term risks and opportunities).

3. Investment selection (choosing appropriate investments under each asset class).

All these activities are intended to help achieve the objectives.

Return objectives and risk objectives

Investment objectives come in different shapes. The two sides of objectives are *return* and *risk*. One of the fundamental principles of investing is that the higher the risk the higher the expected return. Higher target return requires a higher risk level (no pain no gain, no guts no glory). In other words, without accepting enough risk the portfolio will not generate corresponding returns.

Therefore, there are two sets of investment objectives: *return objectives* and *risk objectives*. The two are related and should align. Investors should not expect a certain level of return without accepting the corresponding level of risk.

Investment constraints

Alongside the objectives, there are five categories of *investment constraints*:

1. Investment horizon

2. Liquidity

3. Tax considerations

4. Legal and regulatory factors

5. Special circumstances

The investment objectives and constraints guide investors in planning, constructing, managing and reviewing portfolios. The investment objectives and constraints set the rules of the investment management process. Meeting the investment objectives within the investment constraints should be used as a metric for evaluating success or failure.

Summary

-   Investment objectives are the starting point and must be defined before formulating an investment strategy.

-   Investment objectives describe the *return* that investors aim to achieve, the acceptable *risk* and the *constraints* within which investments should be managed.

-   The fundamental principle of investing is that higher (lower) expected return requires a higher (lower) level of risk.

-   Investment objectives include return objective and risk objectives. Investment constraints include investment horizon, liquidity, tax considerations, legal and regulatory factors and special circumstances.

-   The investment objectives and constraints guide all the investment decisions and form the metric for evaluating success or failure.

1. RETURN OBJECTIVES

The reason for investing is to make money. Generating a return from investments is the objective on which most investors focus. Most investors care less about the specific methods that portfolio managers use and care more about whether the outcome matches their investment objectives and expectations.

The amount of money that investors wish to earn can be articulated in terms of monetary value (such as $100) or percentage (such as 10%). The advantage of using a percentage measure is that it relates the money earned to the money or capital invested[13]. Clearly, earning $1000 on a $1 million portfolio (1% of 1% or 1 basis point, which is 1/10,000) is easier relative to earning $1000 on a $1000 portfolio (100% return). The monetary return is the same but the percentage return is materially different.

Return is also time dependent. It must be linked with a time period over which it should be generated. Earning 10% over one year is very different to earning 10% over three years[14]. Therefore, return should be stated with a clear reference to a time period.

For example, an individual investor has a portfolio of $1 million. The investor requires $50,000 income per annum (5%) and aims to grow the portfolio by $20,000 or 2% per annum above inflation (the expected annual inflation rate is 2%). The required total return to pay income, grow the capital and maintain the portfolio's purchasing power is 9% per annum. This allows for 5% paid out as income, 2% reinvested for capital growth and 2% reinvested for increasing the portfolio's value in line with inflation. This is a simple example of setting a return objective in *total return* terms and linking monetary values with a percentage return and a time period.

Maintaining purchasing power and meeting spending needs are often institutional investors' fundamental long-term investment objectives. Let's take as an example a not-for-profit organisation that exists to promote its mission.

A charity with a mission of fighting cancer, for instance, may sponsor research to find a cure for cancer, support people with cancer and their families, and advertise ways to reduce the risks of contracting the disease. The charity needs funding for its activities from two sources: contributions and return on the charity's portfolio (endowment).

The charity raises contributions, which are added to its portfolio, through fund raising activities. The charity spends a certain amount of money each year to promote its mission (spending rate, which can be stated as a percentage of the portfolio's net asset value). In some countries not-for-profits need to spend a minimum amount each year by law in order to keep their favourable tax status. The aim of the law is preventing not-for-profits from accumulating assets without promoting their mission.

The charity needs to balance promoting its mission in the present and in the future (some organisations have a finite life, but others need to support a mission in perpetuity). Balancing current and future spending is required to ensure that assets are not completely depleted due to excessive spending at present at the expense of future generations.[15] James Tobin wrote that "the trustees of endowed institutions are the guardians of the future against the claims of the present. Their task in managing the endowment is to preserve equity among generations"[16]. Therefore, maintaining the purchasing power of the portfolio and aiming to grow it in real terms (above inflation) is important, in particular when the investment horizon is long.

The total return objective of a not-for-profit is calculated using the formula:

Required Total Return = Spending Rate + Inflation + Real Return − Contributions + Expenses

For example, the total return objective can be 5% (spending rate) + 2.5% (inflation) + 2.5% (real growth) - 3% (contributions as a percentage of the portfolio's value) + 1% (expenses) = 8%.

The portfolio needs to generate an average target return of 8% per annum. In some years the return may be higher and in others lower. In this example the charity needs equity-like returns and must take corresponding investment risk.

Not all investors have specific return objectives in mind. Investors may just wish to grow their portfolio without specific cash outflow needs or a required return. For example, an individual saving for retirement aims to accumulate as much in assets as possible. The objectives are maintaining the purchasing power of investments, growing their real value and avoiding losses as much as possible. This individual focuses on long-term accumulation of assets (capital preservation and growth) without thinking of a long-term specific target return. The objective focuses more on risk than on a specific return since the main concern is avoiding risks that may materially reduce the portfolio's value, preventing a sustainable source of income after retirement to maintain a minimum standard of living.

Caution is needed, however, when deriving investment objectives by assessing the willingness to take risk, as this may be misleading. Investors may be greatly affected by emotions of recent events, such as the fear of a bear market or the greed of a bull market. Their real risk aversion may thus be distorted.

Investors should try to project the annual withdrawals from the portfolio, the required minimum portfolio value (e.g. capital requirements for an insurance company or a bank) and derive the required return. They should evaluate what happens if the objectives are not met. This is the first step of assessing investment risk. The risk of not meeting the required cash flows and portfolio's value levels should be minimised. Investors need to think of contingency plans (such as repositioning the portfolio or changing the investment objectives) for if and when the portfolio is not on track to meet its objectives.

Total return versus income

Total return and income are two different ways of thinking about return objectives. Income includes payments in the form of interest on bonds, dividends on equities and rent on property. Total return includes appreciation in the value of investments (capital gains) as well as the reinvestment of income. Income is often stated as yield, which is income as a percentage of investment price (e.g. 10% yield means an income of $100 from a $1000 investment, or 5% dividend yield means that a stock priced at $100 pays $5 in annual dividends).

Some investors require income from their portfolio. For example, retired investors may focus on generating income to supplement retirement benefits or as a sole source of income. On the other hand, an employed investor, who earns a regular salary, may wish to focus more on the portfolio's capital appreciation since regular income from the portfolio is not required.

When investors are more focused on capital appreciation, interest and dividends should be reinvested to generate additional returns in the future. When income is removed from a portfolio it depletes its assets and potential future returns are diminished. When income is reinvested, future growth potential is higher. When the return on reinvested income is not as high as expected (e.g. due to falling interest rates) investors face reinvestment risk and total return may disappoint.

Over long time periods, the difference between price appreciation (excluding reinvestment of income) and total return (including reinvestment of income) may be significant. It is important, for example, to use total return indices when comparing portfolio returns with those of benchmarks[17].

Figure 1.1 compares the cumulative price appreciation and total return of the S&P 500 Index from January 2000 to June 2012. The chart uses a log scale so a percentage return has the same impact irrespective of its position on the y-axis. As can be seen, the difference is material and becomes more so as the investment horizon gets longer. Total return over the period is 16.9% and price appreciation is -7.3%, a difference of 24.2% due to reinvestment of dividends. Dividends were the main driver of equity returns over the last decade.

Figure 1.1 – cumulative price appreciation and total returns of the S&P 500 Index[18], January 2000 to June 2012

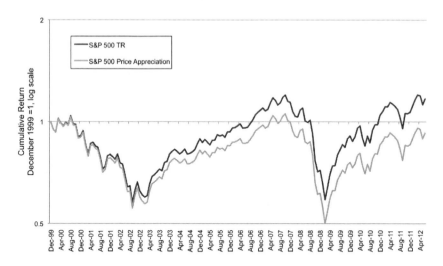

Source: Bloomberg, S&P 500.

Portfolios can generate income not sourced from interest or dividends, but rather from selling or liquidating some assets and paying the proceeds as income. There are some differences, however, between generating income via interest and dividends, and liquidating assets; most notably taxation and transaction costs. Liquidating assets may attract capital gains tax (CGT), which may differ from the tax rate on interest and dividends (it could be higher or lower). Liquidating assets may involve transaction costs. For example, selling real estate may be a costly and long process. When relying on liquidating assets liquidity must be considered as selling certain investments may take time and involve material costs.

Cultural and economic conditions may have an impact on investors' tendency to focus on income or total returns. Investors in Japan, for example, often focus on a portfolio's income because of the low interest rates on deposits and savings in Japan. The aging population, which requires income generation in retirement, and the diminished ability of the working force to support the retired population are also factors in this – such investors are less focused on capital preservation and more on high income. Another example is an endowment, focused on income to pay for ongoing projects and expenses to promote its mission.

Unless income is an explicit objective, return objectives should be expressed in total returns.

Desired versus required return

The distinction between a desired and required return depends on the specific needs and circumstances of each investor. A *desired return* is nice to have, but not a must. It is an aspiration, not a necessity. For example, achieving a return for buying a fancy yacht may be desired, but not required (unless the yacht is required for a skipper's livelihood). Another example is a desire to achieve a return that places a portfolio manager in the top quartile among peers, while a place above median would be sufficient for the health of the portfolio manager's business.

A *required return*, as its name implies, is necessary to achieve. Not achieving it would have an adverse impact on the well-being of private investors or severe business consequences for institutional investors. For example, achieving a return to make a payment on a mortgage is required, not only desired, as missing the payment may lead to foreclosure of the residential home. A return that places a portfolio manager above the median of the peer group may be required to keep the portfolio manager in business. An insurance company must be able to meet payments on insurance claims. This is the reason that regulators impose strict rules for capital adequacy for organisations such as insurance companies, pension plans and banks; to reduce their insolvency risk. Meeting these capital requirements is required for survival, not only desired.

When setting investment objectives required and desired returns should be clearly distinguished. Every effort should be made to achieve required returns. This may mean purchasing bonds whose maturity and principle match expected cash outflows (e.g. a $10,000 mortgage repayment in a year's time can be met by purchasing a one year maturity bond with a $10,000 principle) or assuming a risk level to materially increase the likelihood of meeting required return objectives. On the other hand, excessive risk taking to meet desired returns should be avoided, in particular if it reduces the probability of meeting required returns.

Absolute versus relative return

Return objectives can be set in either absolute or relative terms. *Absolute* return can be a stated percentage return per time period (target return) either without a reference to any variable rate (e.g. 5% per annum) or with a reference to a variable rate, such as cash or inflation (e.g. 5% above LIBOR[19] per annum). The latter is often known as a *cash-plus* or *inflation-plus* objective.

A return objective in *relative* terms is a goal to outperform an agreed benchmark. This type of return objective can be stated as a percentage return per time period over an agreed benchmark (e.g. 3% per annum above the S&P 500 Index or FTSE 100 Index). Most actively-managed, long-only[20] portfolios have a relative return objective.

The choice between absolute and relative return is critical. It determines the risk level of the portfolio, its shape, the behaviour of the portfolio manager and investment results.

The term *absolute* return may be confusing. Sometimes it is interpreted as a promise to generate a positive return (i.e. avoiding negative returns) year after year, but at other times it refers to a target total return objective that is not relative to any benchmark (e.g. 5% per annum over a rolling three years). In this second case negative returns in some years should be expected and the aim is to generate the target absolute return over the investment horizon. Instead of absolute return this second approach should be labelled *irrelative return*. These different ways of thinking about absolute return objectives may be misleading and the difference between positive and a target total return must be clarified.

A cash-plus or inflation-plus absolute return portfolio often needs to assume substantial levels of risk to achieve its objectives. For example, when the cash rate is 4% and the return target is 4% above it after fees, the portfolio is targeting 8% net of fees (i.e. 9% or 10% gross of fees). This return is similar to that of equities and the portfolio needs to assume equity-like risk to have a chance of meeting its target return. This portfolio is likely to have years of negative returns. Investors who expect this absolute return portfolio to deliver a positive return are bound to eventually be disappointed and possibly pursue legal action for the portfolio being mis-sold as low risk with a guaranteed positive return. Clarifying the return objectives and risk level of such a portfolio from the outset is crucial.

During the 2008 credit crunch and financial crisis, for example, the value of many investments, such as equities, corporate bonds, hedge funds and commodities, substantially fell. Many absolute return portfolios delivered large negative returns, ending up with many very disappointed investors. When most asset classes fall together, multi-asset, diversified, absolute return portfolios normally fall as well.

In relative return space there are two sets of risk: absolute and relative. Either increasing or decreasing absolute risk (i.e. risk without a reference to a benchmark) may increase relative risk (i.e. risk with reference to a benchmark). For example, changing the asset allocation to 60% equities and 40% bonds, when the benchmark is 50% equities and 50% bonds, increases both absolute and relative risk (the higher allocation to equities increases absolute risk and the portfolio's asset allocation does not match that of the benchmark, hence higher relative risk). Conversely, changing the asset allocation to 40% equities and 60% bonds reduces absolute risk but still increases relative risk compared to the benchmark allocation of 50% equities and 50% bonds.

In absolute return space, on the other hand, the portfolio is *benchmark agnostic* and relative risk to a benchmark is irrelevant. Reducing absolute risk is a risk reduction exercise since relative risk is not a consideration. However, low risk level may result in *regret risk* or *opportunity cost* if markets rally and the portfolio does not participate as much as it would have done with an appropriate risk level. Not taking enough risk is a risk in itself.

Portfolios with a relative return objective should have a benchmark as a starting point, anchor and constraint, as well as for performance evaluation. Portfolios with an absolute return objective have no benchmark to constrain them (unconstrained portfolio). The shape of a relative return portfolio is defined by its benchmark. The risk of a relative portfolio should be set relative to its benchmark (i.e. relative risk) and the portfolio normally has broadly similar risk characteristics to those of its benchmark. The portfolio's relative risk level sets the allowed deviations from the benchmark.

There are advantages and disadvantages to both constrained (relative return) and unconstrained (absolute return) approaches (most decisions in investment management have advantages and disadvantages). Unconstrained portfolios allow more flexibility to portfolio managers, but normally have loose risk controls. Constrained portfolios, on the other hand, are tied to a benchmark and normally have tight risk controls. For example, a corporate bond portfolio with a relative return objective can have high exposure to financials[21] due to their high exposure in the benchmark. An absolute return portfolio can avoid such a concentrated exposure to financials since it does not need to follow the benchmark as closely as the constrained portfolio does.

Skilled portfolio managers should be able to deliver better investment results from unconstrained portfolios. However, unskilled managers may take excessive risks in unconstrained portfolios, causing damage. Some institutional investors must put constraints on their portfolios to meet legal obligations (e.g. limit holdings in certain risky assets). The choice depends on the investor's objectives and level of trust in the manager.

The investment process and decisions of absolute return portfolios with the goal of positive returns are different from those of relative return portfolios. Absolute return portfolios need to protect the downside and hedge the risks of falling markets. These portfolios should use short selling, derivatives or high allocations to cash to try to generate positive returns even when markets are falling, independently of market conditions. The focus is on *capital preservation*.

Relative return portfolios, on the other hand, normally have limitations on shorting, use of derivatives and maximum levels of cash. The portfolio manager should maintain limited deviations from the benchmark while trying to outperform it or meet the return objectives. If a manager in relative space has concerns that markets are to fall, moving large portions to cash to preserve capital may not be an option since it may materially increase relative risk, causing a breach of relative risk objectives.

The decision on whether to use relative or absolute objectives, therefore, has an impact on the behaviour of portfolio managers. Managers seeking relative returns will think twice before reducing the portfolio's absolute risk in falling markets or during weakening economic conditions because of the concern of underperforming the benchmark. In contrast, managers seeking absolute returns may be less hesitant to take risk off the table during times of weakening investment prospects to protect the portfolio's downside. These managers are less concerned about the portfolio's relative return and have more freedom to position the portfolio in a way that should protect the investors' money.

Inflation

For investors with a long investment horizon a fundamental objective is maintaining or increasing their assets' purchasing power[22]. Central to this objective is keeping a check on inflation, as inflation erodes purchasing power over time. For instance, $100 today will not buy the same amount of goods and services in a year's time because of the effects of inflation. With an annual inflation rate of 2%, $100 will be worth only $98 after a year. After 10 years, with a 2% inflation rate per annum, $100 will be worth $82[23]. This $100 portfolio has lost 18% from its purchasing power in 10 years. Inflation can have devastating effects on wealth over long time periods, in particular when inflation is high and even worse during hyperinflation. Therefore, return objectives should explicitly distinguish between *real* (after taking account of inflation) and *nominal* (before taking account of inflation) returns.

Figure 1.2 shows the cumulative total return of US 10-year Treasury bonds from January 1970 to June 2012 in nominal terms and adjusted for US inflation (real terms). The chart vividly shows the perils of inflation. While in nominal terms bonds have returned 8.5% per annum, the return was only 4.0% per annum in real terms.

Figure 1.2 – cumulative nominal and real total returns of US 10-year Treasury bonds[24], January 1970 to June 2012

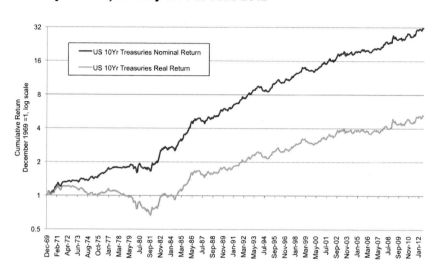

Source: Global Financial Data, USA 10-year Government Bond Total Return Index, US inflation.

Since inflation is an unknown at the outset of managing the portfolio or at the beginning of the performance measurement period, real return includes a variable element (e.g. real return of 5% may mean a total return of 7% when inflation is 2% or 10% when inflation jumps to 5%). Indeed, many absolute return portfolios state their return objective as a percentage return above inflation, instead of cash. This return objective aims to increase the portfolio's purchasing power and grow assets in real terms. Some asset classes should keep up with inflation (real assets such as inflation-linked bonds and real estate). Relative return objectives with respect to a benchmark including such asset classes have a real return element (i.e. inflation hedge).

Nominal return is not adjusted to inflation and already includes inflation in it (e.g. 5% nominal return includes 2% inflation rate and 3% real return). Nominal return objectives may turn out to be a negative real return. For example, a nominal return objective of 4% per annum, when the realised inflation at the end of the measuring period was 5%, results in -1%[25] real return. While the portfolio met its nominal return objectives, the realised return has not even maintained the portfolio's purchasing power.

This example demonstrates the importance of setting up return objectives to reflect the investor's true needs. Investors should think carefully about whether meeting the investment objectives will indeed satisfy their requirements from the portfolio, in particular beating inflation. To do so, investors should assume a sufficient risk level so the expected return would be likely to beat realised inflation, on average. Keeping the portfolio in cash is unlikely to beat inflation.

Indeed inflation is one of the motivations for investing and not holding cash. Investors should consider including real assets, which are positively correlated with inflation, to protect or hedge the portfolio against inflation.

Figure 1.3 shows the cumulative nominal total return of cash (US Treasury bills) from January 1970 to June 2012, as well as cash's inflation adjusted real returns. A stable return of 5.5% per annum has dropped to a measly return of 1.1% per annum when inflation is considered. Nothing more vividly illustrates the impact of inflation.

Figure 1.3 – cumulative nominal and real total returns of US Treasury Bills[26], January 1970 to June 2012

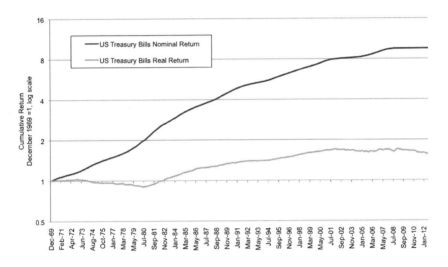

Source: Global Financial Data, USA Total Return T-Bill Index, US inflation.

Fees and costs

An important dimension of returns is fees and costs. When a portfolio manager is hired to professionally manage a portfolio, fees are normally paid to compensate the manager for the investment management services. Fees can range from a few basis points for a passive portfolio tracking a developed equity market (e.g. 5 basis points per annum) to a couple of percentage points for a hedge fund (e.g. 2% per annum). Upfront fees on some retail funds can be as high as 5% (i.e. for every $100 the investor has $95 invested).

Investment management involves other costs such as transaction costs, administration costs, custody costs and so on. Some of these costs depend on the level of portfolio activity or turnover (e.g. transaction costs of trading), others are *ad valorem* and depend on assets under management (e.g. 2% per annum of the portfolio's net asset value or *NAV*), some are linked to performance (e.g. 20% of the excess return over a benchmark or agreed minimum return) and some funds use a combination of these. For instance, many hedge funds use a 2/20 fee structure, meaning 2% asset-based fee and 20% performance fee. Some costs are variable while others are fixed.

The measure of the total fees and costs of running a fund is the *Total Expense Ratio* (TER). The TER should reflect all the expenses, including fees (annual management charge or *AMC*) and costs (e.g. administration, depositary and custodian costs). However, TERs sometimes do not include all the fees (e.g. performance fee) and costs (e.g. transaction costs) and must be carefully scrutinised. Investors should ask portfolio managers whether there are any additional costs that the TER excludes.

Over recent decades the investment management industry has shifted away from a commission-based compensation linked to trading activity to a fee linked to assets under management (AUM). Asset-based fees should be a disincentive to portfolio managers to *churn* portfolios or increase their turnover to generate higher trading commissions (and consequently higher transaction costs) without necessarily benefiting investors[27]. Actively-managed portfolios are expected to have a turnover to add value via changing the portfolio[28]. However, turnover should be in line with the investment management process and objectives, and not excessive. High relative return objectives may require higher turnover than that of lower return objectives, all else being equal (depending on the investment style or strategy).

Investors care about final returns, after fees and costs; this is the net return. A reduction in fees and costs can be a riskless enhancement to net performance and a clear benefit to investors. Nevertheless, reducing fees may be risky if it compromises the quality of the portfolio manager by hiring a less skilled manager (*you pay peanuts you get monkeys*). Negotiating fees, keeping an eye on portfolio turnover and drafting an Investment Management Agreement (IMA) that correctly incentivises portfolio managers to reduce costs are a few of the ways to enhance investment results without assuming additional investment risk.

Compensation structures for managers

Compensation structures influence the motivation and incentives of portfolio managers. One aspect is *principal-agent* issues. In law, an agency relationship is one in which a person (the principal) hires another person (the agent) to perform a task. Because the principal and agent have different preferences or objectives for unobservable actions (e.g. efforts), there is a fundamental conflict that does not arise in the standard economic competitive model, in which all conflicts are internalised through the price system[29].

Professional portfolio managers (agents) manage investments for investors (principals), who delegate to the portfolio managers the authority and responsibility for managing the investments and risks. Investors expect that their preferences will be reflected in the portfolio managers' decisions. The two difficulties are that portfolio managers may not know the investors' preferences and the preferences of portfolio managers may be different from those of the investors.

The first difficulty is relatively readily tackled through clearly defining the investment objectives or the preferences. The second difficulty, however, is the crux of the principal-agent issue as the interests of the principal (the investors) and the agent (the portfolio managers) may be misaligned. Investors must design a compensation structure that rewards managers for acting in line with the investors' preferences and penalises managers for acting contrary to those preferences.

The essence of the principal-agent problem arises when not only the interests are misaligned, but also when there is incomplete and asymmetric information. Under these circumstances the principal cannot properly monitor the agent's behaviour. Designing a suitable compensation structure then becomes more challenging. For example, measuring the outcomes of investment management activities may be difficult and uncertain. Hence, the outcomes may not reflect the agent's efforts. Rewarding performance may reward luck and not skill.

Performance-related fees

While a performance-based fee aims to align the interests of investors and portfolio managers by rewarding managers for outperformance, this fee structure may have an adverse effect on the managers' behaviour and lead managers to take inappropriate risks. Managers essentially have a *put option* and a long position on the AUM (i.e. limited downside with uncapped upside potential). If a manager outperforms there is a reward (fee). If a manager underperforms the loss is limited; potentially the manager is terminated or fired by the investor. Within investment management firms, portfolio managers should receive a bonus when they meet outperformance targets. When there is a severe underperformance they may lose their job, without a claw back on previous bonuses. The downside for the manager is limited to employment and reputation.

When a portfolio continuously underperforms, termination of the portfolio manager is likely. However, if the manager outperforms strongly, by taking higher risks, a turnaround in performance may occur, the manager may still get the portfolio back to positive territory and gain a performance fee. During times of underperformance managers may be incentivised to take more risks (they have almost nothing to lose) to increase the chances of gaining performance-based fees once more. On the other hand, if the portfolio has a good performance and year-end is getting closer, the manager is incentivised to reduce risk, not risking the outperformance, to finish the year ahead of benchmark and earn a performance fee. These portfolio manager's behaviours are misaligned with investor's interests.

Hedge funds commonly use a *high watermark*. This means that performance fees are paid only if the portfolio's NAV is above its peak (i.e. historic maximum NAV). The aim is to ensure that managers do not get performance fees for poor performance. If the portfolio falls and then recovers, but the recovery does not bring the portfolio back above previous peaks, performance fees are not paid. Prolonged and severe underperformance may incline managers to close funds and open new ones with a new watermark since they know that it can take years to get the old funds back above their peaks and gain performance fees again.

Performance fees versus asset-based fees

Performance-based fees are designed to motivate portfolio managers to outperform since outperformance is rewarded. However, as managers accumulate more assets within their portfolios their hunger to generate outperformance diminishes since the asset-based fee increases. If the asset-based fee is attractive enough, managers will be motivated to accumulate more assets, rather than generating more outperformance. In many instances, accumulating assets is easier for managers with a successful track record than continuing to generate attractive returns.

Another angle of large AUM is that more assets impact the ability to capitalise on investment opportunities as the portfolio reaches its capacity, in particular when it invests in illiquid investments. The amount of capital that can be invested in some investment opportunities, such as small capitalisation stocks and *arbitrage*[30] trades, is limited (too much money chasing too few investments). Therefore, in some cases it is easier to increase the AUM of very large portfolios than to generate outperformance. Portfolios are often closed to new investments when capacity is reached to continue generating outperformance and protecting investors' interests. Asset-based and performance-based fees should balance to ensure the motivation of managers is to make investment decisions with the interests of investors in mind.

An ideal compensation structure is based on a fee adjusted for the risk taken. However, this is challenging to stipulate in an agreement and difficult to measure.

Performance objectives and fee levels

Usually, agreed performance objectives with portfolio managers are set net of fees. For example, outperforming a benchmark by 2% per annum net of 2% management fees translates to a 4% outperformance target gross of fees. One of the reasons for hiring an active manager is beating a benchmark after fees. The fees are the *hurdle rate* that the portfolio must pass. Otherwise, a relatively inexpensive passive portfolio can be used, reducing fees, eliminating the potential for outperformance, as well as reducing the risk of underperformance.

Passive portfolios are bound to underperform the benchmark after fees, although activities such as *securities lending* can enhance returns (and add certain risks). The proliferation of passive investments provides a choice between active and passive investments in most asset classes, except for some investments such as direct real estate, private equity and hedge funds, where passive choices are unavailable or very limited, or manager skill is a factor justifying the investment. Therefore, net of fees investment objectives are sensible as active managers are required to generate sufficient returns to cover fees and generate outperformance.

Fee level has a material impact on investment results, in particular over the long term. Figure 1.4 shows the effects of a fixed fee of 50 basis points and 1% per annum on the performance of the S&P 500 Index from January 2000 to June 2012. Over this time period 50 basis points per annum have accumulated to a total cost of 7.1% and 1.0% per annum to a total cost of 13.7%. Without fees the total return of the index was 16.9%, with a 50 basis points annual fee the total return dropped to 9.8% and with a 1% annual fee the total return was only 3.2%. Even small fees have a large impact when compounded over the years. It is claimed that Albert Einstein once described compounded interest – of which these compound fees are an example – as "the most powerful force in the universe".

Figure 1.4 – cumulative total returns of the S&P 500 Index without fees and with 50bp and 1% fee per annum, January 2000 to June 2012

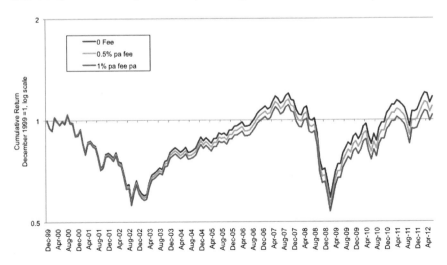

Source: Bloomberg, S&P 500.

Taxes

Taxes are a subgroup of costs. As final investment returns are hit by fees and costs, so they are hit by taxes where applicable. As the famous old saying of Benjamin Franklin goes "in this world nothing can be said to be certain, except death and taxes".

Some portfolios are more tax efficient than others. *Buy and hold* portfolios, holding positions without selling them and consequently not realising capital gains, may be more tax efficient than actively-managed portfolios, buying and selling positions and potentially realising capital gain taxes (CGT). On the other hand, actively-managed portfolios may sell investments at a loss to benefit from loss carry forward to offset CGT liabilities (tax gain/loss harvesting). Investors should use tax-minimising investment strategies when possible.

Tax efficient investments offer more attractive after-tax returns. For example, in the United States local authorities issue municipal bonds. US persons[31] who invest in these bonds are often exempt from federal income tax and income tax of the state by which the bonds are issued. To compare the interest on municipal bonds with that of taxable bonds, which are issued by governments or corporations, the following adjustment is needed:

$$r_m = r_t(1-tax)$$

where r_m is the interest rate of the municipal bond; r_t is the interest rate of an equivalent (same coupon rate and maturity) taxable bond; and tax is the income tax rate on the interest from the taxable bond.

Assuming $r_t = 10\%$ and the tax rate is 30% then a municipal bond needs to have an interest rate of 7%[32] to pay an equivalent interest as that of the taxable bond (all else being equal, such as creditworthiness and liquidity). These bonds demonstrate the impact that taxes or lack thereof can have on final investment results.

All investors should aim to legally minimise their tax bill. This is another way, alongside reducing fees and costs, of enhancing returns without assuming additional investment risk. When formulating investment objectives, investors need to consider after-tax returns and design portfolios to minimise tax liabilities to enhance net of tax returns.

Some investors are taxable (e.g. private investors) and some are tax exempt (e.g. not-for-profit organisations, pension plans and trusts). Taxable investors can often use tax efficient wrappers, such as a retirement savings account, such as 401(k) in the United States, pension plans and Individual Saving Accounts (ISA) in the United Kingdom. Offshore banking[33] and tax avoidance schemes are other ways of minimising investment tax liabilities.

Tax exempt investors do not need to consider taxes, but do need to be careful and manage their investments and business so their favourable tax status is maintained. Taxable investors should consider holding only eligible investments in a tax efficient wrapper and utilising tax minimising strategies, or otherwise be prepared to pay full taxes on their investments.

Return objectives in the presence of liabilities

For pension funds, insurance companies and banks, establishing return objectives has an additional aspect since these investors have a stream of liabilities that must be funded. Usually such organisations use pension consultants or actuaries to determine their required returns as part of an asset liability management (ALM) modelling. ALM models the institution's liabilities based on a set of assumptions and determines the portfolio's required return and risk to match the liabilities and potentially grow the portfolio. ALM needs to account for the institution's liability profile and various risks, such as interest rate risk, inflation risk, credit risk, market risk and liquidity risk, as well as their interrelationships.

The basic idea behind ALM is minimising the mismatch between assets and liabilities, or *surplus volatility*. Surplus is the difference between the value of assets and the value of liabilities. Surplus volatility is the *tracking error*, or relative risk, between assets and liabilities. The objective is to immunise the portfolio against changes in interest rates and inflation. There is a strong relationship between the level of interest rates and the *Net Present Value* (*NPV*) of liabilities. For example, if the duration of the liabilities is 20 years and their NPV is $100 million, then it is expected that for every 1% decrease in interest rates the NPV of liabilities will rise by approximately 20% or $20 million. ALM aims to mitigate this risk by matching the duration of assets that are held to match liabilities with the duration of liabilities. The goal is keeping the value of a portion of the portfolio in line with the value of liabilities.

Return range

While not common, return objectives can be expressed as a range of target returns. For example, cash plus 2% to 5%. The advantage of a range, instead of a single return target, is that it allows for investors to target any point within the range based on market conditions and outlook. When the investor sees ample opportunities to generate returns, higher returns will be targeted. When the investor sees fewer opportunities or when risk level is elevated or uncertainty is high, the low end of the range is targeted. The range does not force the investor to take the same level of risk under all market conditions.

Summary

- Generating returns is the objective of investing.

- Return objectives should be defined in percentage terms of the portfolio value, with a time period over which they should be measured and met and preferably in total returns, unless income is a specific objective.

- Investors should project required cash withdrawals, and target real growth rate and expected inflation to derive the required return.

- Not all investors have a specific target return (e.g. individuals saving for retirement). The focus in this case should be on long-term risk (e.g. inflation risk and market risk).

- Price appreciation excludes reinvestment of income. Total return includes reinvestment of income (e.g. interest and dividends). Total return benchmarks should be used to evaluate portfolios.

- Desired and required returns should be distinguished. Portfolios should be designed to meet required returns. Desired returns are nice to have, but not a must.

- The choice between absolute or relative return objectives has an impact on risk, the portfolio's shape, the portfolio manager's behaviour and results.

- Absolute return portfolios are normally unconstrained while relative return portfolios are constrained as they are anchored to their benchmark. The choice between absolute and relative depends on the investment objectives and the portfolio manager's skill.

- A fundamental objective of every portfolio, if the investment horizon is long, is maintaining the purchasing power and keeping up with inflation.

- Fees, costs and taxes materially impact final returns and must be considered when defining return objectives and designing portfolios.

- Fee structure (asset or performance based) has an impact on the alignment of interests between investors and portfolio managers (agent-principal problem) and the incentives and risk taking of managers.

- Two of the ways to enhance returns without increasing investment risk are reducing fees and costs and minimising taxes.

- The presence of liabilities changes the way investors should think about return objectives. Return objectives should match the liabilities.

- Each investor has unique needs to which return objectives should be tailored. One size does not fit all.

2. BENCHMARKS

Setting a benchmark

Return objectives must be linked to the investor goals and liabilities. Setting a benchmark closely reflecting the goals and liabilities (i.e. the investment policy) and then managing the portfolio relative to this benchmark links the portfolio to the investment objectives and allows the evaluation and monitoring of investment results. The portfolio objectives can be stated as an outperformance target and a relative risk (*tracking error*) with respect of the benchmark, linking the portfolio to the benchmark, and consequently to the investor goals and liabilities.

When the investment objectives are relative the portfolio return is compared to that of an index or a basket of indices (composite benchmark). When the objectives are absolute with a reference to cash or the inflation rate, this rate is compared with portfolio return. When the investment objective is an absolute target return the benchmark is that target return (e.g. 5% per annum). In this case portfolio return above 5% is a success while portfolio return below 5% has missed the target. The benchmark should always represent the portfolio's investment objectives.

If a portfolio returns 10% and its benchmark 8%, the portfolio has outperformed by 2%. Whether this result is good or not depends on the objectives (if the outperformance target was 5% this is not a good result). If a portfolio returns -10% and its benchmark -20%, the portfolio has outperformed by 10%. This can be a very good result, but the return is still negative, causing disappointment. Assessing relative returns should be aligned to the investment objectives and investor expectations.

Even for portfolios without a benchmark investors should be interested in how other investments or asset classes performed. For example, an absolute return portfolio returning 4% is a good result when equity markets returned -15% and cash returned 1%. However, 4% is not a good result when equity markets returned 15% and cash returned 5%. These are unofficial benchmarks to gauge the *opportunity cost* of investing in the absolute return portfolio. Investors could have left the money in cash or invested in equity markets as these were the other readily available opportunities and the returns from these assets are the opportunity cost or returns that could have been achieved elsewhere.

An appropriate benchmark for an active portfolio manager is the portfolio that the manager would hold in the absence of any information or insights about the future performance of the securities in the investment universe[34]. In other words, the benchmark represents the portfolio's *neutral* positioning and lacking a good reason the portfolio should not deviate from its benchmark holdings.

Benchmarks can define the portfolio's investment universe. Such a benchmark can be a passive index, like the S&P 500, FTSE 100 or MSCI Europe Index. The portfolio manager selects a limited number of securities from the benchmark's constituencies (not all of them, otherwise the portfolio closely replicates the benchmark and the potential for outperformance is small), securities outside of the benchmark (*out-of-benchmark*) if the portfolio's mandate permits it and security weightings. Alternatively, the benchmark can represent a peer group of other portfolios with similar characteristics to those of the portfolio. In this case the benchmark is not a passive index, but rather the median or average performance of other similar portfolios, some of which are actively managed. The objective here is to do better than the average of the peers or the competition.

Portfolios investing in a single asset class, such as equities, can choose an appropriate published index as a benchmark. For example, portfolios investing in UK equities can use the FTSE All Share or MSCI UK Index as a benchmark. Portfolios investing in US equities can use as benchmark the S&P 500 Index (if the universe is stocks of large companies), the Russell 3000 Index (if the universe includes stocks of large and small companies) or the MSCI North America Index (if US and Canadian equities make up the universe).

Benchmark choice becomes more difficult when the asset class is not regularly traded on an exchange (e.g. real estate, private equity and infrastructure) or when the assert class is very heterogeneous (e.g. hedge funds, which are not an asset class). In such cases the index is based on estimates and valuations (since quoted prices of its constituencies are unavailable) and it does not represent the entire investment universe of the asset class (e.g. real estate indices cannot include all buildings representing the property market).

Composite benchmarks for multi-asset portfolios

Multi-asset portfolios invest in more than a single asset class. The benchmark for such portfolios is normally a basket or a composite of a few indices, each representing one of the asset classes in the portfolio. The weight, or allocation, to each asset class is determined by the portfolio's investment strategy. The benchmark weights can be set by strategic asset allocation, ALM modelling, arbitrary fixed allocations reflecting the desired target long-term asset mix, allocation with a desired risk level, or the average peer group allocation. The *composite benchmark* should represent the investment objectives or investment policy of the multi-asset portfolio.

For example, Table 2.1 illustrates a composite benchmark of a multi-asset portfolio for a UK-based investor.

Table 2.1 – illustrative composite benchmark for a UK based multi-asset portfolio

Asset class	Benchmark weight	Index
North America Equities	25%	MSCI North America
Europe ex. UK Equities	10%	MSCI Europe ex. UK
UK Equities	5%	MSCI UK
Japan Equities	5%	MSCI Japan
Pacific ex. Japan Equities	2.5%	MSCI Pacific ex. Japan
Emerging Market Equities	2.5%	MSCI Emerging Markets
Domestic Government Bonds	15%	FTA British Government All Stocks
Corporate Bonds	10%	iBoxx £ Non Gilts All Maturities
Global High Yield	2.5%	Barclays Capital Global High Yield
Global Developed Bonds	5%	Barclays Capital Global Aggregate
Emerging Market Debt	2.5%	JP Morgan Emerging Market Debt Plus
Real Estate	5%	IPD UK
Commodities	2.5%	UBS-DJ Commodity
Hedge Funds	2.5%	HFRI Fund Weighted
Cash	5%	LIBOR £ 1 Month
TOTAL	**100%**	

The relative weights of each asset class in the composite benchmark change over time. For example, assume a benchmark starting with an allocation of 50% equities and 50% bonds. Equities return -10% and bonds return 5% in one year. The new benchmark weights are now 46% equities and 54% bonds[35]. The composite benchmark needs *rebalancing* rules (benchmark rebalancing as opposed to portfolio rebalancing).

One common approach is keeping the benchmark weights unchanged (i.e. 50% equities and 50% bonds). This assumes continuous rebalancing to the target weights. However, as the weights of the asset classes in the portfolio change and cannot continuously rebalance, maintaining fixed benchmark weights is an impractical assumption that causes the portfolio weights to drift from those of the benchmark.

Portfolio weights are likely to drift from those of the benchmark for three reasons:

1. Different asset classes perform differently.

2. The portfolio may have a different asset allocation to that of the benchmark.

3. The investments in the portfolio are unlikely to perform in the same way as the passive indices representing the asset classes in the benchmark (relative risk of each investment).

This drift is overstated if the benchmark weights remain fixed. An alternative approach is to float the benchmark weights using the returns of indices, representing each asset class. This is a more accurate representation of benchmark weights over time. Periodic benchmark rebalancing or re-fixing to original target weights should be done when the portfolio is rebalanced to its target weights.

When the portfolio is managed against liabilities the liabilities' value can form a benchmark to which the portfolio's value is compared. The objective is for the assets' value to surpass that of the liabilities (i.e. avoid shortfall or maintain a positive surplus). A portion of the benchmark can represent the liabilities. For example, a defined benefit pension plan can characterise its aggregate liabilities in terms of *duration* (based on the expected amount and timing of cash flows).

A corresponding fixed income portion of the composite benchmark with similar characteristics to those of the liabilities (e.g. duration, credit quality and currency) matches some of the portfolio assets to the liabilities. For example, a pension plan with liabilities valued at $10 million with an average duration of 8 years can have a portion of the benchmark, with a value of $10 million, represented by government bonds with 8-year duration. The liabilities are effectively a short position in government bonds within the benchmark. The other portions of the benchmark, if the portfolio has a value over $10 million (i.e. the pension plan has a surplus), can include other asset classes based on optimised asset allocation aligned to the investment objectives, perhaps to generate real asset growth (i.e. growth or return assets). Duration matching is only a crude estimate and ALM modelling normally uses more sophisticated methods.

Characteristics of a valid benchmark

A valid benchmark should ideally have the following characteristics[36]:

- *Unambiguous.* The underlying constituents are known and their weightings in the makeup of the index are clear.

- *Investable.* It is possible to forgo the use of active investment management and rely on an index tracker to replicate performance. Investors can get exposure to the entire benchmark and track it without actively selecting securities to try to replicate it (or beat it).

- *Measureable.* The benchmark return can be quantified in numerical terms over a given time horizon.

- *Appropriate.* The benchmark correctly measures the performance of the investment strategy or the portfolio manager's investment style.

- *Reflective of current investment opinions.* The portfolio manager has current investment knowledge of the securities or *factor exposures* that make up the benchmark.

- *Specified in advance.* The makeup of the benchmark is disclosed prior to the start of the evaluation period.

In many cases, in particular for multi-asset portfolios, benchmarks do not comply with all of these criteria. Benchmarks may be ambiguous and unspecified in advance since their constituencies may not be clearly defined (e.g. inclusion of securities in style indices depends on the definition of the style) or the weightings of the constituencies are not known with certainty (e.g. peer group averages, which are baskets of actively-managed portfolios).

They may not be investable since they may include investments such as real estate, private equity and hedge funds. They may be immeasurable since the prices of their constituencies are based on valuations and not on published prices (e.g. real estate, private equity). Multi-asset portfolios normally have exposure to some of the problematic asset classes in terms of benchmarking and therefore their composite benchmarks are likely to be invalid. Nevertheless, a benchmark is needed even if it does not meet all the characteristics of a valid benchmark. Its limitations should be noted.

Hedge fund indices

Not all asset classes have indices fulfilling all the characteristics of a valid benchmark. Hedge funds (which are not an asset class) do not have valid benchmarks. Hedge funds are a heterogeneous group of funds and it is difficult to group them together in an index using a set of rules. There are different hedge fund strategies, but even constructing strategy indices, each representing a different strategy, faces serious challenges. Some hedge funds hold illiquid investments, so it is difficult to price them to calculate the index price; some funds are not widely distributed, so their performance is not publicly published; and some funds are ephemeral as they have a finite life or they just go bust at some point. Therefore, it is impossible to produce hedge fund indices that have all the characteristics of a valid benchmark.

Most hedge fund indices are based on databases of reported results from hedge funds that follow particular strategies. The main differences among these indices are: the rules or selection criteria for inclusion in the index (e.g. track record, AUM); strategy categorisation; the weighting scheme (e.g. equally or AUM weighted, as there is no market capitalisation for hedge funds); and investability.

Hedge fund indices come in three varieties:

1. Non-investable

2. Investable

3. Replication indices

Non-investable indices are more representative of the hedge fund strategy than other index choices. However, since their performance is partially based on hedge fund managers' skill and due to various biases, it is impossible to track them; consequently they are not investable through passive trackers.

Investable indices enable investors to track them, normally through derivative-based structures. However, the index provider needs to invest in relatively liquid hedge funds to be able to deliver the performance of the hedge fund basket. This comes at the expense of limited representation of all the hedge funds in the strategy.

Replication indices aim to replicate statistical properties of hedge funds through statistical modelling of historic returns (such as *data mining*). However, they do not replicate hedge fund returns, in particular since returns are heavily dependent on non-replicable manager skill.

Hedge fund indices have a number of biases because they are based on reported results of hedge funds employing each type of strategy, in a similar way to peer groups. These biases include *reporting bias* (results are self-reported by hedge funds and may be inaccurate or based on the fund manager's valuations); *survivorship bias* (poorly performing hedge funds typically go out of business, dropped from the index, leaving only hedge funds with a good track record, thus overstating index returns); *backfill bias* (fund managers may backfill missing historical data with simulated results and when a hedge fund is added to the index its entire history is added); and classification of some hedge fund strategies may be unclear (hence the indices do not compare like with like).

A classic example of reporting bias in hedge fund indices is the fall of Long-Term Capital Management (LTCM) in 1998. LTCM was a hedge fund founded in Greenwich, Connecticut. The principals of the fund included Myron Scholes and Robert Merton, who shared the 1997 Nobel Memorial prize in economic sciences, for developing, in collaboration with the late Fischer Black, the Black and Scholes option pricing model. LTCM was classified as a fixed income arbitrage hedge fund. During August 1998 the fund lost over 40% ($2.1 billion) of its capital, of which $550 million was lost on a single day on 21 August 1998. However, the Dow Jones Credit Suisse Fixed Income Arbitrage Hedge Fund Index lost only -1.46% that month[37]. It appears that given the AUM size of LTCM it chose not to participate in the index and its spectacular failure was omitted from the index return. (The book *When Genius Failed*[38] by Roger Lowenstein tells the full, fascinating story of the rise and fall of LTCM.) Hedge fund indices are thus not completely reliable.

One way to overcome some of these biases is using a fund of hedge fund index, which is less exposed to them[39]. The performance of funds of funds (FoFs) includes: the performance of underlying funds that do not report their performance to the index (lower selection bias); the track record of ceased underlying funds (lower survivorship bias); and when a FoF invests in a new underlying fund the previous track record of the underlying fund is not added to that of the FoF (lower backfill bias). However, FoFs are exposed to a double layer of fees (one at the FoF level and a second at the underlying fund level), therefore understating the index return.

Market-value weighted indices are likely to have less severe biases than un-weighted (equal-weighted) indices since large funds are more likely to survive than small ones (lower survivorship bias) and usually have been around longer (lower backfill bias). According to 2011 research by Roger Ibbotson et al[40], because most hedge fund indices (such as HFRI[41] and Dow Jones Credit Suisse) are created on the fly, the researchers believe that their return biases are much smaller than those in historical databases.

Figure 2.1 compares the cumulative performance of Dow Jones Credit Suisse Global Macro Hedge Fund Index and HFRI Macro Index. Both indices represent the same hedge fund strategy (global macro). While the correlation between the indices is 0.72, there are visual discrepancies in their performance and their total returns over the measuring period differ markedly. The choice between two hedge fund indices representing the same strategy is therefore not straightforward.

Figure 2.1 – cumulative return of the Dow Jones Credit Suisse Global Macro Hedge Fund Index and HFRI Macro Index, January 1994 to June 2012

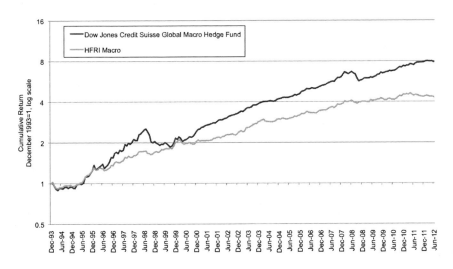

Source: Bloomberg, Dow Jones Credit Suisse, HFRI.

No solution addresses all the issues with hedge fund indices. When choosing an index to represent hedge funds in multi-asset portfolios the main choices are either:

1. Use a hedge fund index and accept its limitations (in particular when the objective is measuring performance of a hedge fund portfolio relative to its peers).

2. Instead of using a hedge fund index use an index linked to the investment objectives (such as cash plus when the objective is generating a positive return).

Neither choice is ideal.

Peer group benchmarks

Often, multi-asset portfolios are benchmarked against peer group sectors. Peer group benchmarks include the performance of different portfolios, grouped together into categories or sectors, based on their characteristics. In the multi-asset sectors these characteristics include the minimum and/or maximum investment in equities and fixed income, and maximum exposure to foreign currencies. Normally, peer group providers regularly (monthly or quarterly) publish the peer members' returns, mean/median return and average asset allocation. The number of peers in each sector is critical since a small number of peers means that a large outlier can impact the peer group average, which may not be statistically robust.

Peer groups are usually comprised of actively-managed portfolios. They include active decisions by managers. Peer group indices lack most of the characteristics of a valid benchmark since they are ambiguous, not investable and not specified in advance.

In the United Kingdom the most common peer group providers are the Association of British Insurers (ABI) and the Investment Management Association (IMA). ABI and IMA offer various multi-asset peer sectors with different ranges of equity allocations and therefore different levels of risk. Each peer group sector can be viewed as defining the broad risk level of its peer members. This enables investors to invest in portfolios whose risk characteristics broadly match their risk appetite. If viewed as providing the general risk level, peer group indices can be used to benchmark portfolios broadly matching certain investment objectives (i.e. the peer benchmark sets the broad risk level, deriving the range of expected returns).

As an example of the risks of peer group benchmarks, in Ireland the Mercer survey is the most common and well-known peer group index. The survey includes only about 15 members. The members use the asset allocations of the survey as a guide to their asset allocation and they aim to outperform the survey.

Entering the 2008 credit crunch and financial crisis, many funds in the peer group had an overweight to Irish equities, bonds and property (all three asset classes crashed during the financial crisis) relative to a global benchmark because of the home bias of most funds in the Mercer survey. The absolute performance of the balanced managed funds in the survey was very disappointing for the investors in the funds. The funds were described as "balanced" but this was an inappropriate mislabelling since they did not have a healthy balance across different global asset classes to maintain proper diversification. This example demonstrates the risks of herding, home bias, mislabelling and potential disappointment with peer group benchmarks.

Multi-asset portfolios benchmarked against peer groups should have a performance target and relative risk with respect of the peer group. However, many portfolios that are marketed relative to peer groups are not explicitly managed against these peer groups, but rather managed against composite benchmarks. These portfolios have undefined relative risk to the peer group as usually there is no link between the composite benchmark and the peer group. Under these circumstances, the portfolios' performance may deviate substantially from that of the peer group.

There are a few shortcomings in using peer benchmarks:

- The asset allocation weights of the peers are known only when they are published on a monthly or quarterly basis and they may change between publications since they are actively managed.

- The composition of some asset classes, such as alternative investments, is not published and needs to be estimated.

- The asset allocations of the peers are self-reported and may be erroneous.

- Peer group index providers may misclassify some securities. For example, the peer index may show an allocation of 40% to global bonds, while in reality the allocation is less than 10% due to misclassifying domestic bonds as foreign.

- Benchmarking to a peer group causes herding since some portfolio managers do not wish to deviate too much from the pack.

- Peer group returns suffer from survivorship bias, in particular when portfolios are compared to peer group medians over long time periods (e.g. 3 and 5 years).

The advantages of peer group benchmarks are that they enable: portfolio managers to compete with each other on a level playing field; investors to compare like with like (more or less); and competitors to compete with each other and not with passive benchmarks. If peer group benchmarks are used to set a broad risk level and the portfolio is managed explicitly to the peer group benchmark then it can help anchor the portfolio to certain risk characteristics.

Pricing time and relative returns

The comparison of the performance of portfolios with that of indices may be distorted due to the portfolios' pricing time. Often, a portfolio's pricing time is not the end of the trading day. For example, a portfolio can be priced at 2:00pm while the trading day ends at 4:30pm. The performance of the portfolio misses the last 2.5 hours of the trading day. The performance of these last couple of hours is not lost but is included in the portfolio's next valuation day. The performance is included, however, in today's index performance.

Most portfolios report performance on a monthly basis. When there is a large movement in markets during the last couple of hours of the month, this movement is included in the index's performance, but excluded from that of the portfolio. When there is a drop (rise) in markets during this time, the portfolio's relative performance is overstated (understated) since the index drops (rises) but this drop (rise) is only recorded in the portfolio the following month. Since the last couple of hours' performance is included in the portfolio's performance in the next month there is a mismatch in performance (this mismatch is naturally adjusted over time)[42]. This potential distortion in relative performance needs to be understood.

Another issue with this phenomenon is that it may inflate absolute and relative risk measurements that are based on monthly returns as performance is overstated in some months and understated in others relative to the benchmark. When evaluating portfolio performance, this phenomenon needs to be remembered.

Fundamental weighted indices

The most commonly used type of index is market-value or market capitalisation weighted. The main shortcoming of this index type is that it tends to have a high concentration in stocks with high market capitalisation. For example, the top 10 stocks in the S&P 500 Index have an allocation of approximately 20% of the index (i.e. 10 out of 500 stocks or 2% of all stocks have one-fifth weight of the index). Hence, a large proportion of index return and risk are driven by a small number of stocks.

Market capitalisation weighted indices tend to get even more concentrated during market bubbles. For example, today 20% of the S&P 500 Index is exposed to the information technology sector. During the build-up of the late 1990s high-tech bubble the allocation to this sector reached nearly 35% of the index. A portfolio closely following a market capitalisation index may end up with a concentrated exposure to a small number of stocks or to overvalued assets due to a bubble such as this.

One of the ways to address the biases of market capitalisation indices is through fundamental weighted indices (FWI). In FWI securities are weighted by economic fundamental factors or accounting figures, such as sales, earnings, book value, cash flows and dividends. FWI commonly use a combination of several fundamentals. The philosophy of FWI is that fundamentals are more accurate estimators of a company's intrinsic value than its current market capitalisation, since the capitalisation is driven by the price that the market gives to the company's securities.

Index construction methodologies

Each passive index represents an asset class (such as equities and bonds). The index is not actively managed and its constituents are included in the index based on a set of rules. For example, the S&P 500 Index includes the stocks of the 500 companies in the United States with the largest market capitalisation. Economic forces determine which securities are included in the index. Successful companies that the market prices highly will have sufficient market capitalisation to be included in the distinguished club of the S&P 500.

There are different methodologies for constructing indices. Investors should know them to understand the biases in indices and how to use indices in multi-asset portfolios. The three common methodologies of index construction are:

1. Price-weighted

2. Market-value weighted

3. Un-weighted (equally weighted)

A *price-weighted* index is calculated as the arithmetic average[43] of the prices of the securities in the index. The index adds together the market price of each security and then divides this total by the number of securities in the index. Such an index assumes that investors purchase one share of each security in the index. The index performance is more impacted by movements in securities with a high price than those with a low price. Hence, the index is biased to securities whose price is high without any true economic sense. The two most well-known price-weighted indices are the Dow Jones Industrial Average (DJIA) in the United States and the Nikkei 225 in Japan.

A *market-value weighted* (value-weighted or market capitalisation weighted) index is calculated by summing the current total market value or market capitalisation (security price times the number of securities outstanding) of all the securities in the index. This sum is divided by a similar sum as of the selected base period. Finally, this ratio is multiplied by the index's base beginning value. Such an index assumes a proportionate market value investment in each security in the index. Firms with greater market capitalisation have greater impact on the index return than do firms with lower market capitalisation. Market cap weighted indices are very common. Some of the well-known indices are the S&P 500, NASDAQ composite, FTSE 100 and the MSCI indices.

In an *un-weighted* index all securities are equally weighted. The index assumes that investors maintain an equal monetary investment in each security. Changes to the index are calculated as either a geometric or arithmetic average percentage return in the price of each security in the index.

The performance of market cap and equally weighted indices can vary materially. Figure 2.2 compares the performance of the S&P 500 Index (market cap) with an equally weighted index of the 500 constituencies of the S&P 500 Index.

Figure 2.2 – cumulative total return of the S&P 500 Index and equally weighted index of the 500 constituencies of the S&P 500 Index, January 1990 to June 2012

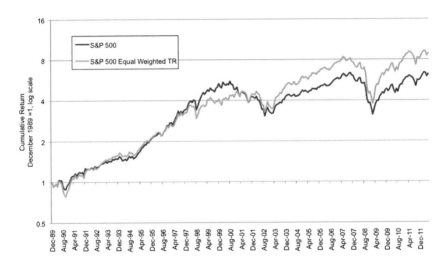

Source: Bloomberg, Lipper, S&P 500, S&P 500 Equal Weighted TR.

Bond indices

Bond indices are more difficult to create and maintain than equity indices for several reasons:

- Compared to the universe of equities, there are many more issues of bonds. The reasons are that many firms have only one common stock but several issues of bonds. Also, governments issue bonds but do not issue equity.

- The variety and characteristics of outstanding bond issues are continually changing. Bond maturities change with the passage of time and firms issue new bonds and call existing ones constantly. Bonds have a wider variety of characteristics (e.g. embedded options) than equities do. The world of bonds, or fixed income, is ever changing and evolving. Entities always look for creative ways to borrow money.

- The price volatility of bonds changes because it is measured by the bond's duration, which changes with the bond's maturity and the market yield curve.

- Due to the lack of continuous trading in bonds, there are challenges in pricing all the individual bond issues in the index's universe.

Benchmark linked to investment objectives

The choice of a benchmark for multi-asset portfolios is an opportunity to clearly link the portfolio to its investment objectives. It may be a composite benchmark representing return and risk objectives and liabilities. Such a benchmark explicitly ties the investor needs to the portfolio.

Summary

- Portfolios should have a benchmark, linking them with the investment objectives, monitoring and evaluating investment outcomes and defining the investment universe.

- Benchmark choice is not trivial, in particular for multi-asset portfolios.

- A valid benchmark should follow certain criteria (it should be unambiguous, investable, measureable, appropriate, reflective of current investment opinions and specified in advance). However, in many cases, such as hedge funds and peer groups, benchmarks do not follow these criteria and raise a series of challenges.

- Investors and portfolio managers should fully understand the benchmark and how the portfolio performance is measured against it.

- Market cap indices can suffer from concentration risk and the concentration tends to increase when bubbles develop. Fundamental Weighted Indices (FWI), which are weighted by company fundamentals, are one way to address the biases in market cap indices.

- Investors should select or construct a benchmark that is linked to the investment objectives of the portfolio.

In the next chapter the focus moves to risk, the other side of return. Return and risk objectives must go side by side and one cannot live without the other. The chapter will discuss risk objectives, define risk, review different types of risks and introduce a variety of topics as a basis for the following chapters.

3. RISK OBJECTIVES

The second set of investment objectives, after return, is risk. Risk is a less familiar, more abstract concept than return. Although it is natural for investors to focus on returns, as that is what they seek to achieve from investing, risk must not be neglected; to earn money risk must be taken.

Risk should be deemed not only as an unwanted consequence of investing (the dark side of investing), but also as a necessary, scarce resource, as only by taking risk can investors generate returns[44].

The objectives of this chapter are to explain risk and review some of its different definitions and types. Only when risk is understood can informed investors decide on the appropriate risk level and types of wanted and unwanted risks in their portfolios.

Risk tolerance

Risk tolerance is a combination of the willingness and ability to accept risk. *Willingness* is the subjective tolerance to risk and it depends on the personality of individual investors or the collective personalities of members of investment committees or the board of directors of institutional investors. Willingness to take risk depends on investors' knowledge, expertise and experience with investing. Some people can live with risk more than others, depending on their psychological profile and circumstances. For example, an entrepreneur who starts a private business normally has a higher risk tolerance, at least in career choice, than an employee. However, the entrepreneur may be very risk averse with personal wealth because of the lack of a stable salary and the high risk already taken in the private business. The employee, on the other hand, while being more risk averse with career choice, may take more risk with private wealth because of a stable salary. Personalities and circumstances determine the willingness to take risk and how well risk-taking investors sleep at night.

An *ability* to accept risk is the objective assessment of how much risk investors can take. For example, retired individuals cannot afford to lose 50% of their portfolio since it jeopardises the ability to generate sustainable future income. Ability to take risk is a function of the investment horizon. A longer investment horizon usually means higher ability to take risk, since there is more time to recoup losses. However, although a 25-year-old investor may have a long investment horizon (i.e. 40 years to retirement) the ability to take risk may be low due to lack of wealth. So ability to take risk is also a function of the size of assets. All else being equal, when investors' wealth is large relative to the portfolio more risk can be taken. When the portfolio is large relative to spending needs and liabilities, a greater ability to take risk is likely.

The other dimension of ability to take risk is the *need to take risk*. An endowment with a certain spending rate needs to take a risk level that is expected to generate sufficient returns to match the spending rate, as well as to grow the portfolio so it is not depleted due to spending and inflation. Some investors must remain invested to generate required returns and to do so they need to take risk.

The risk tolerance of institutional investors is normally driven by objective factors such as spending rates, liabilities and minimum capital requirements. The risk tolerance of individual investors is normally driven by a combination of objective factors and subjective, complex psychology and emotions. Some investors have a high appetite for risk (risk seekers) while others are risk averse.

Definition of risk

The simple definition of risk is the probability of not achieving investment objectives (shortfall) or the chance of disappointment. If investors expect a reasonable outcome, then risk is the likelihood of falling short of this outcome.

Risk comes in many forms. When the return objective is positive real returns, one risk is unexpected higher realised inflation (*inflation risk*) resulting in negative real returns. When the objective is a return of cash plus 4% by investing in a diversified portfolio of equities and corporate bonds, negative equity market returns (*market risk*) and defaults of corporate bonds (*credit risk*) are risks that may cause the portfolio to miss its target or generate negative returns.

When the portfolio has a relative return objective, one risk is underperforming the benchmark due to unsuccessful active investment decisions by the portfolio manager (*manager risk*). When an investor needs to make a payment on a mortgage but at time of payment the portfolio has no sufficient cash and only illiquid investments that require few months to sell, the risk is lack of liquidity to make the payment (*liquidity risk*). The bottom line is that what matters to investors is whether the portfolio is likely to meet its investment objectives.

For portfolios with relative return objectives, successfully beating their benchmark in a falling market may still disappoint investors. Outperforming a falling benchmark may still mean a negative absolute return. Clarifying the risks and educating investors to truly understand risks is essential and may mitigate the need for unpleasant conversations. Investors must understand that portfolios with relative risk objectives or passive index trackers may fall when markets fall.

When index trackers do not fall with markets, they are likely to have breached their objective of tracking the index. Outperformance is not always a good result.

As assuming too much risk may lead to disappointing returns in falling markets, not assuming enough risk may lead to lagging returns in rising markets. Holding high levels of cash when markets rally causes *cash drag* (cash return is lower than that of other investments). *Opportunity cost* may be the result of defensiveness relative to a benchmark when it appreciates, or missing an investment opportunity. However, if you lose an opportunity you may still have enough capital for another opportunity, but if you lose your capital you may not have another opportunity. Mitigating downside risk to survive is more critical than mitigating upside risk not to miss an opportunity.

Regret risk is the risk of regretting an investment decision whose outcome is disappointing. This does not mean that the decision was a wrong one, but rather that the investor regrets making it. Judging a decision should be based on the available information to support it and the circumstances at the time when it was made. This should be remembered when scrutinising investment decisions with the benefit of hindsight. Evaluating investment decisions is an opportunity to learn from past mistakes and improve future investment decisions. Feeling regret may be the result of both good and bad decisions. Regret is an emotion that should be managed by clarifying what the *reasonable expectations* are from each investment decision.

While risk is the chance of not achieving the investment objectives at the end of the investment horizon, the path or the journey matters (*path dependent*). A fall in a portfolio's value, even long before the end of the investment horizon, may mean termination of the portfolio manager, even if there are still good chances of meeting the objectives. Investors may be trigger happy and rush to fire managers, not giving them a second chance.

Losing considerable assets early in the investment horizon may mean that the portfolio has a slim chance, or no chance, of reaching its objectives because of depleted assets. Losing considerable assets later in the investment horizon may mean that the portfolio does not have enough time to recover loses. Portfolios may deviate from their target risk level, needing to be steered by changing their investment mix so that they are *de-risked* or *re-risked*. Risk should be evaluated frequently to ensure that the portfolio is on track.

Risk is different from *uncertainty*. Uncertainty is commonly defined as meaning that the future is unknown and immeasurable, while risk is commonly defined as meaning that the outcome within a possible distribution of returns is unknown, but it is measureable. So uncertainty is risk that is immeasurable[45]. Uncertainty cannot be modelled but risk can be modelled using probabilistic or stochastic models. When the outcome is uncertain, there is no way of forecasting what is going to happen. When the outcome is risky, the deterministic result is unknown, but there are tools to estimate the range of potential results. When investors are uncertain of the potential investment outcome they speculate, gamble or place a bet. Speculating is not investing and investors should stay away from uncertain investments. When investments are risky, investors should take a calculated chance and assess whether they wish to take the risk with its potential reward. Risky investments are the bread and butter of investing.

Risk measurement and risk management are focused on the distribution of potential investment returns. Once the distribution is estimated, risk can be evaluated since the probabilities of different investment returns can be calculated. One challenge is accurately capturing the distribution of all potential outcomes. Another challenge is that most standard statistical distributions, such as the normal distribution, do not capture the true distribution of financial markets and investment returns.

Absolute versus relative risk

Risk can be defined in absolute or relative terms, or sometimes as a combination of both. Absolute risk is more appropriate for portfolios with absolute return objectives and relative risk is more appropriate for portfolios with a relative return objective.

The choice between absolute and relative depends on the investment objectives. Some investors are focused on beating a benchmark, such as portfolio managers, who need to compete with peers to stay in business. Such portfolios should have a relative risk measure. Other investors are concerned about losing money or not achieving their absolute return objectives. Absolute risk measures are more appropriate in this case. Even when portfolios have only relative risk measures, the difference in absolute risk levels between a portfolio and its benchmark should be considered as a supplementary risk control (i.e. portfolio volatility should not deviate too much from that of the benchmark).

Multi-asset portfolios often combine multiple risk measures. When assets are allocated to different portfolio managers, each manager is likely to be assigned a benchmark and relative risk and return objectives. Each manager's performance is evaluated relative to benchmark. For example, US equities are allocated to a US equity portfolio manager, who is tasked with outperforming the S&P 500 Index within a certain tracking error.

The overall multi-asset portfolio, on the other hand, may be more focused on *downside risk*. Absolute risk measures are therefore appropriate for the overall multi-asset portfolio. The risk of multi-asset portfolios is an aggregation of the risks of their underlying investments and the way they allocate across investments. The absolute risk of multi-asset portfolios is made up of different risks, some of which are relative. Combining relative risks when overall portfolio risk is absolute leads to suboptimal portfolios[46].

Standard deviation

The most common absolute risk measure is volatility as measured by standard deviation of returns. Standard deviation is a statistical measure of the dispersion of returns around the arithmetic mean or average return (the average of squared deviations from the mean[47]). If mean return is the expected outcome, standard deviation can be used to measure the probability of better or worse outcomes than expected.

When returns are normally distributed[48] standard deviation has very useful statistical properties. Approximately 64% of observations lie within one standard deviation of the mean; approximately 95% of observations lie within two standard deviations (and should happen once every 44 days if the standard deviation is of daily observations); and approximately 99% of observations lie within three standard deviations of the mean. Close to 100% (99.994%) of observations lie within four standard deviations. A five standard deviation event is very uncommon when the distribution is normal and should happen only once every 13,932 years.

For example, if the distribution of returns is normal, the portfolio mean annual return is 10% and the annualised standard deviation is 5%, then in 64% of years the expected return is 5% to 15% (10% +/- 1*5%), in 95% of years the expected return is 0% to 20% (10% +/- 2*5%) and in 99% of years the expected return is -5% to 25% (10% +/- 3*5%). A return below -5% or above 25% is very unlikely (once in 100 years) if the standard deviation and expected return are accurate and the distribution of returns is normal.

Figure 3.1 illustrates a normal distribution with a mean of 10% and standard deviation of 5%, highlighting the area under the distribution of one standard deviation away from its mean. Approximately 64% of observations fall under this area.

Figure 3.1 – normal distribution (μ=10%, σ=5%) with the area of one standard deviation from the mean highlighted

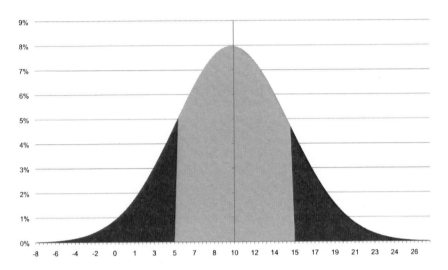

Criticisms of using standard deviation as an investment risk measure include the idea that the normal distribution assumption of investment results is unrealistic; and that the standard deviation symmetrically penalises negative and positive returns. That is to say returns of -5% and 25% are treated in the same way. This criticism has led to a proliferation of alternative risk measures (e.g. Value-at-Risk and semi-variance). Nevertheless, standard deviation is still widely used. It does give a good indication of investment risk level, in particular when the distribution of returns is reasonably close to a normal distribution.

Volatility is commonly stated as *annualised* standard deviation. Using monthly returns, it is easy to annualise standard deviation by multiplying monthly standard deviation by the square root of 12[49] (the number of months in a year). Daily standard deviation is annualised by multiplying it by the square root of 252 (the average number of trading days per year). Weekly standard deviation is annualised by multiplying it by the square root of 52 (the number of weeks in a year).

Some investors think that risk over the long term is lower than over the short term since the expected return is higher with more time, market ups and downs are ironed out and there is more time to recover losses. However, the formula for annualising standard deviation shows that over time risk increases by the square root of time. The good news, however, is that returns increase with time too, so return per unit of risk increases by a factor of the square root of time ($t/t^{0.5}=t^{0.5}$). Mathematically, a longer investment horizon is more efficient than a short one.

For example, for a portfolio with expected annual return of 10% and volatility of 5% the ratio of expected return to expected risk is 2 (10%/5%). Over 10 years, the compounded expected return is 159% = $(1+10\%)^{10}$-1 and the volatility is 17.3% = $5\%*10^{0.5}$, giving a return to risk ratio of 9.2^{50}.

Different asset classes have different long-term average volatilities. The long-term annualised standard deviation of monthly returns of cash is less than 1%, that of 10-year government bonds is around 8% and that of global developed equities is around 15%. The volatility of global emerging market equities is around 25%.

The following charts in Figure 3.2 show the dispersion of monthly returns of the S&P 500 Index, US 10-year Treasury bonds and US Treasury Bills (with a normal distribution superimposed on the histograms). The charts visualise how volatility captures the dispersion of returns for these asset classes. As can be seen, the dispersion of equity returns is higher than that of bonds, whose dispersion is higher than that of cash. The dispersion of the returns of cash is very narrow. The distributions of equity and bond returns are close to a normal distribution, but they are not perfectly normally distributed.

Figure 3.2 – distributions of monthly returns of equities, bonds and cash, January 1970 to June 2012

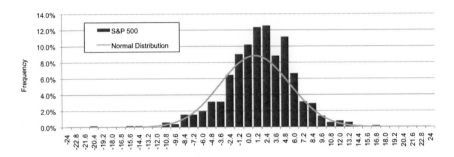

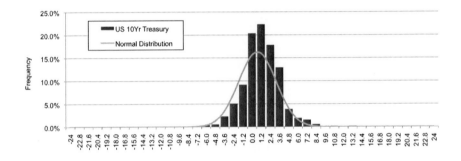

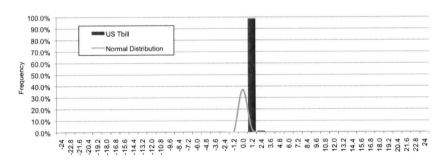

Source: Bloomberg, Global Financial Data, S&P 500, USA 10-year Government Bond Total Return, USA Total Return T-Bill Index.

Variable volatility

Volatility changes over time (non-stationary) depending on market conditions. Historic volatility depends heavily on the measurement time period. For instance, equity market volatility during 2006 (a relatively stable year for equities) was lower than the volatility during 2008 (the year of the collapse of Lehman Brothers and the credit crunch).

Figure 3.3 shows the rolling volatility of US equities, government bonds and cash using a window of 36 months of returns. As can be seen, volatility is volatile.

Figure 3.3 – rolling 36-month volatility of the S&P 500 Index, US 10-year Treasury bonds and US Treasury bills, January 1970 to June 2012

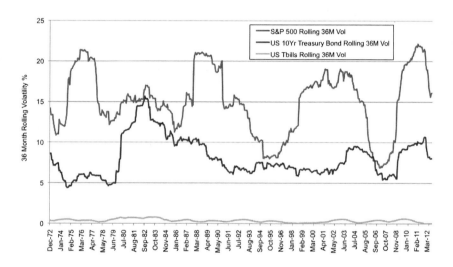

Source: Bloomberg, Global Financial Data, S&P 500, USA 10-year Government Bond Total Return, USA Total Return T-Bill Index.

VIX

The Chicago Board Options Exchange Market Volatility Index (VIX) is a measure of *implied volatility* of traded options on the S&P 500 Index. Often called the *fear index*, it provides an indication of equity market volatility in the United States. When markets fall volatility usually increases, and vice versa. The VIX Index reached its all-time peak during 2008.

Implied volatility is the market's forward-looking expectation for volatility as it is priced in traded options. Historic volatility, on the other hand, is realised volatility calculated from past returns.

Figure 3.4 shows the levels of the S&P 500 Index and the VIX Index. Equity market drops feature an increase in implied volatility. The VIX Index visually demonstrates the volatility of volatility.

Figure 3.4 – prices of S&P 500 Index (LHS) and VIX Index (RHS), January 1990 to June 2012

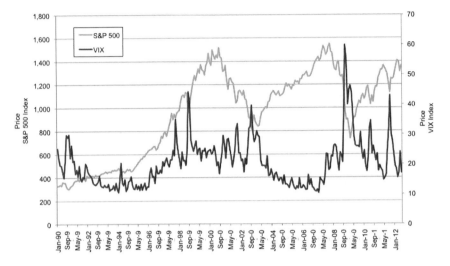

Source: Bloomberg, S&P 500, VIX.

Stating risk objectives

Stating a risk objective using volatility sets a limit on the expected dispersion of expected returns, both to the downside and to the upside. Annual returns within a range of +/- 2% are not as risky as annual returns within a range of +/- 15%. Over the long term, investments with certain (not all) types of risks are expected to compensate investors for these risks and generate higher returns compared to less risky alternatives. The opposite of this may happen and investments with higher risk may generate much lower returns than investments with lower risk during certain times.

Tracking error

Tracking error or tracking risk is a common relative risk measure, based on standard deviation. It is used to measure how closely a portfolio tracks its benchmark. Tracking error is the volatility of returns relative to a benchmark (excess returns). To calculate the annualised tracking error from monthly returns, for example, the monthly standard deviation of relative returns (i.e. the difference between the monthly portfolio and benchmark returns) is calculated and then annualised by multiplying it by the square root of 12. The result is annualised tracking error, which has the same statistical characteristics as those of standard deviation.

$$\text{Tracking error} = \text{Standard deviation}(r_{portfolio} - r_{benchmark})$$

A tracking error of 0% means that a portfolio perfectly tracks its benchmark. The expected excess return, or *alpha*, is 0% as well. Tracking error of 0% is unrealistic since it is normally impossible to perfectly track a benchmark (unless the benchmark consists of a small number of investments that are held in the portfolio at exactly the same weights as those of the benchmark). Tracking error is required to generate alpha and without it the portfolio's expected return is that of the benchmark, minus fees and transaction costs, plus noise or an error factor. Portfolios must be different to the benchmark in order to generate different (hopefully higher) returns.

Passive trackers, such as passive funds or Exchange Traded Funds (ETFs), typically have a tracking error between 0.1% and 0.5% in the case of liquid, developed equity markets, or closer to 1.0% or higher in the case of emerging market equities. Actively-managed equity portfolios typically have a tracking error of 3.0% to 6.0%. Assuming a normal distribution of relative returns, portfolios with a tracking error of 5.0% should perform +/- 10%[51] around the benchmark 95% of times. Active portfolios with a tracking error of 8% to 10% are considered aggressive or *benchmark agnostic*. Relative risk objectives determine the expected relative performance of a portfolio with respect to its benchmark.

Portfolios with high tracking errors have a volatile relative performance. When compared to peer group sectors, such portfolios are more likely to be in the first and fourth quartiles than in the second and third quartiles because they have large relative returns (positive or negative). Due to the volatile relative performance, portfolio managers of such portfolios may frequently move from being heroes to zeros and vice versa, depending on their relative results.

Tracking error has an upside and a downside. Higher tracking error means more potential outperformance and underperformance. Many investors prefer a more stable relative performance and hence a milder relative risk is likely to better suit their investment objectives.

While tracking error is normally used to measure how an active or passive portfolio tracks an index, for illustration purposes the returns of MSCI North American Index and S&P 500 Index are used to demonstrate the tracking error between the two indices. The two indices include different securities (e.g. MSCI North America includes Canadian stocks, and the number of stocks and the rules for including stocks in each index are different) and their performance differs. The annualised tracking error between the two indices is 1.8%. This means that 95% of annual relative returns are expected to lie within +/- 3.6%.

Figure 3.5 shows the cumulative performance of the two indices. The correlation between them is very high (0.99). However, over time their performance can differ markedly.

Figure 3.5 – cumulative return of MSCI North America Index and S&P 500 Index, January 1970 to June 2012

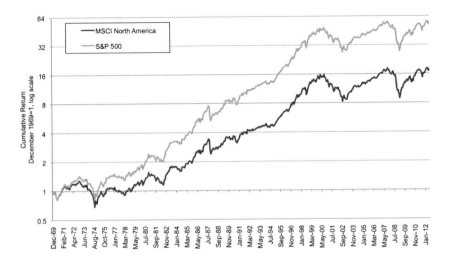

Source: Bloomberg, MSCI North America, S&P 500.

Figure 3.6 shows the distribution of relative monthly returns between the two indices. As expected, with a tracking error of 1.8% the dispersion of monthly relative returns is low.

Figure 3.6 – distribution of monthly relative returns between MSCI North America Index and S&P 500 Index, January 1970 to June 2012

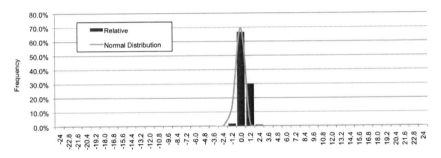

Source: Bloomberg, MSCI North America, S&P 500.

Figure 3.7 shows the z-scores of the relative annual returns of the two indices. The z-score quantifies the number of standard deviations (σ) of each observation (x) from the mean (μ) of the dataset.

$$Z = (x - \mu) / \sigma$$

While there are 23% annual relative returns with z-scores higher than 2 (under a normal distribution 5% is expected), most annual relative returns are below two standard deviations from the mean.

Figure 3.7 – z-scores of annual relative returns between MSCI North America Index and S&P 500 Index, January 1970 to June 2012

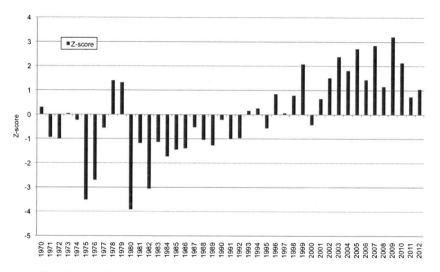

Source: Bloomberg, MSCI North America, S&P 500.

Tracking error limits the flexibility of portfolio managers to deviate from the benchmark. With low tracking errors portfolios hold similar securities with similar weights to those of their benchmarks. The portfolios are constrained or anchored to their benchmarks. Conversely, with high tracking errors portfolios have more flexibility; they can hold different securities with different weights than those of their benchmarks. These portfolios are unconstrained relative to benchmark. Through tracking error investors can control the portfolio's deviations from the benchmark.

Tight relative risk targets limit the ability of portfolio managers to avoid collapses in markets. When there is only an absolute risk target, managers can diverge from the benchmark when its volatility increases in a market crash (if they are quick enough to react and have the skill to take action before the crash or soon after its beginning). When a portfolio is tightly anchored to its benchmark a dive in the benchmark will take the portfolio with it.

Investors should not be concerned only with negative relative returns. High positive relative returns may be a concern if they breach the expected relative return as per the portfolio's tracking error. For example, a portfolio with a tracking error of 2% returning 6% excess return in a year should raise concerns since it is a three standard deviation event, which should happen only once every 100 years. High relative returns may indicate that the portfolio is not managed within its tracking error boundaries.

Often, tracking errors are set and reported *ex ante*. However, when measured *ex post* they may vary from the *ex ante* estimates. Plausible explanations for the variation include risk measurement models not capturing the true tracking error (*model risk*), changes to the portfolio after reporting the *ex ante* tracking errors, distorted relative returns because of timing of pricing and changing market volatility causing a change to the tracking error. *Ex ante* tracking error is only a guide and realised tracking error is likely to be different.

The following formula for calculating tracking error demonstrates the link between market or benchmark volatility and tracking error.

$$TE_p = (\sigma_p^2 + \sigma_b^2 - 2\rho\sigma_p\sigma_b)^{0.5}$$

where TE_p is the portfolio's tracking error, σ_p is the standard deviation of portfolio returns, σ_b is the standard deviation of benchmark returns, and ρ is the correlation between portfolio and benchmark returns.

The formula clearly shows the direct and positive relationship between tracking error and benchmark volatility. That is the higher the benchmark or market volatility, the higher the portfolio's tracking error, and vice versa, all else being equal.

The formula also demonstrates the negative relationship between correlation and tracking error. Higher correlation between the portfolio and benchmark means lower tracking error, all else being equal. This is intuitive as higher correlation indicates more similar returns between the portfolio and benchmark and hence lower tracking error. However, high correlation does not necessarily mean low tracking error because tracking error depends on the volatility of investments as well.

Fat tails

The convenient statistical characteristics of standard deviation and tracking error depend on the assumption that the distribution of returns is normal (Gaussian distribution). In practice, however, financial markets misbehave and their returns do not always follow a normal distribution. Events which should happen once in hundreds or thousands of years happen much more frequently.

Table 3.1 shows the number of monthly returns of the S&P 500 Index within intervals of the number of standard deviations away from the mean from January 1926 to June 2012. The S&P 500 Index has an average monthly return of 0.93% with a monthly standard deviation of 5.53% (not annualised). While the distribution of returns is quite similar to a normal distribution, monthly returns four, five and even eight standard deviations away from the mean have occurred.

If returns were normally distributed, returns more than four standard deviations away from the mean would not be expected to occur frequently (perhaps only once during the last 100 years). Yet, during the measuring period nine monthly returns were four and above standard deviations away from the mean.

Table 3.1 – distribution of S&P 500 Index monthly returns, January 1926 to June 2012

Standard deviations from mean	Return (%)	S&P 500 Index		Normal distribution	
		Number of observations	Percentage of observations (%)	Number of observations	Percentage of observations (%)
8	45.2	1	0.1	0	0.0
7	39.6	2	0.2	0	0.0
6	34.1	0	0.0	0	0.0
5	28.6	1	0.1	0	0.0
4	23.0	0	0.0	0	0.0
3	17.5	11	1.1	1	0.1
2	12.0	86	8.3	22	2.1
1	6.5	445	42.9	141	13.6
0	0.9	375	36.1	709	68.3
-1	-4.6	91	8.8	141	13.6
-2	-10.1	16	1.5	22	2.1
-3	-15.7	5	0.5	1	0.1
-4	-21.2	4	0.4	0	0.0
-5	-26.7	1	0.1	0	0.0
-6	-32.2	0	0.0	0	0.0
-7	-37.8	0	0.0	0	0.0
-8	-43.3	0	0.0	0	0.0

Source: Bloomberg, S&P 500.

The tails of a normal distribution include a known percentage of observations out of the entire distribution (e.g. about 99% of observations are within +/- three standard deviations from the mean; 1% of observations are in the tails). When the distribution is not normally distributed, there may be more observations in its tails than is expected under a normal distribution. The tails of such distribution are therefore *fat*. They have more weight and volume than expected.

If the distribution is not symmetrical, or *skewed*, with more observations in its left tail, which has returns lower than the mean return (the dark side of the distribution), it could mean trouble. The distribution is negatively skewed. Not only are the tails fat, but also the left tail is fatter. Under such a distribution extreme negative events are more likely to happen and when they do happen they may be more extreme than expected under a normal distribution (e.g. five standard deviation events may occur every couple of years instead of every thousand). *Black swans*, which are supposed to appear once in a blue moon, suddenly appear frequently. This is *fat tail risk*.

The first conclusion is that standard deviation and other risk measures relying on a normal distribution do not capture all the risks of actual market behaviour. The second conclusion is that standard deviation should be adjusted for fat tails and complemented by other risk measures. The third conclusion is that fat tail events should not be called fat tail events since they occur much more frequently in financial markets than is expected under a normal distribution. This means that these events are not at the extreme tail of the true distribution of financial market returns, but much closer to its middle. The distribution of financial market returns is not normal and the distribution that most standard risk models use is inaccurate.

Return distributions

Return distributions can be described by their four *moments*:

1. Mean

2. Standard deviation

3. Skewness

4. Kurtosis

A normal distribution is described by its first two moments, mean and standard deviation, since its skewness and excess kurtosis (kurtosis minus three) are zero.

The *mean*[52], the first moment, is the arithmetic average return. The mean is the investment's expected return (the location of the distribution's peak). If a portfolio has n monthly returns, r_t, the mean return (μ) is the sum of monthly returns, Σr_t, divided by n:

$$\mu = \Sigma r_t/n$$

Standard deviation[53], the second moment, is a measure of the dispersion of returns around the mean and is calculated by the formula:

$$\sigma = [(r_t - \mu)^2/n]^{0.5}$$

Skewness[54], the third moment, is a measure of the distribution's symmetry and is calculated by the formula:

$$S = (r_t - \mu)^3/n\sigma^3$$

Negative skewness means that the distribution is asymmetric, tilting to its left, with more returns to the left of its mean than to its right. A distribution with negative skewness has a long left tail. Skewness is not a robust statistic because it is greatly affected by *outliers* (low-frequency, high-impact events) as their values are raised to the power of three. Skewness is highly dependent on the measurement period.

Kurtosis, the fourth moment, measures the extent of the peaks and tail heaviness of a distribution relative to those of a normal distribution. The formula to calculate kurtosis is:

$$K = (r_t - \mu)^4/n\sigma^4$$

A normal distribution has kurtosis of three. Excess kurtosis[55] is kurtosis minus three. Distributions with kurtosis of three are *mesokurtic*. If the kurtosis is greater than three, the distribution is *leptokurtic*. If its kurtosis is less than three, it is *platykurtic*. *Leptokurtosis* is often associated with distributions that are simultaneously peaked and have fat tails. *Platykurtosis* is often associated with distributions that are simultaneously less peaked and have thinner tails. Similar to skewness, kurtosis is not a robust statistic; in fact it is even less so than skewness since outliers are raised to the power of four and it is heavily dependent on the measurement period.

When the distribution is not normal, all four moments should be used to describe it and more accurately capture risks. There are relatively simple ways to adjust standard risk measures for fat tail risk[56].

Downside risk measures

Since standard deviation is a statistical risk measure that is easily misunderstood by investors lacking knowledge in statistics, it may be helpful to translate it to a downside or shortfall risk measure. A simple mathematical calculation is all that is needed for the translation of standard deviation and expected return into a probability of surpassing or falling short of a certain return over a certain investment horizon.

If returns are normally distributed, the probability of exceeding a target return, x, given the portfolio expected return, μ (the small Greek letter mu), and the standard deviation of returns, σ (the small Greek letter sigma), is calculated using Microsoft Excel[57] and the formula:[58]

Probability of exceeding x = NORMSDIST (($μ$ – x)/$σ$)

For example, the probability of exceeding 5% for a portfolio with expected return of 8% and standard deviation of 5% is 72.6%. The probability of falling short of the target is 27.4% (1 - 72.6%).

This calculation is valid only when the returns are normally distributed and the expected risk and return assumptions are a true reflection of reality. The output of the calculation is as good as its inputs (garbage in, garbage out or GIGO). The result of the calculation is valid for a single time period (i.e. if the expected return and risk are for one year, the probability is for one year as well).

Multi-period returns

To calculate the probability of exceeding a target return over multi-periods a lognormal distribution should be used. A lognormal distribution is a probability distribution of a random variable whose logarithm is normally distributed.

For the lognormal distribution the location and dispersion properties are more readily treated using the geometric mean[59] and standard deviation than the arithmetic mean. To calculate returns over multiple time periods a geometric, rather than arithmetic, average should be used because of the compounding of returns (e.g. calculating a five-year return from annual geometric average returns). Arithmetic return is a better estimate for a single time period matching the time period of the average (e.g. expected annual arithmetic average return is appropriate for expressing the expected return over the next year). It is easy to transform the arithmetic expected return and standard deviation into geometric ones.

Define $σ_A$ as the portfolio arithmetic standard deviation and $μ_A$ as the arithmetic expected return. To transform $σ_A$ to geometric standard deviation, $σ_G$, the following formula[60] is used:

$$σ_G = (LN(1 + (σ_A/(1 + μ_A))^2))^{0.5}$$

To transform μ_A to geometric μ_G the following formula is used:

$$\mu_G = LN(1 + \mu_A) - (\sigma_G)^2/2$$

To calculate the probability of exceeding a target return, x, over n time periods the following formula is used:

$$\text{Probability of exceeding } x = 1 - NORMSDIST((LN(1+x)-\mu_G)/(\sigma_G/(n^{0.5})))$$

Greek letters, by the way, are very popular in finance; probably the economists' envy of physicists and mathematicians, who are real scientists.

The portfolio above (8% expected return, 5% volatility and 5% target return) has a probability of 72.1% of exceeding the target return over one year using a lognormal distribution. This is very close to the calculation using the normal distribution (72.6%). The probability for this portfolio of exceeding 5% per annum over a five-year period is 90.5%.

As the time horizon increases from one to five years the expected return increases by approximately a factor of five while risk is increased by approximately a factor of the square root of five (2.24). Therefore, the probability of exceeding the target return increases as the time horizon increases.

Table 3.2 shows the portfolio's probabilities of exceeding different target returns over different investment horizons.

Table 3.2 – probabilities of exceeding target returns over different investment horizon, μ=8%, σ=5%

Target return probabilities %				
		Investment horizon (years)		
Target (% pa)	1	2	5	10
10	33.7	27.6	17.4	9.2
5	72.1	79.6	90.5	96.8
0	95.0	99.0	100.0	100.0
-5	99.7	100.0	100.0	100.0
-10	100.0	100.0	100.0	100.0

If an investor's *minimum acceptable return (MAR)* is a negative return in 1 in 20 years, then the risk and return characteristics of the portfolio are appropriate since the probability of exceeding 0% over one year is 95%. This method can be used as a tool to discuss the probabilities of exceeding MAR and identify appropriate expected return and risk combinations to define return and risk objectives.

Transforming standard deviation to a probability of exceeding a target return or MAR helps investors to better grasp the meaning of volatility. For example, a portfolio with a standard deviation of 10% and expected return of 5% has a probability of 67.9% of exceeding 0% over one year (32.1% chance of a negative return) and a probability of 85.1% of exceeding 0% per annum over five years (14.9% chance of a negative return). The same portfolio has a probability of 94.2% of exceeding -10% over one year and a probability of close to 100% of exceeding -10% per annum over five years.

Does the last example guarantee exceeding -10% over five years because the probability is 100%? The answer is no. This calculation is an estimate, assuming a lognormal distribution of returns, as well as that the risk and return assumptions are accurate and fixed. The risk and return assumptions are average, forward-looking, *ex ante* assumptions and there is no guarantee that they truly reflect the realised, *ex post* risk and return.

This demonstrates the danger of spurious accuracy in investments. Most forward-looking estimates are assumption-based *estimates*. The accuracy of mathematics is limited in an uncertain area, such as investments. Deterministic, single results should often be replaced by probabilistic distributions of potential results. If someone appears too confident in mathematical models supposedly predicting the future, caution and suspicion are probably warranted.

Confidence intervals

Another helpful transformation of risk and return assumptions is transforming them into *confidence intervals* of exceeding a certain return over a certain investment horizon. The expected return with a certain confidence interval (CI) over n number of years is calculated using the formula:[61]

Expected return $= EXP(\mu_G + (NORMSINV(CI)*(\sigma_G/n^{0.5}))) - 1$

The portfolio in the example above (5% standard deviation and 8% expected return) should exceed a return of 0% over one year at the 5% confidence level and exceed a return of 4.3% per annum over five years at the same confidence level. A 5% confidence level translates to 1 in 20 so the portfolio should lose more than 0% in only 1 in 20 years.

Table 3.3 shows the confidence intervals for the portfolio.

Table 3.3 – confidence intervals of expected returns over different investment horizon, μ=8%, σ=5%

Confidence intervals				
				Investment horizon (years)
Confidence level	1	2	5	10
95%	16.4	13.8	11.6	10.5
75%	11.3	10.3	9.4	9.0
50%	7.9	7.9	7.9	7.9
25%	4.6	5.5	6.4	6.8
5%	0.0	2.2	4.3	5.3

Over a five-year horizon the expected return at the top 95% level is 11.6% per annum, the median expected return is 7.9% per annum and the expected return at the bottom 5% level is 4.3% per annum. The analysis shows the range of likely returns over different confidence levels and different investment horizons.

Value-at-risk

Value-at-risk (VaR) is a common risk measure, in particular for institutional investors such as banks which need to aggregate profit & loss (P&L) risk across different activities into a single risk measure or summary statistic[62]. VaR states the amount that could be lost under normal market conditions, over a certain time period at a certain confidence level. For example, a 30-day 95% VaR of -5% means that a portfolio should lose no more than -5% over any 30 days, with a 95% confidence level. A loss of more than -5% is expected in 5% of times, or in 1 in 20 periods of 30 days.

VaR depends on two parameters:

1. Confidence level

2. Time horizon

The choice of the parameters depends on the application of VaR. If VaR is used to report risk, the parameters can be arbitrarily chosen, as long as they are consistent (i.e. across time and portfolios to compare like with like). If VaR is used to determine capital requirements (e.g. the amount of assets an insurance company needs to hold to cover its liabilities), the parameters must be chosen with extreme care. The confidence level must be high enough so the probability of exceeding the VaR is low. The horizon should be related to the liquidity of assets, the time required for orderly liquidation, the time required for sourcing additional funding or the time required for other corrective actions. In other words, the organisation needs to be able to cope with a loss as measured by VaR since such a loss may happen under normal market conditions.

Methods for calculating VaR

There are three methods for calculating VaR:

1. Variance-covariance method

2. Historical method

3. Monte Carlo simulation method

1. Variance-covariance method

The first method for calculating VaR is the analytical method or the *variance-covariance method*. Under the assumption that returns are normally distributed, the distribution of returns can be described only by two parameters (the first two moments): expected return and standard deviation. Expected return, μ, and standard deviation, σ, can be translated to VaR as per the variance-covariance method by the formula:

VaR (95% confidence) = $\mu - 1.65^*\sigma$

VaR (99% confidence) = $\mu - 2.33^*\sigma$

Under the normal distribution, standard deviation and VaR can be used interchangeably; the former focuses on the entire distribution and the latter on its left tail. For example, a portfolio with an annualised standard deviation of σ = 10% and expected return of μ = 10% has a 95% 1-year VaR of -6.5% (10% - 1.65*10%).

If the value of the portfolio is £1 million, then its 95% 1-year VaR is -£65,000. The portfolio is likely to lose less than -£65K over any one year, with a 95% confidence, or the portfolio is likely to lose more than £65K in 1 in 20 years.

The advantages of the mean-variance methodology are its simplicity, ease of calculation and intuition. The disadvantages are that it assumes a normal distribution of returns and it is based on risk and return assumptions that may be inaccurate (it relies entirely on point estimates of the portfolio's expected return and standard deviation).

Figure 3.8 shows the normal distribution of returns for a portfolio with an annualised standard deviation of σ = 10% and expected return of μ = 10%. The left side of the distribution shows the area below the 95% VaR of -6.5%.

Figure 3.8 – normal distribution with the left tail below the 95% VaR of - 6.5% highlighted

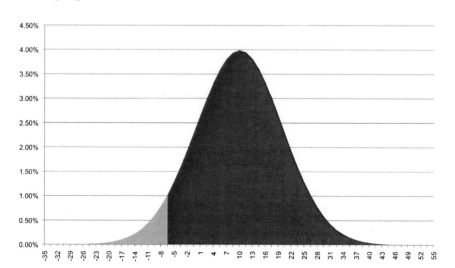

2. Historical method

The second method for calculating VaR is the *historical method*. Under this method historical returns are organised in a histogram, which shows the percentage of past returns falling under different intervals or bins (e.g. percentage of monthly returns between 0% and 1%, percentage of monthly returns between 1% and 2%, and so on).

Focusing on the left tail of the histogram distribution, VaR is the historic return that fell into the required confidence level. For example, if 5% of a portfolio's historic monthly returns fell below -10% then the 95% monthly VaR is -10%.

The advantages of the historic method are its simplicity and that no assumptions about expected risk and return are needed since it is based on historic, realised returns. The disadvantages are that it assumes that history is going to repeat itself, it requires a statistically significant history of returns (which may not be available for new investments) and it is highly dependent on the measuring period. Market characteristics (such as volatility, correlations, yields and so on) are not fixed. Calculating VaR based on recent history or a chosen time period may be misleading (it may overestimate or underestimate risk).

3. Monte Carlo simulation method

The third method for calculating VaR is the *Monte Carlo simulation method*. This method involves developing a model of future hypothetical returns and running multiple trials through the model. Monte Carlo simulation refers to any method that randomly generates trials. The hypothetical trials are then organised in a histogram and, similar to the historical method, VaR is calculated.

This method is useful when analytically calculating VaR is impossible, a history of returns is unavailable or when historical returns are not representative of likely future outcomes. Calculating VaR of portfolios that include derivatives, such as options, often requires the Monte Carlo simulation method. The return profile of such portfolios is not normally distributed because of the asymmetry of the derivatives' returns or because the derivatives are too complex to incorporate in the mean-variance method. The main advantage of this method is its flexibility. Its main disadvantage is that it relies on assumptions and the ability to model future hypothetical returns (*model risk*).

Applying VaR

Similar to standard deviation, it is easy to scale or translate VaR from one time period to another by multiplying VaR by the appropriate square root of time. For example, a one-day VaR multiplied by the square root of 21 (the average business days in a month) gives the monthly VaR. A one-month VaR multiplied by the square root of 12 gives an annual VaR.

Similar to VaR in absolute space, investors can calculate relative VaR to measure the risk of underperforming a benchmark. To do so, return is substituted by relative return and standard deviation is substituted by tracking error.

Standard deviation is less useful for measuring the risk of portfolios with asymmetric distributions, while VaR is beneficial in such cases since it captures the left tail of the distribution. However, if the left tail is thin and extends far out to the left, VaR does not capture the true risk of the distribution since it is not a worst case return as it does not focus on the extreme of the distribution. *Conditional VaR* (CVaR) or expected shortfall looks at the likely return when it exceeds VaR. CVaR is the average return below VaR. For example, if the 95% VaR is -5% and the average return in the 5% area of the left side of the distribution is -8%, then CVaR= -8%.

VaR is the expected negative return at a point on the distribution of returns based on VaR's confidence level (95%, 99%). This negative return is expected to happen once every so often under normal market conditions. CVaR estimates the expected negative return beyond VaR's confidence level. CVaR, similar to VaR, is not the worst return that can happen. To model the worst case, stress testing is required.

Stress testing

Stress testing is a simulation technique used on portfolios to evaluate their reaction to different market conditions, in particular conditions of financial crisis – it defines a scenario and checks the potential impact on the portfolio should the scenario occur. Some regulators require institutional investors, such as banks and insurance companies, to stress test their portfolios to maintain adequate capital to cover potential losses under extreme, but plausible, events.

Three methods of stress testing

There are three common methods for generating scenarios for stress testing:

1   Historic extreme event method

2.   Risk factor shock method

3.   External factor shock

Under the *historic extreme event method*, the portfolio's return is hypothesised under the recurrence of historic stressful events. The portfolio's current positions and risk exposures, or *risk factors*, are modelled with the historic event's returns of markets and/or risk factors. That is, the stress test simulates what would have happened to the portfolio with its current holdings had the historic event occurred today.

Good recent events for stress testing include Black Monday in 1987, the LTCM blow-up and Russian debt default crisis in 1998, the bursting of the high-tech bubble in 2000, the 11 September 2001 terrorist attack, the 2008 credit crunch and the European sovereign debt crisis of 2011. It is useful for the purpose of this testing method that financial markets seem to provide a stress scenario at least once a decade.

The advantage of this method is that it is based on scenarios of real historical financial crises. The disadvantage is that it cannot hypothesise the next financial crisis. The number of historical financial crises or observations is not *statistically significant*[63] in modelling the characteristics of the next one.

With the *risk factor shock method*, the investor shocks any risk factor (risk exposure) in the portfolio by a chosen amount. The exposure of the portfolio to the risk factor remains unchanged. The adjusted returns of other risk factors are modelled through a *covariance matrix* based on their correlation with the shocked risk factor. Finally, the hypothetical impact on the portfolio is calculated.

For example, a change in inflation rate can be chosen as a risk factor. The investor shocks inflation by 10%. Through the covariance matrix the model adjusts other risk factors (such as interest rates and currency exposure) to the rise in inflation.

The stressed return of the portfolio is then calculated with its current holdings under the simulated changes to the different risk factors.

The advantage of this method is its flexibility to check how the portfolio could behave when certain risk scenarios happen. This is a powerful way to understand the portfolio's exposure to different risks. The investor can then take action to control unwanted risks. The disadvantage of this method is that it requires the hypothetical or theoretical modelling of financial crises.

Using the *external factor shock* method, instead of shocking a risk factor, the investor shocks any index (such as equities, government bonds and corporate bonds), macro-economic series (such as oil price) or a custom series (such as exchange rates). Using regression analysis or the covariance matrix, adjusted asset class returns are calculated and used to calculate the hypothetical portfolio return. This method is flexible, intuitive and easily done with Microsoft Excel (it is similar to *backtesting*).

Using a combination of the methods

The recommended method for stress testing is a combination of some or all three methods since each one reveals different aspects of potential stressful events. The choice depends on what the investor wants to learn from the stress test and the available resources at the investor's disposal.

The external factor shock method and historic extreme event method can be easily implemented by backtesting the portfolio using monthly returns of indices representing the portfolio's different asset classes. Hypothetical scenarios (such as equity markets falling 25%) can be tested for the external shock method. Real historic scenarios can be tested for the historic extreme event method. All that is needed is Microsoft Excel and monthly index returns. The risk factor shock method requires more sophistication since the portfolio's exposures to different risk factors need to be derived using a *multi-factor model*.

Table 3.4 shows a simple example of historic stress testing of a portfolio with an allocation of 50% US equities, 40% 10-year US Treasuries and 10% US Treasury bills. Using indices representing each asset class and their historic monthly returns, the portfolio performance is calculated.

Table 3.4 – historic stress testing of 50% equities, 40% bonds and 10% cash portfolio

Event	Start month	End month	S&P 500	US 10-year treasury	US T-bills	Portfolio
1970s bear market	Jan-73	Dec-74	-37.4	7.6	15.9	-16.4
1987 crash	Oct-87	-	-21.5	5.7	0.4	-8.4
1997 Asia crisis	Aug-97	-	-5.6	-1.8	0.4	-3.5
1998 Russian default	Aug-98	-	-14.5	3.9	0.4	-5.6
2000 high-tech bubble	Apr-00	Feb-03	-41.5	38.5	9.9	-10.2
2008 credit crunch	Sep-08	Feb-09	-41.8	8.6	0.1	-20.4
2011 European crisis	Aug-11	Sep-11	-12.1	8.2	0	-2.9

Source: Bloomberg, Global Financial Data, S&P 500, USA 10-year Government Bond Total Return, USD Total Return T-Bill Index.

Stress testing should be used to increase the probability of portfolios performing reasonably well under different scenarios. It is unlikely to be feasible to position portfolios to outperform under all scenarios and still meet their investment objectives under the central scenario. For example, for a portfolio to outperform under a market crisis scenario conservative positioning or hedges should be put in place. If the central scenario, however, is constructive or positive on risk assets, conservatism and costly hedges are likely to cause the portfolio to lag.

Stress testing is helpful in supporting decisions such as removing or hedging some risks that may result in the ruin of the portfolio (*risk of ruin* is unacceptably high risk; if materialised the portfolio may not be able to recover its losses), selecting investments that should do well or provide some protection under certain scenarios, and preparing plans of action on how to react quickly to certain scenarios. Investment management is centred on making reasonable decisions under uncertainty, while considering the risks. Stress testing can inform such decisions.

By stressing portfolios relative to their investment objectives, a link is created between risk and objectives. Portfolios' investment objectives should be represented by a benchmark or modelling of liabilities. Both portfolio and benchmark positions are stressed under the same scenarios and the portfolio's relative return is calculated. This is one method for calculating *shortfall risk* (the risk of not meeting objectives). Shortfall risk equates to the probability of a loss times the magnitude of a loss and is calculated with the following formula:

Shortfall risk = Probability(loss) x amount of loss

Investors need to consider the probability and magnitude of each scenario, estimate the financial impact on portfolios and decide accordingly on appropriate actions.

Other downside risk measures

Maximum drawdown

Other downside risk measures include *maximum drawdown*[64]. Drawdown measures the historic fall from peak to trough during a specific time period and vividly illustrates the investment's downside risk. However, the shortcoming of drawdown is that it is based on historic experiences that may have no predictive power.

Figure 3.9 shows the historic drawdowns of US equities and 10-year Treasury bonds (real returns). During the inflationary 1970s, bonds experienced drawdowns almost as severe as those of equities. Since inflation has been under control, equities have experienced much more severe drawdowns relative to bonds.

Figure 3.9 – drawdowns of real returns of the S&P 500 and US Treasury bonds, adjusted for US inflation, January 1970 to June 2012

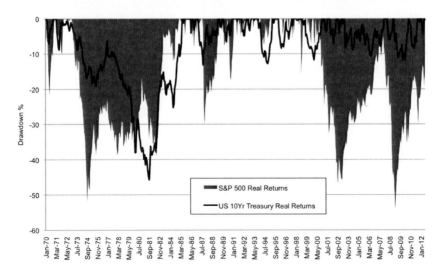

Source: Bloomberg, Global Financial Data, S&P 500, USA 10-year Government Bond Total Return, US inflation.

Semi-variance

Another alternative downside risk measure is *semi-variance*. Semi-variance aims to overcome the criticism that standard deviation panelises both negative and positive returns in the same way. It measures the dispersion of returns that fall below the mean or target return. Semi-variance is the average of the squared deviations of values that are less than the mean or the target return. The formula for semi-variance is:

$$SV = \Sigma(x - r_t)^2/n$$

where n is the number of returns below the mean or target return, x is the mean return or target return; and r_t is the realised return in period t below x ($r_t < x$).

Semi-variance panelises only for undesired retunes, below the mean or target, and completely ignores returns above the mean or target. The disadvantages of semi-variance are that it does not have the attractive statistical properties of standard deviation and it uses only part of the observations. Semi-variance ignores some of the historical information, hence weakening the robustness of its statistical inference.

Risk measurement and risk management

So far the focus has been on ways to measure risk, the ability of different risk measures to effectively communicate and measure portfolio risk, and how to translate risk objectives into risk measures. The prerequisite for controlling risk is identifying, communicating, quantifying and understanding risks. This is the role of risk measurement[65]. Risk management covers the actions that investors choose to take to control risks.

Categories of risk

This section considers the main risk categories when thinking about risk objectives. The four main risk categories are:

1. Market risk

2. Credit risk

3. Liquidity

4. Operational risk

1. Market risk

Market risk is the risk of missing the investment objectives due to movements in the prices or values of investments.

Prices do not always equal values. Price reflects by how much the market is valuing an investment, whereas value is how much it is worth or its *intrinsic value.*

Often the price is too high (overpriced) or too low (underpriced) relative to value. Warren Buffett described this as "price is what you pay, value is what you get."

Valuation is the process of determining or estimating value. The value needs to be estimated or modelled since it is unknown (investments do not come with a value tag). The valuation may by overvalued or undervalued relative to the true value. Valuations by different market participants drive supply and demand forces, and consequently the price of investments. Both the price and value of investments fluctuate and this is market risk. Investors may buy overpriced or overvalued investments whose price subsequently falls. The Holy Grail of investing is buying low and selling high, but buying high and selling low is often the result.

Market risk includes four sub-categories:

(a) Equity risk

(b) Interest rate risk

(c) Currency risk

(d) Commodity risk

(a) Equity risk

When investors invest in equity of a company, they really make two investments, one in the company and a second in the equity market (*equity risk*). The risk of the company (the *diversifiable, idiosyncratic, unique* or *specific risk*) can be diversified away through proper diversification. The market risk or *systematic risk*, however, is not diversifiable and it must be accepted when investing in equities. There are exceptions, such as equity market-neutral hedge funds, which aim to remove directional equity market risk exposure and instead aim to have pure manager alpha. It is challenging to remove the equity market risk for such funds and many fail to do so.

The equity market price level, or overall prices of equities within an index, is determined by demand and supply. Rationally, the level of the equity market should be driven by the *expected* fortunes of companies, of which equities are partial ownership stakes, and economic factors, which affect the overall fortunes of companies across the economy. Equity markets can fall because of weakening prospects for companies and/or the economy.

For example, two basic assumptions to evaluate equities are the *discount factor*, which is used to calculate the present value of future cash flows (dividends and equity final selling price or terminal value) and should reflect the risk of the cash flows, and the *growth rate* of future cash flows (growth of earnings, from which dividends are paid). Equity prices can fall because of an increase in the discount factor (e.g. due to re-pricing of company risk or increase in interest rates) and/or a fall in the growth rate (e.g. due to weaker company-specific or economy-wide growth prospects).

Equity risk is driven not only by rational factors, but also by irrational ones. One challenge in estimating all the necessary variables for equity evaluation stems from the unpredictable, periodically irrational behaviour of markets. Demand and supply are driven by fear and greed, sentiment and the aggregate psychology of investors in the market.

The assumption that markets are efficient (the Efficient Market Hypothesis or EMH) and incorporate all information immediately in security prices gives a lot of credit to investors. EMH basically assumes that investors use valuation models, formulate assumptions based on news, incorporate all the news immediately into the valuation models, act on informed decisions and do not let emotions affect them. It is sometimes amusing when financial news agencies explain the reasons for daily market falls or rallies as if they are always rational. Different investors have different reasons to buy and sell securities, and consequently create supply or demand that impacts markets.

Most markets are fairly efficient, but not as efficient as EMH presumes and not as rational as standard economic theories assume they are. Market risk has a large element of mass psychology. Rational analysis of information often fails to model equity risk. Even when investors do thorough analysis, markets can still move unexpectedly due to panic or euphoria.

(b) Interest rate risk

One of the prominent market risks in fixed income is *interest rate risk*. The prices of government bonds are determined by three main risk factors:

1. Interest rates

2. Inflation

3. Creditworthiness

Interest rates are used in valuation models of government bonds as the discount factor of future cash flows (coupons or interest and principal repayment). Changes in interest rates change bond valuations (e.g. increasing interest rates cause bond prices to decrease and vice versa). Government bonds can be viewed as derivatives on interest rates as their prices are derived from interest rate levels (*duration* measures the sensitivity of a bond's price to interest rates as *delta* measures the sensitivity of a derivative's price to the price of the underlying).

Inflation and expectations for future inflation are a function of the dynamics between short-term and long-term interest rates. Short-term interest rates are controlled by central banks[66]. Central banks do not control long-term interest rates, which are set by market forces (supply and demand). If inflation expectations increase, long-term interest rates will increase to compensate investors for higher inflation risk, which erodes the purchasing power of nominal bonds' future cash flows. Inflation affects interest rates, which in turn affect the price of bonds.

(c) Currency risk

Currency risk is an integral part of every global portfolio. Foreign investments are typically denominated in foreign currencies and currency fluctuations can have a large impact on investment returns. For example, a US-based investor whose base currency is dollars invests in UK equities, where the currency is pounds. The UK equity market rises by 10% (measured in pounds) but the GBP/USD exchange rate increases by 5% (i.e. it takes more dollars to buy each pound, or the dollar has depreciated by 5% against the pound). The return to the investor measured in dollars is 5% (10% - 5%), or more precisely 4.5%[67].

When investing in global equities currency risk can be accepted. Equities are risky anyway, they are a *risk asset*, and currency risk may not dramatically change their risk level. On the other hand, when investing in foreign *conservative assets* (safe-haven assets), such as foreign government bonds, currency risk may significantly change their risk level.

For example, a foreign developed government bond, issued by a credible sovereign, may have a standard deviation of 5% in *local currency* or when currency exposure is hedged back to the portfolio's base currency. However, when currency risk is added (i.e. currency is unhedged) the standard deviation of such a bond may double to 10% or even triple to 15%, reclassifying it from a conservative asset to a risk asset (with equity-like volatility). Currency risk, which is a managed risk since it can be hedged, should be considered as an additional asset class in global portfolios. Currency exposure entails upside opportunities and downside risks.

(d) Commodity risk

Commodity risk, as its name implies, is linked to prices of commodities. Commodity prices have historically been driven by supply and demand, as well as by inflation. Companies that use or produce commodities have an exposure to commodity risk since they need to buy or sell them to operate a business.

Economic factors determine the demand for commodities. For example, healthy economic activity and growth lead to higher commodity consumption, higher demand and higher prices. There are also long-term trends that affect demand, such as the growth in commodity consumption in countries such as China. The supply side is determined by the availability of commodity resources.

The impact of certain events or factors on prices of commodities and other asset classes can differ. For example, a drought may be bad news for equities but good news for commodity prices as it may drive prices up due to falling supplies. When OPEC[68] decides to cut the production of oil it may negatively impact global economies, equities and bonds (due to increasing oil prices and inflation), but positively impact investors holding oil. Commodity prices naturally rise with inflation over time. Inflation spikes may hurt equities and in particular fixed income, but support commodity prices.

Over recent decades more investors and speculators have entered the commodity market. Trading of commodities by financial professionals, such as hedge funds, sometimes weakens the economic link between commodity prices and true demand and supply; that is to say commodity prices can fluctuate and deviate from true value due to financial speculation.

While investing in commodities introduces risks, there are potential investment benefits attached to including commodities in portfolios and assuming commodity risk, such as diversification, expansion of the investment opportunity set and an inflation hedge.

Managing market risk

One way to mitigate market risk is through diversifying portfolios across different investments. The bursting of the 2000 high-tech bubble taught investors a lesson about market risk. Many believed that this occasion was different; *the old economy is dead, long live the new economy.* They claimed that old valuation models were obsolete and dot-com companies would continue to grow and grow forever. The valuations and share prices of internet companies without any profit or foreseeable profits ballooned. Many investors jumped on the bandwagon and shifted all their portfolios to technology stocks, throwing diversification out of the window. When technology stocks crashed, it was a painful lesson in market risk and the need to always keep risk in mind and control it.

Market risk in multi-asset portfolios is managed through several methods. SAA or investment policy sets the long-term market risk level by allocating the portfolio to different asset classes with different long-term risk levels, taking into account the interactions among them. TAA adjusts the asset allocation and portfolio risk level to short-term market conditions. Investment selection picks investments with appropriate risks within each asset class. Portfolio construction aggregates and considers the market risks of all the components and their interactions. Lastly, risk management techniques such as diversification, hedging and insurance are used to control risk.

Diversification is achieved through asset allocation and investment selection. *Hedging* is implemented through derivative markets for most asset classes. For example, a long exposure to the FTSE 100 Index can be hedged by shorting FTSE

100 futures contracts. The currency risk for a US-based investor investing in the FTSE 100 Index can be hedged by shorting forward contracts on the GBP/USD exchange rate. Losses on the long equity or currency position are offset by gains on the short position (the hedge). Conversely, gains on the long position are offset by losses on the short position.

Insurance can be implemented through purchasing put options, for example. Instead of shorting index futures contracts, out-of-the-money put options on the index are purchased to insure the portfolio against falls in the index. The option's asymmetric payoff maintains the upside. However, insurance has an upfront cost or a premium.

2. Credit risk

The 2008 credit crunch has taught investors never to forget credit risk; it lurks in many places, in different guises.

Credit risk is the possibility of a loss for a lender or creditor due to a borrower not making payments as promised. A *credit event* may be *default* (the borrower failing to pay interest or principal), *debt restructure*, such as the borrower postponing payments of promised cash flows, or *haircut* (i.e. reduction in the amount of promised cash flows, such as paying 80 cents on the dollar). A credit event that triggers payment under a *Credit Default Swap* (*CDS*)[69] is defined in the legal documents of the CDS and must be carefully read to understand under what circumstances the CDS pays. It is not always clear on the face of it.

For corporate and some government bonds, credit risk or *default risk* determines their valuations, in addition to interest rates and inflation. Compared to equivalent safe-haven government bonds, corporate bonds usually need to pay higher interest rates or yield to compensate investors for credit risk. Corporate bond valuations depend on the valuation of the corresponding government bonds and the spread, which should reflect the credit risk, as well as liquidity.

Figure 3.10 shows the yields on US Treasuries, AAA and BAA rated corporate bonds since January 1970. BAA corporate bonds have to offer a higher yield than AAA corporate bonds and government bonds to attract investors (i.e. convince them to lend money to the company) and compensate them for the credit risk. At times of financial stress, such as during the 2008 financial crisis, the spread between riskier bonds and government bonds widens as credit risk increases. The spread reflects the level of how the market prices credit risk.

Figure 3.10 – yields on US Treasury bonds, AAA and BAA rated corporate bonds, January 1970 to June 2012

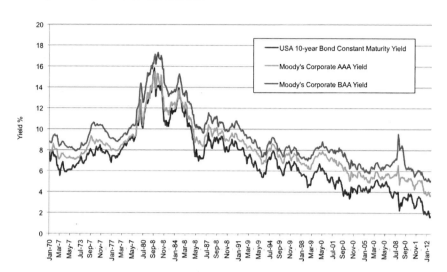

Source: Global Financial Data, USA 10-year Bond Constant Maturity Yield, Moody's Corporate AAA Yield, Moody's Corporate BAA Yield.

Credit risk is analysed and published by credit rating agencies, such as Standard & Poor's (S&P), Moody's and Finch. The main criticism of credit rating agencies is that their ratings are backward and not forward looking. During the 2008 financial crisis investment grade rated firms, such as Lehman Brothers, filed for bankruptcy. As the 2010 European sovereign debt crisis unfolded, the true credit risk of government bonds or sovereign debt of countries such as Portugal, Ireland, Italy, Greece and Spain (known as the *PIIGS*) became apparent. Countries with investment grade credit ratings were on the verge of bankruptcy. The limitations of credit agencies mean that professional corporate bond investors normally use their own analysis to assess the credit risk of bonds.

Credit risk can be hedged using the derivative market (CDS). However, this is not as simple as hedging currency risk, for example. CDS are not available on every corporate issue and sometimes CDS on a corporate bond index must be used to hedge the credit risk of individual corporate bonds. This introduces *basis risk* because of differences between the credit risk of the individual issues in the portfolio and that of the CDS underlying corporate bond index. Additionally, the CDS market is not as liquid as the forward currency contract market. Nevertheless, large portfolios of corporate bonds are often required to hedge credit risk using CDS since selling the underlying bonds may be expensive due to poor liquidity.

3. Liquidity risk

Liquidity risk is one of the least understood risks since it is not captured by most risk measures. Nevertheless, it is one of the most dangerous risks. Liquidity risk includes two types of risk. The first type is *funding liquidity risk* or cash flow risk and it refers to the ability to raise or retain the debt required for financial leveraged positions, meeting *margin calls*[70] or paying portfolio redemptions.

The second type of liquidity risk is *asset liquidity risk*, which is the ability to buy or sell investments in the necessary size, at the prevailing market price, in a timely manner. Liquid investments can be purchased and sold at reasonable transaction costs at any time at the prevailing market price. Illiquid investments, on the other hand, do not have these features. It may be a costly and lengthy process to trade them.

Liquidity is valuable since it gives investors flexibility, or an option. Options in finance, and generally in life, are valuable. Investors demand a premium as compensation for investing in illiquid investments or for assuming illiquidity risk, either through a discount on the price of investments and/or superior returns compared to equivalent liquid investments (this is termed a liquidity premium).

Funding and asset liquidity risks can interact in a toxic combination. Falling markets may induce margin calls or redemptions. If portfolios do not have sufficient cash, assets must be sold or liquidated. If the sold positions are illiquid or large relative to normal market transactions (volume), the sales put further pressure on prices and trigger more margin calls or redemptions. This vicious circle may end up in a liquidity crisis.

Markets can turn illiquid very quickly at stressful times, just when liquidity is most needed. When many investors wish to sell their holdings at the same time, for example when markets fall, there are unlikely to be willing buyers and liquidity may quickly dry up. The 2008 credit crisis saw the credit markets stop functioning and investors could not sell their holdings in corporate bonds while seeing the credit markets fall.

Hedge funds were another prime example of an illiquidity crisis during 2008. Some hedge funds invest in illiquid assets. When markets fell in 2008, some investors wanted to redeem their hedge fund holdings. Many hedge funds could not meet those redemptions (similar to a bank run), had to freeze all redemption requests and created side pockets to hold illiquid investments. Investors could not sell their holdings. Many hedge funds were forced out of business and their investors lost all their investments, some of which had been marketed as low-risk investments with bond-like volatility.

During times of financial crisis investors often wish to quickly sell risky positions and buy safe-haven investments, such as government bonds and gold. When many investors rush out of risk assets to conservative ones (a flight to quality) some assets, such as corporate bonds, real estate and hedge funds, may run into a liquidity crisis. In a market of sellers only, prices fall, more investors try to sell and prices plunge even further. Supply overwhelms demand. At some point, when the crisis is approaching its end, very attractive buying opportunities may emerge since the market is oversold. The challenge is identifying that the crisis is indeed reaching its end.

When purchasing a structured product, such as a principal protected product with 100% capital protection, the small print of the terms usually discloses that capital is protected only if the product is held to its maturity, which may be a few years. If investors need or want to sell the product before maturity the proceeds from the sale may not cover the purchasing price and the principal is not protected. This is another example of liquidity risk. Liquidity is a major factor to consider when evaluating structured products.

Not all investors value liquidity in the same way. Different investors have different risk tolerances to liquidity risk. It depends, as always, on the specific circumstances of each investor. Short-term investors normally need liquidity. Long-term investors, on the other hand, can tolerate more liquidity risk and illiquidity. With skill, long-term investors may turn illiquidity into an advantage and profit from the liquidity premium.

Liquidity and liquidity risk depend on the size of the investment and its nature. Marginal, small holdings in an investment are more liquid than large holdings. Trading substantial holdings requires skill to avoid an adverse market impact[71]. Large investors can be penalised when requiring liquidity and benefit when supplying liquidity to the market.

Investors who may need to liquidate some of their portfolios to meet short-term obligations and liabilities, whether expected or unexpected, should carefully consider liquidity risk. Sufficient portions of the portfolio should have low liquidity risk or be completely liquid in the form of cash, government bonds or large capitalisation equities. Investors need to maintain flexibility in their portfolios to be able to react to market developments. Illiquidity is inflexibility, or flexibility at a high price. Using cash, derivatives and highly liquid investments, such as certain ETFs, as well as limiting the exposure to illiquid investments, are ways to maintain liquidity and flexibility, and control liquidity risk.

4. Operational risk

Operational risk is defined as the "risk of direct or indirect loss resulting from inadequate or failed internal processes, people and systems or from external events"[72]. This definition includes legal risk. Operational risk arises from human errors and ineffective operations. Some examples of operational risk events include fraud, market manipulation, improper trading, fiduciary breaches, account churning, physical damage to assets, system failures, data entry errors, accounting errors and so on. Asset management firms rely on their back office and middle office (operations, IT, finance, accounting and human resources) and compliance departments to help them mitigate and control operational risks. A failure in these areas can easily affect the entire firm and its clients.

One classic example of an operational risk event is the downfall of Barings Bank, which was the oldest merchant bank in London. In 1995 the bank collapsed after one of its employees, Nick Leeson, lost £827 million due to unauthorised speculative trading at the bank's Singapore office. Internal controls and audit by the bank failed and Leeson was able to operate without any supervision from London and without any risk controls over his activities. There are plenty of other such examples[73].

Operational risk is unrewarded by markets, unlike other risks, such as market, credit and liquidity risks. There is no operational risk premium, as there are equity, credit and liquidity risk premiums. Those risks are a resource since controlled and calculated risk taking should generate returns over time. Operational risk only has a downside without any upside (except perhaps for the lawyers who benefit from court litigations following operational risk debacles). Operational risk is an unwanted risk and should be mitigated as much as possible.

Managing operational risk is challenging. The ways to manage it are conducting due diligence on the operational capabilities of asset management firms (operational due diligence on unregulated hedge funds is especially critical) and including sections in Investment Management Agreements (IMAs) to cover risk controls, insurance and indemnity clauses in case an operational risk event results in losses. One primary goal is confirming that there are processes, checks and balances in place to make it easier for people to do the right thing and hard to do the wrong thing. Robust processes and procedures can help mitigate and control operational risk.

Fixed income risk measures

The major factor driving the price of investment grade bonds is interest rates. Fixed income instruments have a set of risk measures to quantify their price sensitivity to changes in interest rates or yield. These measures are particularly useful when setting risk objectives for the fixed income portion of portfolios and when managing assets in line with liabilities.

Duration measures the sensitivity of a bond price to changes in interest rates. It is only an approximate measure since it assumes that all interest rates across the yield curve[74] move in parallel at the same time. This is an unrealistic assumption as yields do not move in tandem. The short side of the yield curve is much more volatile than its long side.

Duration in years times the change in interest rates equals the estimated change in the bond price in percentage terms. For example, the price of a bond with duration of 5.8 years will change by 5.8% for every 1% change in interest rates.

Duration is a weighted average of the time until the bond cash flows. A zero-coupon bond with a maturity of 10 years has duration of 10 years. The larger the coupons of a bond relative to its principal, the shorter the duration is since the weighted average of the time of the interest and principal payments is shorter relative to the maturity of the bond. Cash has duration close to zero.

Convexity measures the sensitivity of bond duration to changes in interest rates. Duration is the first derivative and convexity is the second derivative of changes of bond price with respect to changes of interest rate. Convexity measures the rate of change of duration to changes in interest rates.

Generally, the higher the convexity the more sensitive the bond price is to decreasing interest rates and the less sensitive it is to increasing rates. As interest rates change, the bond price is unlikely to change linearly. Instead, it changes in a curved function of interest rates. The more curved the function, the more inaccurate the duration is as a measure of the price sensitivity to changes in interest rates. Duration is an approximate sensitivity measure for small and parallel changes in interest rates across the entire yield curve. When the changes in interest are large and not parallel, convexity supplements duration to estimate the change in bond price due to change in interest rates.

Figure 3.11 shows the price of a bond (principal $1,000, coupon 5%) for different *yield-to-maturities* (YTM)[75]. The slope of the curve is the duration of the bond. The curve is not a straight line because of convexity. The slope of the curve is different for each point and the change of the slope is the bond convexity.

Figure 3.11 – bond price for different yield-to-maturities

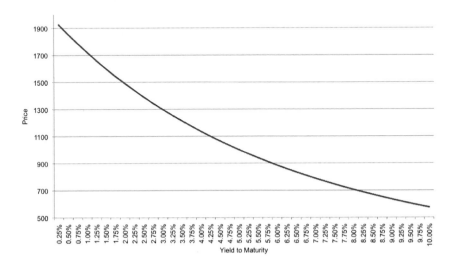

The formula for calculating the estimated change in bond price due to a change in the yield is:

$$\%\Delta P = -D\Delta y + 0.5C\Delta y^2$$

where $\%\Delta P$ is the percentage estimated change in bond price, D is modified duration[76], Δy is the change in yield and C is convexity[77].

As the formula shows, a bond price with a positive convexity falls by a lower percentage when interest rates increase. Most conventional bonds have positive convexity. However, certain fixed income instruments, such as Mortgage Back Securities (MBS), may have a negative convexity.

Floating Rate Notes (FRNs), whose coupons are variable and change with interest rates, have a very short duration. Their duration is calculated to the next time the coupon is adjusted, normally on a quarterly basis. FRNs have relatively low interest rate risk.

A *callable bond* is a bond that allows the issuer to call and redeem it before its maturity. The issuer has a call option on the bond. Duration and convexity calculations for callable bonds need to consider the call feature.

Liabilities are a stream of cash flows that the portfolio needs to pay in the future. Instead of cash inflows from a bond, liabilities are a stream of cash outflows, or a short bond position. Interest rates have a large impact on the present value of liabilities.

Duration and convexity are commonly used to express the risk of liabilities. *Duration matching* is a simple way to immunise a portfolio to its liabilities. Holding bonds with the same value and duration as those of the liabilities links changes to the value of liabilities due to interest rate changes with the value of assets and reduces the risk of a deficit.

The Greeks

When portfolios include derivatives, the Greeks are commonly used as measures of the sensitivity of the prices of derivatives, such as options, to changes in underlying factors. The common measures are denoted by Greek letters, hence the name the Greeks.

- *Delta* (Δ) measures the rate of change of a derivative's price with respect to the change of the price of the underlying (e.g. the sensitivity of the price of a call option on the S&P 500 Index to changes in the price of the index). Delta is the first derivative of the derivative price with respect to the underlying asset price.

- *Gamma* (Γ) measures the rate of change of delta with respect to the change of the price of the underlying. Gamma is the second derivative of the derivative price with respect to the underlying asset price. Delta is similar to bond duration and gamma is similar to bond convexity. Delta and gamma refer to derivatives and underlyings, while duration and convexity refer to bonds and interest rates.

- *Vega* (v), which is not a real Greek letter, measures the sensitivity of the derivative's price to changes in volatility.

- *Theta* (Θ) measures the sensitivity of a derivative's price to time (*time decay*).

- *Rho* (ρ) measures the sensitivity of a derivative's price to changes in interest rates.

Bad risk and good risk

Risk in financial markets can be bad or good for investors[78]. It can be bad if it causes non-repairable damage. For example, if interest rates go up and the investor suffers a permanent capital loss on a government bond or the credit rating of a company deteriorates and the value of its corporate bond falls without prospects for a reversal, this is bad risk.

Risk can be good, on the other hand, if it creates opportunities and attracts a long-term premium. Volatility causes prices to temporarily diverge from values and then opportunities are created for investors to generate alpha. Beta volatility is compensated by the markets over the long term.

Summary

This chapter aims to demonstrate that there is no one single risk measure that captures all the risks of investing. Mathematics alone, as sophisticated as it may be, does not reveal all risks. Common sense and judgment, informed by quantitative risk measures and qualitative risk assessment, are necessary to understand and manage risks.

Investors need to decide which risks are wanted and which are unwanted. Wanted risks are those that should be compensated and which can generate returns over time. Portfolios should maintain controlled exposure to such risks. Unwanted risks should be controlled, mitigated or avoided. When establishing risk objectives, investors need to understand and articulate all the risks that they are willing to take to generate returns, the level of acceptable risk, and risks that they are concerned about and wish to mitigate or avoid.

- Risk objectives are the second set of investment objectives, alongside return objectives.

- Each investor has a different risk tolerance made up of willingness and ability to take risk.

- Expected return and risk must align as risk level determines return level.

- Risk is falling short of investment objectives or the chance of a disappointing outcome. Risk depends on each investor's expectations (the level of expectations drive the level of disappointment).

- Standard deviation measures the probability for an outcome to be better or worse than the expected outcome (mean).

- Volatility is a common measure of absolute risk and tracking error is a common measure of relative risk.

- Because the distribution of investment returns may have fat tails and investors are concerned about downside risk, measures such as VaR focus on the left side of the distribution (downside).

- The worst return distribution combines negative skewness and high kurtosis. This means that, on average, there are more negative returns (the distribution is asymmetrically skewed to its left) and when they happen they are more negative than the normal distribution expects (fat tails).

- VaR is not a worst case risk measure and should be supplemented by stress testing to evaluate potential extreme negative returns.

- Investment management is centred on making reasonable decisions under uncertainty, while considering the risks. Stress testing can inform such decisions.

- Some investments, such as bonds and derivatives, have their own sets of risk measures.

- The main risk categories that investors should consider are market risk, credit risk, liquidity risk and operational risk.

- Markets should compensate investors over time for assuming market, credit and liquidity risks.

4. RATIONAL OR IRRATIONAL MARKETS

Standard financial theories assume that investors are rational and markets are efficient. Behavioural finance has a different view. Investors are human beings; emotions and *cognitive biases* (patterns of deviation in judgment that occur in particular situations due to humans' mental behaviour) drive their decisions and they are not rational machines.

Investors need to understand their behaviour in order to formulate their investment objectives. Only when they understand their investment psychology can they understand how to frame their return and risk objectives, how they are likely to react to different market conditions and investment outcomes, and how to make their investment decisions. Behavioural finance is instrumental in understanding the behaviour of markets, so that more informed investment decisions can be made.

Efficient market hypothesis

The efficient market hypothesis (EMH) claims that financial markets are efficient by incorporating information into security prices very quickly. EMH was developed by Professor Eugene Fama[79] in the early 1960s. There are three levels of EMH:

1. *Weak EMH* claims that security prices reflect all historic publicly available information. Therefore, technical analysis, which relies heavily on past performance, should not generate any excess returns.

2. *Semi-strong EMH* claims that security prices reflect historical public information and instantly reflect new public information as it becomes available. Therefore, fundamental analysis, which analyses publicly available information, should not generate any excess returns.

3. *Strong EMH* claims that security prices not only reflect all publicly available information, but also insider information. Therefore, any active management should not generate alpha. In other words, if strong EMH is valid then there is no value in active investment management.

In his book *A Random Walk Down Wall Street*[80], Burton Malkiel, an economist from Princeton University, emphasised the *random walk hypothesis*[81]. Malkiel claims that security prices typically exhibit a random walk and portfolio managers cannot consistently outperform the market average return[82]. This would mean that security selection is fruitless.

According to the classical economic paradigm, as described by Paul Samuelson[83] in a 1965 article[84], the combination of efficient markets and random walk theory means that any attempt to forecast future stock patterns over any horizon is fruitless as successive price changes are independent over time. This would mean that dynamic asset allocation is useless.

EMH is not a random walk. EMH claims that market prices randomly fluctuate around a drift. A security's price tomorrow is equal to its price today times expected return, which is based on current information. As per EMH the only way to earn higher returns is by taking higher risks. Expected return is a function of expected risk, which is a function of current information.

EMH assumes that all investors are rational, they process information in the same way and security prices reflect information quickly and accurately. Many markets have become more efficient in recent decades with increasing information flow via the internet, globalisation and a rising number of sophisticated market players, such as hedge funds. Hence, according to EMH it is even harder to add any value through active management.

Behavioural finance, however, suggests that markets are not efficient since they are affected by cognitive biases and irrational behaviour of investors, who are not necessarily rational. Empirical research suggests that there is publicly available information, such as price to earnings (P/E) ratios, which can predict performance over the long term. Experience also suggests that in some areas of investment management, such as hedge funds and private equity, manager skill and active management can consistently generate alpha net of fees. Behavioural finance offers hope for active management.

The practical reality is that in spite of EMH, skilled managers can, arguably, consistently deliver alpha. The challenge is identifying and selecting these skilled managers. This suggests that alpha sources can be added to portfolios of diversified betas. These alphas are uncorrelated with the betas, hence reducing risk through diversification, and enhancing returns. Investors should be compensated for beta risks (systematic risks) as per EMH and can gain additional returns through alpha.

Behavioural finance

Behavioural finance is the study of the financial behaviour of practitioners. As the name implies, in contrast to standard finance it focuses on the cognitive psychology that drives the actual behaviour of financial decision makers at the individual level. Behavioural finance helps to make sense of where market anomalies come from. By learning behavioural finance, investors can avoid the traps or errors that others frequently make, as well as learning how to identify and benefit from market conditions that are driven by behavioural finance and not by standard financial theories, such as market crashes and bubbles. The occurrence of bubbles and crashes are evidence that EMH does not hold at all times. Understanding common behaviours also enables better assessment and scrutiny of investment advice, recommendations and commentary that others make.

Standard finance is based on the tenets that investors are rational, expected utility maximisers. Any departure from these models is random and self-cancelling. If investors are irrational, arbitrageurs quickly step in and move prices back to equilibrium. Standard finance predicts that prices move chaotically (random walk[85]), news is incorporated rapidly into security prices, active management does not add value (EMH) and investors are indifferent between dividends and capital gains[86]. If standard finance is accurate, then none of the following should happen: non-random security price movements, arbitrage opportunities, dividends, bubbles, excessive trading and volatility, home country bias, active management, and irrational biases and cognitive errors.

Anomalies in markets

Major anomalies do occur and can be detected in markets though – such as the January effect, small company effect, price momentum, price drift following earnings announcements and poor returns on IPOs. Arbitrage opportunities do occur, such as closed-end funds (traded at discount or premium to NAV), on-the-run versus off-the-run bonds and excess returns on high interest rate currencies. It does appear that markets are not perfectly efficient and rational.

Table 4.1 tries to answer whether there is a January effect. The average monthly return of each calendar month of the S&P 500 Index from January 1926 to June 2012 is calculated. None of the average monthly returns is statistically significantly different than zero (all the standard deviations are much higher than the averages). Without drawing any robust statistical conclusions, on average, July, December and April have higher average returns than January. Perhaps investors are happier during the summer holiday, Christmas, New Year and Easter (albeit the old saying "sell in May and go away" due to the historical underperformance over May to October relative to November to April).

However, the two months with the highest median returns are December and January (the averages are impacted by outliers). September is the only month with negative average returns. Perhaps the end of summer turns investors gloomy.

Table 4.1 – historic statistics of monthly returns of the S&P 500 Index, January 1926 to June 2012

Month	Average %	Standard Deviation %	Median %	% Positive
January	1.48	4.75	1.99	63.2
February	0.18	4.26	0.48	55.2
March	0.81	5.03	1.22	66.7
April	1.65	6.69	1.28	63.2
May	0.20	5.71	0.89	60.9
June	1.08	5.35	0.36	60.9
July	1.90	6.19	1.61	59.3
August	1.15	6.22	1.43	61.6
September	-0.72	6.01	0.01	50.0
October	0.61	6.22	1.05	62.8
November	1.05	5.25	1.49	62.8
December	1.79	3.62	1.93	79.1

Source: Global Financial Data, S&P 500.

The following sections cover some behavioural biases. These biases help explain the behaviour of investors and their reactions to different experiences, opportunities and risks, as well as to different market environments. If markets do not behave as predicted by standard finance, investors need to understand behavioural finance to better understand markets. Behavioural finance has two components: *cognitive biases* in investor behaviour and *prospect theory*. Standard investors, as per financial theory, are rational. Behavioural investors are not irrational; they are just normal human beings.

Prospect theory

Prospect theory[87] is based on two concepts:

1. Mental accounting
2. Loss aversion

Mental accounting

Mental accounting refers to the tendency of humans to classify activities under separate categories or accounts. For example: good investments, bad investments; children's education account, mortgage account; and so on. Investors treat the accounts as if they were independent, ignoring the interrelationships among them. Independent investment decisions are made for each account without considering the impact of decisions on the entire portfolio or the impact that one account may have on the others. By ignoring the interrelationships among different accounts (account aggregation) investors may not efficiently manage their portfolios, miss diversification opportunities and end up with poorly diversified portfolios.

For example, investors may decide to hold a significant amount of cash in their pension account, although material cash is already held at their bank account. Not considering cash holdings across different accounts may end up with a high allocation to cash and missed investment opportunities. Investors may invest in real estate in their investment account without considering that their home also gives them investment exposure to this asset class. The potential result is poor diversification and highly concentrated exposure to real estate.

Another example for mental accounting is the preference for dividends. Modigliani and Miller claim that investors should not have a preference between dividends and capital gains in a world without transaction costs and taxes (the *dividend irrelevance theorem*[88]). Capital gains tax is normally lower than income tax on dividends and therefore dividends should actually be less attractive. Nevertheless, investors classify dividends in the income mental account and prefer them. Another way to generate income is selling stocks. However, stocks are part of another mental account and the two accounts are separated in investors' minds.

Loss aversion

Loss aversion refers to the tendency of investors to be less risk averse when faced with potential losses and more risk averse when faced with potential gains. This means, for example, that investors tend to favour a potential for breaking even by accepting a risky possibility of a gain rather than accepting a small loss and selling.

An example can help demonstrate the asymmetric nature of loss aversion. You need to choose between two investments, either a certain $1 million profit or a 50% chance of $2.2 million profit and 50% chance of zero profit. What would you choose?

The choice is based on the personal preference of each investor. Most people, however, will choose the certain profit rather than taking the risk of earning zero under the second option. The second option has an expected payoff of $1.1 million (50%*2.2 + 50%*0), higher than the $1 million profit of the first option. Choosing the first option is therefore irrational under standard finance. This behaviour is driven by loss aversion.

Now you need to choose between two new investments, either a certain loss of $1 million or a 50% chance of a $2.2 million loss and 50% chance of zero return (breaking even). What would you choose this time? Most investors will choose the second option. This time they are risk seeking, since the second option is riskier (expected loss of $1.1 million) than the first. Most people would hope to break even and not lose anything by choosing the riskier option. When faced with a profit or loss people's behaviour and loss aversion are different. Loss aversion is asymmetric.

Prospect theory claims that utility (satisfaction) is convex in the loss domain and concave in the gain domain (as Figure 4.1 illustrates). *Losing is more painful than the satisfaction of profiting.* People take more risk to avoid losing than to seek profiting.

Figure 4.1 – value function

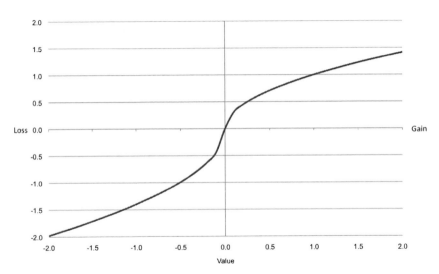

Regret and pride

The fear of regret refers to the pain felt after making a bad decision and the seeking of pride refers to the joy felt from making a wise decision. Behavioural investors regret decisions that result in lost money or a missed opportunity and feel pride when decisions make money. For example, if a portfolio is rebalanced to its target weights and a security is sold before its price later appreciates by 100%, rational investors should not feel regret. The decision was part of the investment management process and it was the right decision based on the information available when making it. Behavioural investors do feel regret though, due to the lost opportunity.

Investors tend to keep holding stocks that fall in value for too long. Rational investors assess each security in portfolio context and hold or sell it based on its future prospects. These investors do not hesitate to sell a losing security if it has no role in the portfolio or its future prospects are poor. Behavioural investors, on the other hand, look at each security in isolation, try to keep holding to break even and refrain from selling a losing security, since it is admitting a failure. This is also an example of mental accounting, distinguishing between a loser account and winner account, or realised and unrealised losses. As long as the security is not sold it is still in the unrealised losses account. Once sold at a loss it moves to the realised losses account and inflicts regret and pain.

As regretful investors may hold losing securities too long and sell winners too early, proud investors may sell winners too soon to realise a profit and achieve the pride associated with it. This is known as *disposition effect*[89] (investors are predisposed to selling winners too early and holding on to losers too long). Both of these decisions are irrational from a tax standpoint. By selling winners capital gains tax rises. By not selling losers, the investor is not using losses as write-offs against reported capital gains. Irrational, emotional behaviour costs money.

Company specific new versus economy-wide news

When news about the overall economy is released, there is no evidence of feelings of regret or the seeking of pride affecting investors' actions. On the other hand, feelings of regret and pride are strong during times of company specific news releases relating directly and uniquely to securities held in investors' portfolios. These contrasts indicate that regret and pride are linked to the degree to which investors feel that they have *control*. Company specific news is viewed as being directly related to the specific prior decision of buying the particular security. Therefore, regret and pride are strong when the company releases information. Economy-wide news, on the other hand, is not seen as related to any specific prior decision to buy individual securities. Economy-wide events are considered to be out of investors' control and do not produce strong feelings of regret and pride related to individual security purchases.

Representativeness

Representativeness[90] refers to the behavioural tendency of simplifying decisions by treating a particular event or characteristic as representative of future success or failure. For example, investors tend to view a good company as a good security. Investors see a company with good historical profitability as representative of a good security. These investors may hold portfolios consisting of securities of good companies. However, security prices of companies with good historical profitability may already price in past profitability and underperform the broad market due to disappointment in the company's current and expected profitability. Security prices reflect future expectations, not historic results. Representativeness may thus have negative effects.

Another example of representativeness is investors' tendency to chase hot performance. This bias causes investors to invest in securities, portfolio managers or markets that have performed well recently. This investment style is called *momentum*. However, past winners may be future losers. Chasing returns may lead to bubbles and markets may overshoot above fair-value, ending in disappointment when they fall from unsustainable highs.

Reference points

Behavioural investors use reference points or anchoring when making buy and sell decisions. Investors often evaluate alternative investment choices not in terms of potential outcomes, but rather in terms of potential returns relative to a reference point. Decisions may be manipulated using the reference point. If the reference point is the price at which a security was bought, investors may use this as a reference point to evaluate whether to sell or keep holding the security based on the gain or loss relative to the reference point, rather than based on the security's future prospects.

For example, a stock priced at $100 is held by two investors. The first investor bought the stock for $80 and the second for $120. Both investors have the same portfolio and investment objectives. The stock's future prospects are poor. The first investor is much more likely to sell the stock than the second one since the first investor sells at a profit and the second sells at a loss. Each investor has a different reference point.

The price of the stock drops by $10. Which investor is going to feel more pain? The second investor's loss has increased by $10 and the first investor's gain has decreased by $10. The second investor is going to feel more pain as the agony of a loss is more powerful than the joy of a gain (prospect theory).

Familiarity, quality and availability

Investors tend to show a behavioural bias of purchasing securities of companies with which they are familiar. Investing in familiar companies or countries is easier and makes investors feel more comfortable. Examples of familiarity are investing in large domestic companies or the investor's home country. Investors may end up with a portfolio with a heavy *home bias*, that is overweight in large (familiar) companies and underweight in international markets and small caps.

Some investors invest their savings in the stocks of the companies in which they work since they know their company well. In this case, familiarity may result in high concentration in one stock whose risk is highly correlated with the investors' employment. The portfolio, salary and retirement benefits are all exposed to the unique risk of one company.

Investors tend to be over-influenced by quality. They prefer well managed, successful companies over less well managed ones and find it difficult to judge the trade-off between quality and price. Investors also tend to focus on availability (i.e. focus on analytical material that is at hand). However, lower quality and less available securities often present opportunities in terms of valuations, growth prospects and markets with lower efficiency, and therefore higher prospects for value from active management. Changing bad management means upside potential for the company's stock price.

Lack of self-control

Lack of self-control refers to the tendency to become caught up in the actions of the crowd (referred to as *herding*). For example, many investors during the 1999 and 2000 technology hype invested in high-tech stocks, although they were at extreme valuations, in order to join the trend. Those investors lost dearly when the bubble eventually burst in March 2000. Investors tend to lose their self-control when they see their colleagues making profits from their investments in fashionable and hot investments.

Clear and contrarian thinking, asking what can go wrong and wondering whether what most investors do is sensible are some of the ways to retain self-control.

Overestimating the precision and importance of information

Investors must rely on available information. The problem, however, is that information is rarely complete or precise. Information arrives randomly, with noise or error. Investors must make decisions based on the information that they access. The behavioural issue is that investors often assume that the information that they have is correct, precise and complete. Therefore, they overestimate the precision and importance of the information. It is not uncommon for investors to make investment decisions based on information found in internet chat rooms or even tips from taxi drivers. Even when a source of information has no credentials, investors may rely on it.

Law of small numbers

Behavioural investors tend to overweight the representativeness of a small number of observations and overestimate their precision. For example, investors may choose a portfolio manager based on successful short-term performance without considering a long-term track record. Another example is using a small number of observations to calculate statistics without acknowledging that they are statistically insignificant.

Calculating any statistic, such as standard deviation or correlation, from monthly returns is statistically insignificant unless there are at least 36 returns (i.e. three years of data). Calculating standard deviation from the returns of 12 months, for example, is statistically insignificant and cannot be used to reach conclusions.

Overconfidence

Overconfident investors think that the information they have is better than average, that they are better able to read and skilfully interpret information than the average investor, and that they have better than average forecasting abilities. When asking a group of portfolio managers whether they think that they are better than the average portfolio manager, for example, far more than 50% will say yes, although statistically 50% are below median.

The problem is more severe when investors feel that they have control over managing their portfolios. This behavioural bias makes investors overconfident, thinking that they are smarter than they really are. They believe that they can time the markets and the highs and lows of security prices. Investors without skill are better off passively investing than trying to outperform the market through active management. Lack of skill normally results in unnecessary portfolio turnover, random noise and poor performance due to transaction costs.

Overconfidence leads investors to be too certain of their forecasts and their ability to control situations. Overconfident investors do not fully recognise or assign proper value to the uncertainty associated with complex investment analysis. Investors underestimate the uncertainty of their forecasts and the risk associated with their decisions. Their portfolios may be poorly diversified and overly concentrated since overconfident investors have strong conviction in a few investment ideas.

Daniel Kahneman[91] said that "the human mind is a pattern-seeking device, and it is strongly biased to adopt a hypothesis that a causal factor is at work behind any notable sequence of events"[92]. For example, when tossing a fair coin six times, which sequence of head (H) and tails (T) is more likely: HHHTTT or HTHTTH? Most people would say that the second sequence is more likely to occur since it appears random while the first sequence appears systematic. However, both have an equal probability of occurring (three heads and three tails). People perceive patterns where none exist (e.g. finding a correlation between the snow fall in Montana and returns of the New York Stock Exchange) and they have too much confidence in their judgment of uncertain events.

Optimism

What do the following have in common: lotteries, smoking and active management? Most people's beliefs are biased in the direction of optimism. Optimists exaggerate their talents, underestimate the likelihood of bad outcomes over which they have no control and are prone to an illusion of control. They tend to underestimate the role of chance and to misperceive games of chance as games of skill.

Overconfidence and optimism is a dangerous combination. Overconfident and optimistic people tend to underestimate risks and exaggerate their ability to control events. These people tend to play the lottery, since they believe that they are likely to win; they smoke, since they underestimate the risks of smoking (the "it won't happen to me" syndrome); and they believe in active management, since they think that they have the skill to select securities or talented portfolio managers to beat the market.

House money, snake bite, trying to break even and endowment effects

House money refers to the winnings of a gambler. Gamblers treat their winnings as house money, not their own money. Since the winnings are not treated as their own money, they tend to take large risks with their winnings. Behavioural investors tend to treat investment gains as house money and take more risks.

Snake bite refers to the reluctance to take risks after experiencing losses. Once a person has been bitten by a snake, the person tends to avoid entering locations with snakes. Investors may tend to avoid risky investments once they have experienced a loss in the market. Portfolio managers with a recent bad track record may be hesitant to take risks, adversely affecting their judgment and chances of generating excess return.

Trying to break even refers to investors' desire to recoup large losses in a quick, very high-risk investment. This is the opposite of a snake bite and investors who experienced large losses may tend to take excessive risk to try to recoup the losses.

The endowment effect refers to the tendency of investors to place higher value on what they own than on identical items that they do not own. Investors tend to ignore emerging risks related to investments that they own and make decisions with the preference of maintaining their holdings in the investments that they have already made. Selling the original investment causes pain or a feeling of loss. Investors fall in love with their investments and they do not objectively and rationally decide whether to keep holding them. Emotions therefore interfere with objectivity.

Hindsight bias

The media is very confident when analysing markets. Prior probabilities are adjusted toward the posterior probabilities[93]. In other words, everything was obvious and predicted, after the fact. The writing was on the wall. Hindsight bias is also known as the illusion of predictability. It leads to overestimation of what portfolio managers could or should have done to make money or avoid losing it. Managers rationalise ex post events that were not forecasted ex ante.

It is much easier to explain events after they occur than to predict them before they occur. Will Rogers described what could be done with perfect hindsight and a time machine: "don't gamble. Take all your money, buy a good stock and hold it until it goes up, then sell it. It if doesn't go up, don't buy it".

Poor probability calibration

Investors tend to underestimate the randomness and volatility of financial markets. As Nassim Taleb argued in his book *Fooled by Randomness*[94], investors are often unaware of randomness and explain random outcomes as non-random. Investors anchor their estimates in the recent past and tend to underestimate the frequency of extreme outcomes (fat tails) in financial markets[95].

Investor myopia and high frequency performance monitoring

Investment should be a long-term endeavour. However, many investors suffer from investor myopia (short sightedness). They are fixated by recent events at the expense of the long-term picture, leading them to irrational decisions that are detrimental to their long-term investment needs and objectives. The combination of myopia and loss aversion causes investors to panic because of short-term losses, losing the patience to ride them out and focus on long-term prospects. They monitor their investments in high frequency.

With more frequent monitoring of rolling returns, the probability of observing seemingly extreme results is higher (as illustrated by Figure 4.2, the number of negative rolling returns increases as the rolling period is shorter). This may lead to costly actions such as strategy revisions or manager terminations, increasing transaction costs with detrimental effects on manager incentives[96].

Figure 4.2 – S&P 500 rolling 12-month and 36-month total returns, January 1970 to June 2012

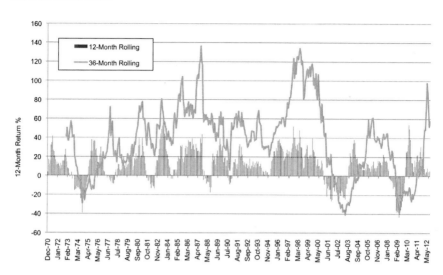

Source: Bloomberg, S&P 500.

With technological development over the last decade, investors can check their portfolio's performance online on a daily basis. However, investing is a long-term activity and frequent monitoring is unproductive.

Adaptive market hypothesis

All these behavioural biases and asymmetry between the pain of losing and joy of gaining lead investors to irrational and emotional behaviour. According to behavioural finance, financial markets are irrational and inefficient. Standard finance theories, which are based on the assumption that investors are rational and markets are efficient, do not necessarily hold in real life.

In 2004 Andrew Lo[97] suggested a theory to bridge the difference between EMH and behavioural finance. He named it the Adaptive Market Hypothesis (AMH).

AMH is based on concepts of evolution, such as competition (investors compete for investment opportunities), adaptation (investors adapt to new economic conditions) and natural selection (the survival of the fittest). It proposes that most behavioural biases, which claim that investors are irrational, are actually consistent with the adaptation of investors to new economic conditions using simple heuristics[98].

Investors adapt to ever-changing market conditions. A generation of investors who have not experienced a bear market are likely to be less risk averse than those who have experienced a bear market. People adapt like animals, following our most fundamental instincts. A cat that is fed and treated nicely by humans will not be afraid of people. A cat that is beaten by people will be afraid of humans. Animals adapt based on their experiences. Humans do so too. Once you get caught by a speed camera on a road, you are less likely to break the speed limit on that road. We all learn from our mistakes.

Contrary to the EMH theory, which claims that investors maximise expected utility and have rational expectations, AMH claims that since optimisation is costly and humans are limited by their computational abilities, they make choices that are satisfactory, not optimal. Humans know that they have reached a satisfactory point through trial and error, and natural selection. Individuals develop heuristics to reach investment decisions and as long as the economic environment remains stable the heuristics eventually adapt to yield approximately optimal decisions. If the economic conditions change, however, the heuristics are not suitable to the new conditions any more. Under these circumstances markets observe behavioural biases, which appear to be irrational behaviour. However, this is not irrational behaviour since it was rational under the previous economic conditions. Investors need to adapt to the new conditions through an evolutionary process.

AMH claims that security prices are based on information reflecting a combination of economic conditions and the number and nature of the groups of investors in the market (species). Investors compete for limited resources (economic profits). This ecological system is dynamic and constantly changes. Under AMH, investment strategies undergo cycles of profitability and loss in response to changing business conditions, the number and types of investor groups and available opportunities. Fear and greed and other emotions are a natural response to different market conditions. Emotions are part of animals' survival instinct through the evolutionary process.

The implications of AMH are that the link between risk and reward is unstable (as the economic conditions, number and types of investors and regulatory backdrop change, so do investors' risk expectations, including the equity risk premium); arbitrage opportunities do exist from time to time; investment strategies have good and bad periods; innovation is key to survival; and finally "survival is the only objective that matters". As Warren Buffett put it, "in order to succeed you must first survive".

The role of the advisor

One role of portfolio managers or financial advisors is to be the rational investor. Customers may be the behavioural investor and the advisor's role is to be the responsible parent. Advisors must ensure that their customers do not make investment decisions based on behavioural biases, such as selling when panicking or buying when everyone is herding.

Advisors need to refrain from being overconfident and make their customers aware of the uncertainty and risks involved in investment decisions. Advisors should not be overoptimistic about investment choices and communicate the realistic probabilities of success and failure. They must not rely on spurious relationships in data, and should be humble, realistic and honest about their skill to make investment decisions. Advisors need to consider all the relevant information and the background to understand their customers' risk aversion.

When purchasing investments, advisors need to make it clear what the selling strategy is and take a long-term view if this fits their customers' investment horizon. Advisors need to educate their customers not to focus on short-term fluctuations in prices and should seek to maximise the customers' overall well-being, including emotional and financial health. The reasons to have a disciplined investment management process are to overcome behavioural finance influences and biases. Professional portfolio managers or financial advisors should be less influenced by emotions.

Advisors have a fiduciary duty to their customers. A *fiduciary duty* is a legal or ethical relationship of confidence or trust regarding the management of money or property between two or more parties. The role of portfolio managers or financial advisors is to consider the interests of their customers above any other interest, such as the advisors' profit, relationships with other parties and personal interests. As doctors are entrusted with their patients' health, financial advisors are entrusted with their customer's wealth. Customers entrust financial advisors with taking care of their money; their life savings. Advisors owe the beneficiaries of this money to take good care of it. Above everything else, advisors need to be honest with their customers.

Daniel Kahneman and Mark Riepe offer this checklist for financial advisors[99]:

- Encourage clients to adopt a broad view of their wealth, prospects and objectives.
- Encourage clients to make long-term commitments to policies.
- Encourage clients not to monitor results too frequently.
- Discuss the possibility of future regret with your clients.
- Ask yourself if a course of action is out of character for your client.

- Verify that the client has a realistic view of the odds, when a normally cautious investor is attracted to a risky venture.

- Encourage the client to adopt different attitudes to risk for small and for large decisions.

- Attempt to structure the client's portfolio to the shape that the client likes best (such as insuring a decent return with a small chance of large gain).

- Make clients aware of the uncertainty involved in investment decisions.

- Identify the aversion of your clients to the different aspects of risk and incorporate their risk aversions when structuring an investment programme.

The role of a portfolio manager

Financial Advisors or IFAs advise customers on how to manage portfolios (advisory). Portfolio managers have discretion on managing portfolios (discretionary). Customers have granted portfolio managers the freedom to make investment decisions on their behalf, under an agreed set of parameters. Customers pay for these services and should expect professional service. The fiduciary role of portfolio managers is to manage portfolios for the customers' benefit and to protect the customers' interests.

Portfolio managers are professional investment managers who should not be affected by behavioural finance. However, portfolio managers are also humans. Customers must ensure that the best portfolio managers are chosen, given the resources that they have available, and that an appropriate governance process is in place to ensure that portfolio managers act in the best interests of the customers.

Conclusion

Understanding the behavioural biases affecting most investors and the markets is necessary to formulate realistic return and risk objectives. Only through understanding investment psychology do investors grasp the true meaning of return and risk, and manage their expectations.

When formulating investment objectives investors need to keep their behavioural instincts and biases in mind. They should aggregate accounts to consider them together (avoiding mental accounting); remember the asymmetry of loss aversion (prospect theory); focus on future prospects of investments and their role in the portfolio (avoiding representativeness and reference points); consider that a bear market potentially inflicts excessive pessimism and bull markets encourage excessive optimism; think contrarian (avoiding following the herd); do not be overconfident; consider the statistical significance of numbers; and keep a clear and critical head. *Keep calm and carry on.*

Summary

- Investors need to understand their investment behaviour to formulate their investment objectives.

- EMH suggests that active management does not add value since markets are efficient. Behavioural finance suggests that markets are not completely efficient and active management can potentially add value.

- According to EMH the only way to earn higher returns is by taking higher risks. Expected return is a function of expected risk, which is a function of current information.

- Understanding the behaviour of market participants, who are affected by cognitive biases and prospect theory, helps investors identify risks and opportunities.

- The main financial behaviours include: mental accounting; the pain of losing outweighs the satisfaction of gaining (prospect theory); risk aversion is asymmetric (investors are more risk averse when faced with potential gain and less risk averse when faced with potential loss); representativeness; and overconfidence.

- Investors are not rational robots as assumed by standard finance. Supply and demand are sometimes replaced by fear and greed as the forces that drive markets.

- AMH tries to bridge between EMH and behavioural finance, suggesting that markets have periods of irrationality and this is part of the evolutionary process of investors adapting to changing market conditions.

- One of the roles of investment advisors is guiding investors and helping them to avoid the traps of behavioural finance. This includes not panicking when markets fall; not selling in a rush at the bottom; not jumping on the bandwagon; and not following the herd and buying at or near the peak.

- Apply common sense, clear thinking and think contrarian before you act. Always ask what can go wrong.

- Investors tend to be too pessimistic when markets fall and too optimistic when markets rally. As Warren Buffett said "be fearful when others are greedy and greedy when others are fearful". While difficult, remember how the rational, objective investor would have analysed each situation and see beyond the fog of emotions.

- Investment management is about buying low and selling high. However, behavioural biases often drive investors to buy high and sell low.

- If investors lack skill then passive investment is the answer since active investment without skill only creates random noise and transaction costs.

- Portfolio managers have discretion to make investment decisions in portfolios on behalf of clients, under an agreed set of parameters. Portfolio managers are the rational professional investment managers and should not be influenced by behavioural finance. However, portfolio managers are also humans and their behaviour should be monitored and controlled.

The next section aims to introduce the basic theories that explain how return and risk are linked. Return objectives and risk objectives must be aligned. Investors should not expect returns without the appropriate risk level. If investors cannot assume the required level of risk, they should not expect the corresponding level of returns. *If you can't stand the heat, get out of the kitchen.*

5. THE RELATIONSHIP BETWEEN REWARD AND RISK

Investors do not want risk but they must accept it. Some accept more risk than others, depending on their risk appetite. Logically, investment risk should be compensated. Had risk not been compensated by markets, investors would have not taken it. If cash and equities had the same return, there would have been no reason to invest in equities instead of cash.

Intuitively, the higher the risk, the higher the expected return. Historically, over long time periods, this rule normally stands and taking risk has been compensated by the market. Small capitalisation equities generated higher returns than large capitalisation equities, which generated higher returns than corporate bonds, which generated higher returns than government bonds, which generated higher returns than cash. Over many time periods holding cash has not even beaten inflation and therefore cash has not even preserved its purchasing power, generating negative real return. Cash is not a risk-free asset class when inflation is taken into account.

The next few sections review some of the financial theories that attempt to link risk and return, how they have been criticised when applied to the reality of financial markets and their insights.

Capital Asset Pricing Model (CAPM)

The Capital Asset Pricing Model (CAPM) sets a theoretical expected or required return of investments. The model links expected return with investments' non-diversifiable or market risk (systematic risk). The CAPM was published by William Sharpe in 1964[100]. Sharpe received the 1990 Nobel Memorial Prize in Economic Sciences, together with Harry Markowitz and Merton Miller, "for his contributions to the theory of price formation for financial assets"[101].

An investment's non-diversifiable risk is often represented by the Greek small letter β (beta). Beta is calculated using the formula:

$$\beta = COV(r_i, r_m)/\sigma^2_m$$

where r_i is the investment return, r_m is the market return, $COV(r_i,r_m)$ is the covariance between the investment returns and market returns, and σ^2_m is the variance of the market returns.

Beta measures the sensitivity of investment returns to market returns or relative volatility. When beta is zero, investment and market returns are independent. When beta is above 1.0 investment returns are more volatile than those of the market and when beta is below 1.0 investment returns are less volatile than those of the market. For example, a security with a beta of 1.20 is 20% more volatile than the market on average. When the market increases by 1% the security increases by 1.2%, on average. The correlation (ρ) between the investment and market returns is calculated using the formula:

$$\rho = COV(r_i,r_m)/\sigma_i\sigma_m$$

which means that another way to express beta is through the formula:

$$\beta = (\sigma_i/\sigma_m)\rho$$

where σ_i is the volatility of investment returns, σ_m is the volatility of market returns, and ρ is the correlation between investment and market returns.

This formula shows that beta depends on the relative volatility of investment returns to that of market returns, and the correlation between investment and market returns.

CAPM states that an investment's expected return, r_i, is:

$$ri = rf + \beta(r_m - r_f)$$

where r_f is the return of a risk-free asset (cash or government bonds; risk-free without liabilities can be cash and with liabilities can be government bonds with a similar duration to that of the liabilities) and r_m is market return.

According to CAPM, the expected return of an investment is a function of the risk-free rate, plus the investment's beta with respect of the market, times the expected excess (above risk-free rate) return of the market.

For example, assume a risk-free rate of 4% and expected market return of 8%. An investment with beta of 0.8 is expected to return 7.2%[102], an investment with beta of 1.2 is expected to return 8.8% and an investment with beta of 0 is expected to return 4% (the risk-free rate). An investment with beta of 1 is expected to return 8% (the market return).

Beta is easily calculated by regressing the investment's historical returns with respect of market returns. The slope of the fitted line from the linear least-squares regression is beta[103]. The point where the line intercepts the y-axis is alpha.

In corporate finance CAPM is commonly used to estimate the required rate of return on securities (such as equities and bonds) to determine the discount factor to calculate their present value, taking into account their appropriate risk level. However, some drawbacks of beta are that it does not capture all the risks of a security, it assumes that returns are normally distributed and there are shortcomings of estimating beta from historical returns.

Beta, like other risk measures, is not stationary and changes with time, as Figure 5.1 illustrates (showing the rolling beta of US equities and Treasury bonds with respect of global equities).

Figure 5.1 – rolling 36-month beta of US equities and US Treasury bonds with respect of global equities, January 1970 to June 2012

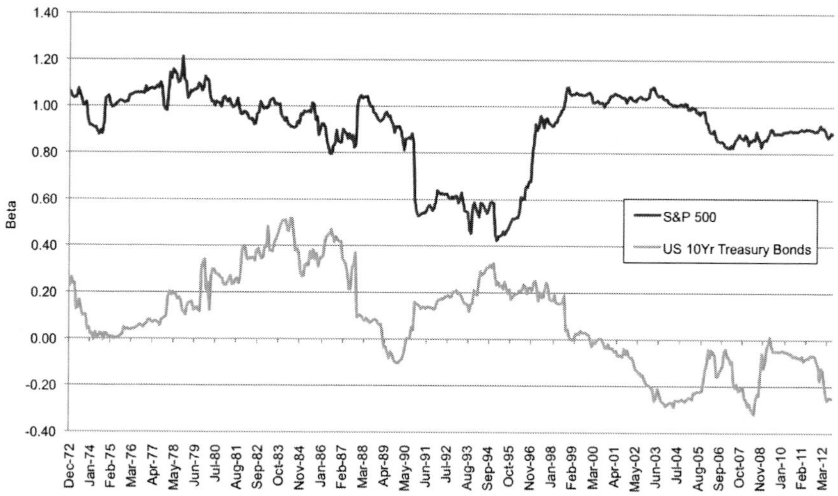

Source: Bloomberg, Global Financial Data, MSCI World, S&P 500, USA 10-year Government Bond Total Return.

CAPM helps demonstrate the relationship between expected risk and return. The main four insights from CAPM are that:

1. The higher the expected risk the higher the expected return

2. If no risk is taken (beta = 0), cash-like or risk-free returns are expected

3. Investors are compensated only for systematic risk (as defined by CAPM)

4. Investments should be analysed in portfolio context (CAPM assumes that all investors hold the diversified market portfolio and each investment's systematic risk relative to this portfolio determines expected return)

As per CAPM, investment risk has to be measured in the context of marginal contribution to risk with respect of the diversified market portfolio.

CAPM claims that not all risks are expected to be compensated by the market. Risks that can be diversified away (idiosyncratic risks) are not compensated, while only the non-diversifiable, systematic risk is compensated (CAPM does not allow for alpha). According to CAPM, the market does not compensate investors for risks that they do not need to take and can be easily removed through proper diversification.

CAPM criticism

CAPM has many shortcomings and has attracted criticism, mostly because of the unrealistic assumptions underpinning it. CAPM assumes that the market portfolio is a market capitalisation weighted portfolio consisting of all the assets in all markets. This would include *all* assets, such as equities, bonds, real estate, human capital, intellectual property, art and so on. In practice, however, such a market portfolio is not investable and is unobservable.

This criticism is the basis for a famous paper by Richard Roll from 1977 and is generally referred to as *Roll's critique*[104]. In practice, the market portfolio is substituted by an index as a proxy and it does not include every asset in the world. For example, for calculating the beta of a stock that is a constituent of the S&P 500 Index, this index is used as a proxy for the market portfolio.

Other unrealistic assumptions on which CAPM is based include the assumptions that: returns are jointly normally distributed; standard deviation of returns is an adequate risk measure; all investors have access to the same information and have the same risk and return expectations; all investors are rational; and there are no taxes or transaction costs (frictionless world).

In practice, investment returns are not normally distributed. Standard deviation is an inappropriate single risk measure when returns are not normally distributed, when investors are concerned about downside risk or shortfall risk, and when there are other risks that are not captured by standard deviation (such as liquidity risk).

Not all investors have access to the same information and they have different views and expectations about markets (Edgar Fiedler once said "ask five economists and you'll get five different answers"). Investors are not always rational and behavioural biases affect their judgment and investment decisions. There are plenty of frictions to trading, such as taxes and transaction costs, investors cannot borrow and lend at the risk-free rate and there are restrictions on short-selling. The real world is very different than the theoretical world of CAPM.

Therefore, CAPM is a theoretical model that does not accurately work in the real world. Nevertheless, CAPM is useful in several ways. Beta is a helpful statistic that measures the *directionality* of investments (investments with a beta above 1.0 are directional while investments with a beta close to zero are not directional or *market neutral*) and it links the correlation and the volatility of investment returns with that of the benchmark (*variability*). Beta should not be used as a main risk measure, but it can complement others.

CAPM should be used by investors who have no forecasting abilities to formulate expected returns of investments. If investors have forecasting ability, they should not use CAPM to derive expected returns since there are better ways to do so. If investors think that they have forecasting abilities, but they do not, they may end up with overly concentrated portfolios, biased because of their spurious forecasts and views. They would be better off pretending that they had no forecasting abilities.

Multi-factor models

CAPM uses only the market return as a single factor to calculate expected investment returns (it is a single factor model). Multi-factor models are used to explain the returns of investments using more than a single factor or exposure. Multi-factor models are used to construct portfolios with certain desired characteristics with exposures to certain factors, and to control and explain portfolio return and risk.

When constructing a multi-factor model the challenge is deciding on the number and nature of the factors. The Fama and French model[105], for example, uses three factors:

1. Size of firms

2. Book-to-market values (i.e. value versus growth investment style)

3. Excess return on the market

Investors typically use historical returns and a multiple least-square regression to estimate the beta coefficient or *factor loading* for each factor, but this may inaccurately predict future values. Models should be tested on out-of-sample data and use more robust methods for estimating the coefficients.

To illustrate this, the monthly returns of HFRI Macro Index are regressed on monthly returns of indices representing US equity size and style, inflation, bonds, cash and commodities over the time period January 2000 to June 2012. As Figure 5.2 illustrates, the multi-factor model is then tested on the out-of-sample time period January 2011 to June 2012:

HFRI Macro = 0.57 + 0.02*Russell 1000 Value − 0.13*Russell 1000 Growth − 0.13*Russell 2000 Value + 0.22*Russell 2000 Growth − 0.70*US Inflation + 0.01*Citigroup US WGBI − 0.16*BofA ML US Corporate Master + 0.34*Barclays Capital Global Aggregate + 0.31*US T-Bill + 0.13*DJ–UBS Commodity

Figure 5.2 – multi-factor model, January 2000 to June 2011 for in-sample and January 2011 to June 2012 for out-of-sample

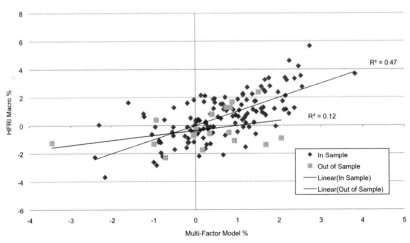

Source: Bloomberg, Global Financial Data, HFRI Macro, Russell 1000 Value, Russell 1000 Growth, Russell 2000 Value, Russell 2000 Growth, US inflation, Citigroup United States WGBI TR, BofA Merrill Lynch US Corporate Master TR, Barclays Capital Global Aggregate Bond TR, USA Total Return T-Bill, Dow Jones UBS Commodity.

Multi-factor models can be divided into three main categories:

1. Macroeconomic models

2. Fundamental models

3. Statistical models

Macroeconomic models compare investment returns to such economic factors as employment, inflation and interest rates.

Fundamental models analyse the relationship between investment returns and their underlying microeconomic factors or financials (e.g. industry classification, market capitalisation, style, earnings and so on).

Statistical models attempt to determine which factors best explain investment returns by extracting the factor loadings from observable returns using statistical methods, such as *principal component analysis* (PCA). However, assigning economic interpretation to statistical factors is difficult.

Arbitrage Pricing Theory (APT)

The *Arbitrage Pricing Theory* (APT) is an equilibrium asset-pricing theory[106] that sets the expected return of investments based on a linear multi-factor model. The expected rate of return from APT is used to evaluate the asset. According to the law of one price identical assets or risks should sell at the same price. The current asset value should therefore equal the expected end of period value discounted at the discount rate implied by APT because the model ensures that the asset value has the same price as that of the proportionally combined factors. If the price diverges from value, arbitrage should bring it back in line with its correct valuation according to APT.

The model assumes that markets are in equilibrium. Equilibrium exists when demand and supply forces cause market prices to stay at levels corresponding to expected or required returns (i.e. sellers and buyers are both satisfied and market prices correctly reflect this balance). In equilibrium, prices equal values as evaluated by sellers and buyers. When markets are not in equilibrium, demand and supply force the market back to equilibrium (i.e. when there are more buyers than sellers prices rise and when there are more sellers than buyers prices decline).

The APT formula is:

$$r_i = a_i + b_{i1}F_1 + b_{i2}F_2 + \cdots + b_{in}F_n + \varepsilon_i$$

where r_i is the return on asset i, a_i is a constant for asset i or its alpha, b_{ik} is the sensitivity of asset i to factor F_k or its beta to factor F_k, and ε_i is the asset idiosyncratic random shock with expected mean zero (the error term).

Similarly to CAPM, the linear factor betas can be quantified through a multiple linear regression of historical returns with respect of the factors or other techniques. Unlike CAPM, APT does not specify the identity and number of factors (CAPM uses a single known factor). It is up to the investor to identify the appropriate factors. Guidelines for such factors include: the impact of the factors on asset prices should be manifested in their unexpected movements, the factors should represent influences that cannot be diversified, timely and accurate information on these variables is required, and the relationship between the asset and the factors should be theoretically justifiable on economic grounds.

Chen, Roll and Ross[107] identified the following macroeconomic factors as significant in explaining security returns: unanticipated inflation; unanticipated changes in GDP as indicated by an industrial production index; unanticipated changes in investor confidence because of changes in risk premium in corporate bonds; and unanticipated shifts in the yield curve. Only unanticipated changes are significant in explaining returns since expected changes are already priced into security prices.

The main insight from APT and other multi-factor models is that, unlike CAPM, there is more than one beta or risk factor. APT suggests that there is more than one source of systematic risk, which should be compensated by markets, as well as constant, a_i. So a_i can be a portfolio manager's alpha.

The main lesson from these models is that investors need to construct diversified portfolios with as many sources of imperfectly correlated betas (systematic risk factors) as possible and then combine them according to their risk appetite. Each systematic risk should be rewarded by the market.

Risk-adjusted performance measures

As return and risk are closely linked – and one should not be considered without the other – it is common to measure performance using ratios of reward per unit of risk, or risk-adjusted performance measures. The objective of investing is maximising some risk-adjusted return measure. Normally, portfolios have a risk budget, which is the range of allowable risk, with the objective of generating the highest return within the boundaries of the risk budget. In other words, the objective is maximising return for a certain level of risk.

The numerator of risk-adjusted performance ratios is a reward measure, such as absolute return, excess return over a risk-free rate or active return relative to a benchmark. The denominator is a risk measure, such as an absolute, relative or downside risk measure. Investors are compensated more for each unit of risk taken as the risk-adjusted performance measure is higher. Risk-adjusted performance measures are commonly used to evaluate investments and portfolio managers. Since managers take different levels of risk, by using these measures it is possible to better compare performance across managers.

The two most common risk-adjusted return measures are:

1. The Sharpe ratio
2. The information ratio

1. Sharpe ratio

Mean-variance optimisation and its graphical representation as the *efficient frontier* is used to identify portfolios with the highest reward to risk, as measured by standard deviation. William Sharpe introduced in 1966[108] a measure defined as the ratio of excess return or risk premium above the risk-free rate per unit of risk as measured by standard deviation. The formula for the Sharpe ratio is:

$$S = (r - r_f)/\sigma$$

where S is the Sharpe ratio, r is portfolio return, r_f is risk-free rate and σ is standard deviation of portfolio returns.

The Sharpe ratio can be calculated ex ante using expected risk and returns or ex post based on historical risk and returns. The higher the Sharpe ratio, the more optimised or efficient the portfolio as per mean-variance optimisation.

Some of the shortcomings of the Sharpe ratio are that it is meaningless when returns are negative and portfolio managers may play the ratio[109]. Some of the ways to play it are: lengthening the time intervals for measuring volatility, such as from daily to monthly or quarterly, and hence underestimating volatility and overestimating the ratio; smoothing returns that are based on appraisals or valuations, therefore dampening volatility; and using option techniques to change the return distribution (e.g. writing options, assuming the default or liquidity risks and increasing the Sharpe ratio as long as the manager is lucky). Bearing in mind these shortcomings, of which investors should be aware, the Sharpe ratio is useful when employed appropriately[110].

2. Information ratio

Similar to the Sharpe ratio, the information ratio is a risk-adjusted performance measure, but instead of being used in absolute space it is a measure in relative space. The ratio gives the active return (excess return above benchmark) per unit of relative risk as measured by tracking error. The formula for the information ratio is:

$$IR = (r - r_b)/TE$$

where IR is the information ratio, r is portfolio return, r_b is benchmark return and TE is tracking error.

Ex ante the information ratio uses expected active return and relative risk, while ex post the information ratio uses historic or realised return and risk. As with any ratio, it is important to use the same measuring period in the denominator and numerator (e.g. annualised active return and annualised relative risk).

The information ratio forms the basis for linking relative return objectives with relative risk objectives. Assume, for example, that the portfolio's return objective is to outperform the peer group benchmark by 2% per annum since empirically this outperformance level is needed, on average, to place the portfolio in the first quartile among its peers. Historically, the portfolio manager has achieved an information ratio of 0.50. From the return objective and information ratio the manager needs a risk budget (tracking error) of 4% (tracking error = return/information ratio = 2%/0.5 = 4%) to achieve the return objective. The tracking error should have a range, such as 1% to 7% (+/- 3%). Therefore, from the return objective and assumed information ratio, the risk objective is derived as target tracking error of 4% within a range of 1% to 7%.

There are many other risk-adjusted performance measures such as *Jensen's alpha,* the *Sortino ratio*[111], the *omega ratio*[112], the *Calmar ratio*[113] and so on. Some ratios attempt to address the asymmetric distribution of returns (e.g. the Sortino ratio is popularly used with hedge funds). As there are many ways to measure risk, there are many reward-to-risk ratios.

Alpha

Alpha is commonly used to describe active or excess return above benchmark (outperformance). However, the true definition of alpha is excess return of active management adjusted for risk. Alpha is the return above a passive, investable benchmark with a comparable risk level to that of the portfolio (i.e. risk comparable benchmark). This ensures that alpha captures only the additional value that portfolio managers added through investment decisions, such as security selection, and not through excess risk taking.

Jensen's alpha is an example for adjusting alpha to risk taken by portfolio managers in the form of beta risk. The formula for Jensen's alpha is:

$$? = r_p - (r_f + \beta(r_m - r_f))$$

where ? is Jensen's alpha, r_p is portfolio return, r_f is risk-free rate, β is portfolio beta and r_m is market or benchmark return.

The alpha is not simply r_p - r_m (excess return over benchmark), but rather is adjusted to the portfolio's beta risk.

The challenges with measuring alpha are how to measure risk, how to adjust the portfolio to risk and that the benchmark should be a passive investable asset. In practice, alpha is commonly used just to describe the excess return over benchmark, r_p - r_b. Excess return, active return and alpha are all interchangeable ways to describe the outperformance of investments or portfolios above their benchmark.

Summary

- The theoretical link between risk and return is intuitive. Investors must assume risks to generate returns above those that would come from cash.

- CAPM links returns with systematic risk as measured by beta.

- Assuming diversifiable risks is not compensated according to CAPM.

- In practice, the CAPM market portfolio is unobservable and is replaced by an index, with respect to which the security's beta is measured.

- CAPM demonstrates that higher risk attracts higher return.

- Multi-factor models aim to formulate expected returns or explain investment returns based on more than a single factor. According to multi-factor models there is more than a single systematic risk that is compensated by the market.

- According to multi-factor models non-systematic risk, such as manager alpha, can also contribute and explain investment returns.

- Investors should construct diversified portfolios with as many sources of imperfectly correlated betas as possible, as well as alphas, and then combine them according to their risk appetite.

- Risk-adjusted performance measures, such as Sharpe ratio and information ratio, link return and risk in a ratio to measure and communicate reward per unit of risk.

- The information ratio is used to derive the relative risk objective from the relative return objective.

- Alpha is excess return of active management adjusted for risk.

6. INVESTMENT CONSTRAINTS

The two sides of investment objectives (return and risk) do not capture all investors' requirements and desires. Investment constraints are the other considerations that should be factored into the investment policy alongside return and risk. Each investor has a range of needs and wishes that have to be taken into account when formulating an investment strategy and when managing a portfolio. Investment constraints cover those need and wish factors.

Investment constraints restrict the range of investment choices. Typically, constraints may adversely affect the ability of skilled portfolio managers to generate returns. However, they are required to reflect investors' needs and desires or to intentionally constrain portfolio managers.

Constraints can be divided into *internal constraints* (determined by investors) and *external constraints* (determined by outside entities such as regulators and beyond the control of investors).

The five categories of constraints

When professional portfolio managers manage portfolios, an Investment Management Agreement (IMA), Investment Policy Statement (IPS) or prospectus lists the objectives and constraints. It is common to divide the constraints into five different categories:

1. Investment horizon

2. Liquidity

3. Tax

4. Legal and regulatory

5. Special circumstances

The constraints, as with the investment objectives, may change over time or when circumstances change. Therefore, the process of setting up the constraints and objectives is dynamic and they should be reviewed at regular intervals, or when necessary.

1. Investment horizon

Investment horizon is the time period during which the investment objectives should be achieved. As a rule of thumb, a longer investment horizon means higher risk tolerance. For example, when the investment horizon is short, say six months, investing in equities may be imprudent since there is insufficient time to recoup any losses or shortfalls relative to investment objectives. The longer the investment horizon, the longer the time available to recoup such shortfalls. Furthermore, equity markets are highly unpredictable over short time frames and investing in them for six months is betting, punting or speculating, rather than investing.

Another common rule of thumb is that private investors should hold equities in a percentage of 100 minus their age. So a 25-year-old investor should hold 75% equities and an investor who is 75 should hold 25% equities. This rule demonstrates the inverse relationship between investment horizon and risk. However, it is not recommended to blindly follow this rule since the percentage of equities in portfolios should be determined by the investment objectives and the specific circumstances of each investor, not by a simple fit-all formula such as this.

Professional portfolio managers often specify a time horizon over which their performance is measured and evaluated. For example, a manager may have an objective of outperforming a benchmark by 2% per annum over rolling 3-year periods. This means that the manager needs to generate average alpha of 2% per year over every 3-year period. If the manager falls short of the objective in any one year, there is an opportunity to perform above the target return in the following years and still meet the overall objective. The longer investment horizon (three years) provides the manager with more flexibility and opportunities to meet the objectives.

This objective structure reduces the likelihood of a manager being fired for failing to meet investment objectives in a single year. Managers should be given sufficient time to add value and myopically evaluating them over short time periods is unconstructive both for the manager and for investors, since replacing managers is costly. Typically, it may be more worthwhile to work with managers to try to improve performance instead of firing them when there is a potential for improvement. Managers should be evaluated over a full economic cycle to judge their performance during bull and bear market conditions. At minimum, managers should be evaluated over at least one year, unless there are valid reasons to evaluate their performance over shorter time periods.

Some investors have a very short investment horizon; for example, investors who need to pay a down payment on a house in six months. This short investment horizon dictates the risk level of the portfolio (low), investment selection (potentially bonds with six month maturity) and liquidity needs (high). The short investment horizon really does constrain the investment choices. Investment strategies for short-term investors are markedly different than those for long-term investors.

Some investors have very long investment horizons or perhaps even perpetual ones, such as pension plans, insurance companies and charities. Their portfolios can take higher risks, the investment universe is broader and liquidity needs are lower compared to portfolios with short horizons. Such investors can invest a portion of their portfolios in illiquid securities (e.g. private equity) and benefit from a liquidity premium.

Investment horizon can be divided into a few different horizons or segments. Each horizon may require a different investment strategy. For example, a 50-year-old who plans to retire in 10 years has at least two investment horizons: 10 years to retirement and 30 years of retirement. Potentially, a third horizon after the person's death includes planning for managing the estate through a trust arrangement.

Longevity risk is the risk of longer life than expected (while over the long-term we are all dead, in investment management even a longer life is a risk). If a person lives beyond expectations, then the retirement investment horizon may be much longer than originally planned. The person may not have enough assets to support the longer life. Defined benefit pension funds and insurance companies, for example, face longevity risk since they may pay more pension benefits than expected if pensioners live longer.

Under some tax regimes the holding period of securities may determine whether realised gains or losses fall under the capital gains tax (CGT) rate or income tax rate[114]. The difference in the holding period may have a material impact on tax returns.

In summary, investment horizon impacts:

- Risk level
- Investment universe
- Investment choices
- Investment strategy

This is one of the most influential factors on the way investments are managed.

2. Liquidity

Liquidity is the proportion of the portfolio that investors need to be able to sell or liquidate (turn into cash) within a certain (usually short) time period. Some examples for liquidity concerns are a down payment for a home, tuition fees for children's education, bills for emergency hospital treatment, income during retirement, and any liability payment.

Liquidity is divided into unexpected and expected needs. *Unexpected* needs require cash reserves for unexpected events (e.g. a medical emergency or an immediate need to replace a car), as well as for capitalising quickly on investment opportunities (e.g. real estate investors need cash to be able to quickly pay a down payment on an attractive property in a hot property market).

Expected needs require a portion of the portfolio to be invested in highly liquid securities to be able to meet liabilities (e.g. mortgage payments). Expected liquidity needs can be further divided based on whether their timing and magnitude are known or unknown. For example, a general insurance company needs to meet claims on car accidents and fire damages. Using stochastic models actuaries calculate the amount of assets that need to be held in liquid securities to meet those claims, whose amount and timing are unknown. The general insurance company's portfolio is likely to be invested in liquid fixed income instruments with a low risk level and high liquidity given the profile of the short-term stream of liabilities.

When purchasing a residential home, cash buyers who do not need a mortgage would have an advantage over buyers who need a mortgage, all else being equal. The high liquidity of the cash buyer is a competitive advantage since they can complete the transaction quicker.

Liquidity costs money. When portfolios hold cash instead of investments with higher expected returns, there is an *opportunity cost* for not investing in the higher-yielding investments. This is particularly true when short-term interest rates are low and the expected return from cash is low. Some investment vehicles, such as closed-end funds, may offer high liquidity. However, it comes at a cost, in particular when the underlying investments of the vehicle are illiquid.

For example, a closed-end fund investing in direct property may offer daily liquidity but the fund's price may be offered at a significant discount to the portfolio's net asset value (NAV). Therefore, investors who sell their holdings may receive much less than their share in the value of the underlying assets. Some vehicles have different prices for buying units (*bid price*) and selling units (*ask price*). The difference between bid and ask (the bid-ask spread) reflects, inter alia, the price of liquidity.

A long investment horizon allows for holding illiquid investments, which should pay a *liquidity premium*. Markets tend to compensate investors for assuming certain types of risks, such as liquidity risk and systematic risk. Many famous university endowments in the United States (e.g. Yale and Harvard endowments) have made a name by investing in illiquid assets, such as private equity and absolute return strategies. The requirement for liquidity may come at a price and the ability to bare illiquidity may be a benefit.

High liquidity needs usually indicate lower risk tolerance. It is likely to affect the performance objectives, in particular in a low interest rate environment. The expected returns of cash and short-term bonds are low when interest rates are low. High liquidity needs mean higher allocation to those asset classes and lower expected returns for portfolios.

3. Tax

As Albert Einstein put it, "the hardest thing in the world to understand is income tax". For high net worth individuals, the complexity of global taxation opens the door for complex tax planning, offshore banking and trust structures. Tax planning can materially enhance after-tax investment returns.

Tax planning includes: tax efficient portfolio management (e.g. low turnover to minimise realising taxable profits and using realised losses to offset capital gains); tax efficient structuring (e.g. tax efficient wrappers and offshore banking); selecting investments and holding periods to differentiate among the tax rates on interest, dividends and capital gains (e.g. holding an investment for more than one year so CGT applies to gains); differentiating between current income and retirement income tax rates (e.g. holding an investment in a pension scheme to defer taxation until retirement); estate tax planning (e.g. trust structures to avoid inheritance tax); and positioning portfolios to reflect the potential for tax legislation to change.

Philanthropic donations are a way to reduce tax liabilities while supporting charitable causes. In many countries not-for-profit organisations enjoy favourable tax treatment and donations by individuals to those organisations come with tax benefits. The areas of philanthropy, wealth management and tax are closely related and offer many opportunities for tax planning for donors. Philanthropy is an extension of wealth management and it serves one of the financial objectives of wealthy individuals.

Tax-exempt institutions may need to manage their portfolios in certain ways to maintain their status. For example, not-for-profit organisations in the United States need to spend a statutory minimum amount from their portfolio each year to maintain their tax-exempt status. Some tax-exempt institutions are taxed on Unrelated Business Income (UBI) and need to carefully consider their businesses to avoid attracting tax. Tax concerns affect not only the way portfolios are managed, but also how business is conducted.

In the United Kingdom some off-shore retail funds must maintain a reporting status to be tax efficient for UK retail investors. Reporting status means that investors need to pay CGT on distribution of income, rather than income tax, as long as the fund and investors meet certain criteria. This can mean a significant saving in taxes.

Legally reducing taxes on investment returns is one of the only ways of enhancing investment returns without increasing investment risk.

4. Legal and regulatory

Investment management is a heavily regulated industry. Some investors, in particular institutional investors such as insurance companies, pension plans and banks, must operate within a heavy regulatory environment. The regulations are typically aimed at assuring the institutions' solvency. The regulations cover capitalisation, reserves and processes. Naturally, legal and regulatory factors have a material impact on investments. A trust, for example, may require that no more than 10% of its assets are distributed to its beneficiaries each year.

Legal and regulatory constraints include limits on the way portfolios are managed (e.g. capped income distribution or a minimum spending rate), allocation to specific assets (e.g. capped allocation to below investment grade bonds or requirements to hold a minimum cash reserve) and the ability to access certain investments (e.g. ineligibility of real estate and commodities in UCITS funds). Some investments may be completely prohibited for legal and regulatory reasons.

Two influential regulatory developments affecting institutional investors are Solvency II and Basel III. Solvency II is a European regulatory regime for insurers. The Solvency I regime was introduced in the early 1970s and defines capital requirements by specifying simple blanket solvency margins. Volatility and uncertainty in the estimated value of liabilities is addressed in a fragmented way using broad assumptions that often do not reflect the underlying risk. This simplistic design means that Solvency I lacks risk sensitivity and does not capture a number of key risks. It does not ensure accurate and timely intervention by supervisors and it does not facilitate optimal allocation of capital.

Solvency II aims to change the capital requirements of the insurance industry and introduce new risk management requirements and enhanced allocation of capital to risk. The goals of Solvency II are to: more effectively help protect policyholder interests and the stability of the financial system as a whole by making firm failures less likely; increase the efficiency in the use of capital by improving returns; and achieve a more efficiently priced market for insurance products, making it easier for firms to do business across the European Union[115].

The Basel Committee on Banking Supervision (BCBS) is the primary regulatory forum for commercial banking. The committee was established in 1974 by central bank governors of G10 countries. The committee does not have formal supervisory authority. It is composed of representatives from central banks and national and banking regulators, such as the Federal Reserve Board and the Bank of England (BoE). The most important regulatory requirement for banks is in regard to capital holdings. Regulatory capital is required to cover unanticipated losses. It is a safety net in case asset value falls below that of liabilities or assets cannot be liquidated quickly enough to meet liabilities. The two difficulties in defining regulatory capital are deciding on the level of sufficient capital and what actually counts as capital.

Basel III is a new global regulatory standard on bank capital adequacy and liquidity agreed by the members of the BCBS. Basel III was developed in response to the deficiencies in financial regulation revealed by the 2008 global financial crisis. Its aim is to strengthen bank capital requirements and introduce new regulations on bank liquidity and leverage.

These regulations have a significant impact on the way large institutions manage their assets, as well as a material impact on the economy.

5. Special circumstances

The final category of investment constraints is special or unique circumstances. This is a catch-all category, covering anything that is not covered by the other constraints that investors need or wish to take into account when managing their assets. The list of examples is endless.

Islamic investors, for example, may wish that their investments follow *Sharia Law*. This includes a layer of ethical rules in portfolios, such as restrictions on leverage, investments in companies whose business is related to alcohol or pork, gambling and vices, speculation using derivatives (Sharia prohibits gambling) and day trading.

Socially Responsible Investing (SRI) or sustainable or ethical investing, seeks to generate returns while promoting social good. SRI favours investing in securities of companies that support the environment, human rights, consumer protection and diversity. The idea is that such companies have a sustainable future and therefore generate attractive long-term returns.

Many organisations, such as charities, wish to invest in companies that are considered ethical. They screen their investments so they exclude companies that are involved in tobacco, alcohol, gambling, adult entertainment, defence and animal cruelty. Interestingly, there are funds specialising in vice investing (gambling, smoking and pornography) and some of these funds have been generating benchmark-beating returns.

Impact of investment constraints

Investment constraints hurt the ability of skilled portfolio managers to generate alpha by limiting their flexibility. Not all views and investment decisions can be implemented under constraints. If portfolio managers cannot invest in the entire universe as per the benchmark, then performance may lag or benefit from constraints outside the manager's control.

For example, if a manager cannot invest in companies related to oil exploration because the investor does not want to support companies that damage the environment, the portfolio may lag its benchmark when oil stocks rally. If the investor does not want the portfolio to invest in bonds that are below investment grade and due to a credit crunch they fall, then the portfolio may outperform due to the constraint, but not because of the portfolio manager's skill. If the investor has a need to hold substantial cash to support liquidity needs, the portfolio may lag its benchmark when other asset classes perform well due to a cash drag. The investor must understand and accept the negative, or inadvertently positive, impact that constraints may have on performance.

When investors are unsure about manager skill, constraints are necessary to keep managers in line with the investors' objectives. Investors, however, need to think carefully before adding constraints, since they reduce the potential alpha of skilled portfolio managers. Trusted managers should be as unconstrained as possible to be able to add more value.

Summary

- Investment constraints complement the return and risk objectives to cover all the requirements and desires of investors from their investments.

- Investment horizon materially impacts the appropriate investment strategy, risk level and investment selection.

- Liquidity needs determine the portion of the portfolio invested in highly liquid investments, such as cash and government bonds.

- Tax concerns may have a large impact on after-tax, realised returns. Minimising tax is one of the only ways to enhance investment results without increasing investment risk.

- Legal and regulatory factors are influential in the heavily regulated investment management industry and are mostly out of investors' control.

- Generally, constraints limit the ability to generate returns but are needed to tailor portfolios to investor and regulatory requirements.

- Constraints may have positive or negative impact on performance. Investors need to understand this and consider it when evaluating portfolio managers and when setting the constraints.

PART 2
SETTING AN INVESTMENT STRATEGY

Once the investment objectives and constraints are established and documented, the next step is formulating the investment strategy. Part 2 moves on to look at this next step in the investment management process.

INTRODUCTION

An investment strategy is a plan to achieve the investment objectives under the investment constraints. It is a set of rules, procedures and tactics designed to guide investment decisions with the goal of achieving the investment objectives. While strategy is the overall plan for achieving the objectives, tactics are the steps to advance towards the objectives. Strategy provides the framework for action and tactics define the actions.

The two main components of investment strategy are Strategic Asset Allocation (SAA) and Tactical Asset Allocation (TAA). SAA sets the long-term asset allocation for the portfolio while TAA adjusts the asset allocation to short-term considerations, such as risks and investment opportunities. Investment strategy also covers investment selection, to populate each asset class with appropriate investments, and risk management.

For example, the long-term investment objectives may be beating inflation and growing the portfolio by 2% per annum. The investment constraints are excluding bonds below investment grade and alternative investments. The investment strategy may thus include SAA that allocates the portfolio to asset classes that keep up with inflation (e.g. inflation-linked bonds) and asset classes that provide growth over the long term (e.g. equities). Commodities, whose value normally increases with inflation, are excluded due to the constraints that do not permit investing in alternative investments. The expected return of the asset allocation is 4.5% per annum (2.5% for inflation and 2% for real return).

TAA tweaks the allocation between equities and bonds based on the stage in the economic cycle and the view on whether equities should outperform or underperform bonds over the short term. Investment selection picks the actual investments under each asset class (e.g. active or passive equities) and ensures that all bonds are above investment grade, as per the constraints. Risk management guides the portfolio to the investor's risk tolerance. The required risk level is not too high (the return objectives are relatively conservative), while enough risk should be taken to achieve the objectives.

Investment strategies may be defensive, with the aim of preserving capital or meeting liabilities, or aggressive, with the aim of growing capital. Often, the strategy is somewhere in the middle or combines defensive and aggressive elements. Investment strategies for multi-asset portfolios are a balancing act between return and risk.

Summary

- Investment strategy is the plan to achieve the investment objectives under the investment constraints.

- Investment strategy is a set of rules, procedures and tactics designed to guide investment decisions with the goal of achieving the investment objectives.

- Investment strategy includes SAA and TAA, as well as investment selection and risk management.

The following chapters will cover all the ingredients of investment strategy – SAA, TAA, investment selection and risk management – as well as examples for special investment strategies for special circumstances, objectives and market conditions.

7. STRATEGIC ASSET ALLOCATION

Strategic Asset Allocation (SAA), often referred to as policy allocation, is the appropriation of funds across different asset classes. It is a process of determining the long-term (hence strategic) target allocations to the available asset classes. When the investment horizon is short term, SAA may be inappropriate since it is based on long-term asset class assumptions on expected return and risk (the horizon of underlying assumptions must match that of the investment strategy). Nevertheless, portfolios still need an asset allocation that can be determined by other methods, such as liability matching, when SAA is inappropriate.

A wealth of academic research claims that SAA is the most significant driver of portfolio risk, more so than security selection and market timing. Through SAA, portfolios are aligned with investors' long-term investment objectives and constraints, balancing risk and reward, and diversified across different asset classes, benefiting from the risk-mitigating effects of diversification. Asset allocation is a way to change portfolios' reward-to-risk profile and it is usually the first step in formulating an investment strategy.

Asset allocation involves estimating the expected return and risks of investments, as well as the interactions among them, and choosing a combination of investments with the highest likelihood of efficiently meeting the investment objectives (i.e. highest expected return per unit of risk). SAA determines a portfolio's long-term expected return and risk, excluding the potential benefits of TAA and investment selection. Hopefully, TAA and investment selection will add to portfolio returns.

Some investors include in SAA only the three traditional assets class: equities, bonds and cash. Expanding the investable universe beyond these three asset classes may improve SAA's risk/return characteristics. Asset classes with low correlation to the three traditional ones contribute the greatest benefits. Adding other investment types, such as real estate, hedge funds, private equity and commodities, benefits from expanding the investment opportunity set and enhancing diversification. However, it also introduces risks and challenges in modelling these asset classes. SAA analysis needs a proxy for each asset class to model its return, risk and correlations. For some of these non-traditional asset classes no appropriate indices are available and including them in SAA analysis raises modelling challenges.

Adding additional asset classes has a diminishing marginal contribution to diversification. A small allocation to an esoteric asset class in an already well diversified asset allocation may have negligible impact on risk and return but material impact on complexity. A cost-benefit analysis is necessary in this case.

The goal of the SAA process is determining the long-term exposure to available asset classes. The definition of an asset class is blurry. One definition is that asset classes provide exposure to different betas or sensitivities to factors such as stock markets, currencies, interest rates, inflation, maturity, credit spreads, volatility and so on. Beta exposes the asset class to passive, systematic risks that should be compensated by a return. This return does not rely on portfolio manager skill or active management and does not require high fees to be paid. Each asset class includes a bundle of different beta exposures. The SAA process determines how to expose portfolios to different betas by combining different asset classes, taking into account the investment objectives and constraints.

Summary

- Asset allocation is the allocation of funds across different asset classes.

- Asset allocation involves estimating the expected return, risks and correlations of investments and choosing a combination with the highest likelihood of efficiently meeting the investment objectives.

- Expanding the investment universe beyond equities, bonds and cash by adding investments such as real estate, hedge funds, private equity and commodities benefits from expanding the investment opportunity set and enhancing diversification.

- The goal of the SAA process is determining the long-term exposure to available asset classes or how to expose the portfolio to different betas, taking into account the investment objectives and constraints.

8. HISTORICAL PERFORMANCE OF ASSET CLASSES

We do not know what is going to happen in the future. We do know, however, what has happened in the past and this is the first step in understanding what may happen in the future. George Santayana said "those who cannot remember the past are condemned to repeat it." You need to know the past to understand the present and to understand the present to predict the future.

History teaches us about the way different asset classes behave, their return and risk characteristics, and the interrelationships among them. Portfolios are invested to generate returns in the future. Before exploring the methodologies to position portfolios for the future, however, the first step is examining the history of different asset classes and their combinations.

Figure 8.1 shows the cumulative performance (based on monthly total returns) of the three traditional asset classes in the United States: equities (S&P 500 Index), 10-year (constant maturity) government or Treasury bonds and Treasury Bills (T-Bills), measured in US dollars ($) from January 1970 to June 2012. It also shows inflation (Consumer Price Index or CPI) for the same period. Indices are used to represent each asset class (assuming passive, buy and hold investment, with all dividends and interest reinvested, without transaction costs, fees and any potential alpha).

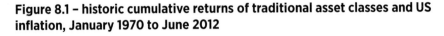

Figure 8.1 – historic cumulative returns of traditional asset classes and US inflation, January 1970 to June 2012

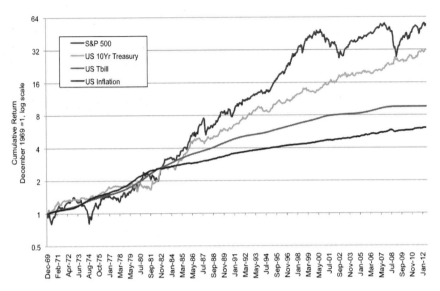

Source: Bloomberg, Global Financial Data, US Bureau of Labor Statistics, S&P 500, USA 10-year Government Bond Total Return, USA Total Return T-Bill, US Inflation.

We can see from the chart that $1 invested in the S&P 500 Index at the beginning of January 1970 would have grown to $54.6 by the end of June 2012. The S&P 500 Index returned 9.9% per annum over the period. $1 invested in US 10-year Treasuries at the beginning of the period would have grown to $31.8 by the end of the period. This is an annualised return of 8.5%. $1 invested in US T-Bills (money market or cash) over the same time period, would have grown to $9.6, an annualised return of 5.5%. The average inflation per year over the period was 4.3%. $6.1 in June 2012 could buy goods and services worth only $1 in January 1970. In other words, $1 in January 1970 is worth 16 cents in June 2012. Inflation over the period was 509%.

The results show that over this particular time period investing in US large capitalisation equities was rewarded more than investing in 10-year government bonds and investing in bonds was rewarded more than keeping the money in cash. Long-term investing in the S&P 500 Index during this time period was handsomely rewarded.

The line representing the cumulative performance of equities is bumpier than that of bonds. The line representing cash is much smoother than those of equities and bonds. The bumpier the line is, the riskier the asset class is.

Table 8.1 shows the performance per annum (annualised geometric mean[116]), annualised standard deviation (volatility) and correlations of the monthly total returns of the S&P 500 Index, US 10-year government bonds and US T-Bills (as well as US inflation). The standard deviation of equities is higher than that of bonds, whose standard deviation is higher than that of cash. Taking more risk during this time period was rewarded with higher returns, as would be expected according to financial theories, such as CAPM.

Table 8.1 – historic return and risk characteristics of traditional asset classes and inflation, January 1970 to June 2012

	S&P 500	10-Yr Gvt Bonds	T-Bills	US Inflation
Performance (% pa)	9.9	8.5	5.5	4.3
Volatility (% pa)	15.66	8.48	0.92	1.28
Sharpe ratio	0.28	0.36	0.00	-0.87
Correlation				
S&P 500	1.00	0.11	0.01	-0.09
10-Yr Gvt Bonds	0.11	1.00	-0.01	-0.17
T-Bills	0.00	-0.01	1.00	0.45
US Inflation	-0.09	-0.17	0.45	1.00

Source: Bloomberg, Global Financial Data, US Bureau of Labor Statistics, S&P 500, USA 10-year Government Bond Total Return, USA Total Return T-Bill, US Inflation.

Figure 8.2 uses the same indices and asset classes. However, this time the time period is January 2000 to June 2012. The results are materially different. The S&P 500 Index massively underperformed government bonds. Over this time period taking equity risk has not been rewarded, the equity risk premium (equity return over government bond or cash return) was negative and investors would have been better off keeping their money in bonds and cash. Cash had a positive *nominal* return during the period but a negative *real* return; cash did not even beat inflation.

Figure 8.2 – historic cumulative returns of traditional asset classes and US inflation, January 2000 to June 2012

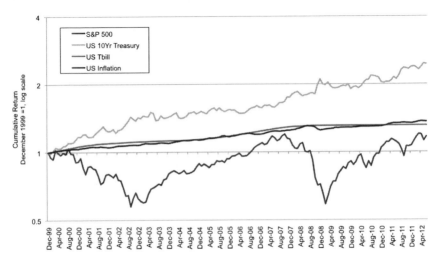

Source: Bloomberg, Global Financial Data, US Bureau of Labor Statistics, S&P 500, USA 10-year Government Bond Total Return, USA Total Return T-Bill, US Inflation.

The two main conclusions from these charts and tables are that investing results are highly dependent on the time period and that risk is not always rewarded. Had it been always rewarded, we would not have called it risk.

Another insight from Figure 8.2 is that US large capitalisation stocks have moved sideways since January 2000, virtually returning nothing in nominal terms and delivering a negative real return. This has been a lost decade for passive, buy and hold investing in US equities (active management could have made money or lost money).

Figure 8.3 shows the historic return and risk (volatility) of a variety of asset classes from January 1994 to June 2012. It can be seen that different asset classes have different risk and return characteristics.

Figure 8.3 – historic return and risk of different asset classes, January 1994 to June 2012

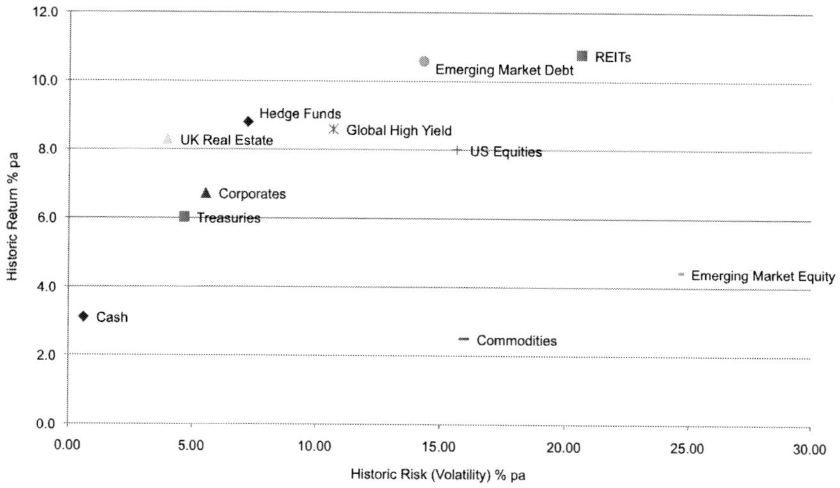

Source: Bloomberg, Global Financial Data, Lipper, USA Total Return T-Bill, Citigroup United States WGBI TR, BofA Merrill Lynch US Corporate Bond Master TR, Barclays Capital Global Aggregate Bond TR, Barclays Capital Global High Yield TR, JPM Emerging Markets Bond Index Plus EMBI+ Composite, S&P 500, MSCI Emerging Markets, Dow Jones UBS Commodity, HFRI Fund Weighted Composite, FTSE NAREIT Equity TR, UK IPD TR All Property.

Do equity markets behave?

The question of whether equity markets behave or misbehave depends on the definition of proper behaviour. CAPM and other finance theories expect risk to be rewarded, at least over the long term. Equity markets are expected to trend upwards with time. The normal distribution expects a nice, symmetric, bell-shaped distribution of returns. So, do equities behave?

Figure 8.4 shows the cumulative performance of the S&P 500 Index from January 1926 to June 2012. As can be seen from the chart, market crashes are an integral part of investing in equity markets. When the index returns are adjusted for US inflation, equities can move sideways for more than a decade or two. Twenty years of equities moving sideways is not what financial theories expect.

Figure 8.4 – historic cumulative returns of the S&P 500 Index in nominal and real terms adjusted for US inflation, January 1926 to June 2012

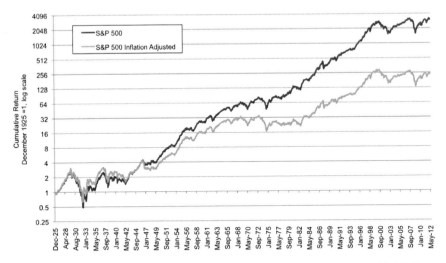

Source: Bloomberg, Global Financial Data, US Bureau of Labor Statistics, S&P 500, US Inflation.

Figure 8.5 shows the drawdowns of the S&P 500 Index from 1926 to 2012. Drawdowns of more than -20% are common. Drawdowns of -30%, -40% and -50% are not as common, but are part of equity investing.

Figure 8.5 – historic drawdowns of the S&P 500 Index, January 1926 to June 2012

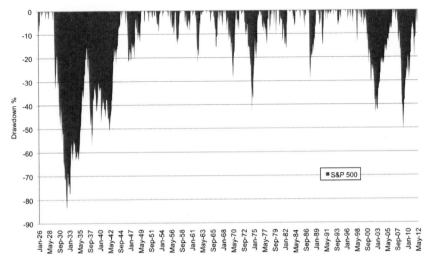

Source: Bloomberg, Global Financial Data, S&P 500.

Table 8.2 shows the 20 worst monthly returns of the S&P 500 Index since January 1926 and the number of standard deviations from the index mean return. Violent negative monthly returns, far away from the mean in terms of number of standard deviations, are part of the reality of investing in equity markets[117]. If equity markets are expected to behave as predicted by normal distribution, then they indeed misbehave.

Table 8.2 – worst monthly returns of the S&P 500 Index, January 1926 to June 2012

Monthly return %	Date	# SDs from mean
-29.48	Sep-31	-5.50
-24.51	Mar-38	-4.60
-23.52	May-40	-4.42
-22.61	May-32	-4.26
-21.53	Oct-87	-4.06
-19.74	Apr-32	-3.74
-19.66	Oct-29	-3.72
-17.98	Feb-33	-3.42
-16.80	Oct-08	-3.21
-16.12	Jun-30	-3.08
-14.46	Aug-98	-2.78
-13.81	Sep-37	-2.67
-13.74	Dec-31	-2.65
-13.50	Oct-32	-2.61
-13.24	May-31	-2.56
-13.24	Mar-39	-2.56
-13.04	Nov-29	-2.53
-12.64	Sep-30	-2.45
-11.52	Sep-74	-2.25
-11.33	Mar-32	-2.22

Source: Bloomberg, Global Financial Data, S&P 500.

Bubbles and market crashes

Stories of financial disasters and crises have several benefits. Firstly, realising the impact and frequency of financial disasters helps remind investors during good times that things may turn really nasty. Often during good times everyone is optimistic, forgetting past disasters and that the next crash is waiting to happen. As John Galbraith wrote in his book *A Short History of Financial Euphoria*[118], the free-enterprise system drives markets to euphoric bubbles and then to crashes.

Secondly, understanding how and why disasters occur helps investors learn from the mistakes of others. Mistakes are costly and learning from those of others is an opportunity to learn from mistakes without paying the same price they did. As per Oscar Wilde, "experience is the name everyone gives to their mistakes"[119]. Mistakes are experience, which is intuition. Thirdly, stories of epic blunders make good investtainment (invest-entertainment). Everyone loves a good story.

Idiosyncratic risk and *systematic risk* must be distinguished. Idiosyncratic risk is related to one firm and is generally under the control of the firm and its management. Systematic risk, on the other hand, is shared across the market and a systematic event is generally a result of a policy error by a government, inappropriate economic policies and/or misplaced macroeconomic incentives. The focus when we talk about bubbles and crashes is on systematic events that swept entire markets.

Alan Greenspan, with the help of Robert Shiller's *Irrational Exuberance*[120], employed the term 'irrational exuberance' to describe financial bubbles. On 5 December 1996, Greenspan, then Chairman of the Federal Reserve Board, asked a rhetorical question:

> "but how do we know when irrational exuberance has unduly escalated asset values, which then become subject to unexpected and prolonged contractions as they have in Japan over the past decade? We as central bankers need not be concerned if a collapsing financial asset bubble does not threaten to impair the real economy, its production, jobs and price stability".

Markets did not like Greenspan's question and fell (only modestly relative to the sorties below). Nevertheless, irrational exuberance has become a phrase describing the top of a speculative bubble. Most financial crises are the aftermath of a bubble bursting.

Arguably, the first recorded bubble was the Tulip Mania in the Netherlands. It was a time when the contract prices for tulip bulbs reached extraordinary highs. At the peak of the bubble in 1637 some bulbs were sold for more than 10 times the annual salary of a skilled craftsman. In February 1637 the prices of the contracts suddenly collapsed.

In 1711 the South Sea Company was incorporated in Britain. The company was granted the monopoly to trade in Spain's South American colonies and in exchange assumed the national debt that England incurred during the War of Spanish Succession. Speculation in the company stocks led to a bubble, which was known as the South Sea Bubble. The bubble exploded in 1720 and many investors lost their fortunes. Sir Isaac Newton, whose law of gravity ironically says that what goes up must come down, was one of the investors in the company.

Newton invested early in the company's stocks, making a large profit by selling early. However, Newton watched friends and colleagues around him continuing to invest and making more money. Perhaps overtaken by greed, Newton invested again in the company and this time invested much more than the amount which he had profited earlier. He even borrowed to invest more (i.e. invested on margin or levered his position). Unfortunately, he invested soon before the bubble burst. From July to September 1720 the share price completely plumbed and he lost a substantial portion of his wealth. Even one of the greatest geniuses in history could not identify a bubble, predict when it would burst and overcome his greed. Newton said of this: "I can calculate the movement of the stars, but not the madness of men".

The 1929 Wall Street Crash was one of the most devastating stock market crashes in history. It marked the beginning of the Great Depression that affected all Western countries and which did not end until America entered World War II in 1941. The 1920s (the Roaring Twenties) were a time of wealth and excess and many investors believed that the stock market would continue to rise forever. The Dow Jones Industrial Average (DJIA) increased by about 500% in the six-year period ending 3 September 1929. On Thursday 24 October 1929, known as *Black Thursday*, share prices fell 11%. On Monday 28 October, known as *Black Monday* (more Black Mondays are to follow), the DJIA Index fell 13%. The next day (*Black Tuesday*) the DJIA Index lost another 12%. The volume of stocks traded on that day was a record that was not broken for nearly 40 years.

The market reached its bottom on July 1932. Between September 1929 and June 1932 the S&P 500 Index fell more than 83% (interestingly, the S&P 500 Index rebounded by more than 90% during July and August 1932). Milton Friedman claimed that what made the great contraction so severe was not the downturn in the business cycle, trade protectionism or the 1929 stock market crash. Instead, he suggested the banking system collapse during three waves of panic over the 1930 to 1933 period plunged the United States into the Great Depression.

The 1970s bear market lasted between January 1973 and December 1974. Affecting all major stock markets in the world, particularly the United Kingdom, it was one of the worst stock market downturns in modern history. The S&P 500 Index fell by more than 37% and the FTSE All Share Index by more than 69% during this time period (interestingly, the FTSE All Share Index rebounded by almost 90% during January and February 1975). The crash came after the collapse of the Bretton Woods system[121] over the previous two years, with the associated Nixon Shock[122] and the dollar devaluation under the Smithsonian Agreement[123]. It was compounded by the outbreak of the 1973 oil crisis in October of that year, when an oil embargo was proclaimed following the decision of the United States to supply the Israeli Defence Force during the Yom Kippur War.

The next infamous *Black Monday* occurred on Monday 19 October 1987. Stock markets around the world crashed. The DJIA Index lost 22.6% in one day. The most popular explanation for the crash was program trading, mostly portfolio insurance strategies, which sell stocks when their prices fall.

In July 1997 the Thai baht collapsed when the Thai government decided to float the baht and cut its peg to the dollar. Thailand was effectively bankrupt before the collapse of the baht due to its out-of-control foreign debt. The crisis quickly spread to other countries across South East Asia and was known as the Asian financial crisis. The International Monetary Fund (IMF) stepped in and initiated a $40 billion programme to stabilise the currencies of South Korea, Thailand and Indonesia, which were particularly hit by the crisis. By 1999 the economies of the countries were beginning to recover. During the crisis the South Korean won collapsed by 34%.

A year later, in 1998, two events occurred. The first event took place on 17 August 1998 when Russia defaulted on its sovereign debt (Russian default crisis). The second event was the collapse of Long-Term Capital Management (LTCM), a hedge fund, which lost $4.6 billion in less than four months after the Russian default crisis. In September 1998 the New York Federal Reserve Bank invited major investment banks to engineer a bailout for the hedge fund in order to prevent the destabilisation of the stock market. A complex mix of derivatives, speculative investments and leverage utilised by LTCM threatened the entire financial system.

In 2000 the infamous dot-com, high-tech or internet bubble burst. The low interest rates in 1998 and 1999, the hype around the internet and the claims that the old economy was dead helped push the NASDAQ composite to soaring highs. On 10 March 2000 the NASDAQ composite peaked at 5,048, more than a 100% increase on its value a year previous. The NASDAQ composite started falling after the United States federal court declared Microsoft a monopoly. This was the beginning of a long equity bear market. On 11 September 2011 the terrorist attack on the World Trade Centre in New York City and the Pentagon occurred. The bear market continued until March 2003 when stock markets hit a bottom and a bull market began. Between April 2000 and February 2003 the S&P 500 Index fell by more than 41%. Between March 2003 and May 2008 it was up by more than 83%.

The credit crunch occurred in 2008. The crisis was triggered by the bankruptcy of Lehman Brothers, but its build up was the housing bubble in the United States, sub-prime lending, deregulation, an increased debt burden on households and governments, financial complexity (derivatives and structured securities), and mispricing of risk. It is considered the worst financial crisis since the 1929 Great Depression. It led to the collapse or near-collapse of large financial institutions, unprecedented bail-outs by governments and a long-lasting global recession. The magnitude of the crisis had not been predicted by officials and most economists. Federal Reserve Chairman Ben Bernanke said in March 2007 that "at this juncture, the impact on the broader economy and financial markets of the problems in the subprime market seems likely to be contained". In May 2008 US Treasury Secretary Henry Paulson said in an interview "I do believe that the worst is likely to be behind us". Between September 2008 and February 2009 the S&P 500 Index lost almost 42%. Between March 2009 and April 2011 it rallied by almost 94%.

The valuable lessons that these crises teach us are that bubbles are part of financial markets, investors are not always rational, greed and fear are strong forces, even smart people cannot predict the markets, at times of crisis governments and central banks often need to step in and help the free markets, and few standard deviation events, or tail events, occur much more often than they should according to statistics. When markets rise and it seems too good to be true, it usually is too good to be true. Historic crashes are also helpful for conducting stress testing.

It is worth noting the strong and rapid recoveries following most crashes. Sometimes it is better to stay invested after experiencing a crash, rather than panicking and disinvesting. Missing the rally after the crash may have a huge impact on portfolio performance and long-term wealth accumulation.

Claiming *this time is different*, during both good and bad times, is usually wrong. Each time is indeed different, since the circumstances are never the same. However, the general conditions pushing markets into crisis are similar and usually have happened before, in particular when looking at the very long term[124]. People tend not to learn from past mistakes. While history is insightful, as markets evolve historical relationships evolve and cannot be used as a guide for the future. Investors need to evolve with markets and while learning from history is important, the current circumstances must be analysed and differentiated from historical events.

The lesson from history

Markets definitely go thorough episodes of irrationality. Risk has been compensated in the past. However, the last decade is concerning. Two big bubbles have exploded and markets have experienced the biggest financial crisis since the Great Depression. This time should not be different and equity markets should recover as they did in the past – there have been other decades during which risk has not been compensated. For example, from the middle of the 1960s to the middle of the 1980s the US equity market has moved sideways when adjusted for inflation. However, with unprecedented low interest rates, an unprecedented level of public debt in Western economies and unprecedented equity market crashes all occurring within one decade, is this time not different? Investors need to think about risks carefully. The first years of the second decade of the 21st century are different. We have never been here before.

Summary

- History teaches us about the future.

- In the past, over the long term, taking risk has been rewarded by returns. Equities have outperformed bonds, which have outperformed cash.

- The situation may be very different over different time periods, during which equities can severely underperform bonds and cash, and cash may not even keep up with inflation.

- Bubbles and market crashes occur more often than suggested by statistics and the normal distribution. It is difficult to predict crashes, even for experts, and portfolios should be positioned so a crash will not result in ruin. Stress testing can assist in doing this.

- If a portfolio has suffered a crash, it is often better to remain invested since on many occasions crashes have been followed by strong recoveries.

- Time in the market is often more valuable than timing the market.

9. COMBINING ASSET CLASSES

Multi-asset portfolios combine asset classes. This is the essence of multi-asset investing. The performance and risk of a diversified portfolio are the average of those of the different asset classes.

Table 9.1 shows the performance[125], volatility, Sharpe ratio and maximum drawdowns of the three traditional asset classes (equities, bonds and cash) and three asset allocations that combine them in different proportions. The data are based on monthly total returns from January 1970 to June 2012. The asset allocations assume fixed allocations, rebalanced to target weights on a monthly basis.

Table 9.1 – single asset and asset allocation historic return and risk characteristics, January 1970 to June 2012

	Single asset classes			Conservative	Moderate	Aggressive
	US T-Bills	US 10-Yr Gvt Bond	S&P 500	25% Equity, 70% Bonds, 5% Cash	60% Equity, 35% Bonds, 5% Cash	75% Equity, 20% Bonds, 5% Cash
Performance (% pa)	5.5	8.5	9.9	9.0	9.5	9.7
Volatility (% pa)	0.9	8.5	15.7	7.5	10.2	12.0
Sharpe ratio	0.00	0.36	0.28	0.47	0.40	0.35
Max drawdown (%)	0.0	-15.8	-50.9	-12.1	-29.8	-38.7

Source: Bloomberg, Global Financial Data, S&P 500, USA 10-year Government Total Return, USA Total Return T-Bill.

The naming of multi-asset portfolios is a controversial issue. Thinking of some typical asset allocation labels: *conservative* may not be really conservative to all investors; *capital preservation* may not preserve capital; *balanced* may not be well balanced across different asset classes; and *income* may be quite aggressive and not generate a lot of income. Other popular names such as *adventurous*, *dynamic* and *strategic* may mean different things to different investors.

The names may be misleading and the characteristics of each portfolio should be carefully examined to determine its true risk level. The risk level is subjective, as it depends on each investor's willingness to take risk and each investor has a different ability to take risk.

The return and risk analysis in the table offers a few insights:

- Higher equity allocation means higher risk level of the asset allocation (both in terms of volatility and maximum drawdowns). Equities are a source of risk and return in diversified portfolios.

- Combining a number of asset classes reduces the risk of the asset allocation relative to that of equities.

- The *conservative* asset allocation has a lower risk (7.5%) than that of bonds (8.5%), although it has a 25% allocation to equities. Allocating some of the portfolio to risk assets may reduce overall risk due to diversification benefits.

- The performance of all asset allocations lies between those of bonds and equities. Diversification averages performance.

The risk-adjusted performance (Sharpe ratio) of all three asset allocations is higher than that of equities and, except for the aggressive allocation, than that of bonds. Giving up performance relative to equities was compensated by a reduction in risk. The allocations are more efficient than equities since they offer a higher unit of performance per unit of risk. Overall, during the specific time period used for the analysis, investors would have been better off diversifying their portfolios when reward/risk is considered.

Figure 9.1 plots the three asset classes and the three asset allocations on the risk (x-axis, standard deviation) and return (y-axis) plane. The line is not the efficient frontier but just a line drawn from cash to equities, through the three allocations. The chart shows that bonds are an inefficient asset class on a standalone basis since it is possible to combine bonds with other asset classes and generate higher return for the same level of risk. The aggressive asset allocation, for example, is more efficient than equities since for a small reduction in return (0.2%) risk is materially reduced (3.6%).

Figure 9.1 – single asset and asset allocation historic return and risk, January 1970 to June 2012

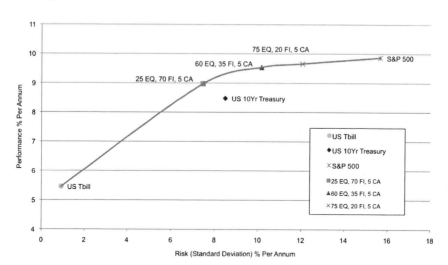

Source: Bloomberg, Global Financial Data, S&P 500, USA 10-year Government Total Return, USA Total Return T-Bill.

Figure 9.2 shows the cumulative performance of equities, bonds and the *moderate* asset allocation. The performance of equities is much bumpier than that of bonds since equities are more volatile. The bumpiness of the *moderate* allocation lies between those of equities and bonds, showing that its risk lies somewhere in the middle. The risk and return of a combination of two asset classes lies between the risk and return of each asset class on a standalone basis (depending on the allocation to each asset class).

Figure 9.2 – equities, bonds and the moderate asset allocation cumulative return, January 1970 to June 2012

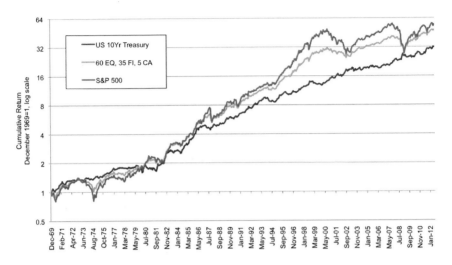

Source: Bloomberg, Global Financial Data, S&P 500, USA 10-year Government Total Return, USA Total Return T-Bill.

Figure 9.3 shows the drawdowns of equities, bonds and the *moderate* asset allocation. Equities have dramatic drawdowns while those of bonds are much more subdued. As expected, the drawdowns of the *moderate* allocation lie in the middle.

Figure 9.3 – equities, bonds and the moderate asset allocation drawdowns, January 1970 to June 2012

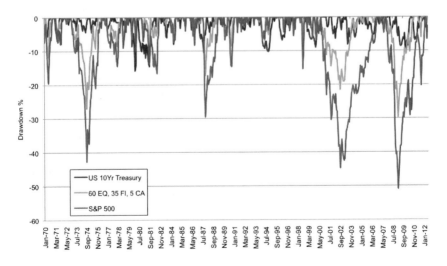

Source: Bloomberg, Global Financial Data, S&P 500, USA 10-year Government Total Return, USA Total Return T-Bill.

There are instances where combining two asset classes generates a higher return and a lower risk than those of each of the asset classes separately, as Figure 9.4 and Table 9.2 demonstrate. Combining 50% global equities (MSCI World Index) and 50% commodities (DJ-UBS Commodity Index) over the time period January 2001 to December 2011 produced a portfolio with higher return (2.4%) than that of equities (2.2%) and commodities (1.9%), and lower risk (15.2%) than that of equities (17.1%) and commodities (17.8%). The correlation between global equities and commodities was 0.51. This is a diversification bonanza. The time period was chosen intentionally to make a point as during many other time periods combining equities and commodities results in lower risk than that of equities or commodities, but with lower return than that of equities.

Figure 9.4 – cumulative returns of global equities, commodities and a 50/50 portfolio, January 2001 to December 2011

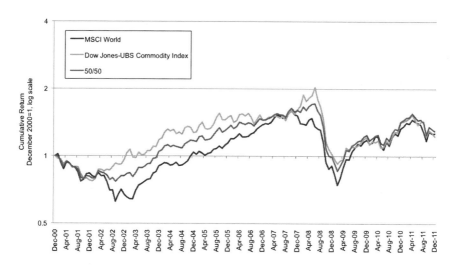

Source: Bloomberg, MSCI world, Dow Jones UBS Commodity.

Table 9.2 – global equities, commodities and a 50/50 portfolio historic return and risk characteristics, January 2001 to December 2011

	MSCI World	DJ-UBS Commodity	50/50 Portfolio
Performance (% pa)	2.2	1.9	2.4
Volatility (%)	17.1	17.8	15.2
Sharpe ratio	0.01	0.00	0.03

Source: Bloomberg, MSCI world, Dow Jones UBS Commodity.

The attractive benefits of combining asset classes depend on the interdependencies among them. Had all asset classes performed exactly the same, there would be no point in combining them. Since they do not perform in the same way, as demonstrated in Figure 9.5 (showing the annual performance of equities, bonds and cash), diversification works.

Figure 9.5 – annual returns of US equities, Treasuries and Treasury Bills, January 2000 to June 2012

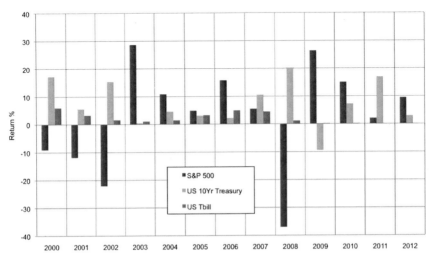

Source: Bloomberg, Global Financial Data, S&P 500, USA 10-year Government Total Return, USA Total Return T-Bill.

Diversifying across asset classes

Diversification reduces some risks (idiosyncratic risks). Skilled investors should expose their portfolio to idiosyncratic risks since if they are right, the potential returns are higher than the average return that diversification achieves. However, investors who have no skill in selecting idiosyncratic risks (e.g. selecting a limited number of stocks) should diversify their portfolios. Diversification is one of the only ways of reducing some portfolio risks without paying for insurance or hedging.

Diversification delivers average, not spectacular, returns. If the objective is getting rich from investing, diversification does not serve this purpose. If the objective is reducing volatility then diversification does serve this goal. For wealth generation, a concentrated portfolio may be needed. For wealth preservation, a diversified portfolio may be needed.

Portfolios should hold diversified sources of systematic risks, or betas, to benefit from diversification and the expected compensation (risk premium) for assuming these risks. However, as the performance of equity markets over the last decade shows, a simple buy and hold strategy does not seem to work as it did in the past. Since asset classes can experience very long spells of flat performance and material drawdowns, a dynamic process of switching among sources of systematic risk is required to preserve and grow capital. This is achieved through dynamic SAA and TAA.

Summary

- Diversifying across a number of asset classes with differing performances reduces idiosyncratic risk.

- The risk-adjusted performance of a well-diversified portfolio is typically superior (more efficient) to that of an undiversified portfolio.

- Diversification delivers average, not spectacular, returns.

- Concentrate portfolios for wealth generation and diversify portfolios for wealth preservation.

- Asset classes can move sideways for decades and experience material drawdowns. Therefore, a dynamic process of managing the exposure to systematic risks is required to preserve and grow capital.

This section has demonstrated the intuition behind diversification. The next section aims to quantify the benefits of diversification and highlight some of its shortcomings.

10. DIVERSIFICATION

Diversification in layman's terms is *not putting all your eggs in one basket*. It is the process of seeking different sources of return and combining them based on their risks and interdependencies. The interdependency among investments must be imperfect to benefit from the risk-reduction of diversification.

Correlation (ρ, the Greek letter rho) is a measure of linear interdependency[126]. Correlation of +1.0 means a perfect positive linear relationship (i.e. when one investment moves up or down the second one moves in the same direction) and correlation of -1.0 means a perfect negative linear relationship (i.e. anti-correlation, when one investment moves up or down the second one moves in the opposite direction). Correlation has a value between -1.0 and 1.0 in all other cases, indicating the degree of linear relationship between the investments. As it approaches zero the linear relationship is weaker. The closer the correlation is to either -1.0 or 1.0, the stronger the linear relationship.

Many investments exhibit high correlations. For example, equities of different companies tend to move together because company earnings are affected by the same economic developments and discount factors (used in equity valuation models) are affected by economy-wide interest rates. Government bonds and equities, on the other hand, have lower correlation since they react differently to economic developments. Economic slowdown is bad news for equities since dividends and earnings growth may fall but good news for government bonds since interest rates and inflation rates may ease. Cash has a low correlation with equities since cash has stable, positive nominal returns, while returns of equities fluctuate.

Emerging market equities tend to move in tandem under a general risk aversion to emerging markets as investors rush to sell risky assets and buy conservative, safe-haven assets (flight to quality) such as government bonds, dollars, Swiss francs and gold. Often during a widespread equity sell-off correlations among equities increase because most of them fall. When correlations increase there are fewer opportunities for active managers to add value since all securities move in the same direction and security selection is consequently less effective. It is common that at time of crisis, historical correlations break and move toward 1.0. Just when diversification and active management are most needed, they fail investors. This does not mean, however, that diversification does not work in the long term.

Modern Portfolio Theory

Harry Markowitz introduced the concepts behind Modern Portfolio Theory (MPT) in his seminal 'Portfolio Selection' article[127] of 1952 (MPT is more than 60 years old, hardly modern anymore) and mathematically showed the risk reduction benefits of diversification. The world of investment management changed forever.

A portfolio's *expected return* is simply the weighted average (mean) of the expected returns of the individual investments in the portfolio. For example, a portfolio holding 60% equities with an expected return of 8% and 40% bonds with an expected return of 5%, is expected to return 6.8% (60%*8% + 40%*5%). For a multi-asset portfolio the formula for expected return is:

$$r_p = \sum w_i r_i$$

where r_p is the portfolio expected return, w_i is the weight to asset i and r_i is the expected return of asset i.

Portfolio *return* is the proportionally weighted combination of the returns of the asset classes. The relationship or interdependency between asset classes does not change the overall portfolio's expected return. The weight to each asset class and each asset class's expected return determine the overall portfolio's expected return.

As Markowitz showed in his paper, *expected risk*, as measured by standard deviation or variance (variance = σ^2), *does* depend on the relationship among asset classes, as measured by correlation. For example, a portfolio holding 60% equities, whose standard deviation is 15%, and 40% bonds, whose standard deviation is 5%, with 0.20 correlation between them, has a standard deviation of 9.6% as per the calculation:

$$\sigma = (0.6^2 0.15^2 + 0.4^2 0.05^2 + 2*0.6*0.4*0.15*0.05*0.2)^{0.5} = 9.6\%$$

A simple weighted average of the two standard deviations equals 11% (60%*15% + 40%*5%) and this would have been the portfolio risk had the correlation between equities and bonds been 1.0 (perfect correlation; no diversification benefits). The imperfect correlation thus reduces portfolio risk.

For a multi-asset portfolio the formula for expected risk is:

$$\sigma_p^2 = \sum w_i^2 \sigma_i^2 + \sum\sum w_i w_j \sigma_i \sigma_j \rho_{ij}$$

where σ_p^2 is the expected portfolio variance, w_i is the portfolio weight to asset i, σ_i is the standard deviation of asset i and ρ_{ij} is the correlation between the returns of asset i and j.

Portfolio variance is made of two components. The first component $\Sigma w_i^2 \sigma_i^2$ is not reduced by diversification and is a function of the allocations to investments and their volatilities. The second component $\Sigma\Sigma w_i w_j \sigma_i \sigma_j \rho_{ij}$ is affected by correlation and lower correlation or higher diversification means higher portfolio risk reduction.

It is worthwhile giving an example of the formula for a three-asset portfolio:

$$\sigma_p^2 = w_a^2\sigma_a^2 + w_b^2\sigma_b^2 + w_c^2\sigma_c^2 + 2w_a w_b \rho_{ab}\sigma_a\sigma_b + 2w_a w_c \rho_{ac}\sigma_a\sigma_c + 2w_b w_c \rho_{bc}\sigma_b\sigma_c$$

where σ_p^2 is the portfolio variance, w_a, w_b and w_c are the weights of investments a, b and c, σ^2a, σ^2b and σ^2c are their variances and ρ_{ab}, ρ_{ac} and ρ_{bc} are the correlations between each pair of investments.

The standard deviation is the square root of the variance.

One insight from portfolio risk calculations is that when diversifying, investors need to ensure that portfolios are indeed diversified across imperfectly correlated assets. Holding stocks of two companies in the same industry in the same country may not be true diversification since these two stocks are likely to be highly correlated. Their returns are going to be driven by the same factors. One factor is market return, which is used in CAPM, and cannot be diversified. The two stocks share this same factor with different (but perhaps similar) exposures (betas) to it. Other common factors may include size, style, industry, country and currency factors. To truly diversify portfolios, investors need to choose investments and asset classes with exposure to different factors and drivers of performance.

How many investments are needed for diversification?

Assuming average standard deviation for each investment (σ), average correlation among investments (ρ) and an equally weighted portfolio with N investments, the formula for calculating portfolio variance simplifies to:

$$\sigma^2\rho = \sigma^2\rho + \sigma^2(1 - \rho)/N$$

The total portfolio risk can be broken down to two components: $\sigma^2\rho$ and $\sigma^2(1-\rho)/N$. The former component cannot be reduced by increasing the number of investments and represents the market or systematic risk. The latter component can be reduced by increasing the number of investments. As the number of investments increases, the latter component reduces quickly.

Assuming average standard deviation of 40% and average correlation of 0.20, when including 30 securities in a portfolio most of the risk reduction benefits through diversification are achieved[128] (as demonstrated in Figure 10.1).

Figure 10.1 – portfolio volatility and number of investments. Assuming average volatility of 40%, average correlation of 0.20 and equally weighted portfolio

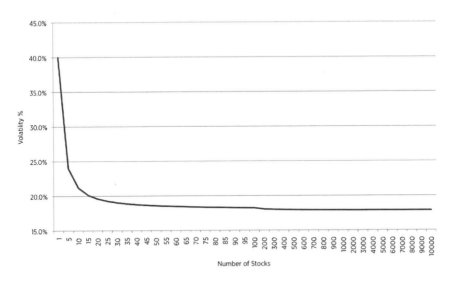

Using MPT in practice

MPT can be used for a simple asset allocation process. Portfolio expected return and risk are calculated based on the Capital Market Assumptions (CMAs – the expected return, risk and correlation for the universe of asset classes). Portfolio optimisation can be used to identify allocations with the highest possible return for a certain level of risk or the minimum required risk for a certain level of return. This process is *mean-variance optimisation* and is easily done through an optimisation tool such as Microsoft Excel Solver for a limited number of asset classes.

When the number of asset classes is relatively large, more powerful computer software may be needed for optimisation as the number of variables increases rapidly (a portfolio with n assets has n expected returns, n standard deviations and $(n^2-n)/2$ correlation coefficients). Optimisation methodologies based on multi-factor models have been developed to reduce the number of variables. However, with the increasing power of computers, optimising multiple investments is not an issue any more.

Mean-variance optimisation has several shortcomings. It usually leads to asset allocations in which the majority of holdings are concentrated in a small number of asset classes that make up the investment opportunity set (often the results contradict the common sense of diversification). Also, it does not consider liabilities (although they can be modelled into the optimisation through negative or short assets), it is based on the assumption of normal distribution and it is a single period model, while most investors have multi-period objectives. Nevertheless, optimisation is used to identify efficient asset allocations, at least as a starting point.

Based on the CMAs, MPT quantifies the expected risk and return of asset allocations and it is possible to align them with the investor objectives. Once the investor objectives are determined, MPT helps in formulating an investment strategy and guiding investors in choosing an efficient asset allocation with the lowest expected risk while targeting the return objective or the highest expected return for an acceptable level of risk.

Investment constraints can be incorporated into the investment strategy through matching the investment horizon of the CMAs with that of the investor, adding constraints on minimum cash and liquid assets' levels to address liquidity needs, and defining the investment universe and setting minimum and maximum weights (ranges) to different asset classes to address tax, legal, regulatory and special circumstance constraints.

For example, at least 5% of the portfolio needs to be held in cash, no more than 10% of the portfolio can be invested in alternative investments and no exposure to bonds below investment grade is allowed. All these constraints can be expressed by setting the universe of asset classes (i.e. exclude high-yield and emerging market bonds) and ranges for allocations (i.e. minimum allocation to cash 5%; allocation to alternative investments 0% to 10%).

When a risk-free asset is available, according to Tobin's separation theorem[129], regardless of investors' attitude to risk, portfolios should be split between a portfolio with the highest Sharpe ratio (global market portfolio) and the riskless asset. The portfolio with the highest Sharpe ratio provides the highest possible reward per risk while the overall risk can be adjusted by the split between the portfolio and the riskless asset. According to this theorem all investors should hold the same portfolio. In reality, however, investors hold different portfolios because of differences in investment opportunity set, access to investments, preferences, taxes, advice and locations.

MPT criticism

Similarly to the CAPM, MPT is based on unrealistic assumptions. It assumes a frictionless world without trading transaction costs and taxes; that investors can take any position (including unlimited shorts), lend and borrow at the risk-free rate and liquidity is limitless; that all assets, including human capital, can be traded on the market; that all investors are rational and have the same investment horizon, measures of risk, information and a desire to hold diversified portfolios to reduce risk; and that politics and investor psychology have no effect on markets. All these assumptions are unrealistic. Nevertheless, even when these assumptions are relaxed, MPT is used to calculate portfolio expected return and risk and is a basis for most asset allocation techniques.

One shortcoming of MPT is that its sole risk measure is standard deviation. Not only does standard deviation assume that returns are normally distributed (ignoring the distribution's higher moments), but it also does not capture risks such as liquidity risk.

The solution for accounting for the limitations of standard deviation as a risk measure is adjusting it to higher moments or using downside risk measures. The solution for accounting for liquidity risk is explicitly considering it. For example, the expected portfolio cash outflows should be matched with the allocation to liquid investments and the time to liquidate positions, ensuring that the portfolio has sufficient liquidity to meet its liabilities.

Another shortcoming of MPT is that it assumes a single investment horizon and a static asset allocation during this horizon. This is normally an unrealistic assumption since investors have multiple time horizons. The solution is using a dynamic asset allocation process that is updated with market developments and investor circumstances.

Evaluating securities in portfolio context

One insight from MPT is evaluating investments in portfolio context. In a well-diversified portfolio investments should not be considered in isolation. Rather, their impact on the entire portfolio should be considered. Each investment's contribution to portfolio return and risk is the evaluation metric.

Using the example of equities with a volatility of 15%, bonds with a volatility of 5% and a correlation of 0.20 between them, adding equities to a 100% bond portfolio actually reduces portfolio risk. While equities in isolation are a risk asset, with a volatility of 15%, allocating 5% to equities in the portfolio reduces volatility from 5.0% to 4.95%. The 95%/5% bond/equity portfolio has a lower risk than the 100% bond portfolio.

Assuming the expected return of equities is 8% and that of bonds is 5%, the 95%/5% bond/equity portfolio's expected return is 5.15%, while that of the 100% bond portfolio is 5%. The diversified portfolio not only has a lower expected risk but also a higher expected return (a higher risk-adjusted expected return). Investing in equities does not always increase risk. It depends on the portfolio to which they are added.

Global diversification and where it is needed the most

The performance of each local equity market is affected by the economic conditions and fortunes of its country or region, so equity markets across national borders should exhibit imperfect correlation. Global equity investing should enjoy diversification benefits. Furthermore, diversifying internationally expands the investment opportunity set and benefits from global trends, such as the development of emerging markets and the rise of China.

While historically, international diversification has been a source for diversification benefits, the correlation across international equity markets has increased in recent decades because of globalisation, global corporations and global economic developments with increasing cross-border impact. World markets have become increasingly integrated.

Figure 10.2 shows the rolling 36-month correlation between the returns of the S&P 500 Index and the FTSE All Share Index from May 1962 to June 2012. While the average correlation in the 1960s was 0.30, it is 0.88 since the beginning of the 2000s. The benefits of international diversification have diminished. Nevertheless, international markets are still imperfectly correlated and international diversification can still add value.

Figure 10.2 – rolling 36-month correlation between US and UK equities, May 1962 to June 2012

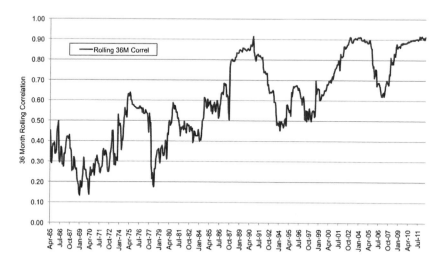

Source: Bloomberg, S&P 500, FTSE All Share.

Many portfolios of both private and institutional investors have a large *home bias*. Investors whose domestic market is large, developed and diversified tend to have a higher home bias than investors whose domestic market is small, developing and concentrated. Behavioural finance may explain home bias as a familiarity bias. Implied returns from portfolios with a home bias show that some investors tend to have higher return expectations from domestic markets and higher perceived risk of foreign markets.

Some objective factors such as taxation, transaction costs, capital controls, restrictions on foreign investments and availability of information were barriers for international diversification in the past, but the impact of these factors has diminished over recent decades. Another reason for home bias is currency risk, although it is easily manageable through hedging.

One rationale for home bias from standard finance is that as the local market is more diversified and includes more global corporations, the benefits of international diversification are less material. As Figure 10.3 shows, the volatility of highly developed local markets, such as those of the United States, United Kingdom, Switzerland and Australia, is in line with the volatility of global equities (as represented by the MSCI World Index). The volatility of smaller local markets, such as Sweden, Hong Kong, Norway and Ireland, on the other hand, is higher than that of global equities. For these markets global diversification is more important. Irish investors, for example, should diversify their portfolios globally.

Figure 10.3 – volatility of regional equity markets compared to that of global equities, February 1999 to June 2012. Light bar: MSCI World Index measured in local currency. Dark bar: MSCI regional Index

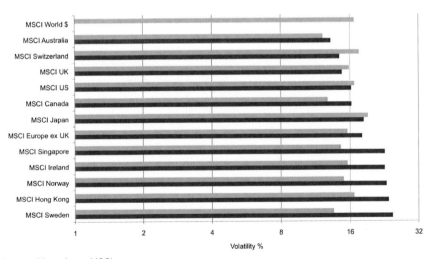

Source: Bloomberg, MSCI.

To illustrate the effects of different allocations between domestic and international equities, Figure 10.4 shows the volatility of different domestic and foreign combinations for the US, UK and Japanese equity markets. Based on experience, over a limited historic time period, the minimum volatility is achieved for Japan with 50% domestic and 50% foreign; for the United Kingdom with 70% domestic and 30% foreign; and for the United States with 80% domestic and 20% foreign.

The bias to the UK domestic market is driven by the low volatility of the domestic market relative to foreign markets. The opposite is true for Japan. For a US investor, the benefits of international diversification are less material. Nevertheless, there are still benefits for diversifying internationally even for US investors, whose local market is the most diversified in the world.

Figure 10.4 – volatility of a mix of domestic and global equities, January 1988 to June 2012

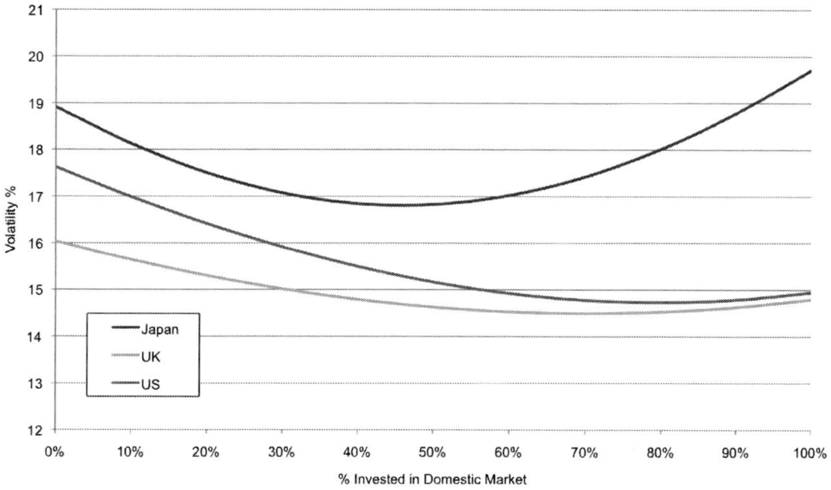

Source: Bloomberg, MSCI.

An alternative to diversifying globally by geographic regions is diversifying across global sectors[130]. However, it is questionable whether global sector diversification has any benefits over regional diversification[131].

The importance of asset allocation

The main process for achieving diversification in multi-asset portfolios is asset allocation. Many academic studies compare the impact of asset allocation, security selection, market timing and other factors on the return and risk of portfolios. Two famous studies by Gary Brinson et al from 1986[132] and 1991[133] claim that on average asset allocation determines 91.5%, security selection 4.6%, market timing 1.8% and other factors 2.1% of the *variance* of portfolio returns (as graphically illustrated by the pie chart in Figure 10.5). The Brinson studies talk about portfolio variance, not return.

Figure 10.5 – determinants of portfolio variance

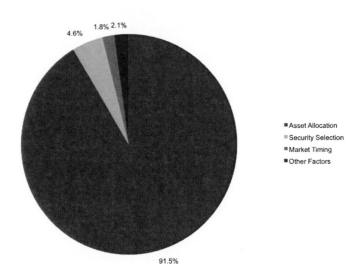

Roger Ibbotson and Paul Kaplan tried to answer three questions in their study in 2000[134]. The first was how much of variability of returns *across time* is explained by SAA or investment policy. In other words, how much of portfolios' ups and downs SAA explains. Their answer was 90%. This is the same question that the Brinson studies addressed and Ibbotson agreed with Brinson. Interestingly, the exposure to capital markets, as represented by the S&P 500 Index, explained on average about 75% of portfolios' variability of returns. Therefore, exposure to capital markets seems to be the factor explaining the variability of returns, on average, more than the exact choice of SAA.

The second question in the Ibbotson study was how much of the variation in return *across portfolios* is explained by SAA. In other words, how much of the variation in return between two portfolios is explained by differences in their policy? The study's answer was 40%. The focus here is not on volatility of returns, which is a measure across time, but on cross-sectional volatility of returns, which is a measure across portfolios at the same time.

The third question in the Ibbotson study was what proportion of the return level is explained by policy. This is the ratio of portfolios' policy return to portfolios' actual return. The answer in the study was 100%. This means that, on average, active management does not add value. This conclusion is in line with William Sharpe's paper[135] the 'Arithmetic of Active Management'. Other papers are harsher and conclude that on average active management reduces returns and increases volatility[136].

The main conclusion from the studies is that asset allocation is a major driver of long-term returns and risk. Average investors generate returns since markets tend to go up over time and asset allocations expose portfolios to capital markets. Skilled or lucky portfolio managers and unskilled or unlucky managers cancel each other out. Hence, active management is argued to not add value on average. While this is true for the average investor, investors who have skill in selecting investments or portfolio managers who consistently outperform can generate considerable returns thorough active management.

While asset allocation is undoubtedly important, investment selection does not fall behind. In a 60%/40% equity/bond portfolio, with 8% equity expected return and 5% bond expected return, the expected portfolio return is 6.8%. Moving 10% from bonds to equities (70%/30% equity/bond) the portfolio's expected return increases to 7.1%. In the original 60/40 portfolio, if equities outperform the 8% hurdle by 1%, the portfolio's expected return is 7.4%. Equity outperformance of 1% has a larger impact on portfolio return than a 10% increase in the allocation to equities. Assuming equity volatility of 15%, volatility of bonds of 5% and a correlation of 0.20 between equities and bonds, changing the asset allocation to 70/30 increases portfolio risk from 9.6% to 10.9%. An increase of 3% in equity risk (from 15% to 18%) is enough to increase the risk of the original 60/40 portfolio to 11.4%.

These calculations show that active management within an asset class can have a larger impact on portfolio return and risk than material changes to asset allocation. The challenge, however, is picking portfolio managers who add alpha (outperform) more often than the times that they add a negative alpha (underperform). Active management and investment selection can have a substantial impact on portfolio results.

Indeed, the debate on the importance of asset allocation continues. James Xiong, Roger Ibbotson et al published an article in 2010[137] claiming for equal importance of asset allocation and active management. In the article portfolio total returns are decomposed into market return, asset allocation policy return in excess of market return and returns from active portfolio management. Using time-series and cross-sectional analysis, the article suggested that *market return* is the most important determinant of total return. However, the article examined the results for specific peer groups after removing the market return component of total return and found that asset allocation policy returns in excess of market return and active portfolio management are equally important. Multi-asset investing must get both the asset allocation and investment selection right.

The Yale Model

The Yale Model was developed by David Swensen and Dean Takahashi. Swensen has been the Chief Investment Officer (CIO) of the endowment fund of Yale University since 1985. The Yale Model is described in Swensen's 2000 book *Pioneering Portfolio Management*[138]. The model divides portfolios into five or six broadly equally weighted portions, each invested in a different asset class with low correlations among them. This model was one of the pioneering implementations of multi-asset investing and MPT in a renowned portfolio as the model diversified assets across investments with low correlation to benefit from diversification.

The model recognised that liquidity should be avoided since it comes at a price of lower expected returns. The endowment allocated to illiquid asset classes, such as private equity, to benefit from the liquidity premium.

In his 2005 book *Unconventional Success*[139], Swensen advised investors to construct portfolios allocated to six core asset classes with low correlation among them and a bias to equities, rebalance the portfolios on a regular basis and in the absence of confidence in active management to add alpha, utilise low-cost passive investments, and keep a watchful eye on costs and fees.

The Yale Model suggests that investors can formulate SAA without using optimisation techniques (although the Yale endowment does use mean-variance optimisation and other quantitative techniques[140]). The diversification across asset classes is more qualitative and intuitive than quantitative and, as long as common sense is applied correctly, should provide diversification.

Diversifying across a number of asset classes that should have low correlation with each other, such as equities (domestic and foreign), fixed income (government bonds, inflation-linked bonds and corporate bonds), real assets (real estate and commodities), alternative investments (hedge funds and private equity) and cash, is likely to deliver well diversified portfolios. MPT and the formulas for expected risk and return can be used to check that the asset allocation matches the investment objectives.

Risk-based asset allocation

When thinking about diversification and asset allocation, investors can separate their assets into three buckets or risk accounts:

1. Safe bucket

2. Market risk bucket

3. Risky bucket[141]

The *safe bucket* includes assets that the investors cannot afford to lose or risk. Safety first is the objective. Investors are completely risk averse with respect of these assets and risking them may jeopardise the investor's future, standard of living and financial well-being. The safe bucket includes assets such as a residential house, human capital and cash reserves. These assets are the individual's life savings and retirement assets or institutional investor's assets held to match liabilities or meet regulatory requirements.

The benchmark for this bucket should represent low risk and conservatism such as cash, the inflation rate or inflation-linked government bonds. The investment objective is maintaining the purchasing power of assets without risking capital (i.e. capital preservation). The downside risk of the assets in the safe bucket should be protected by insurance where applicable (home insurance and life insurance). Cash should be invested in deposits in large, creditworthy institutions (that are *too big to fail*). Inflation-linked and conventional government bonds issued by countries with high and stable credit ratings (avoiding countries like Greece) should be used to match liabilities.

The second bucket is the *market risk bucket*, which includes assets that investors can afford to risk and wish to invest in with the objective of real growth over time (i.e. capital growth). The risk level of this bucket depends on the investor's risk appetite. The assets should be well diversified across different sources of beta and alpha. The main risks are market, credit and liquidity risks. The assets in this bucket could include savings, investible assets, and surplus assets of a pension fund. Investors should apply the principles of multi-asset investing to the assets in this bucket, including SAA, potentially TAA and investment selection. The benchmark should reflect the investment objectives for this bucket (e.g. a composite benchmark representing the long-term investment policy or SAA).

The third bucket is the *risky bucket*, or speculative or aspirational bucket. This bucket should make up a relatively small portion of investors' entire wealth or assets (less than 20%, preferably less than 10%). However, in some instances this bucket comprises the majority of investors' portfolios (e.g. entrepreneur's private business). Investors should be willing and able to risk the assets in this bucket, aspiring to earn considerable returns. If successful, the investments in this bucket may increase the investor's standard of living.

The assets in this bucket may include single stock investments, private equity, real estate and other concentrated positions. The bucket is not diversified because diversification reduces risk but also averages expected returns. To earn high returns a concentrated or even leveraged portfolio is needed. Investors who are keen to be actively involved in managing their portfolio can do so within the risk bucket. Investors should use their expertise in a specialised niche to select investments. For example, entrepreneurs invest in new start-ups, high-tech industry specialists select stocks using their industry knowledge and real estate developers select properties. Leverage is an option but it should be contained within this bucket without potentially spilling over and affecting the other two buckets. There is no clear benchmark for this bucket and its performance should be assessed on an absolute return basis with the expectation of very high returns (sometimes measured in increments of 100%).

Investors can dynamically move assets across the three buckets. For example, if the value of liabilities falls (e.g. when interest rates increase the present value of liabilities decreases), assets can be moved from the safe bucket to the market risk bucket as less assets are needed to match liabilities. If investments in the risky bucket realise a profit and the investor wishes to de-risk the portfolio and take profits, assets can be moved from the risky bucket to the market risk bucket. As investors approach retirement assets should be moved from the market risk and risky buckets to the safe bucket. The allocation across the buckets changes to match an investor's preferences, objectives and circumstances.

The risk-based asset allocation methodology enables investors to holistically consider all their assets (including home and human capital), assigning the appropriate risk level and investment techniques to each asset group. The methodology builds on the cognitive bias of *mental accounting* by separating assets into different accounts with different risk and return objectives. However, through acknowledging that assets are separated into different accounts and not ignoring their interrelationships, investors can manage the risk of their entire wealth or assets.

Asset allocation for multiple horizons

Most long-term investors have multiple investment horizons for various parts of their portfolio. A 2010 article[142] suggests that most investors have a series of short-term, intermediate-term and long-term investment objectives that should be addressed with a series of sub-portfolios to meet the particular investment objectives and liabilities of each investment horizon.

For example, an individual may be saving to buy a house next year, accumulating funds to pay children's college tuition in five years and saving for a retirement portfolio to be used in 15 years, all at the same time. Each of these sub-portfolios has different liquidity requirements, expected returns, risk tolerances and investment horizons. The solution is that different asset allocation decisions are applicable for each sub-portfolio rather than at the total portfolio level. The allocation to each sub-portfolio is determined by its spending needs. The appropriate risk measure is not volatility but rather the expected loss relative to investment objectives. Sub-portfolios with a long-term investment horizon should consider the effects of inflation on expected loss.

Concentration and focus investing

The opposite of diversification is concentration, or focus investing. Andrew Carnegie, the famous American industrialist, said "the wise man puts all his eggs in one basket and watches the basket". *Focus investing* is an investment strategy following concepts such as:

- Purchase stocks of companies that have an understandable business, sustainable competitive advantage and good management that has the benefits of shareholders in mind.

- Invest for the very long term. Therefore, the compounding benefits are extended and tax payments are delayed.

- Invest using a margin of safety (i.e. identify stocks with prices below their intrinsic value).

- Concentrate the investment selection and avoid over-diversification. Purchase only high-conviction investments. Invest material time and money in researching each investment.

- Consider risk in terms of opportunity cost and permanent loss of capital. Volatility is not a risk per se; it just indicates how jumpy the journey is going to be. Volatility creates investment opportunities since it creates a mispricing between price and valuation.

Focus investing is not recommended for everyone since it is risky and requires skill. However, if investors want to become rich from investing, diversification delivers average market returns while focus investing may deliver material relative returns (above or below the market average). Focus investing avoids some of the potential pitfalls of diversification, such as over-diversification, which may lead to elimination of all alpha and an expensive market tracker.

Two of the most well-known followers of focus investments are Philip Fisher, the father of growth investing and the author of the famous book *Common Stocks and Uncommon Profits*[143], and Warren Buffett.

Summary

Like in many other areas of investing, the answer to diversification is grey, not black or white. Diversification has mathematically proven benefits. For most investors, who have no extraordinary skill, diversification works. For some extraordinary investors (see Warren Buffett), concentration makes more sense. Successful entrepreneurs concentrate their portfolios on a single private equity investment. They have a talent and/or luck. For most non-extraordinary investors, diversification is beneficial.

- Diversification is a way to reduce portfolio risk without sacrificing all investment return. This is one of the few proven ways to enhance risk-adjusted returns (alongside reducing fees, costs and taxes).

- Imperfect correlation is the key to diversification.

- MPT mathematically quantifies a portfolio's expected return and risk, based on inputs on asset class expected return, risk and correlation (Capital Market Assumptions or CMAs).

- MPT enables investors to calculate expected risk and return of portfolios to match them with the investment objectives.

- MPT has shortcomings since it uses volatility as a single measure of risk, it relies on unrealistic assumptions and it is based on a single investment horizon. Nevertheless, it is widely used, and rightly so, since it is simple, intuitive and does provide the framework for more sophisticated optimisation techniques.

- Investments should not be evaluated in isolation but rather in portfolio context (i.e. their impact on the risk and return of the entire portfolio should be considered).

- While the benefits of international diversification have diminished over recent decades due to increasing correlations across international markets, it still has risk-reducing benefits and it expands the investment opportunity set. International diversification is more important for investors whose home market is undiversified.

- Asset allocation is the main driver of portfolio risk and returns over the long term. However, investment selection can have a material impact on overall portfolio results. The challenge is selecting performing investments or portfolio managers who consistently add alpha.

- The Yale Model suggests allocating the portfolio across four to six asset classes that have low correlation with each other.

- The risk-based asset allocation methodology splits assets across three buckets: *safe*, *market risk* and *risky*. Each bucket has different risk and return objectives. The safe bucket includes assets that investors cannot afford to lose. The market risk bucket includes a diversified multi-asset portfolio. The risky bucket includes concentrated positions, in high risk/high potential reward investments that investors can afford to lose.

- Investors with multiple investment horizons, each with different set of investment objectives and liabilities, can divide their total portfolio into sub-portfolios, each managed to investment objectives and liabilities matching the different investment horizons.

- Every investment strategy or asset allocation methodology should be modified as market and investor circumstances change.

- Focus investing is about concentrating, not diversifying, portfolios. This investment strategy is appropriate for skilled investors who wish to generate higher than average market returns. Concentrated portfolios are likely to diverge from average market return, either above or below it.

The following chapters explore the steps of the SAA process:

1. Formulating the inputs or the Capital Market Assumptions (return, risk and correlation) for different asset classes

2. Optimisation or modelling techniques

3. Dynamic SAA processes to adjust SAA to current market conditions and multiple investment horizons

Dynamic SAA is the key to avoid a static, buy and hold portfolio. Portfolios should be relevant to current market conditions, to which they are linked via dynamic SAA and its Capital Market Assumptions.

11. CAPITAL MARKET ASSUMPTIONS

Modern portfolio theory provides the methodology for calculating the expected return and risk of portfolios and deriving efficient asset allocations through an optimisation process. The success of MPT heavily depends on formulating forward-looking, underlying asset class assumptions that have a high correlation with actual future results (*information coefficient*).

The inputs for the SAA process are the Capital Market Assumptions (CMAs), including expected return and risk for each asset class and the correlations among them. The *strategic* aspect of SAA (*Strategic* Asset Allocation) means that it has a long horizon of 5 to 10 years and the horizon of the CMAs needs to match it. Most methods for formulating CMAs are systematic and quantitative driven since the aim is forecasting market return and risk over the long term. Conversely, TAA aims to forecast tactical, short-term market movements. The next sections will review some of the methods for establishing CMAs.

CMAs based on history

Many investors naïvely extrapolate historic average returns into the future to formulate CMAs. History, however, is a poor predictor of future returns. Taking the average return of any market and extrapolating it to establish an expected return is likely to fail. It may be right for a couple of years by chance, but it will be wrong most of the time. (Repeating a bet enough times wins once in a while.)

Figure 11.1 shows the annualised geometric average return of 10 years of monthly returns of the S&P 500 Index and plots the subsequent average of realised 10 years of monthly returns. As can be seen, history is not a good predictor of expected returns. Equity returns fluctuate.

Figure 11.1 – historic and subsequent 10-year returns, January 1926 to June 2012

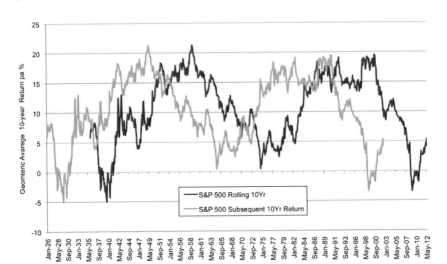

Source: Bloomberg, Global Financial Data, S&P 500.

The scatter chart in Figure 11.2 plots the historic average 10-year S&P 500 Index return (x-axis) and subsequent 10-year average return (y-axis). The R^2 (coefficient of determination[144]), which measures how much of the variability of the second series is explained by the first series, is very low (0.04), indicating close to zero correlation between the two series. The information coefficient of historical returns is very weak as a predictor of future returns.

Figure 11.2 – historic and subsequent 10-year returns with a liner regression line, January 1926 to June 2012

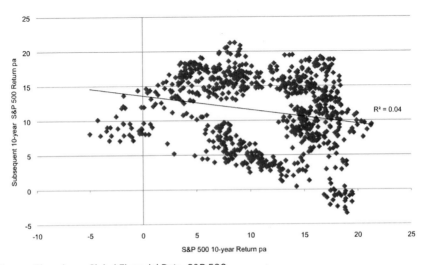

Source: Bloomberg, Global Financial Data, S&P 500.

Figure 11.3 shows the compounded annual return (geometric mean) over each decade since the 1920s of US equities (S&P 500 Index), 10-year Treasury bonds and US Treasury Bills (T-Bills). Figure 11.4 shows the annual arithmetic average returns over each decade of those three asset classes. As the charts illustrate, performance from decade to decade differs. Hence, the returns over the last 10 years are a poor predictor of the returns over the next 10 years, whether a geometric or arithmetic average is used.

Figure 11.3 – historic geometric average returns over each decade, 1920s (from January 1926) to 2010s (to June 2012)

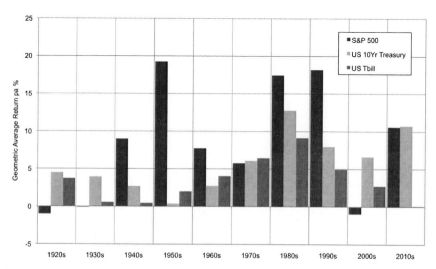

Source: Bloomberg, Global Financial Data, S&P 500, USA 10-year Government Bond Total Return, USA Total Return T-Bill.

Figure 11.4 – historic arithmetic average returns over each decade, 1920s (from January 1926) to 2010s (to June 2012)

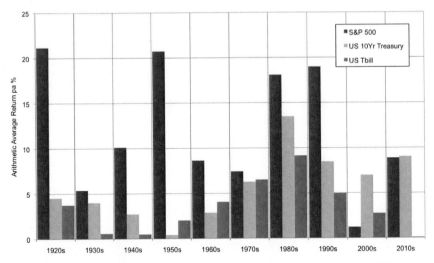

Source: Bloomberg, Global Financial Data, S&P 500, USA 10-year Government Bond Total Return, USA Total Return T-Bill.

Nevertheless, there is value in history. After all, history is what we know and we should learn from it. Figure 11.5 shows the historic annualised *standard deviation* of 10 years of monthly returns of the S&P 500 Index and the subsequent 10-year annualised standard deviation. While volatility is not stationary (it changes), history is a good indication for the risk level of different asset classes over long time periods. Since the 1950s the standard deviation of the S&P 500 Index has been range bound around 15%.

Figure 11.5 – historic and subsequent 10-year volatility, January 1926 to June 2012

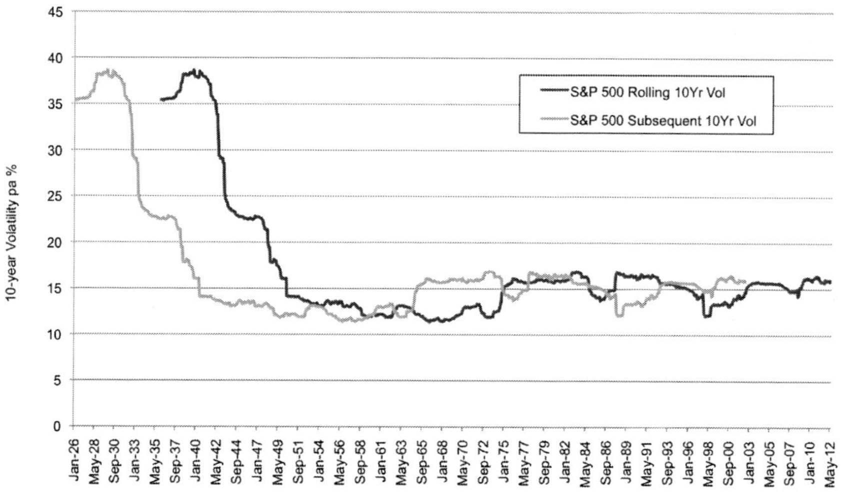

Source: Bloomberg, Global Financial Data, S&P 500.

Figure 11.6 shows the volatility of returns over each decade since the 1920s of US equities (S&P 500 Index), 10-year Treasury Bonds and US T-Bills. As the chart illustrates, volatility from decade to decade, while it differs, sometimes materially, is more stable than returns. The 1920s and 1930s are two outliers for equities (the Great Depression). The 1980s are an outlier for US government bonds, the volatility of which has increased since the 1950s.

Figure 11.6 – historic volatilities over each decade, 1920s (from January 1926) to 2010s (to June 2012)

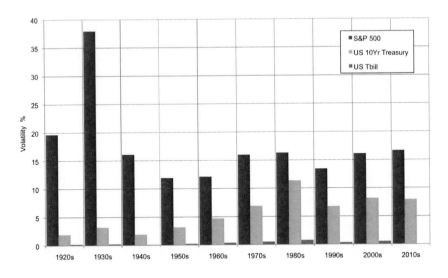

Source: Bloomberg, Global Financial Data, S&P 500, USA 10-year Government Bond Total Return, USA Total Return T-Bill.

Figure 11.7 shows the historic *correlation* between 10 years of monthly returns of the S&P 500 Index and those of US 10-year government bonds and the subsequent 10-year realised correlation. Similarly to standard deviation, correlation is not stationary. Figure 11.8 shows the correlations decade by decade. As correlation may shift markedly from historic levels, historic correlations are a poor predictor of future correlation.

Figure 11.7 – historic and subsequent 10-year correlation between US equities and bonds, January 1926 to June 2012

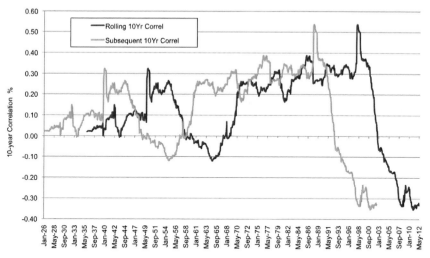

Source: Bloomberg, Global Financial Data, S&P 500, USA 10-year Government Bond Total Return.

Figure 11.8 – historic correlations between US equities and bonds over each decade, 1920s (from January 1926) to 2010s (to June 2012)

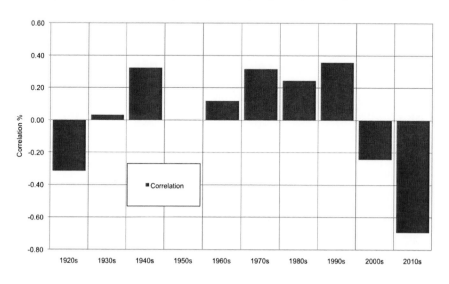

Source: Bloomberg, Global Financial Data, S&P P 500, USA 10-year Government Bond Total Return.

The conclusions are that better methodologies are needed to establish expected returns than naïvely extrapolating historic returns. While it is straightforward to use historical data to project future performance, it is a flawed method. Correlations can wildly change from decade to decade. However, it has been shown that historic risk level is a good guide for future risk level.

The flaws of constant CMAs

Often, investors use long-term average returns and adjust them based on an assessment of future prospects to generate a set of constant or static CMAs. Alternatively, more recent average returns are adjusted toward the long-term average under the assumption of *mean reversion*. For example, the compounded annual return of the S&P 500 Index from January 1926 to June 2012 is 9.8%. The compounded annual return over the last 12.5 years since January 2000 is only 1.3%. Assuming that recent returns are going to revert towards the long-term mean, but are unlikely to reach historic highs, an expected return of 8% per annum for the next decade may seem reasonable (although it is difficult to justify 8% as it is difficult to justify 7% or 9% based on this data).

Three clear weaknesses of this methodology are that:

1. It is based on an unsubstantiated assumption of mean reversion

2. It is driven by a subjective assessment of the future (the long-term average is arbitrarily adjusted downward and the more recent average is arbitrarily adjusted upward)

3. A constant expected return is not robust

The disadvantage of constant CMAs is that they are not adjusted to current market conditions. Using 8% per annum as an expected return of equities, for example, ignores the current state of the economy, short-term interest rates, inflation expectations, levels of dividends, and prospects for earnings and dividend growth.

When the starting point is the top of the economic cycle, equity returns in the next few years are likely to be subdued since normally inflation is high, interest rates are likely to increase, growth is expected to slow down and equity prices are already at elevated levels (high P/E ratios or price to earnings multiples). Under these circumstances 8% is probably overly optimistic. Optimistic or overestimated expected equity returns drive the SAA optimisation process to allocate more to equities, leading to an equity-biased portfolio that is likely to disappoint.

Conversely, when the starting point is the bottom of the business cycle, the opposite is true. Equity valuations are probably cheap at this stage of the cycle, economic growth is likely to accelerate and equity returns in the next few years are likely to be attractive. Depressed expected returns lead to a sub par allocation to equities, defensive portfolios and likelihood of disappointment due to a missed opportunity.

Figure 11.9 shows the rolling 10-year mean annualised performance of the S&P 500 Index. Average performance over periods of 10 years swings wildly and a single, constant figure cannot capture correctly the index performance.

Figure 11.9 – rolling 10-year performance of US equities, January 1926 to June 2012

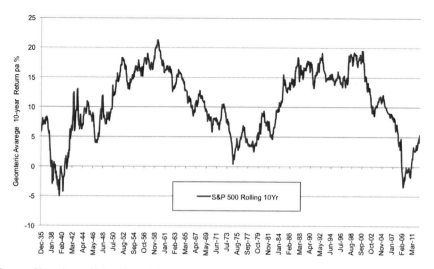

Source: Bloomberg, Global Financial Data, S&P 500.

The 12-month rolling returns of US equities look like a seismograph reading during a 9.5 Richter scale earthquake (as illustrated by Figure 11.10). Annual equity returns are far from static and static CMAs are misleading. A dynamic method that considers the current market conditions and links them to the likely returns over the next 10 years is needed.

Figure 11.10 – rolling 12-month performance of US equities, January 1950 to June 2012

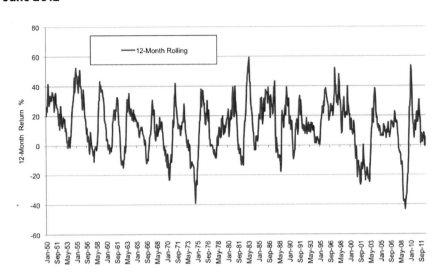

Source: Bloomberg, S&P 500.

Past and future equity returns

Equities are riskier than cash and most types of bonds. Investors, therefore, should be compensated for the excess risk of investing in equities relative to cash and bonds. Investors expect to earn an *equity risk premium* (ERP) for investing in equities. The equity risk premium is the difference between the return of equities and that of cash or government bonds (depending on how the premium is defined). The forward-looking, expected equity risk premium determines the investment policy and the allocation to equities within portfolios. The higher the expected equity risk premium, the higher the expected return of equities and the higher the allocation to equities relative to cash and bonds, depending on the investor risk appetite.

A similar argument holds for bonds relative to cash. Bonds are riskier than cash due to duration risk (interest rate risk) and credit risk. Hence, investors expect a risk premium for investing in bonds instead of holding cash. *Maturity risk premium* is expected to compensate for interest rate risk (longer maturity involves longer duration and higher interest rate risk) and *credit risk premium* is expected to compensate for credit risk.

Several academic studies have researched the historic equity risk premium and debated what risk premium can be reasonably expected in the coming decades. One conclusion is that historic experience may be misleading.

The US markets have the most readily available data to study the historic equity risk premium. Since January 1926 to June 2012 the S&P 500 Index has outperformed US 10-year government bonds by an arithmetic average of 6.0% per annum and a geometric average of 4.3% per annum. The outperformance versus Treasury Bills was an arithmetic average of 8.0% per annum and a geometric average of 6.1% per annum. In a 2005 article[145] William Goetzmann and Roger Ibbotson showed that from 1926 to 2004 US stocks outperformed long-term government bonds by 6.6% arithmetically and 5.0% geometrically. The time period between 2004 and 2011 reduced these long-term averages by approximately 70 basis points.

Academic studies on the future expected equity risk premium give different results. Fama and French[146] claim that equity returns during the 50 years ending in 2000 were higher than what investors should have expected to earn. Stock prices have been bid up to reflect the reduction in future expected returns due to a lower equity risk premium. This means that investors viewed equities as less risky and demanded a lower equity risk premium to compensate them for taking equity risk. As the equity risk premium declined the price of equities was bid upward. Higher current price means lower future returns reflecting the lower equity risk premium. They claim that dividends and company earnings growth are much better predictors of sustainable future equity returns than historic dividends plus capital appreciation. Dividends, earnings growth and sustainable returns will be discussed at length in later sections.

Dimson, Marsh and Staunton from the London Business School in their 2002 book[147] *Triumph of the Optimists* summarised the returns of different asset classes from 1900 to 2000 and concluded that an arithmetic average equity risk premium over government bonds in the United States, the United Kingdom and world equities would fall within a range of between little below 4.0% and little above 5.0%.

In their 2006 study[148] they used a database of long-term returns to estimate the equity risk premium for 17 countries and a world index over a 106-year period. The worldwide equity risk premium is 4.7% over US Treasury bills and 4.0% over 10-year US Treasury bonds. They inferred that investors expect a premium on the world index of about 3.0% to 3.5% on a geometric basis or approximately 4.5% to 5.0% on an arithmetic basis relative to Treasury Bills. In their 2009 study[149] they reported that over the period 1900 to 2008 the equity risk premium versus T-Bills was 5.0% in the United States and the world average was 4.2%. The equity risk premium over bonds was 3.8% in the United States and the world average was 3.4%.

In a 2003 study[150] by Ibbotson and Chen the long-term equity risk premium relative to the long-term government bond yield is estimated to be about 6% arithmetically and 4% geometrically. They claimed that increases in the price/earnings ratio account for only a small portion of the total return of equity.

The bulk of the return is attributable to dividend payments and nominal earnings growth (including inflation and real earnings growth).

The future equity risk premium is unknown as it is impossible to predict it with any certainty. This uncertainty needs to be considered when formulating CMAs that inform the SAA process and the investment strategy. Due to this uncertainty, a simple approach to formulating CMAs may be best since sophistication may not add any value.

Simple building blocks approach

For a simple approach to formulate CMAs, the starting point is the 10-year government bond yield in the investor's base currency (US Treasuries for dollar-based investors, gilts for pound-based investors and German Bunds for euro-based investors). This provides an appropriate benchmark for the level of returns over the next decade since government bond yields can be interpreted as a guide for expected future short-term interest rates, as well as an estimate for the expected returns of 10-year government bonds over the next decade. Robert Arnott et al proposed taking the current yield to maturity as a proxy for bond expected return[151], assuming that the bond is held until maturity.

Figure 11.11 shows 10-year US Treasury yields and 10-year Treasury subsequent 10-year annualised total returns. Ten-year yields are a good estimate of the subsequent 10-year returns (information coefficient 0.96).

In periods of hyperinflation (1970s) and in periods of falling inflation the relationship between 10-year yields and subsequent 10-year returns may break. In the early 1970s inflation spiked unexpectedly and the yield did not anticipate the fall in government bond prices. When inflation got under control during the second part of the 1970s, government bonds rallied and got in line again with the 10-year yield. As inflation has been much better controlled since the late 1970s, 10-year yields should remain a good basis for expected 10-year government bond returns over the next decade.

Figure 11.11 – 10-year Treasury yield and subsequent 10-year Treasury returns, January 1926 to June 2012

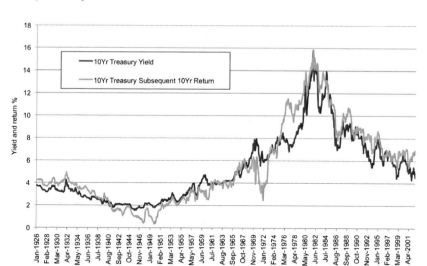

Source: Global Financial Data, USA 10-year Bond Constant Maturity Yield, USA 10-year Government Bond Total Return.

Figure 11.12 demonstrates the goodness of fit (R^2) of current 10-year government bond yields as a base for the expected subsequent 10-year government bond total returns. The R^2 is 0.92 (it rarely goes higher than that in forecasting anything in finance). This is a very high information coefficient. The angle of the regression line is close to 45° meaning that the yield is a good predictor for the level of subsequent 10-year returns, not only for the changes in returns.

Figure 11.12 – 10-year Treasury yield and subsequent 10-year Treasury returns, January 1926 to June 2012

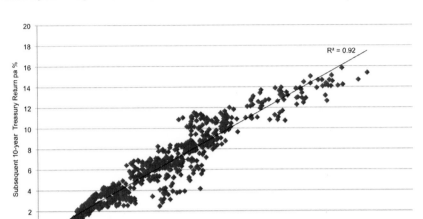

Source: Global Financial Data, USA 10-year Bond Constant Maturity Yield, USA 10-year Government Bond Total Return.

Government bond yields are easily observable on a daily basis. Available, objective market information, such as bond yields and prices, are a good starting point for formulating CMAs since they include the market's collective view and do not rely on subjective interpretations.

For estimating long-term cash returns, 1% is subtracted from the 10-year government bond yield. *Triumph of the Optimists* shows that the historic bond maturity risk premium is 1% above Treasury Bills. In their 2009 study[152], Dimson et al found that the bond risk premium over Treasury Bills is 0.8%.

Figure 11.13 shows the relationship between the 10-year government bond yield minus 1% and subsequent 10-year cash annualised total returns. While there is a visible relationship between the bond yield and subsequent cash returns, with a relatively high information coefficient of 0.77, the estimation error is material.

From the middle of the 1940s until the beginning of the 1980s this methodology underestimated cash returns, while it has overestimated long-term cash returns since the beginning of the 1980s. Structural shifts in inflation rates and consequently in the level of short-term interest rates is the reason behind these under and overestimations.

Figure 11.13 – 10-year Treasury yield minus 1% and subsequent 10-year Treasury bill returns, January 1926 to June 2012

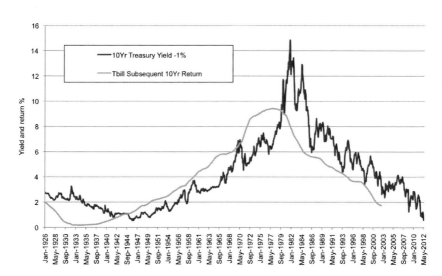

Source: Global Financial Data, USA 10-year Bond Constant Maturity Yield, USA Total Return T-Bill.

There is an easier and more accurate way to estimate cash returns. Current short-term interest rates are a better estimate for cash returns for the next year than 10-year government bond yields minus 1%. Short-term interest rates can be adjusted based on the expected policy of the central bank responsible for the currency[153] in which cash is denominated, depending on whether interest rates are likely to increase or decrease. When inflation is increasing or decreasing and economic growth is expanding or slowing, short-term interest rates are likely to increase or decrease, respectively, and correspondingly the cash return will do likewise.

To avoid considering the views on central banks' policy the 1-year note[154] yield can be used instead to formulate the CMAs for cash over the next few years. Figure 11.14 shows the estimation power of 1-year note yield and subsequent one-year return of cash. The information coefficient is 0.96.

Figure 11.14 – 1-year note yield and subsequent one-year Treasury bill returns, December 1940 to June 2012

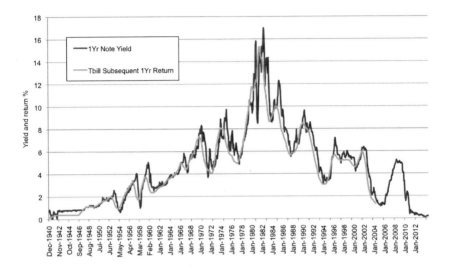

Source: Global Financial Data, USA 1-year Constant Maturity Note Yield, USA Total Return T-Bill.

To estimate the expected return of equities, an equity risk premium should be added to the 10-year government bond yield. The government bond yield in each currency is used to estimate the national or regional equity return (Treasury bonds for the United States, gilts for the United Kingdom and German Bunds for the euro zone). A general equity risk premium of 4% seems reasonable. It is lower than the historic average and in line with academic studies that claim that the future equity risk premium is not expected to be as high as the one that investors have enjoyed during the last 50 years.

This methodology for formulating expected returns using *building blocks* of bond yield, premium for equities and discount for cash is intuitive. When the 10-year government bond yield is low, the expectations are for short-term interest rates to be low over the next 10 years. Hence, cash returns are expected to be low. Low interest rates indicate expectations for subdued inflation[155], weak economic growth, slow or negative growth in corporate earnings and consequently lower equity returns. Low government bond yields mean that the current prices of government bonds are high and hence the expected bond returns are low (once the yield climbs the prices of bonds will decline or if held to maturity the yield to maturity is the expected return of bonds). Conversely, when bond yields are high, the expected returns for the three asset classes are correspondingly high as well.

To estimate the volatility of each asset class the simple building blocks method uses the historical volatility calculated from monthly total returns of representative indices for each asset class over the longest relevant available history (i.e. history since the last structural change in the economy or markets). The same method is used to estimate correlations among asset classes (i.e. calculating correlations between the longest relevant historic monthly total returns). Using historical data to estimate correlation is controversial and crude. Volatility and particularly correlations tend to change over time and historical calculations depend heavily on the time period used.

An example can summarise and illustrate. It is assumed that the investor's base currency is the dollar and the yield on 10-year Treasury bonds is 4%. Therefore, the expected return of equities is 8% (4% + 4%), return of government bonds is 4% and return of cash is 3% (4% - 1%). The standard deviations and correlations are calculated from historic monthly returns of indices representing global equities measured in dollars (e.g. MSCI World Index), Treasuries (e.g. Citigroup United States WGBI TR Index) and cash (e.g. 1-month dollar Libor).

As of the end of June 2012 the 10-year Treasury yield was below 1.7%. Figure 11.15 shows the 10-year bond yield since 1926 as well as its 10-year moving average. Since the end of the 1980s the yield has trended downward (in a government bond rally) and reached a low level not seen since the middle of the 1940s when World War II ended in September 1945.

Based on the yield, the expected return of the three traditional asset classes is very modest for the next decade. Equities are expected to return 5.7%, 10-year government bonds 1.7% and cash 0.7%. With inflation at approximately 2% per annum, bond real return is expected to be negative while for cash it is -1.3%. This is going to be a challenging decade for investors, who will need to look for creative ways to generate returns. However, potentially reassuring is that during the 1950s, following the last time bond yields were so low during World War II, equities rallied very strongly.

Figure 11.15 – 10-year Treasury yield and 10-year moving average yield, January 1926 to June 2012

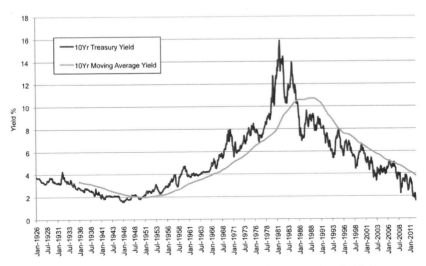

Source: Bloomberg, Global Financial Data, USA 10-year Bond Constant Maturity Yield.

Weaknesses of the simple building block approach

While robust for estimating expected returns of government bonds, intuitive and readily used, this methodology is very simplistic and inaccurate for estimating equity expected returns. Figure 11.16 shows the US 10-year government bond yield plus 4% and the subsequent 10-year annualised return on the S&P 500 Index. As can be seen, this methodology is not an accurate predictor of the next 10 years of equity returns. The reason is that the equity risk premium fluctuates. The information coefficient is only 0.21 and must be significantly increased to take this seriously.

Figure 11.16 – 10-year Treasury yield plus 4% and subsequent 10-year US equity returns, January 1926 to June 2012

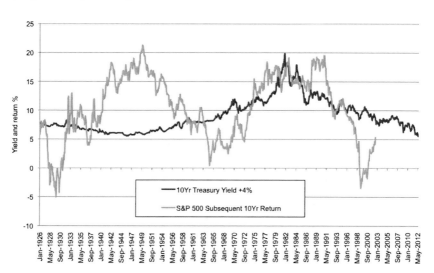

Source: Bloomberg, Global Financial Data, USA 10-year Bond Constant Maturity Yield, S&P 500.

The simple building blocks methodology may incorrectly estimate equity returns since the equity risk premium (ERP) is not constant. Figure 11.17 shows the 10-year bond yield and the cumulative performance of US equities. The low yields of the 1940s marked the start of an equity rally whose magnitude has not been repeated until the 1980s and 1990s.

Following the Great Depression and during World War II risk aversion was elevated, the ERP was high, equities were cheap and bond yields were low. As the world was coming out of the depression and the United States joined the war, risk aversion fell, the ERP fell with it and equities rallied strongly. During the 1970s, bond yields were relatively high by historic standards to that point. However, equity markets moved sideways for almost a decade. During this time period the realised ERP was flat to negative. These historical experiences show that applying a constant ERP to a 10-year government bond yield may be misleading.

Figure 11.17 – 10-year Treasury yield (LHS) and S&P 500 cumulative performance (RHS), January 1926 to June 2012

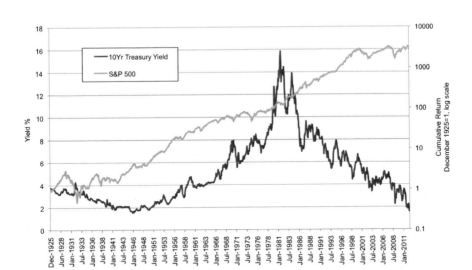

Source: Bloomberg, Global Financial Data, S&P 500, USA 10-year Bond Constant Maturity Yield.

Surely we can do better than this; a more accurate methodology is needed.

Sophisticated approach to establish CMAs

Many methodologies for establishing CMAs are based on a building block approach. Dimson, Marsh and Staunton, for example, break down expected returns into five building blocks[156]:

1. *Expected inflation.* Expected inflation can be sourced from the breakeven rate of inflation-linked bonds.

2. *Real yield on long-term inflation-linked bonds*[157]. Inflation plus real yield is the expected return of long-term nominal bonds.

3. *Maturity premium.* The expected return of bonds minus the maturity premium gives the expected return of cash. The geometric average maturity premium in 17 countries over 109 years ending in 2008 was 0.8%. Dimson et al estimate an average maturity premium of 1% going forward.

4. *Equity risk premium.* Expected return of cash plus the equity risk premium is the expected return of equities. Dimson et al estimate an equity risk premium of 3.0% to 3.5% over cash.

5. *Style premium.* This is an adjustment to capitalisation (small/large cap) or style (value/growth). The expected return of equity plus the style premium gives the expected return on the specific investment style. The style premium can be positive or negative.

Two other sources of returns are *alpha* from skilled portfolio managers and *noise* from unskilled managers. These factors, however, are excluded from CMAs, except for some investments, such as hedge funds and private equity, where alpha assumption (i.e. manager skill) is needed to justify the investment.

While building blocks 1, 2 and 3 are relatively easily obtainable from yields on inflation-linked and nominal government bonds and historical experience, the question still remains how to estimate the equity risk premium (building block 4).

Equity risk premium

Dimson el al[158] break the equity risk premium into three parts: geometric mean of the dividend yield net of real interest rate; annualised dividend real growth; and annualised change in price/dividend ratio over time. The longer the investment period, the more dominant is the dividend yield.

Before we can work on a method to calculate the equity risk premium we need to find a way to calculate the expected returns of equities.

Calculating expected equity returns

Generally, returns of equities are determined by three main factors:

1. Change in valuation

2. Dividend yield

3. Growth in dividends (growth in earnings per share)

Over a one-year horizon, change in valuation dominates equity returns, accounting for more than 60% of returns, while dividend yield and growth in dividends account for about 20% each. As the investment horizon gets longer, however, the weight of dividend yields and dividend growth increases. When the horizon reaches 10 years, the weight of change in valuation shrinks to about 30%. Dividend yields and dividend growth then account for 35% each and are the most important contributors to returns[159]. It is hence possible to reliably forecast equity returns over the long term using dividend yields and growth in dividends.

Dimson et al[160] claim that in the long term, the value of an equity portfolio corresponds closely to the present value of dividends. According to a 2007 article[161] by John Campbell and Samuel Thompson, as valuation ratios, dividend yields contain information that can be used to forecast equity returns under a steady-state assumption.

The Gordon growth model, named after Myron Gordon, who published it in 1959[162], is a simple equity pricing model. It assumes that a company pays dividends, D, that grow at a constant rate, g, and that investors require a rate of return on equities, r, higher than the growth rate, r>g. According to the model the price of a stock, P, is:

$$P = D/(r - g)$$

According to the Gordon model, the price of equity depends on dividends and the growth in dividends. The expected return on equities is therefore dividend yield (P/D) plus dividend growth:

$$r = P/D + g$$

Figure 11.18 shows that dividend yields have explanatory power of equity returns over subsequent 10-year periods. Regressing dividend yield with respect of subsequent equity 10-year total returns gives an R^2 of 0.27 and information coefficient of 0.52. This is already an improvement from the simple building block approach based on 10-year government bond yield plus a constant 4% equity risk premium (the information coefficient was only 0.21), but further improvement is still needed.

Figure 11.18 – dividend yield and subsequent 10-year US equity returns, January 1926 to June 2012

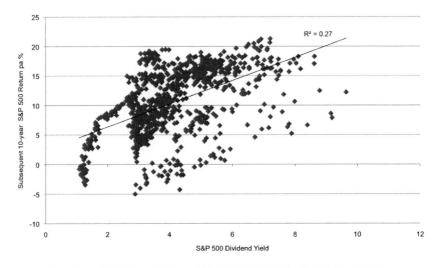

Source: Bloomberg, Global Financial Data, S&P 500, S&P 500 Monthly Dividend Yield.

Dividend yields are a good indicator for the current valuation of equities as they tend to decrease when equity prices increase and decrease when equity prices fall, as demonstrated by Figure 11.19. Dividend yield is the ratio D/P. Dividend payments (D) are more stable than equity prices (P) and therefore when equity prices fall, D/P increases and vice versa. The first building block for formulating expected equity returns is therefore *dividend yield*.

Figure 11.19 – dividend yield (RHS) and equity price (LHS), January 1990 to June 2012

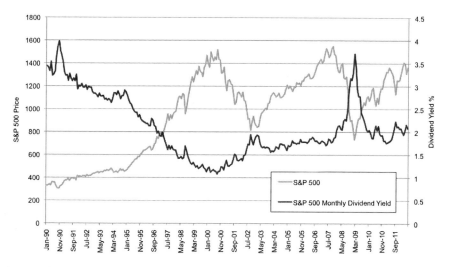

Source: Bloomberg, Global Financial Data, S&P 500, S&P 500 Monthly Dividend Yield.

In the long term, dividends cannot grow faster than the economy; otherwise this would entail corporate profits eventually growing larger than the economy itself. Hence, expected GDP growth is the upper cap for expected dividend and earnings growth rate.

Over the long term, dividend growth lags economic growth. Dimson et al[163] studied a database of stock and bond returns for 17 countries over the 109-year period from 1900 to 2008. They found that real dividends rose by only 0.65% per annum in the world index, which is constructed from the 17 countries. This was more than 1% below global real economic growth, which was approximately 2% per annum over the same period. In the United States real dividends grew at an annualised rate of 1.2% per annum, 2% below the annualised real US GDP growth rate of 3.2%. Others, including Robert Arnott and Peter Bernstein[164], have also written about the dilution of earnings as they pass through to dividend growth.

The second building block for formulating equity expected returns is therefore long-term trend nominal *GDP growth* minus a *dilution factor*. If real GDP growth is easier to estimate, then long-term expected inflation rate should be added as well. Current dividend yields on different indices are readily available. However, sourcing the long-term growth expectations is more difficult. Potential sources for long-term GDP growth are either long-term historic growth rates or forward-looking estimates by organisations such as the OECD and IMF[165].

The price-to-earnings ratio (P/E) is useful in forecasting future stock price changes[166]. On average, decades starting with high P/E ratios, relative to historic average, underperform decades starting with low P/E ratios. Figures 11.20 and 11.21 show the explanatory power of the P/E ratio and its reciprocal the E/P ratio or the earnings yield.

Figure 11.20 – P/E ratio and subsequent 10-year realised return, January 1926 to June 2012

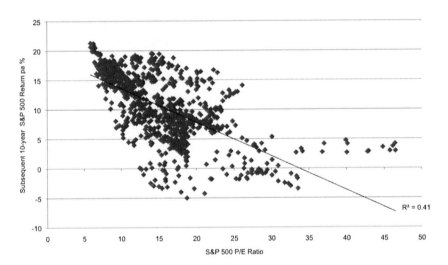

Source: Bloomberg, Global Financial Data, S&P 500, S&P 500 P/E Ratio (As Reported).

Figure 11.21 – E/P ratio and subsequent 10-year realised return, January 1926 to June 2012

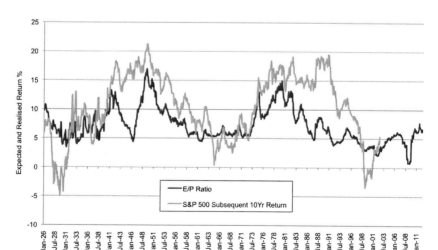

Source: Bloomberg, Global Financial Data, S&P 500, S&P 500 P/E Ratio (As Reported).

Figure 11.22 shows the relationship between E/P ratio and subsequent 10-year annualised equity returns (the information coefficient is 0.67).

Figure 11.22 – E/P ratio and subsequent 10-year realised return, January 1926 to June 2012

Source: Bloomberg, Global Financial Data, S&P 500, S&P 500 P/E Ratio (As Reported).

The third building block for formulating equity expected returns is therefore the *P/E ratio*. The current P/E is assumed to revert back to its long-term average. The P/E effect is hence the expected return per annum for the convergence between current and long-term average P/E and is calculated using the formula:

$$P/E \text{ effect} = (P/E_{LT\ Avg}/P/E_{Current})^{(1/n)} - 1$$

where the P/E effect is the annualised contribution to expected returns due to changes in P/E, $P/E_{LT\ Avg}$ and $P/E_{Current}$ are the long-term average and current P/Es, respectively, and n is the number of years in the investment horizon (e.g. n = 10 for 10-year horizon).

Combing the three building blocks – dividend yield, GDP growth and P/E – the formula for estimating the expected returns on equities is:

$$E(r) = \text{inflation} + D/P + (g - lag) + P/E \text{ effect}$$

where E(r) is the long-term sustainable expected return of equities, inflation is the expected inflation, D/P is the current dividend yield, g is the expected long-term real economic (GDP) growth, lag is the amount earnings growth in market indices is expected to lag overall economic growth and the P/E effect is the contribution to return due to expected changes in P/E ratios.

The formula can be adjusted to different sizes and styles by including a style premium or discount.

There are potential variations and improvements to this formula. Some improvements focus on better estimating the P/E ratio and incorporating the effects of share repurchase and earnings retention rates on dividend yields. However, the formula is simple, easy and practical since it is based on readily available information and does not require adjustments and subjective forecasts.

Figure 11.23 shows the goodness of fit of this methodology. R^2 of 0.44 is a material improvement in the model's predictability power. The information coefficient is 0.67.

Figure 11.23 – expected return and subsequent 10-year realised return, January 1926 to June 2012

Source: Bloomberg, Global Financial Data, S&P 500, S&P 500 Monthly Dividend Yield, S&P 500 P/E Ratio (As Reported), USA 10-year Bond Constant Maturity Yield, USA Inflation Indexed 10-year Bond Yield, US Inflation.

Figure 11.24 shows the clear relationship between expected (using the methodology just introduced) and subsequent 10-year annualised equity returns[167]. This methodology can be used to generate reliable expected returns for equities over the next 10 years. The expected returns are not correct all the time and material estimating error still exists. After all, forecasting equity returns is not trivial. However, this methodology is clearly superior to alternative ones.

Figure 11.24 – expected return and subsequent 10-year realised return, January 1926 to June 2012

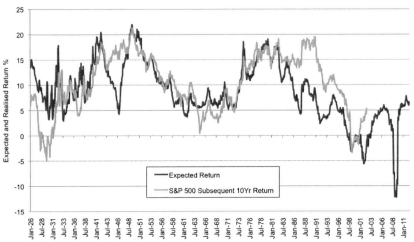

Source: Bloomberg, Global Financial Data, S&P 500, S&P 500 Monthly Dividend Yield, S&P 500 P/E Ratio (As Reported), USA 10-year Bond Constant Maturity Yield, USA Inflation Indexed 10-year Bond Yield, US Inflation.

One way to improve the methodology is to adjust the P/E ratio. First, for the price (P) the average 10-year price of the index (S&P 500) is used instead of the current one. Second, the P/E ratio is calculated using the current earnings (E) and the average 10-year price. Third, the same methodology as above is used to calculate the P/E effect and the expected return of equities. As can be seen from Figures 11.25 and 11.26 the information coefficient has increased from 0.67 to 0.74 and the R^2 from 0.44 to 0.54.

Once in a while this methodology gets it very wrong (e.g. late 1930s, mid-1940s, late 1990s, and 2001). Nevertheless, clearly it has predictive powers.

Figure 11.25 – expected return and subsequent 10-year realised return, January 1926 to June 2012

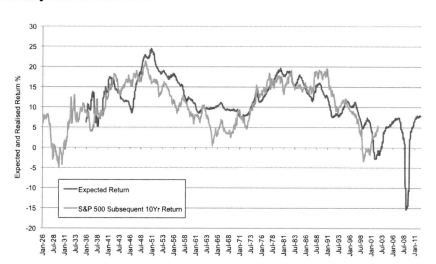

Source: Bloomberg, Global Financial Data, S&P 500, S&P 500 Monthly Dividend Yield, S&P 500 P/E Ratio (As Reported), USA 10-year Bond Constant Maturity Yield, USA Inflation Indexed 10-year Bond Yield, US Inflation.

Figure 11.26 – expected return and subsequent 10-year realised return, January 1926 to June 2012

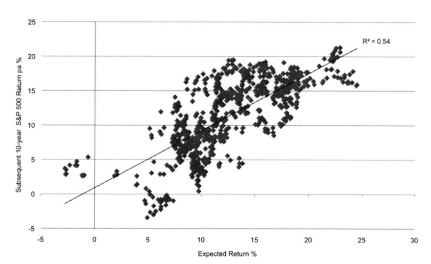

Source: Bloomberg, Global Financial Data, S&P 500, S&P 500 Monthly Dividend Yield, S&P 500 P/E Ratio (As Reported), USA 10-year Bond Constant Maturity Yield, USA Inflation Indexed 10-year Bond Yield, US Inflation.

Calculating the equity risk premium

To calculate the expected equity risk premium (ERP) the appropriate risk-free rate needs to be subtracted from equity expected return. The choice of risk-free rate is important. If the equity expected return is based on a real value, then a real value should be used for the risk-free rate (e.g. real yield of long-term inflation-linked bonds). On the other hand, if the expected return of equity is based on a nominal value, then the risk-free rate should be a nominal value (e.g. yield on long-term conventional government bonds).

Figure 11.27 shows the historic expected ERP over 10-year Treasuries. Unlike the static 4% ERP under the simple building block approach, the ERP is dynamic and changes with time. The average forward-looking ERP over the entire period since January 1926 is 3.6%. However, the average ERP since January 1960 is only 0.2%.

Figure 11.27 – expected equity risk premium relative to Treasury bonds, January 1926 to June 2012

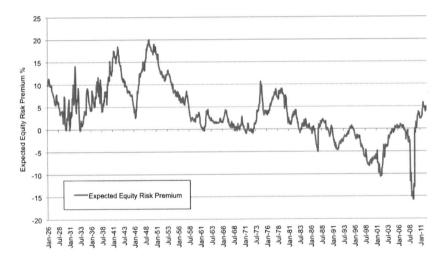

Source: Bloomberg, Global Financial Data, S& P 500, S&P 500 Monthly Dividend Yield, S&P 500 P/E Ratio (As Reported), USA 10-year Bond Constant Maturity Yield, USA Inflation Indexed 10-year Bond Yield, US Inflation.

Example

An example can summarise and illustrate. The objective is estimating the expected return of US equities and their ERP. As of the end of June 2012, the dividend yield on the S&P 500 Index was about 2.1%[168]. The expected long-term US real economic growth (GDP) is assumed to be 3.2%[169]. The lag between real economic growth and dividend growth in the United States is about 2.0% according to Dimson et al. The P/E ratio of the S&P 500 Index was 15.7 at the end of June 2012. The long-term average P/E ratio is 16.8. This implies a P/E effect of 0.7%[170].

The expected *real* equity return is 2.1% + 3.2% - 2.0% + 0.7% = 4.0%. The *nominal* expected equity return is 4.0% plus the expected inflation rate of 2.13% (sourced from breakeven rate of 10-year inflation-linked bonds[171]), giving a total expected equity return of 6.13% per annum.

Since 6.13% is a nominal expected return, to calculate the ERP the risk-free rate based on long-term nominal bonds should be subtracted. The yield on 10-year Treasury was 1.67% as of the end of June 2012. The expected ERP is 6.13% - 1.67% = 4.46%. This relatively high ERP is mostly driven by the historically low yields on 10-year Treasuries.

The expected return on equities can be adjusted to country or region, size and style based on style premiums or discounts. Country risk premium can be estimated through the beta of the regional stock index to the world equity index. Betas tend to cluster around 1.0 with some falling outside the 0.7 to 1.3 range.

As per Dimson et al, small capitalisation stocks have historically outperformed the total market by 1.4% per annum in the United States and 2.3% per annum in the United Kingdom. A reasonable size premium is therefore 1.0% to 1.5%. Value stocks have outperformed the general market by 1.2% per annum since the end of 1926 in the United States and by 1.5% per annum over the entire period 1900 to 2008. The value premium is more sustainable in small cap stocks in both the United Kingdom and the United States. A reasonable value premium is therefore 1.0% to 1.5%[172].

Fixed income expected return

For government bonds, yields with the same maturity and base currency as those of the bonds whose returns are forecasted can be used to make the forecast of expected return. Accounting for the *roll-down* can improve the prediction. Roll-down is the return due to the convergence between the price of a bond and its par as it approaches maturity[173]. Roll-down return is positive when the bond is trading at a discount (the roll-down will pull the price up towards par) and negative when the bond is trading at a premium (the roll-down will pull the price down back to par).

Corporate bonds have a higher yield than equivalent government bonds reflecting the credit risk premium. The lower the credit rating is the higher is the spread between the corporate bond yield and the government bond yield. For corporate bonds, corporate bond yields are used to forecast their expected returns but the yield should be adjusted for default risk. The lower the credit quality, the more important the adjustment is. The bigger the economic stress, the larger the adjustment is. Credit rating agencies, such as Moody's, provide expected default cost for bonds with different credit ratings, including the expected recovery rate, as shown in Table 11.1.

Table 11.1 – historical default cost, 1920 to 2011

Rating	Default Cost %
Aaa	-0.04
Aa	-0.12
A	-0.18
Baa	-0.40
Investment Grade	**-0.23**
Ba	-1.32
B	-3.00
Caa-C	-5.80
Below Investment Grade	**-2.32**

Source: Moody's.

In their 2011 study[174], Dimson et al looked at historic returns, yields and default rates of corporate bonds in the United States over the period 1900 to 2010. Highest rated corporate bonds in the United States returned 0.68% per annum above Treasury bonds between 1900 and 2010. This is close to the historic spread of Moody's Aaa investment grade bonds over Treasuries of 0.7%. The default rate was 0.15%. Default loss is default rate times one minus recovery rate or:

Default Loss = Default Rate*(1 – Recovery Rate)

The recovery rate has averaged 40%. The average annual loss due to defaults is therefore 0.09%. The default rate of Baa rated bonds has been 1.14% and the average for high-yield bonds (i.e. below investment grade) has been 2.8%.

A credit premium on investment grade corporate bonds of 0.68% seems high given the low default rates. This is a risk premium and partially compensates investors for the illiquidity of corporate bonds. Holding a diversified portfolio of corporate bonds should diversify the idiosyncratic risk of default of individual issuers. In 2009 the average default rate on all bonds reached 5.4% and the average on high-yield bonds was 13%. This shows that default rates increase during recessions. Corporate bonds, therefore, have a beta to equity markets since during recession the default rate can increase.

Expected volatility and correlation

Standard deviation should be calculated over the longest relevant time period. Investors should evaluate whether there was a structural change in the market that would have caused standard deviation to change. If it has, standard deviation should be calculated over the longest period since such structural changes. Investors should look at rolling standard deviations to spot structural changes. The quantitative process should be completed by a qualitative rationale. The explanation for the structural change must make sense.

As Figure 11.28 demonstrates, the rolling 36-month volatility of the S&P 500 Index has dramatically shifted following structural changes before the middle of the 1940s (the Great Depression and World War II). Long-term volatility therefore should be calculated using returns since the early 1950s. Annualised volatility over the entire period (including the period January 1926 to December 1949) is 19.2% while volatility since January 1950 drops to 14.6%. The more recent 14.6% seems to better capture the average volatility from the beginning of the 1950s, rather than 19.2%, which seems to be the top of the volatility range.

Figure 11.28 – rolling 36-month volatility of US equities, January 1926 to June 2012

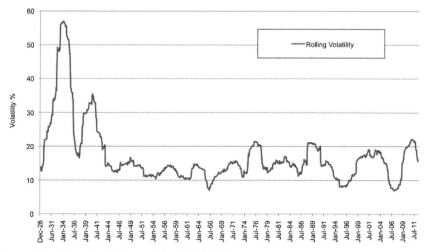

Source: Bloomberg, Global Financial Data, S&P 500.

Standard deviation of historical returns does not capture all investment risk. In order to have a more realistic measure of prospective risk for long-term investors, the following three adjustments can be applied: reflect changes in exposure to risk factors (duration, spread levels); deal with smoothing or mean reversion (horizon effects); and take into account asymmetries in actual return distributions (skewness, kurtosis or fat tails). To adjust for fait tails the Cornish Fisher approximation can be used[175].

Correlation is the most difficult to forecast – it is unpredictable and changes over time due to lack of fundamental value to drive it. Luckily, correlation is the least significant parameter for SAA optimisation. A Bootstrap optimisation technique produces more robust asset allocations to changes in correlation[176].

Pay-out ratios, share repurchase and lag between GDP and earnings growth

Low pay-out ratios (dividends/earnings) and larger stock repurchase programmes portend, but do not guarantee, lower subsequent lag between economic growth and dividend growth (as with many theories in finance, this claim has been challenged[177]). However, the pay-out ratios of the S&P 500 Index over recent years are well below historical average. The lower pay-out ratio can explain as much as 0.4% of the historic 2% lag between US economic growth and US dividend growth. That is, if the companies in the S&P 500 Index had issued about 50% of their earnings over the past five years as dividends, then the historic lag between economic growth and dividend growth would have only been about 1.6%. Fortunately, the smaller pay-out ratio should signal even lower future lag between economic growth and dividend growth. Companies that reinvest most of their earnings ought to grow faster than they would have had they distributed those earnings as dividends.

Companies use a larger share of their earnings to repurchase their stocks than they have done in the past. Companies that use some of their earnings to buy back their stock may be able to afford to distribute more dividends per share in the future than they otherwise would, because stock repurchase programmes result in fewer shares amongst which to distribute future dividends. Therefore, stock repurchase programmes should result in a higher dividend growth rate. Lower pay-out ratios give dividend yields more room to grow, so dividend yields may grow a little faster than they otherwise would. In summary, there is a reasonable basis to expect less of a lag in the United States between future economic growth and dividend growth.

The connection between the pay-out ratio and growth rate can be illustrated by the Gordon equity valuation model. Equity price is determined by the formula:

$$P = D/(r_f + ERP - g)$$

where P is equity price, D is dividend, r_f is the risk-free rate, ERP is the equity risk premium above r_f (r_f + EPR is the equity required or expected rate of return) and g is dividend or earnings growth rate.

Dividing both sides of the equation by E (earnings per share or EPS) gives:

P/E = D/E / (r$_f$ + ERP - g)

where P/E is the price to earnings ratio and D/E is the dividend pay-out ratio (i.e. the percentage of earnings paid to shareholders in the form of dividends).

The equation can be rearranged to:

D/E = P/E (r$_f$ + ERP - g)

The inverse relationship between the pay-out ratio and dividend or earnings growth rate is clear. A lower (higher) pay-out ratio means higher (lower) earnings growth and lower (higher) equity return, all else being equal (e.g. P/E ratio).

Breakeven inflation as a guide for expected inflation

Expected inflation is a critical component in formulating CMAs. Inflation-linked government bonds (linkers) are available in each major financial market. In the United States these bonds are known as *Treasury Inflation Protected Securities* (*TIPS*).

The difference (spread) between the yields of equivalent (same maturity) conventional (nominal) and inflation-linked government bonds is known as the breakeven rate of inflation. This spread is used as a guide for the market expected inflation. However, the spread is affected by a number of factors that may mean that it is not a true market forecast for inflation. These factors include:

- *Inflation risk premium.* The breakeven rate may be higher than the market inflation forecast since it compensates investors for holdings bonds whose price may drop due to an unexpected increase in inflation.

- *Taxes.* The relationship between the yields of linkers and conventional government bonds may be distorted by taxes. The tax treatment of linkers differs among countries. In the United States taxable investors are taxed on both the real yield and the inflation accrual (known as *phantom tax* since investors pay tax on an accrual, which is unrealised income). Therefore, when inflation or expected inflation increases, the bond price needs to fall to keep the after-tax real yield unchanged and the opposite when inflation or expected inflation decreases. Hence, the price and yield of linkers change due to tax reasons and not only due to inflation. In the United Kingdom income is taxed only on the coupon payments of linkers, not on the principal's inflation adjustment. UK taxable investors therefore have an incentive to hold shorter dated linkers as their tax treatment is more favourable than that of short-dated conventional bonds. If the price of linkers is driven by supply and demand of taxable investors, rather than tax-exempt investors, this may influence the price of linkers, their yield and consequently the breakeven inflation rate.

■ *Regulation and liability valuation rules.* Tax-exempt institutional investors (e.g. pension funds and insurance companies) may demand particular maturities of conventional and inflation-linked bonds for liability-matching. This can lead to valuation anomalies. Since arbitrageurs require long time horizons to drive valuations back to fair-values the concentrated demand by institutions can cause differences in breakeven inflation rates for different bond maturities.

■ *Liquidity.* Differences between the liquidity of conventional and inflation-linked bonds may mean that the yield of linkers includes a liquidity premium, distorting the breakeven inflation rate.

■ *Biases in inflation measurements.* The official indices (such as CPI and RPI[178]) used in calculating the uplifted value of linkers can be biased. The biases should be reflected in the breakeven rate of inflation. For example, if it was viewed that linkers were more than compensated for inflation because of biases in the inflation index, their price would be bid up (and their yield bid down) and the breakeven rate of inflation would be higher than the expected rate of inflation.

These factors may cause the breakeven inflation rate to differ from the market expectations of inflation. The effects of these factors may differ across countries and bond maturities. Nevertheless, the breakeven inflation rate is a good approximation for a market inflation forecast. If investors have strong views that the breakeven rate is likely to be either over-optimistic or over-pessimistic, they can adjust the breakeven rate based on their views to get the expected inflation and use it for formulating CMAs.

The inflation-linked market in the United Kingdom has a longer history than that in the United States and is used to demonstrate the differences between nominal and inflation-linked bonds over time (Figure 11.29) and the relationship between the breakeven inflation rate and subsequent 5-year RPI rate (Figure 11.30). While 10-year RPI should be used to be consistent with the 10-year breakeven rate, due to the relatively short history the 5-year rate is used.

Figure 11.29 – 10-year yields of gilts and UK inflation-linked bonds, January 1985 to June 2012

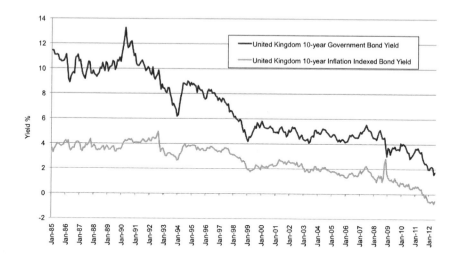

Source: Global Financial Data, United Kingdom 10-year Government Bond Yield, United Kingdom Inflation Indexed Bond Yield.

Figure 11.30 – UK 10-year breakeven inflation and subsequent 5-year RPI, January 1985 to June 2012

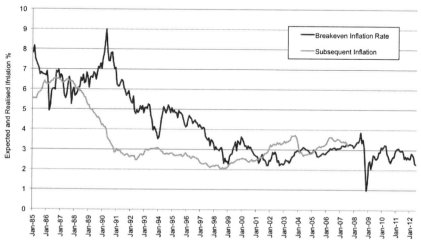

Source: Global Financial Data, United Kingdom 10-year Government Bond Yield, United Kingdom Inflation Indexed Bond Yield.

Views on inflation can affect the decision of how much to invest in inflation-linked bonds since if realised inflation is lower than the breakeven inflation, linkers will underperform conventional bonds, and vice versa. Investors whose risk-free investment is an inflation-linked government bond should have a strategic position in conventional government bonds if they expect conventional bonds to provide an adequate reward for expected inflation and a risk premium above it. In other words, such investors should regard the insurance offered by inflation-linked bonds as too expensive.

CMAs for other asset classes

The principles used to derive CMAs for all asset classes are similar. A yield is a starting point. The long-term expected growth in yield and long-term valuation changes are added. The expected return is adjusted to any risks and special features (e.g. size and style) by applying discounts or premiums.

When these building blocks for different asset classes are difficult to estimate investors have three main choices:

1. *Multi-factor model.* Multi-factor models can be used to derive the CMAs of asset classes using other asset classes for which CMAs are known. Multi-factor models can be as simple as a multiple linear regression, whereby the monthly returns of an asset class are regressed with respect of those of other asset classes. For example, assuming the returns of convertible bonds can be explained by 60% equities and 40% corporate bonds (assuming a delta of 0.60 of the convertibles), the expected return of convertibles is a weighted average of that of equities and corporate bonds (credit). Assuming that the expected return of equities is 6.13% and the expected return of investment grade corporate bonds is the current[179] average yield on AAA US corporate bonds of 3.66% minus a historic default cost of 0.04%, giving an expected return of 3.62%, then the expected return of convertibles is 60%*6.13% + 40%*3.62% = 5.13%.

2. *Black-Litterman model.* The Black-Litterman model[180] can be used to calculate expected returns across various asset classes. However, investors need the market capitalisation of all asset classes to do so.

3. *CAPM.* CAPM can be used to calculate the expected return of an asset class through its beta with respect of an asset class whose CMAs are established. Since the time horizon of CMAs is 10 years, the risk-free rate in CAPM should be the 10-year government bond yield as opposed to cash. For example, the beta between convertible bonds and US equities is 0.74[181]. The expected return of convertibles is therefore 1.67% + 0.74*(6.13% - 1.67%) = 5.0%.

Another choice for formulating CMAs is using subjective views and surveys. Investors can rely on their forecasts for the future or on surveys of expert opinions. However, opinions are subjective and can be greatly influenced by biases, recent experiences and forecasting skills. Different methodologies for deriving CMAs give different expectations. This is the reason they are only expectations and the A in CMAs is for *assumptions*. It is important to use the same methodology across asset classes so the CMAs are consistent to minimise the risk of over or under allocating to asset classes because of model risk.

What CMAs ignore

CMAs estimate the market or index returns (beta exposure) of each asset class. They do not account for the expected *alpha*. Alpha is much more difficult to estimate and it depends on the specific portfolio manager chosen to manage each investment. Skilled or lucky managers may add alpha while unskilled or unlucky managers may add negative alpha or just noise.

Manager skill is often confused with luck or risk taking. For example, managers who consistently overweight equities relative to bonds may appear skilful since equities tend to outperform bonds over time. This is, however, only excessive risk taking if managers do not change the asset allocation. It is skill if managers change the asset allocation at the right times, whereas it is just noise if managers change the asset allocation without any skill. It is difficult to distinguish noise from alpha and skill. Noise increases the volatility of returns, attracts fees, distracts investor attention and wastes valuable time.

For some investments, such as private equity and hedge funds, an alpha assumption is necessary. The merits for investing in these assets depend on manager skill and alpha. Without alpha these investments would not be selected by an SAA optimiser since their attractive risk/reward characteristics depend on manager skill.

Private equity investments are normally assumed to have much higher expected volatility than that of publicly traded equities. However, private equity's higher expected returns depend heavily on the ability of portfolio managers to add alpha. Without an alpha assumption, a mean-variance optimisation process is unlikely to include private equity in asset allocation.

Hedge funds are mostly about manager skill. For hedge funds alpha must be included in the CMAs. Establishing CMAs based only on replicating hedge fund returns with indices of traditional asset classes without assuming alpha results in losing any edge for the hedge funds over those traditional asset classes and is unlikely to warrant any allocation to hedge funds. For hedge funds with an absolute return objective, for example, the return objective can be used as expected return. While using return objective as expected return is not ideal since many managers do not achieve their objectives, the only reason to include an absolute return product in portfolios is high conviction in the manager. If the conviction is high, then using the return objective as input into the asset allocation process is reasonable. This needs to be reviewed after a while to ensure that the manager justifies the conviction.

Another factor that CMAs need to consider is *transaction costs*. In some cases, such as direct real estate, the transaction costs of changing an asset allocation may be higher than multi-year expected returns (e.g. the round trip of buying and selling direct real estate may cost 7%). In other cases, such as private equity, building the position may take a significant amount of time and returns in the first few years are expected to be negative (J-curve). CMAs should take into account both the transaction costs and investment horizon or time required to realise returns on each investment.

CMAs should consider the accessibility to asset classes. While in theory all asset classes are accessible, this is not always practical. Some portfolios cannot hold private equity and hedge funds due to liquidity restrictions; some portfolios cannot hold direct real estate and commodities due to regulatory constraints (e.g. UCITS); some portfolios cannot use derivatives due to regulatory or investor constraints; and some portfolios cannot access all asset classes due to size and limited availability of investment vehicles.

All these factors should be considered when using CMAs to formulate SAA and investment strategy. Alpha assumptions can be added to CMAs as premiums and transaction costs can be reduced as discounts. The systematic process of formulating CMAs must be complemented by judgment.

CMAs for SAA

Over the long-term it is possible to estimate the average expected return and risk of asset classes. This is helpful in understanding what portfolios are likely to return on average over the long-term and at what risk. This is also helpful in understanding which asset classes are cheap and which are expensive based on a systematic, objective process. Through CMAs and SAA the long-term plan for portfolios can be formulated.

Summary

- The inputs (Capital Market Assumptions or CMAs) of the SAA process are the expected return, risk and correlations of asset classes.

- The investment horizon of SAA is long (typically 5 to 10 years) and the CMAs should have the same horizon. The aim is formulating long-term expectations.

- Historic returns are a poor predictor of future returns.

- Historic volatility can be used as a guide to the level of risk of asset classes.

- Correlation is unstable and unpredictable. Using historic correlation is inaccurate. However, correlation has the least impact on SAA results out of the three CMAs.

- A single, constant number for expected return (e.g. equity expected return of 8%) does not consider the current market conditions and the likely returns over the coming years given the current position in the business cycle.

- A simple building block approach to formulate CMAs starts with the 10-year government bond yield in the portfolio's base currency, uses the yield as bond expected return, adds an equity risk premium of 4% to arrive at equity expected return and subtracts 1% to arrive at cash expected return. Standard deviations and correlations are calculated from the longest relevant historical data (since any structural changes in markets) of monthly total returns of indices representing each asset class. This is a simple approach, using current market conditions to formulate CMAs, but it is not accurate for expected returns.

- A more sophisticated building block approach breaks expected equity returns into inflation, dividend yield, trend GDP growth minus dilution (expected growth of earnings) and P/E effect.

- The expected return can be adjusted to country, size and style.

- The yield on government bonds is the expected return for government bonds. The yield on corporate bonds is the expected return for corporate bonds but it needs to be adjusted for the loss due to defaults, which can be estimated from default cost tables of rating agencies.

- Historical standard deviations can be improved as predictors of expected risk by unsmoothing autocorrelated returns and adjusting risk for fat tails.

- Historical correlation can be improved by bootstrapping techniques.

- Inflation is a critical component in formulating CMAs. The spread between the yield on conventional and inflation-linked bonds is the breakeven inflation rate and can be used as a guide to market expectations of inflation. The breakeven rate is distorted because of inflation risk premium, taxation, liquidity premium and preferences by institutional investors for certain bond maturities. Yet, the breakeven inflation is a good approximation for market expectations of inflation.

- Alpha is particularly important for investments that depend on manager skill, such as hedge funds and private equity. CMAs for these investments need to include assumptions about alpha.

- CMAs should also consider transaction costs, time frame to realise investments and accessibility to asset classes for each investor.

The next chapter demonstrates how to put the CMAs into practice to derive optimal SAAs.

12. OPTIMISATION

Optimisation is the process of identifying an asset allocation with either a maximum expected return under a set of constraints (mainly risk), or minimum risk under a set of constraints (mainly expected return). In other words, optimisation is used to derive an efficient asset allocation with the highest possible expected return for a certain risk level or minimum risk level for a target expected return. Optimisation normally requires a quantitative method[182] and a computer program. The optimisation program basically follows an iterative process whereby it tries different asset allocation mixes until the maximum or minimum value is reached while satisfying the constraints (if it is possible to do so).

Microsoft Excel Solver is a basic linear programming optimisation tool for relatively simple optimisations. When more sophisticated optimisations are required, MATLAB or dedicated software can be used. For very simple optimisation it is possible to run a manual iterative process of trial and error to try to identify asset allocations that meet the optimisation criteria.

The efficient frontier

The efficient frontier, which was introduced by Harry Markowitz as part of MPT, is a graphical representation plotting all the efficient asset allocations in the risk/return space. The efficient frontier is an arc, which on its right side has a single, most risky investment. As the arc moves to the left additional investments are added to the mix to reduce risk through diversification.

Figure 12.1 shows a simple illustrative efficient frontier using the three traditional asset classes: equities, bonds and cash. Figure 12.2 shows an efficient frontier with a fourth asset class, alternative investments, added to the mix. The efficient frontier expands upwards. This means that thanks to diversification benefits it is possible to reach a higher expected return for most levels of risk. In other words, the benefit of adding additional imperfectly correlated investments to portfolios is risk reduction through diversification and higher expected return without increasing investment risk.

Figure 12.1 – the efficient frontier with traditional asset classes

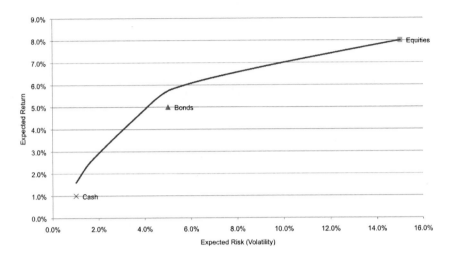

Figure 12.2 – the efficient frontier with traditional asset classes and alternative investments

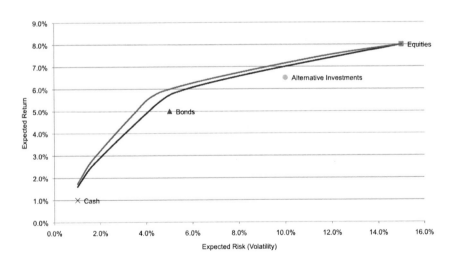

Asset allocations are efficient if they have the highest achievable expected return for a certain level of risk (as defined by volatility of returns) or the lowest possible level of risk for a certain expected return. All asset allocations below the efficient frontier are inefficient or suboptimal since allocations with higher expected return for the same level of risk are available (i.e. there are asset allocations that dominate them).

Asset allocations above the efficient frontier are unachievable since they require asset classes with higher expected return, which are unavailable according to the CMAs. Investors can use the efficient frontier to choose efficient asset allocations given either their risk tolerance (acceptable risk level) or target return.

When combining two efficient asset allocations the blend itself is efficient[183]. This is known as the *two mutual fund theorem* and its implication is that investors can achieve a desired efficient asset allocation by combining two others. For example, if there are two optimised asset allocations, one conservative and a second aggressive, investors can combine the two to achieve a third moderate asset allocation that is also efficient.

The *slope* of the efficient frontier indicates how much more risk is required to generate additional expected return. The slope is determined by the asset classes included in the optimisation and their CMAs. As CMAs dynamically change, so does the slope. A frontier with a steeper slope means more expected return can be generated for taking extra risk (i.e. Sharpe ratio) than a frontier with a flatter slope.

Figure 12.3 shows the efficient frontier and the Sharpe ratio of each asset allocation. On the left side of the frontier, where its slope is steep, taking more risk is compensated by more return and the Sharpe ratio increases rapidly. However, from the point where the slope of the frontier is flatter, the Sharpe ratio falls, meaning taking more risk is not compensated by enough corresponding return. The slope of the frontier is a signal for the amount of risk investors should take through asset allocation. In this example, taking a risk of 4% (standard deviation) gives the most efficient asset allocation with the highest Sharpe ratio[184].

Figure 12.3 – the efficient frontier, expected return (LHS) and Sharpe ratio (RHS)

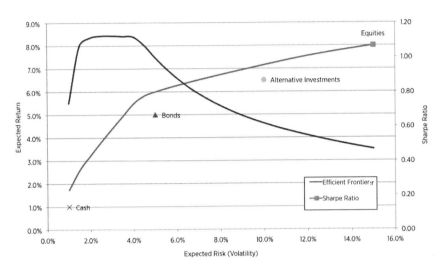

The *curvature* of the frontier depends on the correlations among investments. If the correlations are all equal to 1.00 there are no diversification benefits and the efficient frontier will be a straight line without any curvature. As investments are less correlated (or more negatively correlated) the frontier is more curved.

Typically, efficient frontiers are drawn with a thin line. However, normally more than one combination of assets is efficient or close enough to be efficient for every level of risk. Richard Gold introduced the concept of the *fuzzy frontier*[185] to optimisation of real estate portfolios. The impact of uncertainty on the allocation process, as well as the low quality or unavailability of data, means the results show that the efficient frontier is not singular but plural, or fuzzy.

Numerous statistically dissimilar weighted portfolios may be equally attractive for any given combination of expected risk and return and an allocation range, rather than a specific target allocation, is more realistic. Due to the frontier being highly dependent on CMAs, there is a risk of spurious precision when plotting a thin-lined frontier. A thicker line, as illustrated in Figure 12.4, may be more representative of the plural correct or optimal combinations of asset classes for each risk level. Asset allocations sitting close to the efficient frontier are probably efficient enough.

Figure 12.4 – the fuzzy frontier

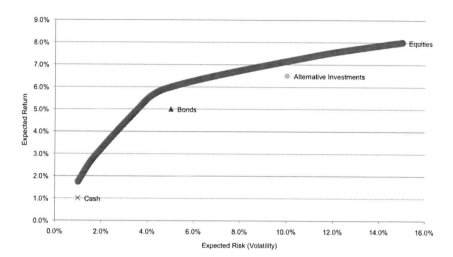

Optimisation in relative space

As optimisation in absolute space optimises expected return over standard deviation to maximise the Sharpe ratio, optimisation in relative space optimises expected relative returns over tracking error to maximise the information ratio.

The starting point for a relative optimisation is a benchmark. The constraint is the tracking error relative to the benchmark and the objective is finding the highest possible information ratio. The optimisation has a risk budget in the form of tracking error and this anchors the asset allocation to the benchmark, ensuring that the asset allocation is not expected to deviate too much from the benchmark's level of risk and allocations.

Figure 12.5 shows an efficient frontier in relative space and the corresponding information ratio for each asset allocation. The benchmark is 50% equities, 40% bonds and 10% cash. Alternative investments are off-benchmark. When tracking error reaches 8% the asset allocation is 100% equities and no further excess return is achievable.

Figure 12.5 – the efficient frontier in relative space, expected return (LHS) and information ratio (RHS)

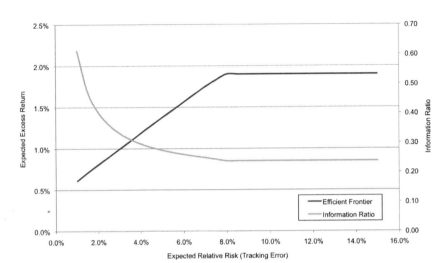

Peer benchmarks

When the benchmark is a peer group index, the process is more complicated. Peer group indices often do not disclose the allocations to all asset classes. For example, the allocation to fixed income may not disclose the breakdown between government and corporate bonds, the allocation to alternative investments may not disclose the breakdown among the different alternative strategies, such as hedge funds, private equity, absolute return, commodities and others, and the answer to the question of whether real estate and convertible bonds are part of alternative investments is sometimes ambiguous.

To address these unknowns assumptions must be made on the breakdown of the peer weights to different asset classes. For example, within local fixed income an assumption based on the breakdown of debt level between government and corporate bonds may be appropriate, such as 60% government bonds and 40% corporate bonds, although this does not necessarily represent the average holdings of actively-managed peers.

Another complication with peer group indices is that updated weights are not always available as the providers of peer indices usually publish them only on a monthly or quarterly basis. The solution is to drift the starting weights on a daily basis using passive index returns representing each asset class. This is only a proxy of reality since it excludes active management results (the members of the peer group are active, not passive) and it ignores asset allocation changes made by the members. However, this is a practical solution.

The only way to be more accurate is to prepare a list of the largest members and update the holdings from available public material (such as fact sheets), although they are normally published only on a monthly basis. The drifting of the weights can be done using actual peer returns rather than passive index returns.

A clear advantage of including SAA in portfolios benchmarked versus peer groups is that the asset allocation is optimised and does not follow the herd. The portfolios offer the highest expected return for a given level of risk. The peer group allocation broadly determines the absolute risk level or the range of accepted risk. Portfolios need to maintain a risk level within that range, while not breaching the constraints of each peer sector (such as limits on maximum allocation to equities or foreign currency). The asset allocation aims to maximise the information ratio and portfolio managers determine the amount of tracking error to allocate to SAA depending on the *risk budgeting process* and the opportunities for SAA to add value.

Utility theory

Utility theory is used to identify an efficient asset allocation matching the investors' risk appetite. Rational investors prefer more to less and they are risk averse. For example, they would prefer $1,000 without uncertainty over a 50% chance of getting $500 and a 50% chance of getting $1,500 (with expected payment of $1,000). One way to represent investors' preferences is through a quadratic utility function[186], representing the expected utility as a function of expected return minus expected risk. The utility (U) derived from investing is:

$$U = r_p - \sigma^2/\lambda$$

where r_p is expected portfolio return, σ^2 is expected variance of portfolio returns and λ (lambda) is investor risk tolerance.

Utility is expected return minus a risk penalty. λ is larger for investors who are less risk averse (i.e. the risk penalty is smaller).

Figure 12.6 shows the required return[187] for the same utility for different levels of risk tolerance (λs). As risk tolerance is lower, more return is required to compensate investors for risk to maintain the same utility.

Figure 12.6 – utility functions with different risk tolerance coefficients, maintaining the same utility level

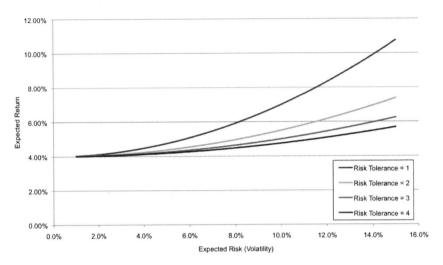

The value of utility is determined by the expected level of utility. The shape of the function (i.e. slope and curvature) is determined by the risk/reward trade-off. Rational investors are indifferent to the position on a utility function (hence its name *indifference curve*) since the risk/reward ratio is constant across all the points on each function (i.e. for assuming more risk investors demand additional returns based on their risk appetite). The slope of the function is determined by the risk aversion. Higher risk aversion means a steeper sloping utility function because much more utility is required to compensate investors for taking additional risk.

Rational investors maximise utility and position their portfolios on the highest possible utility function. Figure 12.7 shows the curves of utility functions for different levels of utility. Investors are indifferent as to the location on each curve but desire to be located on the highest curve possible.

Figure 12.7 – utility functions with the same risk aversion coefficient and different utility levels

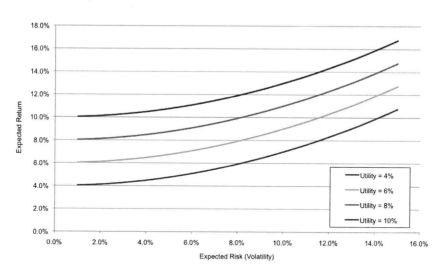

Once the most efficient asset allocation for each risk level has been identified through optimisation, the efficient frontier is drawn. The tangent point between the concave efficient frontier and the convex utility function on which the tangent point lies identifies the investor's optimal asset allocation (illustrated in Figure 12.8).

The efficient frontier represents the highest achievable returns for each risk level. The utility function represents the risk/return trade-off for matching investors' risk tolerance for each level of return. The tangent point between the efficient frontier and the utility function is the investor's maximum risk/return trade-off. It matches the investor's risk aversion coefficient and has the highest achievable utility.

Figure 12.8 – combining the efficient frontier and utility function to identify the efficient asset allocation

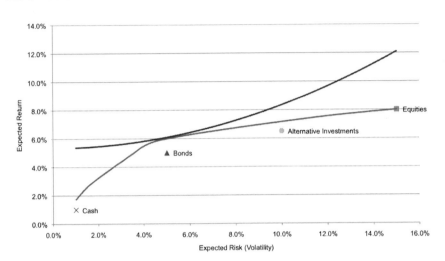

This is the theory for identifying the appropriate point on the efficient frontier. It is challenging and impractical, however, to determine the utility function for each investor as it is an abstract term (for instance, how is λ determined?).

Alternative to the utility function

A practical method that can be used in place of the utility function is to establish the investment objectives (this may be a challenge as well) and match the estimated risk level of the portfolio with the investor's risk objectives, or to identify through the efficient frontier what level of risk is required to meet the return objectives. Since there is a margin of error in estimating CMAs, an appropriate region on the efficient frontier should be located, rather than a single point (the frontier is fuzzy). Then the investor can maximise the expected return or minimise the risk level, identifying a broadly efficient asset allocation satisfying both the return and risk objectives.

It is easy to quantitatively link the probability of exceeding a target return per annum over a certain investment horizon with the efficient frontier and choose the point that maximises this probability.

Figure 12.9 adds to the efficient frontier a chart showing the probability[188] of exceeding a target return of 5% per annum over a 5-year horizon. Taking a risk level of 6.5% maximises the probability and this is the risk level representing the efficient asset allocation for meeting the 5% return objective. Taking higher risk may increase expected return but it reduces the probability of meeting the 5%

target return over the investment horizon. For risk levels below 4% the probability of achieving the target falls dramatically (the expected return is too low). This methodology links return objective, risk objective and investment horizon and helps investors to set the long-term investment strategy for their portfolio with the highest likelihood of meeting the investment objectives.

Figure 12.9 – combining the probability of exceeding target return and the efficient frontier to identify the efficient asset allocation

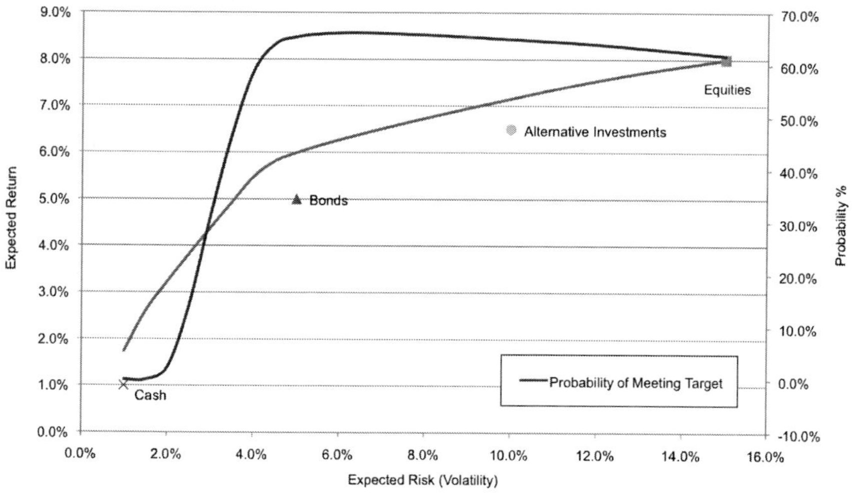

Optimisation for a single asset class

In some cases optimisation may be utilised for a single, heterogeneous asset class to create a customised, optimised benchmark. For example, global developed bonds are an asset class including bonds issued by governments of developed countries, international organisations (such as *supranationals*[189]) and corporations operating in developed countries across the globe. The Barclays Global Aggregate Bond Index commonly represents the asset class. Since the asset class is heterogeneous and includes sub asset classes that have different CMAs, optimisation can be used to reach desired, customised long-term characteristics for the asset class.

For example, Japanese Government Bonds (JGBs) may be out of favour for many years due to the low interest rates in Japan. The prospects for JGBs are grim since they pay a low yield, when interest in Japan eventually increases their prices will fall and they have no prospects for capital gains since interest rates have no room to decrease. Optimisation can underweight or completely exclude JGBs and a new, customised asset allocation can be created for the asset class. The performance of the customised allocation should be compared to that of a standard benchmark (Barclays Global Aggregate Bond Index) to evaluate performance.

Another example of an asset class that is suitable for customisation is emerging market debt (EMD), represented by the JP Morgan Emerging Markets Bond Index (EMBI). There are long-term allocation opportunities between local and hard currency, sovereign and corporate, and nominal and inflation-linked emerging market debt.

Other asset classes may require benchmark customisation because of dislocations in the market. For example, the UK corporate bond market has a large exposure to financials that may be deemed risky following the 2008 credit crisis (or an attractive investment opportunity). Portfolio managers who need to manage portfolios versus a corporate bond index, with a certain tracking error, may not be able to avoid the material exposure to financials without breaching the relative risk budget constraints. Therefore, customising the benchmark by splitting it into financials and non-financials, or reducing the allocation to financials, may be a way to control the exposure to financials. However, this leads to an active position relative to the standard benchmark.

An alternative solution is allowing portfolio managers to manage portfolios or a portion thereof without a tracking error constraint or with a higher tracking error and rely on manger skill to avoid or reduce the high exposure to financials. This may allow managers to hedge risks and avoid unwanted beta risk. Managers must be able to be trusted to use the flexibility to the benefit of investors (skilled managers should be unconstrained, unskilled managers should be constrained or fired). Managers, however, may be reluctant to use the full flexibility since it introduces relative risk (underperformance risk).

Extra flexibility in the credit market should also come with flexibility of using derivatives, in particular for large portfolios. The credit market can suffer low liquidity and derivative markets can alleviate some of the liquidity constraints (but introduce other concerns, such as derivative risks).

Investment horizon

Typically, the investment horizon of SAA is 5 to 10 years. Over short time periods (less than a year), changes in security valuations determine the lion's share of returns. Valuations are driven by supply and demand forces, which are driven by economic conditions (standard finance) and psychology (behavioural finance). When economic activity expands corporations invest and hire more, more people are employed and wages are higher, consumers consume more, and investors invest more in risk assets, pushing their prices upwards. The opposite occurs when economic activity shrinks. Behavioural finance claims that prices are driven by fear and greed, which are driven by investors' sentiment, psychology and behaviour. TAA is the process through which short-term expectations, opportunities and risks are expressed in portfolios' asset allocations. TAA considers the short-term factors that SAA does not consider.

CMAs, the inputs of the SAA process, can be based on 10-year government bond yields, which are the basis for forecasting returns over the next 10 years. CMAs can be based on dividend yields, expected earnings growth and P/E ratios, whose explanatory power is over the long term (more than five years), not the short term. CMAs form expectations of long-term *average* asset class returns and should not be used to forecast returns over short time periods since this is not what they aim to do.

Estimating volatilities over short time periods should follow a different process than the one used for CMAs. *ARCH* and *GRACH*[190] models, taking into account *volatility clustering*[191], may be used to forecast volatility over the short term. These models use much shorter historic horizons (the weighted average age of data is known as *half-life*) than CMAs to forecast short-term volatilities.

It is unrealistic to forecast correlations over the short term because of large estimation error. This is not much more than guessing (*guesstimate*). TAA looks at economic conditions and level of uncertainty to predict correlations and volatility. However, the methodologies for forecasting volatility and correlation through CMAs for SAA are not meant to be used for predictions over short time frames. SAA optimisation is appropriate for the long term and the TAA process is appropriate for the short term.

Since SAA is based on CMAs, which are the expected average return over the next 10 years, the timing of returns in unknown. For example, if expected equity return is 8%, the returns over the first five years may be substantially lower than 8% with higher returns in the last five years, potentially giving an average of 8% return over the entire time period[192]. Therefore, SAA can have long time periods of disappointing performance. It is impossible to use SAA and CMAs for optimising asset allocations for short horizons. Nevertheless, the SAA framework enables objective and systematic assessment of the relative valuation of asset classes for portfolio positioning.

Sensitivity to assumptions

Mean-variance optimisation results are highly sensitive to the inputs or CMAs. The results are most sensitive to expected returns, then to volatility and finally to correlations. The optimisation results are sensitive to an error in the return assumptions 11 times more than to an error in the variance assumption, and twice as sensitive to an error in the variance assumption than to an error in the covariance assumption on average[193]. An error in the inputs may cause material error in the output, which is the efficient asset allocation.

In some cases the output from the optimisation is impractical due to errors in CMAs. For example, overestimating the expected return and/or underestimating the volatility of hedge funds and/or underestimating their correlations with other asset classes, may result in an erroneous optimised allocation invested mostly in hedge funds. Furthermore, the optimisation does not take into account risks that are not reflected in standard deviation, such as liquidity, credit and manager risks. Distorted CMAs may result in concentrated asset allocations with unacceptable risks.

One way to address the optimisation's sensitivity to CMAs is to constrain the optimisation. Constraints can be added on the minimum and maximum allocation to each asset class and let the optimiser find the optimal asset allocation within the constraints. For example, holding minimum cash (e.g. 2%) may be needed for liquidity purposes while without a minimum constraint the optimiser may allocate nothing to cash, in particular when the required expected return is high and short-term interest rates are low. Capping the maximum allocation to hedge funds, for example, is reasonable since reported returns and risks of hedge funds may be misleading and lead to unrealistic CMAs and unjustified high allocations to hedge funds. The disadvantage of constraining the optimiser is that the constraints are subjective and may result in suboptimal results from the optimiser.

Capping the allocation to illiquid asset classes, such as direct real estate, or limiting the changes from current asset allocation due to transaction costs, are other examples of required interventions in the optimisation process to address liquidity risk and transaction costs.

For some investments there is no appropriate proxy in the form of representative indices (e.g. private equity, hedge funds, infrastructure and real estate) and it should be acknowledged that their CMAs may be inaccurate. Investors should check the results of the optimiser and modify the allocation if necessary. The optimiser is a mathematical model that should inform a common-sense driven human decision.

Bootstrapping

Another technique to overcome the optimisation's sensitivity to CMAs is bootstrapping.[194] Bootstrapping gathers many alternative versions of a single statistic that would ordinarily be calculated from one sample. For instance, the correlation between two asset classes is calculated. The problem is that correlation is highly dependent on the measuring period. Measuring correlation over a sample time period of *n* monthly returns provides only one value of correlation. Hence, it is unknown by how much the correlation varies over different time periods.

Instead of relying on a single sample period bootstrapping randomly extracts a new sample of *n* monthly returns out of the N available monthly historic returns (the entire population), where each return can be selected at most *t* times. By repeating this *t* times, bootstrapping creates a large number of datasets that could have been observed in the historic return series and computes the correlation for each dataset. Thus an estimate of the distribution of the correlation is created. The idea is to create alternative versions of correlation that could have been observed in the set of historic returns.

By using bootstrapping the optimisation is made robust (*robust optimisation*) because it is less sensitive to CMAs since they are not based on a single time period. For each set of CMAs under each iteration of the bootstrapping process, an efficient frontier is created. Then from all the hypothetical efficient frontiers, an average efficient frontier is calculated. This efficient frontier is robust and is less sensitive to the measurement period over which the correlation was calculated. The same technique can be used to estimate volatility.

Figure 12.10 shows the distribution of rolling 10-year correlations between US equities and US 10-year Treasuries since January 1970. The correlation over the entire period is 0.11. However, as the histogram shows, most observed 10-year correlations are between 0.25 and 0.40 (over 60% of observations). Therefore a correlation estimate of 0.30 may be more accurate than 0.11. While this is not bootstrapping it demonstrates the benefits of using the entire distribution of observations to estimate values rather than a single statistic.

Figure 12.10 – distribution of rolling 10-year correlations between US equities and 10-year Treasuries, January 1970 to June 2012

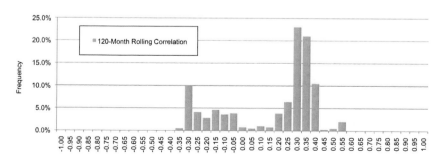

Source: Global Financial Data, S&P 500, USA 10-year Government Bond Total Return.

Resampled optimisation

Resampled mean-variance optimisation combines traditional optimisation with Monte Carlo simulation to account for the uncertainty of CMAs[195]. Resampling uses Monte Carlo simulation to estimate the CMAs for mean-variance optimisation and eventually to create the resampled efficient frontier. The steps for resampling are:

1. Estimating CMAs (returns, standard deviations and correlations)

2. Running a multivariate simulation resulting in a new set of CMAs and efficient frontier

3. Recording the weights and returns of the efficient frontier at predetermined standard deviation intervals (e.g. 1%, 2%, 3% and so on)

4. Repeating steps 2 to 3 more than 1,000 times

5. Calculating the average allocations to each asset together with the average returns for each standard deviation interval

The result is the resampled efficient frontier. The shortcomings of this method are that the asset allocation inherits the estimation error in the original inputs, the method lacks theoretical foundations (there is no reason for the resampled asset allocation to be optimal) and the resampled results may be an active risk versus the benchmark for no reason.

Optimisation based on historical performance

While inappropriate to derive forward-looking asset allocations, optimisation based on historical performance was correct in the past. It can be used to study the effects of including asset classes in portfolios. By using historic returns, volatilities and correlations, investors can experiment with how different allocations to different investments would have performed in the past.

Multi-period optimisation

One shortfall of the long investment horizon of SAA is that some investors or portfolios do not have such a long horizon. Evaluating the success of SAA should take at least five years. Some investors do not have sufficient time to even evaluate whether SAA added value.

One of the main shortfalls of the mean-variance optimisation is that it is a single-period model. Investors optimise the asset allocation for a single time period, which may be long, and retain the allocation for the entire period, without altering it due to developments in markets. The solution is a multi-period optimisation in the form of *dynamic SAA*, whereby the optimisation is done periodically based on updated CMAs that incorporate current market conditions. In addition, asset allocation should be adjusted to tactical views and risks through the TAA process.

Dynamic CMAs and current market environment

CMAs should be linked to the current market environment. When CMAs are based on current 10-year government bond yield, inflation expectations derived from breakeven inflation as implied by inflation-linked bonds, dividend yields, P/E ratios and earnings growth expectations, the CMAs reflect the current market conditions, market expectations and the collective market wisdom as reflected in security prices (i.e. the stage in the economic cycle and market expectations are reflected in current security prices).

For example, at the bottom of the economic cycle, equity prices are low, dividend yields are relatively high, P/E ratios are relatively low and hence the expected return of equities is relatively high. Government bond prices are high, short-term interest rates and bond yields are relatively low and hence the expected return on cash and bonds is relatively low[196]. The opposite occurs at the top of the cycle, with low return expectations for equities and high expectations for cash and bonds.

Dynamic SAA recommendations exhibit *mean reversion*. When equity prices are high the dynamic SAA process allocates less to equities. When equity prices are low, the opposite occurs. Therefore, dynamic SAA tends to sell equities when their prices are high (take profits) and buy when they are low (buying opportunity). Buying low and selling high is the basic principle of active portfolio management.

Dynamic CMAs change based on current market conditions and SAA recommendations change based on these CMAs. Dynamic CMAs link SAA to current market conditions. SAA should be reviewed at regular intervals (quarterly, semi-annually or annually). A good practice is conducting a quarterly or semi-annual review, optimising the asset allocation using updated CMAs and checking the impact of the new asset allocation on the information ratio and Sharpe ratio. If the increase in the reward-to-risk ratio warrants a change to asset allocation, taking into account transaction costs, then the new SAA should be implemented. When looking at the information ratio in relative space, the Sharpe ratio and absolute risk should be considered as well to avoid taking excessive absolute risk relative to that of the benchmark.

SAA should be reviewed on an ad hoc basis when changes in CMAs are material and warrant it and/or when opportunities emerge in the market, requiring implementation in a timely manner. For example, following the 2008 credit crisis prices of corporate bonds became very attractive since the market priced in unrealistic default rates. The yields on corporate bonds were extremely high to compensate investors for the elevated credit risk (i.e. high credit risk premium). This was an opportunity to overweight credit within asset allocations. This may be done through ad hoc SAA review (or potentially through TAA, depending on the portfolio structure and investment process).

SAA implementation is another consideration. Changing SAA through trading underlying physical investments may be expensive, time consuming and disruptive to underlying portfolio managers, in particular in large multi-asset portfolios. Implementing some of the SAA positions using derivatives where possible (e.g. equities and government bonds for which liquid futures contracts are readily available) enables changing asset allocations in a more efficient and timely manner. Large multi-asset portfolios should have the flexibility to use derivatives to be nimble and implement asset allocation changes, as well as to hedge risks quickly and efficiently.

The SAA process is based on CMAs that are formulated through a systematic, quantitative approach, so common sense and qualitative judgment are required to ensure that the process does not automatically invest in unattractive assets or disinvest from attractive ones. The gap between long-term SAA and short-term views should be filled through adjusting the asset allocation to short-term views and risks. Similar to most quantitative, systematic approaches, the SAA process should inform and guide investors, who should apply their judgment to the final investment decisions.

Black-Litterman

The Black-Litterman model was developed in 1990 at Goldman Sachs by Fischer Black and Robert Litterman and was published in 1992[197]. It aims to overcome the shortcomings of MPT, namely unintuitive, concentrated portfolios that mean-variance optimisation generates due to sensitivity to inputs and estimation error in CMAs. The model uses a Bayesian[198] approach to combine intuitive prior[199] market equilibrium expected returns as forecasted by CAPM with investors' subjective views on expected asset class returns.

The resulting set of expected posterior returns (market expected returns plus investor views) can be used in mean-variance optimisation to create robust optimised asset allocations. In other words, the model blends public market data on expected asset class returns with the investor's private views. If the investor does not have a private view, only the public data will be used, or if the investor has views only on a subset of asset classes, these views will be blended with the public views on the full set of asset classes.

Equilibrium

The main source for long-term wealth growth and portfolio returns is economic growth. In equilibrium, all investors should hold portfolios reflecting economic growth. Portfolios would have an asset allocation proportional to asset classes' market capitalisations, which reflect the economy's expected future productive capacity. *Equilibrium returns* are a set of returns that would clear the market. In equilibrium, investment prices equal fair-value. Expected returns, which are the supply side, equal required returns, which are the demand side. Sellers set a price that buyers accept because investments are fairly valued.

The current price of investments determines future returns (i.e. low current price means higher returns and vice versa). All investors who hold a portfolio in proportion to the equilibrium market portfolio would earn returns or risk premiums that would compensate them for investment risk. This is the reason that the market portfolio of CAPM is a market capitalisation-weighted portfolio consisting of all investable asset classes.

Optimal portfolio

A portfolio is optimal when for every investment at the margin the ratio of change in the expected excess return (excess return above risk-free rate) over change in portfolio risk is identical. In other words, allocating less to an investment with lower expected return and more to an investment with higher expected return increases the portfolio risk so the portfolio's new expected return-to-risk ratio is the same as that of the previous portfolio. The portfolio expected risk-adjusted performance has not changed and hence the portfolio was optimised before changing its asset allocation.

If a portfolio is suboptimal it is possible to reduce the allocation to an investment with lower expected return per unit of risk, increase the allocation to a higher returning investment, and adjust the allocation to cash to keep the portfolio risk constant. The expected return of the portfolio has increased without increasing its risk. Therefore, the previous portfolio was suboptimal.

Each portfolio should have a risk budget (e.g. maximum allowed standard deviation or tracking error). Every investment decision should depend on its impact on the portfolio's expected return and marginal impact on portfolio risk. For example, allocating more to equities and less to bonds is likely to increase both expected return and risk of the portfolio. Efficient asset allocation keeps the expected return-to-risk ratio constant due to this change.

The *marginal contribution to risk*[200] of each investment depends on its covariance with all other investments in the portfolio and the allocations to each investment. The marginal contribution to portfolio risk can be calculated if the weight, volatility and correlations of each investment are known.

If a portfolio is optimal the implied expected excess return of each investment must be proportional to its marginal contribution to portfolio risk. This is true since in an optimal portfolio the ratio of expected excess return over marginal contribution to risk is identical for each investment.

Implied returns are the expected returns on each investment that would result in an optimal allocation. Within an efficient portfolio the reward-to-risk of each investment is proportional to its beta with respect of the portfolio. It is possible to reverse engineer the expected returns from an efficient portfolio. This is called *reverse optimisation*. If a portfolio is optimal, it is possible to calculate the implied returns that would lead a mean-variance optimiser to reach the portfolio weights (i.e. the implied returns are used as CMAs).

If the implied returns are in line with expected returns, then the portfolio is optimal. If the implied returns are not in line with expected returns, then the portfolio is not optimal. It is possible to allocate more to investments with expected returns above implied returns and increase the portfolio's expected return.

The idea behind the Black-Litterman model

There are three sources of returns in a portfolio: real risk-free rate, market risk premium (beta) and active manager return (alpha). There are three sources of risks in a portfolio: interest rate risk (usually from portfolio liabilities, which can usually be hedged and therefore this risk is not compensated by the market), market risk (beta risk, which is compensated by the market) and active risk (skill based; uncorrelated with other risks).

CAPM (an equilibrium model) claims that markets are efficient and all investors maximise expected return subject to a risk constraint. Hence, expected excess returns (equilibrium risk premium) of each investment are proportional to its beta. Beta measures the marginal impact of changing the allocation to an investment on the risk of the market portfolio. Beta is therefore the risk measure in the Black-Litterman model.

Global markets are not in equilibrium. Therefore, there are investment or alpha opportunities. When investors take advantage of these opportunities they push investment prices back to equilibrium. For example, when investments are under-priced relative to their predicted equilibrium price, investors purchase them and the demand pushes their price up until it reaches equilibrium price. The equilibrium framework helps investors identify opportunities by enabling them to calculate the required return for taking risk when investing.

Implied returns from public data

The Black-Litterman model starts with the market portfolio. This is a portfolio consisting of all asset classes and weighted by their market capitalisation[201]. The model then calculates the implied returns on the market portfolio. The implied returns are the equilibrium expected excess returns (over cash) as predicted by CAPM. The model calculates expected returns for all asset classes that are included in the market portfolio. This approach of reverse optimisation was proposed by William Sharpe[202] and it flows from his work on CAPM.

According to Sharpe[203], current market values of major asset classes inform forecasts for outcomes because an asset's current market value reflects the collective view of the probabilities of future prospects. According to the semi-strong form of EMH, all public information has been absorbed into the market and is reflected in the pricing of securities. This leads to the traditional CAPM and the existence of equilibrium returns. Capital markets provide unbiased estimates of future prospects[204] or incorporate views about deviations from such estimates[205].

Since the market takes into account all participants' views (consensus views), investors with no private information should have higher conviction in market derived returns. The preferred strategy without superior private views is constructing portfolios based on those returns (*default portfolio*) and managing them passively.

Private investor views

The Black-Litterman model provides a quantitative framework to modify the default portfolio based on investor views. Views can be in terms of expected return of an asset class (different than the implied return) or an expectation that one asset class is to outperform another by a certain total return. The model provides a mathematical framework to incorporate the investor views and the confidence in them. Once the equilibrium returns and investor views are combined, the new set of expected returns is used to optimise the portfolio using a mean-variance optimisation. The idea is to update a prior distribution with given data (investor views) to generate a posterior distribution of expected returns.

Advantages and disadvantages of the model

The advantages of the Black-Litterman model are that it provides a framework to establish expected returns for all asset classes, the expected returns are robust and consistent, there is a framework for incorporating investor views with their confidence and the result is an optimised portfolio that does not suffer from the issues of MPT.

Since the model uses the capitalisation-weighted market portfolio as a starting point and uses reverse optimisation to calculate the expected returns for all asset classes, investors do not need to establish expected returns for each asset class. The model does it consistently across all asset classes. It is based on the assumption that efficient market forces push the market portfolio to equilibrium and therefore equilibrium returns can be calculated. If the market portfolio is out of equilibrium due to irrationality of markets, the model calculates expected returns that represent the current state of the market and identifies opportunities through the expected returns. For example, if an irrational bubble pushed the market capitalisation of equities above equilibrium level, the expected return of equities will be lower and the allocation to equities in an optimised portfolio would be lower, representing the heightened levels of equity market capitalisation.

The disadvantages of the Black-Litterman model are its reliance on CAPM with all its disadvantages and the need to establish the market portfolio, including all asset classes that are to be included in the portfolio. Global market capitalisations of some asset classes are difficult to quantify (e.g. property, hedge funds, private equity and infrastructure). The market capitalisation of some asset classes is zero (e.g. commodity futures). The market capitalisation of government bonds is artificially inflated since governments persuade institutional investors to hold their debt through regulations.

With all of its disadvantages, the model can be used alongside other methodologies as a sense check. Software packages that include the Black-Litterman model are readily available. Investors need to gather the representative market capitalisations of different asset classes and to understand how the model works and what outputs it provides. Once the model is not a black-box its outputs can be helpful, at least to supplement the investor-formulated CMAs.

Reverse optimisation

This section covers the mathematics of reverse optimisation. Some of the calculations are useful not only for the Black-Litterman model, but also for other portfolio analytics. If you are not interested in the technicalities please skip this section.

One of the fundamental tools of multi-asset portfolio analytics is the variance-covariance matrix. The matrix has the variance of each asset across its diagonal and the covariance between each pair of assets in the other cells of the matrix. Covariance is calculated using the formula:

$$\text{Covariance}_{i,j} = \rho_{ij}\sigma_i\sigma_j$$

where Covariance$_{i,j}$ is the covariance between assets i and j, ρ_{ij} is the correlation between assets i and j, and σ_i and σ_j are the volatilities of assets i and j, respectively.

If i = j then the covariance is the variance of asset *i* since the correlation is 1.0 and $\sigma_i\sigma_i$ is σ^2_i. Table 12.1 shows a correlation and covariance matrix for a simple, three-asset portfolio.

Table 12.1 – correlation and covariance matrix

Asset	Weight (w)	Volatility (σ)	Correlation (ρ)			Variance-Covariance (Σ)		
			Equities	Bonds	Cash	Equities	Bonds	Cash
Equities	60%	15%	1.0	-0.1	-0.2	0.0225	-0.0008	-0.0003
Bonds	30%	5%	-0.1	1.0	0.0	-0.0008	0.0025	0.0000
Cash	10%	1%	-0.2	0.0	1.0	-0.0003	0.0000	0.0001

To calculate the standard deviation of the portfolio, matrix algebra is helpful. The formula for variance (square of standard deviation) is:

$$\sigma^2 = w'\Sigma w$$

where w is the vector of portfolio weights, w' is the transpose of w and Σ is the variance-covariance matrix.

The formula for the standard deviation of a portfolio in Microsoft Excel is:

SQRT(MMULT(MMULT(TRANSPOSE(w),Σ),w)))

Since this is an array formula, when entering the formula in Microsoft Excel the buttons Ctrl-Shift-Enter must be pressed together, instead of just the Enter button. The standard deviation of the portfolio in Table 12.1 is 8.96%.

To calculate the implied excess returns the following formula is used:

$$\Pi = \lambda\Sigma w$$

where Π is the vector of implied excess returns, λ is the risk aversion coefficient (i.e. the market price of risk), Σ is the variance-covariance matrix and w is the portfolio weights.

The starting point in the Black-Litterman model is the market portfolio, whose weights are determined by the market capitalisation of each asset.

λ is calculated using the formula:

$$\lambda = (r_m - r_f)/\sigma^2{}_m$$

where r_m is the expected market return, r_f is the risk-free (cash) expected return and $\sigma^2{}_m$ is the variance of the market portfolio.

In the example, assuming expected market return of 4% and risk-free return of 1%, and using the 8.96% standard deviation of the portfolio, λ is 3.74. The implied returns can now be calculated.

Table 12.2 – implied returns

Asset	Implied excess return (Π)	Implied total return
Equities	4.95%	5.95%
Bonds	0.11%	1.11%
Cash	-0.06%	0.94%

The Microsoft Excel formula to calculate the implied excess returns is:

$$\Pi = \lambda * \text{MMULT}(\Sigma, w)$$

The entire range of the three cells for the implied returns should be selected and the buttons Ctrl-Shift-Enter should be pressed together.

To calculate the total implied return, the cash expected return is added to each implied excess return.

When calculating implied returns the starting point is the portfolio's weights, unlike optimisation where the starting point is the expected returns. If the implied returns were used in a mean-variance optimisation the optimised portfolio would have the weights in vector w. The implied returns can be used to assess whether the portfolio's weights are in line with the views that the investor wants to express within the portfolio. If, for example, the implied return for cash is 0.94% while the investor thinks that cash is going to generate only 0.70% then the 10% allocation to cash is too high. If the investor reduces the allocation to cash and recalculates its implied return it will decrease. This process can be repeated until the implied return matches the investor view.

Combining investor views – the Black-Litterman formula

Once the equilibrium expected returns are determined, the next step is to adjust them to the investor views.

Assume that the investor has two views – k represents the number of views. The first view is that the excess return of equities is 6% and the second view is that bonds are going to outperform cash by 2%. These views are going to be represented in the view column vector (Q) with dimension k x 1 (2 x 1 in this case since there are two views).

	6%
Q =	
	2%

The views in vector Q are matched to the asset classes by matrix P_k. If N is the number of asset classes, P_k is a k x N matrix. Matrix P_k looks like this:

	1	0	0
Pk =			
	0	1	-1

The P_k matrix maps the 6% on equities (i.e. the expected return of equities is 6%) and the 2% positive on bonds and negative on cash (i.e. bonds are to outperform cash by 2%).

The next step is calculating the Ω matrix, which is the covariance matrix of the error term. Ω is a diagonal matrix[206]. The value of each variance in the Ω matrix is calculated using the formula:

$$\Omega_k = (P_k \Sigma P'_k)\tau$$

τ is a scalar called the *uncertainty scaling parameter*. This parameter is used to scale the conviction in the investor views relative to the market equilibrium returns. τ can be calculated using the formula:

$$\tau = 1/(n - 1)$$

where n is the number of observations used to calculate the covariance matrix (Σ)[207]. Alternatively, τ can be calculated using the formula[208]:

$$\tau = \# \text{ investor's observations} / \# \text{ market's observations}$$

This formula is based on the concept of the Central Limit Theorem[209], according to which τ should reach its true value when the number of observations approaches infinity. As the number of observations used to derive equilibrium returns (the market) is higher, the accuracy of the derived implied estimates is higher and the uncertainty is lower.

The Microsoft Excel formula to calculate the first value in Ω is:

$$\Omega_1 = \tau^*\text{MMULT}(\text{MMULT}(P_1, \Sigma),\text{TRANSPOSE}(P_1))$$

where P_1 is the first row in the P_k matrix.

The resulting Ω matrix looks as follows:

	0.00056	0
$\Omega =$		
	0	0.00065

Now the new expected return vector E[R] combining the equilibrium return with the investor views can be calculated using the Black-Litterman model. The Black-Litterman formula is:

$$E[R] = [(\tau\Sigma)^{-1}+P'_k\Omega^{-1}P_k]^{-1}[(\tau\Sigma)^{-1}\Pi+P'_k\Omega^{-1}Q]$$

In Microsoft Excel the formula looks like this:

E[R] = TRANSPOSE(TRANSPOSE(Π)+TRANSPOSE(MMULT(MMULT(Σ*
τ,TRANSPOSE(P)),MMULT(MINVERSE(MMULT(MMULT(P, Σ* τ),TRANSPOSE(P))+
Ω),Q–MMULT(P,Π)))))

The formula should be entered covering all cells of the range of the vector of expected returns, pressing together the buttons Ctrl-Shift-Enter. The results are the posterior expected returns (as shown in Table 12.3)[210].

Table 12.3 – Black-Litterman posterior expected returns

Asset Implied	Excess Returns (Π)	New Combined Excess Returns E[R]
Equities	4.95%	5.40%
Bonds	0.11%	0.97%
Cash	-0.06%	-0.11%

The intuition behind τ is clear from the Black-Litterman formula. $\tau\Sigma$ and $P'_k\Omega^{-1}P_k$ represent the confidence that the investor has in the public market equilibrium returns and the investor's private views, respectively. Higher τ gives higher weight to the market views and tilts the portfolio closer to equilibrium returns, giving lower weight to the investor's views.

Optimisation

Some of the methods for producing robust optimised asset allocations are known as *Post Modern Portfolio Theory*. Optimisation quantitatively derives an asset allocation that is likely, over the long term, to generate the highest expected return, on average, for a given level of estimated risk. This is as scientific as asset allocation and formulating investment strategy goes.

Whichever technique is used for SAA, SAA determines the long-term target weights of portfolios, their investment strategy or policy. Through SAA the long-term level of both absolute and relative risk are set. The size of the risk allocated to SAA (i.e. allowable deviations from benchmark weights) relative to other risks, such as TAA and investment selection risks, will be determined as part of the multi-asset risk budgeting process.

The SAA is the first stage of multi-asset portfolio construction. Portfolio construction creates portfolios from asset allocations by including TAA and investments. SAA suggests the allocation to asset classes or betas and portfolio construction populates these betas with actual investments.

TAA alters the long-term asset allocation to benefit from short-term opportunities and to position portfolios for short-term risks. SAA and TAA together determine the asset allocation, which is the top-down process of managing portfolios. The investment selection process fills each asset class with investments and is the complementary bottom-up process. Together they form the investment strategy of the portfolio.

Summary

- Optimisation is a quantitative process used to arrive at an efficient asset allocation with the highest expected return for a given level of risk or the lowest expected risk for a given level of return.

- The efficient frontier is a graphical representation in the expected risk (x-axis)/return (y-axis) space plotting all the efficient asset allocations.

- The efficient frontier can be used to identify asset allocations that match investor's objectives or maximise utility.

- The efficient frontier can be used to assess whether the return and risk objectives are achievable or require adjustment (e.g. more risk is needed to achieve the return objective or lower return should be expected to meet the risk objective).

- While optimisation in absolute space maximises return-to-volatility (Sharpe ratio), optimisation in relative space maximises excess return to tracking error (information ratio).

- Tracking error anchors the asset allocation to the benchmark.

- Optimisation versus peer group has unique challenges since not all the details of the peer benchmark are known. However, the optimisation ensures that the asset allocation is efficient and not just following the herd. The peer benchmark sets the broad risk level of the portfolio.

- SAA can be utilised to optimise single asset classes, such as global developed and emerging market debt or to customise standard benchmarks of asset classes to better fit investor objectives.

- CMAs are used to estimate average asset class returns, risks and correlations over long time periods, not short horizons. To estimate short-term returns a different methodology is needed as part of TAA.

- The process of deriving CMAs is systematic and quantitative. The process of deriving TAA views is normally fundamentally driven and subjective, although it can be informed by quantitative models.

- The SAA framework enables objective and systematic assessment of the relative valuation of asset classes for portfolio positioning.

- Mean-variance optimisation is sensitive to its assumptions (CMAs). The output is most sensitive to return, then to variance and then to correlation.

- One method to address the optimisation's sensitivity to CMAs is constraining the optimisation with maximum and minimum allocations to each asset class. The constraints, however, are subjective and may result in suboptimal allocations from the optimiser.

- Constraints can be used to explicitly incorporate different objectives or limit trading transaction costs following changes to SAA (i.e. constrain deviations from current allocation).

- Bootstrapping is a statistical method of creating a distribution of statistics, such as variance and correlation, from history rather than using a single one that is heavily dependent on the measuring period. Bootstrapping increases the robustness of optimisation to estimation error of CMAs.

- Resampling is another method to overcome the sensitivity of the optimisation to the CMAs and generate more robust optimisations. Instead of bootstrapping, resampling uses a Monte Carlo simulation.

- Optimisation based on historical experience should not be used to optimise forward-looking asset allocations but can be used to test how different asset allocations would have performed in the past.

- Mean-variance optimisation optimises the asset allocation for a single time period only. A dynamic SAA process is used for multiple time periods by updating the optimisation periodically, incorporating dynamic CMAs to reflect current market conditions.

- CMAs are linked to current market expectations and prices, such as bond yields, breakeven inflation and dividend yields, which change over time. This means that the SAA should follow a dynamic process and should be reviewed periodically to link it with current market conditions.

- The Black-Litterman model generates expected returns for asset classes through reverse optimisation of a market capitalisation weighted portfolio based on CAPM. The implied returns are combined with investor views to produce a set of consistent CMAs. These CMAs are then used in mean-variance optimisation to generate robust asset allocations. The model can be used alongside other SAA approaches as a sense check.

This concludes Part 2, setting an investment strategy.

PART 3

IMPLEMENTING A SOLUTION

Part 3 focuses on the third stage of the investment management process, implementing a solution, and discusses how the long-term investment strategy is completed by TAA and implemented through investment selection. Asset allocation is transformed into a portfolio of investments.

TAA can be considered part of setting an investment strategy or an active return-generating investment, which is part of implementing a solution.

While still focusing on the top-down asset allocation, TAA is materially different from SAA and requires a different skill-set and methodologies. TAA ensures that the long-term investment strategy is kept updated with market developments and risks. Investment selection then switches to the bottom-up process of investing the portfolio in actual investments.

INTRODUCTION

Implementing a solution turns the investment strategy into an actual portfolio. Investment strategy includes top-down, long-term SAA, adjusted to short-term opportunities and risks through TAA, and bottom-up policy on the rules and guidelines for selecting investments. Implementing a solution moves to the practical stage of selecting investments, constructing the portfolio and managing it.

Implementing a solution covers TAA, the investment selection process (including manager and vehicle selection) and the investment management process (including portfolio construction, implementation and risk budgeting).

Summary

- Implementing a solution turns the investment strategy, which includes top-down long-term SAA, adjusted for short-term TAA, and bottom-up policy on investment selection, into a portfolio.

- Implementing a solution covers TAA, investment selection and the investment management process.

13. TACTICAL ASSET ALLOCATION

Tactical Asset Allocation (TAA) is the process of deviating from the weights of SAA with the goals of enhancing performance through benefiting from relative value and market opportunities, and mitigating and managing risks. TAA is a risk management tool since it can quickly and efficiently alter the asset allocation to control the exposure to different risks.

Without any short-term views, the default, neutral positioning for portfolios is SAA. SAA is the portfolio's long-term investment strategy. TAA is optional and portfolios should have no deviations from SAA without investor views to support such deviations. If TAA managers have no forecasting ability, the best approach is sticking with SAA and not including TAA. TAA without forecasting skill just adds noise, risks and transaction costs. When investors do not have forecasting skills they should admit it. It is important to know what you know and know what you do not know. As Mark Twain put it "it ain't what you don't know that gets you into trouble. It's what you know for sure that just ain't so".

If investors stick to the same view, eventually they will be right. Perpetual bears or bulls eventually get it right since markets eventually fall or rally. This is, however, not a forecasting skill but rather consistent risk taking or risk aversion. The key for forecasting is consistency. Consistency does not mean perfect foresight, but rather getting it right more times than getting it wrong. Getting it right only rarely does not consistently add value.

The goal of TAA is taking advantage of inefficiencies in the relative prices of securities in different asset classes[211]. Like any other active investment strategy, TAA aims to sell high and buy low by shorting or going long investments with prices above or below fair-value, respectively. TAA normally utilises opportunities in different global markets, such as equities, fixed income, currencies and others. It is commonly called *GTAA* or Global Tactical Asset Allocation.

TAA should enhance the efficient frontier by adding an uncorrelated source of alpha, enhance the diversification in risk composition by adding an additional source of risk and enhance the risk management capabilities by adjusting portfolios to short-term risks.

Table 13.1 illustrates the three potential steps in asset allocation:

1. Benchmark (if different than SAA)

2. SAA

3. TAA

Table 13.1 – illustrative benchmark, SAA and TAA for a UK based multi-asset portfolio

Asset Class	Benchmark	SAA	TAA	Asset allocation
UK equities	30%	39%	-6%	33%
North America equities	10%	8%	1%	9%
Europe ex. UK equities	6%	2%	2%	4%
Japan equities	2%	1%	1%	2%
Asia ex. Japan equities	1%	3%	1%	4%
Emerging market equities	1%	3%	1%	4%
Gilts	15%	5%	6%	11%
Inflation-linked bonds	3%	0%	0%	0%
UK corporate bonds	9%	15%	-5%	10%
Global developed bonds	1.5%	2%	1%	3%
Emerging market debt	1.5%	5%	1%	6%
Real estate	5%	5%	-3%	2%
Commodities	2%	2%	0%	2%
Hedge funds	8%	8%	0%	8%
Cash	5%	2%	0%	2%
TOTAL	**100%**	**100%**	**0%**	**100%**

In Table 13.1 the two largest TAA positions are underweight UK equities and overweight gilts. If UK equities are going to underperform gilts, these two active positions will add value. If UK equities are going to outperform gilts, these two active positions will contribute negatively to performance.

The fundamental law of active management

TAA is an active investment strategy. According to the fundamental law of active management, which was introduced by Richard Grinold in 1989[212], the information ratio (IR) is equal to the *information coefficient* (IC) multiplied by the square root of *breadth* (BR):

$$IR = IC * BR^{0.5}$$

The information coefficient is the correlation between investment decisions and outcomes (i.e. measuring the number of correct investment decisions or the forecasting ability). Breadth is the number of independent (uncorrelated) active decisions in a year. If TAA is narrowly focused on deciding on the relative value of equities versus bonds or cash, then the strategy's breadth is narrow (small number of market timing calls) and its information ratio is expected to be low.

Even when TAA is expanded to calls on different countries around the world, the breadth may still be narrow because of the high correlation among different equity markets. TAA needs to cover as many markets and investments as possible so its breadth is as wide as possible.

Whatever the breadth is, the success of TAA ultimately depends on the information coefficient or the skill of the TAA manager at making investment decisions. Making many wrong decisions may have breadth but it does not add value (it adds noise and transaction costs). Every investor, skilled as may be, does not make all the right decisions. However, the preponderance of decisions should have a positive impact. With skill available, increasing the number of uncorrelated investment decisions should increase the information ratio.

One essential component that is missing from the fundamental law of active management is *market inefficiency*. If markets are efficient, as per EMH, active management cannot outperform the average market return since all investments' prices reflect intrinsic values. One prerequisite for outperformance is market inefficiency since it is needed for mispricing. The only way to beat the market is to identify mispriced investments (as many as possible to generate breadth), value them correctly (information coefficient) and invest accordingly.

Inefficient markets do not guarantee outperformance. For every investor who buys undervalued investments another investor sells them at a loss (zero sum game). Only investors with superior skill can add value in inefficient markets. Investors with superior skill cannot add value in completely efficient markets. So I would add a third element to the fundamental law of active management, market inefficiency (MI):

$$IR = IC*MI*BR^{0.5}$$

Since TAA requires judgment on relative value it is not a market timing strategy, which normally has a low breadth and success ratio. *Market timing* is a strategy that aims to enter the market when it is expected to rise and exit when it is expected to drop. It is very difficult to time the market and getting it wrong may be very costly.

TAA takes advantage of fundamental inefficiencies of prices deviating from fair-value, such as irrational exuberance (bubbles), investors' overreaction to perceived risks (e.g. the 1987 and 1998 equity crashes), investors' slow reaction to new information, and structural barriers, such as home bias. These inefficiencies cause prices to diverge from fair-value and create buying and selling opportunities that TAA aims to exploit.

Filling the gap between SAA and TAA

SAA sets the portfolio's long-term target weights. The next step is deciding when and by how much to deviate from these long-term weights due to short-term considerations. The reasons to deviate from the SAA target weights include: to benefit from short-term market opportunities; to control portfolio risk due to concerns and emerging risks; and to temporarily alter the portfolio's risk/reward profile due to investor requirements. As TAA changes the portfolio's asset allocation, its potential impact on risk and return can be material.

TAA views can be used to alter SAA positions. SAA takes a much longer-term view (5 to 10 years) than does TAA (less than one year) and is based on systematic CMAs and optimisation techniques. TAA, on the other hand, considers fundamental economics and market views. SAA ignores shorter-term considerations, which are reflected in portfolios through adjusting SAA positions based on TAA.

For example, SAA may underweight Japanese equities because of low dividend yields and growth expectations or low 10-year Japanese Government Bond yields, which feed into CMAs. TAA, in contrast, may be bullish on Japanese equities because of growing demand for Japanese products from China and expected weakness of the yen as it may support exporters.

The SAA long-term underweight can be adjusted by increasing the allocation to Japan to a neutral or overweight based on the short-term tactical view. The adjustment can be implemented via derivatives or Exchange Traded Funds (ETFs) so it can be quickly and cost efficiently removed when the TAA view changes and the position moves back to its SAA weight.

Combining long-term SAA and short-term TAA in investment strategy is the key to aligning portfolios with investment objectives over the long-term investment horizon while incorporating short-term considerations. TAA guides the portfolio through the long-term journey of SAA, as does the dynamic SAA process.

Budgeting the risk of TAA

TAA should be considered in the context of the overall portfolio, accounting for how portfolio risk changes due to TAA positions. SAA weights normally set the portfolio's investment policy or benchmark weights. The policy sets the portfolio's long-term risk level while TAA deviates from the policy, altering the portfolio risk level. For example, if SAA allocates 20% to equities and TAA overweights equities by 5% and underweights cash by 5%, the risk level of the portfolio is increased. To control the risk contribution of TAA, it should be allocated an appropriate risk budget so the portfolio's total risk level remains within the risk objectives.

The two ways to control the risk of TAA are to allocate a VaR or tracking error to TAA (so limiting the contribution to absolute risk of TAA or its deviations from SAA weights); or to limit the allowed deviations of each TAA weight from each SAA weight (i.e. asset allocation ranges).

The tracking error approach allows for more flexibility and innovation for TAA since it enables TAA to include asset classes that are not already included in SAA (off-benchmark), it does not limit deviations for any particular asset class and it controls the overall deviations from SAA weights.

Using asset allocation ranges has the function of limiting the deviations of each asset class from SAA weights. Relative risk can be controlled by the width of the ranges (there is a big difference between a range of +/- 2% and +/- 5%). This approach is more constraining than the tracking error approach and it may not capture all risks.

For example, if TAA is limited on the deviations from target equity weight, risk can be increased by taking excessive credit risk. This type of risk taking is not captured by asset allocation ranges but it is better captured by tracking error since it controls overall volatility and not any specific asset class. The advantage of ranges, however, is that investors can limit the deviations in each asset class. Sometimes a combination of the two approaches is used.

TAA overlay versus standalone TAA vehicle

TAA can be implemented through three main methods:

1. Trading underlying investments

2. Derivative overlays

3. Standalone TAA vehicles

1. Underlying investments

Trading underlying investments is implemented through increasing or decreasing the allocations to underlying portfolios or investments. For example, when TAA overweights UK equities and underweights gilts, it is implemented through buying UK equity portfolios or stocks and selling gilt portfolios or gilts. Since

TAA has a short-term horizon, these positions may be reversed quite often. This method is inefficient since it may involve material trading costs and it may be disruptive to underlying portfolio managers as they need to accommodate large cash flows.

One way to mitigate these inefficiencies is including passive, liquid investments in each asset class, such as passive funds or ETFs, and using them as a buffer to implement TAA. ETFs do, however, have management fees and trading them involves transaction costs. However, ETF fees and costs are normally lower than those of actively-managed investments. Views on currencies can be implemented either through buying currency hedged share classes of underlying investments (a combination of hedged and unhedged share classes can be used to reach a desired target hedge ratio) or through using forward currency contracts. Implementing TAA through trading underlying investments is recommended only for multi-asset portfolios that cannot utilise derivatives.

2. Derivative overlays

Derivative overlays use long and short positions in derivatives to implement TAA. For most equity and government bond markets, futures contracts are readily available and forward currency contracts are available to implement currency views. The overlay can use other derivatives, such as options and swaps. However, utilising more complex derivatives requires more sophistication and comprehensive understanding of derivative markets, as well as an adequate operating infrastructure to support such trades and risk management systems to manage risks.

Derivative overlays require cash as collateral for the derivative positions. For example, a TAA derivative overlay on a $2 billion multi-asset portfolio with a 1% tracking error target for TAA and $200 million notional exposure through derivatives requires $20 million cash to satisfy the derivatives' collateral requirements. Ideally, the collateral should be invested in passive vehicles to replicate the benchmark of the multi-asset portfolio to prevent a cash drag on the collateral.

Short derivative positions must be covered by congruent long positions (a tracking error test is applied to ensure that the covering positions are appropriate) to prevent naked shorts. A naked or uncovered short is a short position without holding the corresponding long position. Long derivative positions should be covered by a cash equivalent to the notional amount of the long futures positions to avoid leveraging the portfolio. For example, going long futures on the S&P 500 with a notional of $100 million will require only $10 million as collateral. However, the portfolio should hold an additional $90 million in cash to cover the long synthetic equity position to avoid leveraging the portfolio, unless leverage is permitted and wanted.

An overlay is an efficient way to implement TAA. Its main advantages, compared to trading investments, are that underlying portfolios do not need to be traded (most derivatives are liquid and trading them involves lower transaction costs, except perhaps for illiquid derivatives), underlying portfolio managers are not affected by the overlay (not disruptive), derivative positions are unfunded meaning that they do not need cash to back the notional position (only cash for collateral; hence the overlay is capital efficient) and most derivative markets are liquid.

The disadvantages of an overlay are: it requires more sophistication than trading investments (e.g. reporting portfolio positions, risk management, investor education); futures contracts need to be rolled over when they expire (e.g. every quarter); basis risk (i.e. difference in performance between derivative and intended market exposure); and futures contracts do not include currency exposure (it should be gained through the cash market if desired). Due to rolling costs and broker commissions holding futures positions over the long term may be more costly than buying passive funds.

3. Standalone TAA vehicles

Standalone TAA vehicles are similar to a global macro hedge fund and they fit into the alternative investments allocation of multi-asset portfolios. The vehicle is funded by cash, has the flexibility to implement TAA views without constraints due to the positions in the multi-asset portfolio (i.e. shorts do not need to be covered by congruent longs and longs do not need to be covered by cash) and it has no limitations on leverage since the leverage is contained within the vehicle. While flexibility is an advantage, standalone vehicles cannot alter the multi-asset portfolio's asset allocation, do not complement SAA and cannot be used as a risk management tool (unlike overlays).

Investors can choose between a segregated portfolio and collective investment scheme for the TAA vehicle. Segregated portfolios can be customised for the multi-asset portfolio's requirements (as long as portfolio size is sufficient for a segregated account). Collectives have limited liability that is important due to the leverage and short positions of the TAA vehicle. However, collectives are typically offered to external investors and are not customisable.

If, however, the collective is used solely to implement TAA instead of a derivative overlay across a range of portfolios for a single investor, this can be an efficient TAA implementation. The collective in this case should be the least expensive (e.g. not UCITS compliant) since it does not need to be sold externally.

Advantages and disadvantages of the methods

Each of the three methods has advantages and disadvantages:

- *Complement SAA in setting asset allocation.* Only trading underlying investments and derivative overlays can be used to alter the asset allocation of multi-asset portfolios.

- *Risk management tool.* Trading underlying investments and derivative overlays can be used as a risk management tool, controlling the multi-asset portfolio's asset allocation. Only derivative overlays can be used to hedge and insure against risks. Futures and forward currency contracts can be used to quickly change risk exposures to address emerging risks. For example, if a multi-asset portfolio is overweight equities and risks or uncertainties emerge, risk can be hedged through shorting equity futures contracts. Once the risks have receded, the futures contracts can be quickly closed. Trading underlying investments or changing SAA positions may take time and involve transaction costs. Standalone vehicles cannot be used to manage risks.

- *Risk management of the TAA process.* Derivative overlays account for the correlations with the positions within multi-asset portfolios and have better controls over short positions and leverage compared to standalone vehicles. Standalone vehicles can have more flexibility with shorting and leveraging positions.

- *Performance measurement.* Measuring and evaluating the performance of derivative overlays is more challenging since overlays are constrained by the positions within the multi-asset portfolio. In other words, managers of derivative overlays do not have full control over all the investment decisions because the overlay is constrained by the positions in the multi-asset portfolio.

- *Operational complexity.* Derivative overlays may be more operationally complex. While standalone vehicles may be operationally complex within the vehicle, from the multi-asset portfolio's perspective it is more simple to invest in a single vehicle.

- *Short selling.* One of the advantages of a TAA strategy should be its ability to short sell. Short selling benefits from a fall in investment price. Derivative overlays are usually restricted to short or underweight only long positions within the multi-asset portfolio. A naked or uncovered short is a short position without holding the corresponding long position. The loss potential of a naked short is limitless since investment price may theoretically increase indefinitely and the loss on the short position is uncapped. When the short position is covered, the potential losses on the short positions are offset or covered by the gains on the corresponding long position.

Other considerations are that TAA strategy may have a high level of volatility or tracking error (as high as 30%) and it may put the TAA manager and organisation at risk, there are a limited number of markets and investments that can be included in a TAA strategy and hence there is a concentration risk, and using multiple TAA managers may have diversification benefits and give a higher information ratio (according to the fundamental law of active management more uncorrelated decisions increase the information ratio).

Sizing positions based on conviction and risk

Assume that a $1 billion multi-asset portfolio has a goal of gaining 75bp from a TAA overlay with an assumed information ratio of 0.50. The multi-asset portfolio requires a tracking error of 1.5% from TAA (75bp/0.50). If the TAA strategy has a target volatility of 30% the multi-asset portfolio needs to allocate $50 million to TAA (1.5%/30%*$1 billion). The TAA overlay needs approximately $5 million in cash funding for collateral for the futures contracts and the collateral is put aside for *equitisation*[213] to replicate the benchmark of the multi-asset portfolio to eliminate the impact of cash drag.

The balance of the overlay ($45 million) is used to establish long and short positions. When establishing the long and short positions, the TAA manager needs to take the positions of overall multi-asset portfolio into account and leverage is typically not permitted. Alternatively, 5% can be allocated to a funded TAA standalone vehicle. The positions within the standalone vehicle are not limited by the positions in the multi-asset portfolio.

The positions of each TAA view should be sized according to the conviction in each view while the overall tracking error of TAA should be controlled according to the desired contribution to performance from the TAA strategy.

The ratio between expected risk and contribution to tracking error of each TAA position should be equal across all positions. This ensures optimal position sizing and that each position has the same expected contribution to performance adjusted to its contribution to risk. Achieving such equality in the ratio may be impractical, so aiming for a broadly equal ratio is reasonable.

Medium-Term Asset Allocation (MTAA)

A Medium-Term Asset Allocation (MTAA) process may be included in multi-asset portfolios. The objective of MTAA is adding performance over the medium-term horizon that falls between TAA (less than a year) and SAA (5 to 10 years). The horizon of MTAA is around two years. MTAA includes positions that are not expected to add value over the short term, expected to be held to maturity and may underperform on a marked-to-market basis. This must be understood by investors in order that their expectations are managed and they understand that this process may result in short-term negative contribution to relative performance.

Conclusion

TAA is an important weapon in the arsenal of multi-asset investors, in particular as a tool for adjusting the long-term investment strategy to short-term developments and positioning portfolios to account for short-term opportunities and risks. If done correctly, TAA is a potential source of alpha and a risk management tool. Not all multi-asset portfolios use TAA. Some portfolios maintain positions for the long-term without adjusting. Whether TAA should be included in multi-asset portfolios depends on the investment objectives and the available skills at the investor's disposal.

Summary

- TAA complements SAA to set the multi-asset investment strategy.

- TAA alters SAA with three main objectives: exploiting short-term relative value opportunities across markets to add value; changing the asset allocation to manage risks; and temporarily adjusting the reward/risk profile of the portfolio as required by investors.

- As per the fundamental law of active management, the information ratio equals the information coefficient times the square root of breadth. The success of a TAA strategy depends on the number of investment decisions (breadth) and the investor's forecasting ability (information coefficient).

- TAA should adjust the long-term asset allocation weights to short-term market views and fill the gap between the long and short term. SAA looks at long-term (5 to 10 years) prospects for markets based on a systematic, quantitative process to derive CMAs and optimise the asset allocation. TAA looks at short-term (less than one year) market opportunities and risks, typically based on a combination of qualitative and quantitative processes. SAA and TAA complement each other. TAA considers what SAA ignores.

- The risk level of portfolios should be controlled after allowing for the asset allocation deviations due to TAA.

- TAA should include either an overall tracking error relative to SAA or limitations on the deviations of each asset class from SAA weights (i.e. allocation ranges). The former approach allows for more flexibility.

- TAA can be implemented through trading underlying investments, derivative overlays or standalone vehicles. Trading underlying investments involves transaction costs, which can be mitigated through using passive vehicles, such as ETFs. Derivative overlays are a cost-efficient way to implement TAA, although they are limited by the coverage requirements of the multi-asset portfolio (short positions must be covered by congruent long positions and long positions by cash). Standalone vehicles are flexible (no need for coverage, no limitations on leverage and short selling), however they do not change the asset allocation of the multi-asset portfolio.

- TAA overlays can be used as a risk management tool since they can quickly change the portfolio's asset allocation to control risk exposures.

- The positions of TAA should be sized according to the desired tracking error of the TAA process and its target performance contribution to the multi-asset portfolio.

- The ratio between expected risk and contribution to tracking error of each TAA position should be equal across all positions.

- MTAA is a process whose investment horizon is about two years. Its positions should add value over this investment horizon and may underperform on a marked-to-market basis in the short term.

14. FORECASTING

The objective of forecasting is formulating an objective view of the future direction of investments. It is one of the most challenging roles of investment management, because crystal balls do not work in real life. As Mark Twain said, "it's difficult to make predictions, especially about the future". Many investors erroneously tend to extrapolate recent history and base their forecasts on current sentiment. When markets are up, investors are positive and so are their forecasts. When markets are down, investors are negative.

As has been shown, SAA is based on forward-looking CMAs that are normally derived through a systematic, quantitative process that aims to forecast expected returns, risks and correlations of asset classes (beta exposures) over the long term. TAA is based on fundamental, economic views and/or a quantitative process to derive investment decisions on the relative value or direction of markets and investments over the short term. TAA is an active strategy and its success depends on the skill of the TAA manager to forecast the future.

Three methods of forecasting

There are three methods that are used to forecast markets:

1. Technical analysis

2. Fundamental analysis

3   Quantitative analysis

Many investors combine these methods. For TAA fundamental and/or quantitative methods are the most commonly employed to support investment decisions, while technical analysis is sometimes useful to time the implementation of decisions.

1. Technical analysis

Technical analysis aims to forecast the direction of prices through the study of past market data, in particular prices and volumes of trading. Technical analysis often analyses charts of market prices (technical analysts are referred to as chartists). The objective is to identify price patterns and market trends to try to forecast future patterns. The principles of technical analysis are that market action discounts all available information (technical analysis aims to understand what investors think of that information), prices move in trends, history tends to repeat itself and investors collectively repeat the behaviour of investors who preceded them.

The ability of technical analysis to add value is disputed by EMH in its weakest form, which claims that current market and security prices already price in all past information. The random walk hypothesis claims that technical analysis is futile.

In a paper from 2000 Andrew Lo el al[214] analysed data from the United States from 1962 to 1996 and found that "several technical indicators do provide incremental information and may have some practical value". Behavioural finance may explain the value of technical analysis because investors collectively tend toward patterned behaviour and patterns in prices tend to repeat themselves. If enough investors use technical analysis to support investment decisions it can be a self-fulfilling prophecy.

While the predictive power of technical analysis is questionable and it should not be used as the sole basis for forecasting markets and driving investment decisions, it can be helpful in determining the timing of implementing market views. For example, the *Relative Strength Index* (RSI) is a technical indicator that charts the current and historical strength or weakness of a market based on the closing prices of the recent trading period. It is a *momentum oscillator*, measuring the velocity and magnitude of directional price movements.

Momentum is the rate of the rise or fall in price. RSI computes momentum as the ratio of higher closes to lower closes. Markets that have had more or stronger positive changes have a higher RSI than markets that have had more or stronger negative changes. It can be helpful in timing decisions to overweight or underweight a market, as long as the decision itself is supported by robust fundamental or quantitative analysis.

Another simple technical indicator is a moving average. Figure 14.1 shows the daily prices of the S&P 500 and its 50-day moving average. If a market is above its 50-day moving average it indicates that it may be overbought and if the market is below the moving average it indicates that it may be oversold. When there is a fundamentally-driven decision to overweight or underweight a market, the moving average can help with timing entry and exit decisions (i.e. buy when the market is oversold or sell when it is overbought).

Figure 14.1 – S&P 500 daily prices and 50-day moving average, 31 December 2009 to 30 June 2012

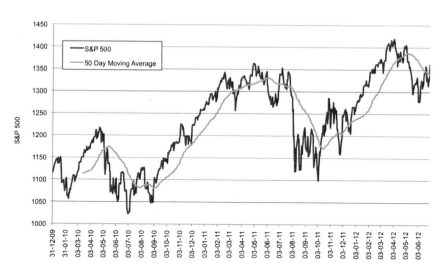

Source: Bloomberg, S&P 500.

2. Fundamental analysis

Fundamental analysis focuses on analysing the state of the economy, interest rates, inflation, corporate earnings, corporate balance sheets and policies of central banks and governments.

When fundamental analysis is used for security selection it normally combines top-down analysis of the general direction of the economy (macro) to formulate views on markets, industries, interest rates and currencies with a bottom-up analysis of specific securities (micro). Bottom-up analysis often ignores the allocations to countries and industries and focuses on selecting individual securities. Depending on the investment philosophy and process, top-down analysis determines the allocation to countries and sectors while bottom-up analysis determines the investments within each country and sector.

When fundamental analysis is used for TAA it normally focuses on the top-down analysis. The analysis covers global economics, including international and national economic indicators and developments, such as GDP[215] growth, inflation, interest rates, currency exchange rates and commodity prices. The result may be a single view on the economy or a number of economic scenarios. The views are then translated into a strategy of long and short positions in different markets and investments. A TAA strategy includes overweights and underweights to equity markets, bond markets, currencies and other markets such as commodities. The strategy can be more granular, making calls on sectors within equities, duration and credit ratings within bonds, sectors within commodities, as well as more thematic investments and trade ideas such as taking advantage of investment opportunities in derivative markets (e.g. mispricing of risk in options).

3. Quantitative analysis

Quantitative (quant) analysis, as its name suggests, involves forecasting market direction using quantitative methods, statistical models, mathematical formulas and algorithms. A common approach in TAA is to use multi-factor models, looking at valuations, momentum, risk level, sentiment, interest rates and yield curve to produce buy and sell signals on different markets, covering equities, bonds and currencies. While some TAA strategies are completely quant driven, a combination of quantitative and fundamental analysis is more robust so the quant signals inform and feed into the fundamental process.

The shortcoming of quant analysis is that it is largely based on observed, historical correlations and trends in market prices. If those correlations and trends break down, due to a reversal or stress in markets causing historic correlations to change, the quant models may fail in predicating inflection points. Quant models also tend to fail when there is a regime change or a structural change in markets.

The pioneer of quantitative finance was Harry Markowitz in his 1952 paper 'Portfolio Selection'[216] when he quantified the concept of portfolio diversification. In 1969[217] Robert Merton introduced stochastic calculus into the study of finance to explain the behaviour of financial markets. With the assistance of Merton, Fischer Black and Myron Scholes developed the Black-Scholes option pricing formula in 1973[218], for which they were awarded the 1997 Noble Memorial Prize in Economic Science. These developments were the foundations of quantitative finance, an area that has developed exponentially over the last couple of decades.

Forecasting markets over the short term

Rudi Dornbusch was fond of remarking that "in economics things take longer to happen than you think they will and then they happen faster than you thought they could". Economists are notoriously bad at making the right calls on markets. Forecasting markets over a short timeframe is extremely difficult. Most professionals have good *forecasting* abilities with the benefit of hindsight after the event, but not using foresight before the event.

Over the long term, equities should deliver positive returns, at least in line with inflation. As population grows, the demand for goods and services manufactured and sold by companies grows. Therefore, just to keep up with the increasing demand, overall companies' earnings should grow. The economy of the United States, for example, has grown at 3.3% over the long term[219]. Companies' earnings are assumed to grow at this pace minus a dilution factor (about 2.0% in the United States). Over the long term equities are assumed to generate expected returns made of dividend yield plus nominal earnings growth. Fixed-income investments, when held to maturity, should deliver a return in line with the yield to maturity after allowing for defaults (credit risk). It is therefore beneficial to hold positions in investments over the long term and deviations from these long-term positions should be supported by solid reasoning.

TAA needs to forecast market returns over the short term. Equity prices are mainly driven by changes in valuations over the short term and not by dividend yields and long-term earnings growth. When fixed income investments are not held to maturity a large proportion of their total return is affected by changes in their valuations (capital gains and losses). Changes in valuations are driven by fluctuations in interest rates, inflation and credit ratings. Forecasting equity valuations, interest rates, credit quality and inflation over the short term is difficult. Forecasting returns over the long term is much easier. Nevertheless, deviating from long-term positions should be supported by high-conviction, short-term views.

One of the objectives of TAA is adding value through altering the asset allocation based on views on different markets. Basically, TAA aims to overweight (go long) undervalued markets and underweight (short) overvalued markets. Determining the fair value of markets is extremely difficult but is required to decide whether markets are over (price > fair-value) or under (price < fair-value) valued.

For example, if equities are expected to outperform bonds, TAA should overweight equities and underweight bonds. Unlike investment selection, TAA does not involve analysing and forecasting returns of individual securities, but rather of asset classes, markets or sectors. TAA can add value under the assumptions that markets are either inefficient all the time (TAA needs to identify mispricings and opportunities) or very efficient but not all the time and therefore any mispricing will correct itself (TAA needs to identify the mispricing before market forces correct it). If markets are efficient all the time, as EMH claims, then TAA and active management in general cannot add value.

Quantitative multi-factor model

The two main ways to forecast market performance for TAA are fundamental and quantitative analysis. Under the *quantitative approach* a quantitative multi-factor model is often used to systematically exploit inefficiencies or temporary imbalances in equilibrium values among different asset classes.

One simple single factor example is screening different equity markets for earnings yield (E/P ratio, the reciprocal of P/E), then going overweight (long) markets with above average earnings yields and underweight (short) those with below average earnings yield. Markets with high earnings yields may be distressed and cheap, and investing in them may benefit from a distress risk premium.

To construct a multi-factor TAA process, investors need to choose which factors to include covering equity, bond and currency markets. TAA multi-factor models should weight the factors and produce positive or negative signals to overweight or underweight markets or investments. The factors and their signals should make economic sense. Commonly used factors include:

- *Valuation.* Screening for earnings yield (ratio of earnings to equity prices). High earnings yield is a positive signal.

- *Momentum.* Comparing the equity return 12 months ago with the return one month ago (the 12th month return is omitted since the market tends to reverse after 12 months). Momentum is an indication of market sentiment. Positive momentum is a positive signal.

- *Term structure* (the slope of the yield curve). The yield on 10-year government bonds minus the 1-month yield on cash. Markets with a steeper term structure tend to outperform those with a flatter one because the slope signals expansion and is positive for equities.

- *Real interest rates.* The yield on 10-year government bonds minus inflation. Markets with higher real interest rates tend to outperform.

- *Interest rate differentials.* Currencies of countries with higher interest rates tend to outperform on average.

These five factors are just an example. Other factors include changes to credit risk premium (e.g. change in the spread between Moody's corporate Baa and Aaa yields), VIX level relative to history and changes to real Personal Consumption Expenditure (PCE)[220]. Investors can use more or fewer factors depending on their beliefs.

Summary

- TAA is an active investment strategy and its success depends on the ability to forecast markets correctly.

- Three methodologies to forecast markets are technical analysis, fundamental analysis and quantitative analysis. Many investors use a combination of all three to support investment decisions. TAA commonly uses the fundamental and/or quantitative methods.

- Forecasting markets over the short term is extremely difficult. Market returns over the long term are driven by dividend yield, long-term economic growth and bond yields to maturity. Valuations are a much more prominent factor in determining returns over the short term. Changes in valuations are difficult to forecast.

- TAA analyses markets and overweights (goes long) undervalued markets and underweights (goes short) overvalued markets.

- The quantitative process is commonly based on multi-factor models that generate buy and sell signals on different markets and investments. Some of the commons factors are valuation, momentum, term structure, real interest rate and interest rate differentials.

15. ECONOMIC CYCLE

Under the *fundamental approach,* research into the economics of markets aims to identify relative value opportunities across markets and investments. Different investments are expected to perform well or poorly during different stages of the economic cycle (business cycle or market cycle).

Four stages of the economic cycle

The economic cycle has four main stages:

1. Expansion

2. Slowdown

3. Recession

4. Recovery

The stages are defined by change in GDP (i.e. GDP grows during expansion and contracts during recession). It is difficult to know which stage the economy is in, which stage it is heading towards and whether the cycle is going to evolve as expected. It is most difficult to forecast the inflection points in the cycle. These are the points where the cycle moves from one stage to the next.

Figure 15.1 illustrates a theoretical, smooth economic cycle[221].

Figure 15.1 – the economic cycle

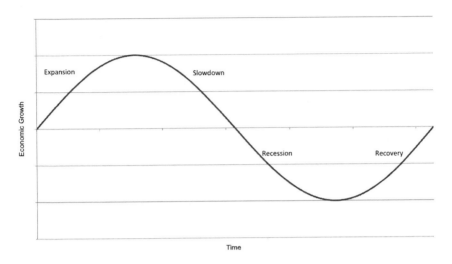

Figure 15.2 shows the year-on-year (YoY) changes to the real GDP of the United States. The economy has been going through cycles of growing and slowing (expanding and contracting during some time periods).

Figure 15.2 – US real GDP YoY changes, January 1946 to June 2012

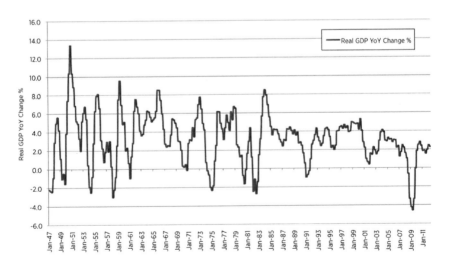

Source: Global Financial Data, United States Real GDP in 2005 Dollars.

According to Keynesian economics fluctuations in aggregate demand cause the economy to reach a short-term equilibrium at levels that are different from the full employment rate of output. These fluctuations express themselves as the economic cycle. Since the 1940s, following the publication of Keynesian economics, most governments of developed countries have considered it to be their responsibility to mitigate the effects of the economic cycle through stabilisation policies.

Figure 15.3 shows the YoY changes to real GDP in the United Stated since 1900. As can be seen, the magnitude of the changes in GDP, or the booms and busts, has considerably decreased since the end of the 1940s.

Figure 15.3 – US real GDP YoY changes, January 1900 to December 2011

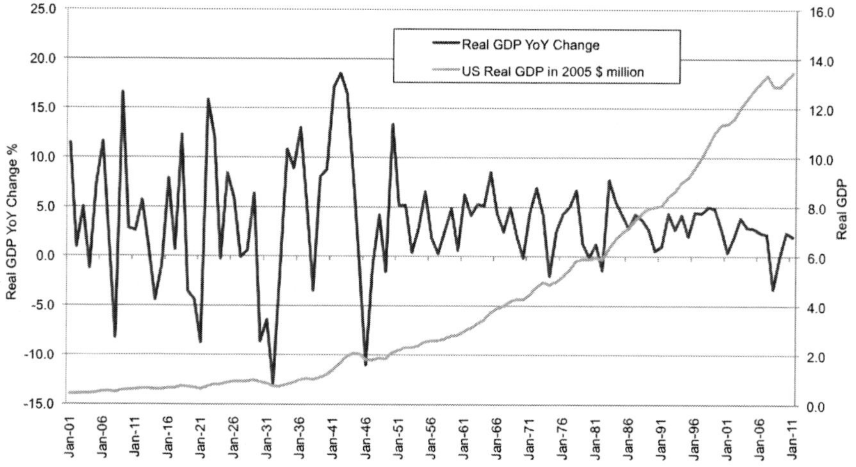

Source: Global Financial Data, United States Real GDP in 2005 Dollars.

According to Keynesian economics recessions are caused by inadequate aggregate demand. Therefore, governments can increase the level of aggregate demand through increasing the money supply (expansionary monetary policy) and increasing government spending or reducing taxes (expansionary fiscal policy). These policies, according to Keynes and his followers, could help brining the economy back to equilibrium.

Neoclassical economists have argued against the Keynesian model since the 1960s. Most notably, Nobel Laureate Milton Friedman argued against the ability of Keynesian policies to manage the economy. Friedman was the main proponent of the monetarist school of economics, arguing for a close and stable association between inflation and money supply. Friedman rejected the use of fiscal policy as a tool of demand management and argued that the government's role in guiding the economy should be restricted.

Friedman and his school of thought supported the free market philosophy, claiming that the markets work without government intervention. The 2008 credit crisis questioned the free market philosophy as governments and central banks had to step in and bail out the global financial system. The invisible hand of the market[222] had lost its way.

Other stages of the economic cycle

There are potential stages of the economic cycle that fall outside of the standard four stages:

- *Stagflation* is a situation in which the inflation rate is high and the economic growth rate slows down while unemployment remains steadily high. This situation is difficult for policy makers since actions designed to lower inflation or reduce unemployment may actually worsen economic growth. Stagflation may occur when the productive capacity of an economy is reduced by an unfavourable supply shock, such as an increase in oil price for an oil importing country. This shock tends to raise prices while slowing the economy by making production more costly and less profitable. Stagflation may also result from inappropriate macroeconomic policies. Central banks may, for example, permit excessive growth of the money supply. During the 1970s the world suffered from stagflation that started with a shock to oil prices and continued as central banks tried to fight the recession using monetary policy that would stimulate the economy.

- *Deflation* is a situation when there is a decrease in the general price level of goods and services. Deflation occurs when the inflation rate falls below 0% (a negative inflation rate).

- *Goldilocks* is an economic situation that is not too hot and not too cold (like the porridge in *The Story of the Three Bears*). Moderate economic growth is sustained as well as low inflation. This allows for a market-friendly monetary policy. A Goldilocks economy is supportive of equities and risk assets, as moderate growth is maintained, as well as of fixed income and conservative assets, as interest rates and inflation are steady.

The output gap

The economic cycle can be defined as the position of the economy relative to its long-term trend. The *output gap* is the difference between the potential output of the economy and its current output (the difference between potential GDP and actual GDP). Potential output is the economy's maximum output without generating inflation. Economic output depends on the availability of resources such as labour, commodities and capital. Economic output is expected to expand with the growth of these resources (e.g. increasing population increases the available labour force). The growth in resources is the economic trend growth rate.

The output gap is typically expressed as a percentage of GDP. A positive output gap means that the economy is producing more than its potential and this is called an *inflationary gap*. It indicates that the growth of aggregate demand is outpacing the growth of aggregate supply, possibly creating inflation. A negative output gap means that the economy is producing less than its potential and this is called a *recessionary gap*, possibly indicating deflation.

The output gap and economic growth rate define the four stages of the economic cycle. In a slowdown the output gap is positive but growth is below its trend. In a recession the output gap is negative and growth is below its trend. In a recovery the output gap is still negative, but growth is above its trend. In an expansion the output gap is positive and growth is above its trend.

Table 15.1 – the stages of the economic cycle as defined by the output gap and economic growth.

The four stages of the economic cycle		Output gap	
		Negative	**Positive**
Growth	**Below trend**	Recession	Slowdown
	Above trend	Recovery	Expansion

While the output gap is not directly observable, there are a number of observable economic factors that indicate whether the economy is heading toward growth or slowdown. Figures 15.4, 15.5 and 15.6 respectively show the relationship between the subsequent 12-month change to real GDP in the United States and the slope of the yield curve (10-year Treasury yield minus 90-day Treasury Bill yield), inverse changes to the level of the 10-year Treasury yield and changes to real Personal Consumption Expenditure (PCE).

Each factor has an economic rationale for its link with changes to GDP. An inverted yield curve (i.e. long-term bonds have lower yield than short-term debt) is a sign for potential slowing economic growth or a recession because the market is pricing in dropping inflation and interest rates. A rise (fall) in 10-year government bond yield level indicates slowing (accelerating) economic growth as the 10-year yield indicates the market expectations for changes in inflation and interest rates (e.g. dropping inflation and interest rates are a sign for recessionary pressures). A rise (fall) in PCE is a leading indicator[223] for accelerating (slowing) economic growth as the US consumer is a major driver of economic growth, both in the Unites States and globally.

Figure 15.4 – slope of the yield curve and subsequent real GDP YoY change, January 1970 to June 2012

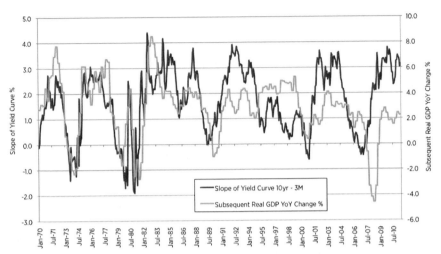

Source: Global Financial Data, USA 10-year Bond Constant Maturity Yield, USA Government 90-day T-Bills Secondary Market, United States Real GDP in 2005 Dollars.

Figure 15.5 – inverse YoY change in level of 10-year Treasury yield and subsequent real GDP YoY change, January 1970 to June 2012

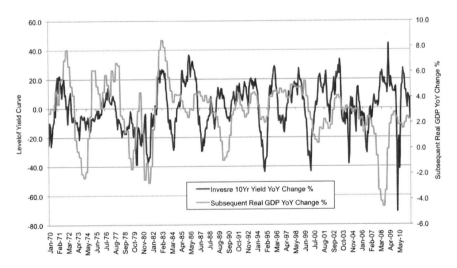

Source: Global Financial Data, USA 10-year Bond Constant Maturity Yield, United States Real GDP in 2005 Dollars.

Figure 15.6 – real personal consumer expenditure YoY change and subsequent real GDP YoY change, January 1970 to June 2012

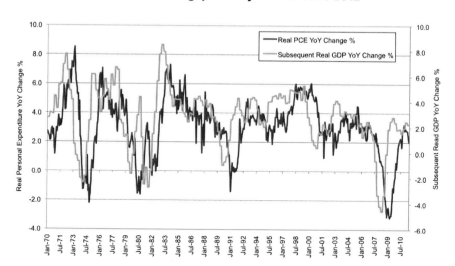

Source: Global Financial Data, Bureau of Economic Analysis[224], United States Real GDP in 2005 Dollars.

There are also a number of common economic indicators that can be used to gauge the likely direction of economic growth:

- The *Purchasing Managers Index* (*PMI*)[225] monitors purchasing managers' acquisition of goods and services. A reading of 50 or higher generally indicates that industry is expanding.

- The *ISM Manufacturing Index* (*ISM*)[226] monitors employment, production inventories, new orders and supplier deliveries. It indicates the health of the corporate sector.

- The *Jobless Claim Report* shows the number of first-time (initial) filings for jobless claims in the United States and indicates the state of the labour market.

- The New Residential Construction Report[227], known as *housing starts*, indicates the number of new houses that have begun to be constructed in the United States. Together with the *Existing Homes Sales Report* it monitors the US housing market.

- The *Retail Sales Report* tracks the dollar value of merchandise sold within the retail trade.

All these economic indicators, as well as others (e.g. inventories, industrial production, unemployment, mutual fund flows) are inputs into the fundamental analysis for formulating expectations for the evolution of the economic cycle.

As an example, Figure 15.7 shows the link between PMI and subsequent real GDP YoY change.

Figure 15.7 – PMI and subsequent real GDP YoY change, January 1970 to June 2012

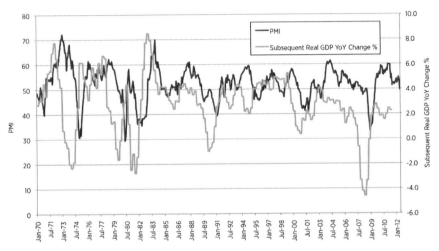

Source: Global Financial Data, Institute for Supply Management, United States Real GDP in 2005 Dollars.

The output gap affects inflation, interest rates and economic growth. When economic activity is below trend, demand is lower than normal, unemployment is higher than normal and companies have excess capacity. This tends to lead to lower inflation and companies tend to reduce prices of goods and services to remain competitive. Central banks are likely to respond to economic activity. When growth is below trend and the output gap is widening during a recession, central banks are likely to cut interest rates and loosen monetary policy as inflation falls.

In recovery, inflation may still be low, but central banks are less likely to reduce interest rates as the output gap is closing. Monetary policy is likely to be accommodative, but stable. When the economy is growing above trend, there are likely to be inflationary pressures and central banks act by increasing interest rates.

Economic cycle and investment assets

Corporate profitability, stock market performance, consumer behaviour, sentiment and capital expenditure (CAPEX) are all affected by inflation, interest rates and economic growth. Therefore, the position in the economic cycle drives the performance of different asset classes. As different asset classes react differently to those factors, their performance diverges depending on the phase of the economic cycle. TAA strategies can benefit from the divergence in performance among asset classes and from different countries being at different stages of their economic cycle. For example, thinking of the four stages of the cycle:

1. *Slowdown.* During a slowdown, equities and bonds perform poorly. Inflation and interest rates are rising, economic growth is slowing and corporate profitability is falling. This combination is negative for both equities and bonds. Cash is the preferred asset class. During times of increasing interest rates and inflation, investors tend to focus on the short term and seek income (dividend yields). Equities that are high quality, with a high dividend yield, should outperform low-quality equities that yield low dividends. Value stocks outperform growth stocks. Oil prices have historically risen during slowdowns, but this may have been the catalyst for a slowdown, not its consequence. Gold may perform strongly since most other asset classes perform poorly. Corporate bonds underperform government bonds because of widening credit spreads.

2. *Recession.* During the early stages of a recession equities typically fall due to weakening corporate profits and pricing in of the recession. Bonds perform well during the early stages of a recession and during its late stages due to falling interest rates and inflation. This is the best time to invest in government bonds. Commodities perform poorly during a recession due to falling demand. However, commodity performance follows long-term super cycles and it is difficult to forecast commodity returns based on the economic cycle. Corporate bonds underperform government bonds.

3. *Recovery.* During the recovery stage monetary policy is still accommodative while growth is strengthening and inflation is still low. This is the best combination for equities, albeit with potential increased volatility as the market is not sure whether the recovery stage has arrived. Small capitalisation equities perform strongly during the recovery stage and outperform large capitalisation equities. Corporate bonds outperform government bonds.

4. *Expansion.* During the expansion stage equities continue to perform well, outperforming bonds and cash. Corporate bonds outperform government bonds.

Figures 15.8, 15.9 and 15.10 show the average quarterly US real GDP changes from January 1970 to June 2012 ranked by percentiles and respectively the average corresponding performance of US equities, 10-year Treasuries and cash during each percentile. Equities perform poorly during recessions and slowdowns. Government bonds perform strongly during stagnated economic growth or recession, while their performance is more modest during periods of strong economic growth. Cash performs most strongly during a recession and expansion.

Figure 15.8 – average quarterly real GDP change and corresponding average US equity return, January 1970 to June 2012

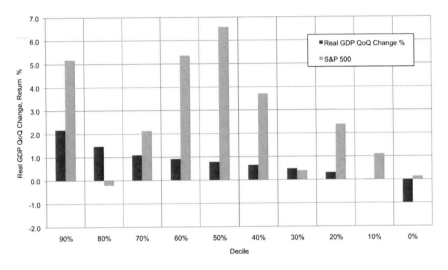

Source: Global Financial Data, S&P 500, United States Real GDP in 2005 Dollars.

Figure 15.9 – average quarterly real GDP change and corresponding average US 10-year Treasury return, January 1970 to June 2012

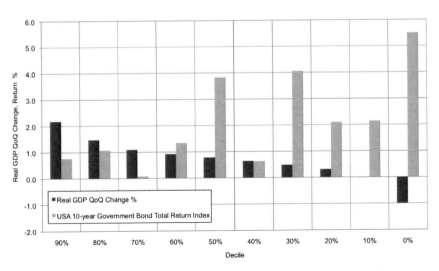

Source: Global Financial Data, USA 10-year Government Bond Total Return, United States Real GDP in 2005 Dollars.

Figure 15.10 – average quarterly real GDP change and corresponding average US Treasury Bill return, January 1970 to June 2012

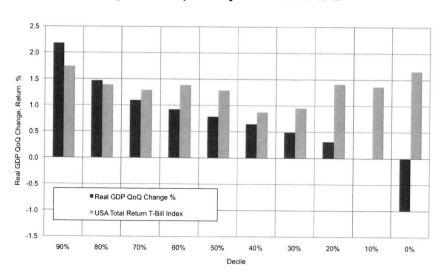

Source: Global Financial Data, USA Total Return T-Bill, United States Real GDP in 2005 Dollars.

Investment clock

A popular way to look at the economic cycle is through the *investment clock*, which was first published in London's *Evening Standard* in 1937. While the investment clock has its flaws (it is a very crude way to look at the economic backdrop), it is a helpful framework to guide investment decisions at different stages of the economic cycle.

Figure 15.11 – the investment clock

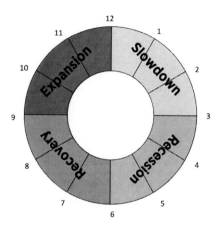

The hours on the clock correspond to the following economic stages:

- *12 o'clock*: The peak of the *expansion* is a time of optimism, greed and excess. Full employment, rapid economic growth, favourable economic conditions and positive sentiment support the real estate market. Investors use leverage to purchase real estate. Commodities are an attractive investment as inflation is on the rise and economic activity creates demand for commodities. Inflation-linked bonds should protect against increasing inflation.

- *1 o'clock*: The economy has moved to the *slowdown* stage of the economic cycle. Rising inflation, demand for capital (e.g. due to leveraged property purchases) and government endeavours to move the overheating economy to a soft landing result in interest rate rises. A policy error of increasing interest rates too rapidly may end up with a hard landing.

- *2 o'clock*: The price appreciation of property and equities is unsustainable as economic activity slows. High interest rates weigh on property prices since the cost of capital is high. Fixed income investments are more attractive now that interest rates are near the upper limit of where they will reach. Equities look less attractive as profitability of companies is pressured due to high interest rates, high commodity prices and high real estate prices. A correction in equity prices is a risk as the risk of a recession (not the recession itself) may be priced into equity prices.

- *3 o'clock*: This is the slowdown's end and the beginning of the *recession*. A correction in the equity market is likely as the market realises that a recession has started and it is priced into equity prices. Slowing economic activity, still high interest rates, a fall in equity prices, negative sentiment and a drop in corporate profitability move the economy to a recession. Commodity prices fall.

- *4 o'clock*: Business confidence and consumer spending fall. Equities do not look attractive. Fixed income and cash are the popular asset classes. Cash is king. A flight to quality pushes government bond prices and gold higher. Safe haven currencies, such as the US dollar, Japanese yen and Swiss franc appreciate.

- *5 o'clock*: Poor economic conditions dampen merger and acquisition and IPO activities. Credit is tight and banks are reluctant to lend. Consumer confidence is at very low levels. Pessimism prevails. Weak demand for goods and services pushes corporate profitability down and results in profit downgrades. When the economy shrinks for two subsequent quarters it is officially in a recession. Fixed income and cash continue to outperform.

- *6 o'clock*: This is the bottom of the cycle. Fear drives investors out of risk assets (equities, commodities and high-yield bonds). Inflation slows, the demand for capital is low and interest rates begin to fall. Individuals and corporations focus on building their balance sheets by reducing leverage and debt (deleveraging). The labour market is under pressure and unemployment is high. Consumers are spending less. Government fiscal and monetary policies often come into play to provide a stimulus to the economy.

- *7 o'clock*: The *recovery* from the bottom of the recession begins with increased government spending and reductions in interest rates. Investors begin to invest again in equities as their valuations are attractive and falling interest rates support equities. Corporate bonds and high-yield are attractive as companies build their balance sheets and deleveraging reduces the supply of corporate and high-yield bonds.

- *8 o'clock*: During the recession, companies were forced to cut costs, lay off employees and become much more efficient. Company profit margins now improve as well as profitability. The economy is starting to grow. Equity prices rise and price-in the expected expansion. This is a good time to buy risk assets, such as equities and corporate bonds.

- *9 o'clock*: The economic cycle moves to the *expansion* stage. Unemployment falls. Commodity prices rise as the growing economic activity creates demand for commodities and inflation rises. Now that interest rates are not at high levels, financing real estate is attractive and real estate prices begin to rise again. This is a less favourable period for fixed income because of rising interest rates and inflation.

- *10 o'clock*: The growing economy and rises in risk asset prices lead to optimism. Many claim that "this time is different" and forget that the slowdown is around the corner. This is a stage in which bubbles are created. Investors may still make handsome gains from risk assets, but the inflection point is getting closer and it is always difficult to predict its exact timing.

- *11 o'clock*: The government spends on infrastructure, jobs are created and the economy is further stimulated as the demand from private sector businesses increases. More employees are hired to cope with the increased demand and required production levels. Low interest rates incentivise businesses to borrow to finance expansion. Wise investors forecast the inflection point that is coming due to the overheating economy, rising inflation, excess hiring and building of over capacity. The peak is nigh.

Global economic cycle

The economies of different countries and regions are interconnected and influenced by each other. The consumer in the United States is one of the most powerful global economic forces. China is the largest producer and exporter of goods. The level of consumption in the United States and Europe determines the level of demand for export-dependent Chinese production and consequently the economic growth of China.

The economic growth of industrial countries, such as China, the United States and Germany, sets the global demand for commodities. The economies of commodity-producing countries, such as global emerging markets, depend on the stage of the economic cycle of industrial countries. The prices of commodities affect inflation. Rising commodity prices may import inflation to commodity-importing countries, such as the United States.

The Federal Reserve fights inflation though increasing interest rates. Rising commodity prices, inflation and increasing interest rates are likely to push the economy into a slowdown and eventually a recession. Consequently, the US consumer is likely to consume less. US recession is likely to drag other countries into a recession since global demand for goods falls. Increasing globalisation has created a global village where local economies affect other local economies.

Countries and regions do, however, grow at different rates and can be at different stages of the economic cycle. Analysing the economies of different countries and regions and the interrelationships and influences among them enables TAA to reach decisions to overweight and underweight different asset classes in different countries around the world.

Economic scenarios versus a single view

Forecasting the long-term performance of markets with some accuracy is difficult, forecasting performance in the short term is even more difficult and forecasting performance precisely on any time scale is impossible.

An alternative methodology is admitting that it is impossible to forecast the performance of markets and instead establishing three or four likely economic scenarios and assigning a probability to each one. Normally, one scenario is a central view with the highest probability. A second is a pessimistic scenario and a third is an optimistic one. A fourth scenario is a possibility. The scenarios should be mutually exclusive and exhaustive. Risk scenarios can be included as well. These are low-probability, high-impact scenarios that may have a material adverse effect on portfolios. Hedges and insurance should be considered to protect against these scenarios.

Expected short-term returns for each asset class are established under each scenario and the expected returns of portfolios under each scenario are calculated. Portfolios should be constructed to perform reasonably well under each scenario and under the average weighted expected return of the different scenarios. Some scenarios are more supportive than others. Portfolios can include hedges or insurance to address scenarios under which their performance is unacceptably poor.

For example, if the main scenario supports investing in risk assets, such as equities, but the more pessimistic scenario expects negative returns on equities, TAA may include an allocation to long-term government bonds that should perform well under the pessimistic scenario and protect the portfolio. Purchasing a put option on equities is also a way to protect the portfolio. However, purchasing an option, or insurance, has a cost (premium) that reduces the portfolio's expected return.

One of the most effective hedges against market crashes is long volatility. Volatility shoots up when markets crash and long volatility makes money. When there is more uncertainty and risk in the market, the price of derivatives increases since they are used to both hedge and speculate. Since the other variables in the derivative pricing model remain fairly stable or adjust over time, implied volatility increases dramatically.

The VIX Index represents implied volatility of exchange traded options on the S&P 500 Index and its level increases at times of market stress. Investors can be long volatility by holding certain derivatives (e.g. call options or futures contracts on the VIX) or shares in portfolios that are long volatility.

Purchasing insurance may be expensive. The price of futures on the VIX is determined by its futures term structure. When current volatility is low, for example, volatility is expected to increase and the futures term structure is upward sloping. VIX futures may still be expensive even though current volatility is low. In addition, rolling the VIX futures adds another layer of costs to the protection strategy. The price of portfolio protection or insurance may cause the portfolio to bleed performance.

Portfolio insurance should also be dynamic. When equity markets fall and the VIX increases, it is expected to decrease quickly when markets stabilise. The VIX futures should be unwound to take profits near the peak of the VIX; otherwise, the profits will be wiped out when the VIX goes back down.

Portfolios should be stress tested under each scenario to assess the potential negative impact and to support decisions on protection, hedges and insurance. Protection costs money, either directly (e.g. premium on insurance) or indirectly (e.g. opportunity cost on a hedge or on holding high-quality, long-term government bonds). A risk/reward analysis should inform the decision making.

The advantages of using several economic scenarios include:

- *Addressing the uncertainty of forecasting.* Economic forecasting is difficult. The uncertainty may be addressed by developing a number of economic scenarios and weighting them by their probabilities.

- *Considering risks.* Alongside a central scenario, which would be the scenario with the highest probability, other scenarios highlight the risks and alternatives to the central scenario.

- *Building more robust portfolios.* The alternative scenarios should inform the portfolio construction process. The goal is to perform well under the central scenario, while ensuring a reasonable performance under the alternative scenarios. The objective of reasonable performance under the other scenarios may reduce the performance under the central scenario due to the costs associated with diversification, hedging and insurance. However, this may prevent a very disappointing result under the alternative scenarios and increase the probability of survival (or reduce the risk of ruin).

- *Focus on capital preservation.* Considering alternative scenarios, as well as more extreme risk scenarios, allows hedges to be implemented with the objective of preserving capital should the central scenario prove incorrect.

The main disadvantage of several scenarios is that when the probabilities assigned to the different scenarios are balanced and the scenarios cover a wide range of potential economic outcomes, it is unclear what the tactical view is. If investors need a single view on the direction of the economy to position portfolios, several scenarios with roughly equal probabilities and views covering all possible outcomes are not helpful.

Thematic investing

Portfolio managers sometimes include thematic investments in their portfolios. Thematic investing involves identifying certain social, economic, industrial, and demographic trends, or *themes*, that may ultimately contribute to the performance of portfolios by benefiting from these trends.

Some examples of themes include investing in companies that are involved in *clean water* production. Clean water is a scarce resource in many countries around the world and it may become even scarcer with time. Companies developing solutions for clean water may pay handsomely to their investors.

Investing in *agriculture* is another example, linked to the global trend of expanding population and depleting agriculture resources. The increasing awareness paid to the environment, global warming and depleting oil reserves should support companies that develop *renewable energy* sources. The continued *technological evolutions and revolutions* in areas such as the internet, electric cars and healthcare provide plenty of themes. Retiring *baby-boomers* is a trend supporting companies in the healthcare sector.

Modern emerging markets are another long-term theme. The economic evolution of emerging markets due to structural shifts including inflation targeting, willingness to accept some exchange rate volatility, fiscal conservatism, increasing flexibility in labour and capital markets, rising numbers of domestic consumers, demographic changes (such as urbanisation), growth of domestic savings and pensions, and infrastructure developments, has put emerging markets as a leading force behind global economic growth. Emerging markets account for over 60% of global economic growth, up from below 40% just over a decade ago. Most portfolios should have exposure to this theme through emerging market equity and debt, as well as potentially through private equity, infrastructure and hedge funds specialising in emerging markets.

Frontier markets are another theme focusing on markets that have not started to emerge yet, such as Africa.

While long term in nature, and hence not tactical, thematic investing is not part of the SAA and would be part of the TAA or MTAA process.

Price and value

The ultimate objective of investing is buying low and selling high. If markets are efficient then price equals intrinsic value and investors can only expect to generate returns in line with risks. There will be no superior returns. However, markets are not always efficient. When investors oversell due to fear (psychological effects) or are forced to sell (e.g. when they are hit by margin calls and must reduce risk positions), securities can be underpriced relative to their intrinsic value. This creates potential buying opportunities. When investors overbuy due to greed, creating bubbles, securities can be overpriced relative to fair value. This is the time to sell or to short. The question is how to determine the intrinsic value to assess whether markets are underpriced or overpriced.

One way to evaluate markets is to compare their yields to historic levels, combined with a forward-looking assessment on whether the yields reflect true risks and whether they are going to mean-revert to previous levels. Contrarian investing such as this is the key for superior returns. However, markets can stay over or under priced for long time periods and taking the contrarian view may result in prolonged disappointing returns.

Figure 15.12 shows the yield on and price of low investment grade high-yield bonds (CCC and below) in the United States. Yields have spiked during market crashes (2000 and 2008) and prices have initially suffered. However, when yields have reached the top and prices have reached the bottom it has been a buying opportunity. This is not straightforward. A rule of investing when yields are above

25%, for example, would have resulted in painful results in the early 2000s, but would have paid off in 2002 and 2008. Combining this rule with forward-looking assessment of the economic conditions and the health of corporate balance sheets could have been beneficial.

Figure 15.12 – price and yield of US junk bonds, December 1996 to June 2012

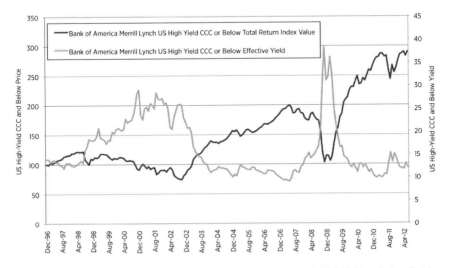

Source: Global Financial Data, Bank of America Merrill Lynch US High Yield CCC or Below Total Return, United States Real GDP in 2005 Dollars Effective Yield.

Figure 15.13 shows the yield and price of 10-year Italian government bonds. The 2011 European sovereign debt crisis saw yields at 7%; a level not seen since 1997. While many investors considered the yield to be a sign of the potential forthcoming insolvency of the Italian sovereign, some investors have seen this as an investment opportunity supported by the belief that the European Union and its policy makers would do everything in their power to protect the union. Indeed, the Italian government has not defaulted on its debt (as of yet) and investors who bought Italian bonds at a bargain at the end of 2011 made a handsome profit.

Figure 15.13 – the price and yield of Italian government bonds, December 1996 to June 2012

Source: Global Financial Data, Italy 10-year Total Return Government Bond, Italy 10-year Government Bond Yield.

It is notoriously difficult to predict the future. It is even more difficult to consistently predict the future. However, the present provides plenty of information in the form of P/E ratios, government bond yields, credit spreads, yield curve slopes and so on. Reading correctly what this information is showing, together with forward-looking analysis, an understanding of market psychology and common sense can help identify investments that are attractively priced relative to other investments and historical levels.

Expectations

Over the short term what matters for investment performance is whether economic or corporate results are above or below expectations. The absolute returns matter less. The equity price of a corporation publishing handsome earnings, but earnings that are below expectations, may fall. The equity price of a corporation posting a net loss, but which is better than a larger expected loss, may rise. Absolute results have an impact over the long term, but over the short term the question is whether the results surprise on the upside or downside.

The Citigroup Economic Surprise Index[228], for example, shows how economic news is compared with market consensus expectations. As Figure 15.14 illustrates, when the news flow turns from positive to negative, the equity market is likely to fall.

Figure 15.14 – the surprise index and US equities, January 2003 to June 2012

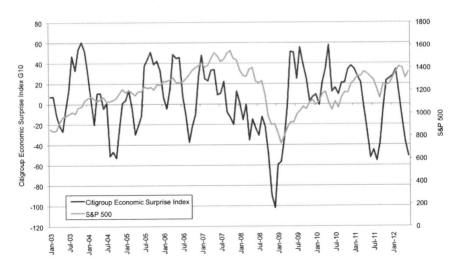

Source: Bloomberg, S&P 500, Citigroup Economic Surprise Index (G10).

Financial stress

An increasing number of tools are becoming available to help investors gauge market conditions. The Bank of America Merrill Lynch Global Financial Stress Index is a calculated, cross market measure of risk, hedging demand and investor flows in the global financial system. Levels greater (lower) than zero indicate more (less) financial market stress than normal.

The index is a weighted average of three sub-indices: the Risk Index, which measures market, solvency and liquidity risk; the Flow Index, which measures asset price momentum of equities, bonds and money markets calculated using investor flows and volumes; and the Skew Index, which measures relative demand for protection against large swings in major global equities and currencies. This index should not be relied upon solely to make investment decisions. However, it is another tool to be used alongside others to support decisions.

As Figure 15.15 illustrates, financial stress reached extreme highs during the 2008 credit crunch and financial crisis as well as during the 2011 European sovereign debt crisis. When financial stress is high, normal economic forces may give way to other forces, such as politics.

Figure 15.15 – Stress Index and US equities, January 2000 to June 2012

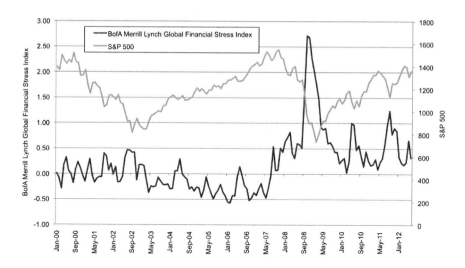

Source: Bloomberg, S&P 500, BofA Merrill Lynch Global Financial Stress Index.

Summary

- Fundamental analysis aims to identify relative value opportunities across markets and asset classes using economic research.

- Different asset classes are expected to perform well or poorly during different stages of the economic cycle. The four stages of the economic cycle are expansion, slowdown, recession and recovery. The challenge is identifying the current stage, the next stage and the inflection points between stages.

- Several economic scenarios, instead of a single view, can be helpful in admitting the difficulty in predicting markets, helping to position portfolios to perform reasonably well under different scenarios and supporting decisions to hedge or insure portfolios to different negative potential outcomes. However, when a single view is needed to position portfolios, several scenarios with roughly equal probabilities and views covering all possible outcomes are not helpful.

- The objective of thematic investing is to benefit from investments that are linked to long-term social, economic, industrial and demographic trends.

When the SAA and TAA are determined, the top-down asset allocation process is completed. SAA and TAA together set the portfolio asset allocation. SAA is the long-term investment policy and TAA adjusts it to short-term considerations.

The process is dynamic and asset allocation should be reviewed regularly. TAA should be altered as and when it is required because of its short investment horizon and objective of quickly capitalising on opportunities and addressing risks. SAA should be reviewed and altered less frequently than TAA due to its long-term investment horizon.

Once the asset allocation is finalised, the next step is to identify the appropriate investments to populate the portfolio, gaining access and exposures to each asset class, as well as aiming to benefit from the potential alpha from investment and security selection. While alpha is not a must, one of the objectives of investing is to try to generate alpha, or to beat the market.

The next sections depart from the top-down asset allocation and shift to the bottom-up investment selection.

16. INVESTMENT SELECTION

Once the asset allocation is decided, the next step in the multi-asset investment management process is selecting investments within each asset class. For example, according to the SAA a portfolio should invest, say, 10% of its assets in US equities, while their benchmark is the S&P 500 Index. The investor can select from:

- Individual constituency stocks of the S&P 500 (e.g. Apple, Exxon Mobil, Microsoft, IBM and so on)

- Off-benchmark US stocks

- ETFs or passive funds tracking the S&P 500 Index

- Actively-managed funds aiming to outperform the S&P 500 Index

- A combination of funds benchmarked against the Russell 1000 Value Index and Russell 1000 Growth Index

- A fund benchmarked against the Russell 3000 Index

- A long futures contract on the S&P 500 Index

- A segregated portfolio managed by a portfolio manager picking stocks

- A combination of some or all of these.

Clearly, there are ample choices. The question that investment selection aims to answer is how to choose from among all these different options.

Investment selection must be linked to the investment strategy. CMAs for SAA are normally derived from historic returns of passive indices, each representing an asset class. The assumption is that the investments under each asset class either have similar return and risk characteristics to those of the passive index used for deriving CMAs, or any difference is understood and considered. Otherwise, the portfolio may have a materially different risk and return profile than that of the investment strategy. The risk is that the portfolio may behave differently than expected as per the investment strategy, which matches the investment objectives. Careful investment selection is necessary to keep the link between the portfolio and the investment objectives.

Actively-managed investments are expected to perform differently (hopefully better) than passive indices. Portfolios using active investments should behave differently than the asset allocation, which allocates to passive indices, otherwise the portfolios are not active. Active investments introduce active risk and the potential for alpha. The portfolio's total active risk should be monitored and controlled so the portfolio's drift from investment strategy is limited. Active risk from security selection can dynamically change through investment selection (e.g. active and passive split).

The flip side of risk is return. Investment selection generates returns. It can generate positive or negative results. While asset allocation is important, investment selection can easily tip the scale between a successful and unsuccessful portfolio. Investment selection directly impacts costs, fees and taxes (the limiting of which is one way to achieve investment risk-free returns). Investors should focus on investment selection as much as they do on asset allocation. Investment selection requires hard work, unless passive investments are used. To gain alpha from security selection a material investment in investment selection is needed. Many famous investors, such as Benjamin Graham[229], Philip Fisher and Warren Buffet, suggest this.

There are numerous choices of different types of investments, ranging from individual securities, through passive index tracking and actively-managed portfolios, to derivatives and structured products. Each investment type is suitable for different circumstances, portfolios and investors. Each has advantages and disadvantages. Each has risks and potential rewards. Investors must understand the choices and make informed investment decisions supported by a philosophy and a process that enable them to reach conclusions that fit their investment objectives.

The assumption of this book is that multi-asset investors do not select individual securities. This is delegated to single asset class portfolio managers or collective investment schemes (CIS) or funds. Multi-asset investors are responsible for selecting managed investments[230], manager selection and portfolio construction, ensuring that all the investment choices fit together across different asset classes. Multi-asset investors must make decisions such as splitting active and passive investments, allocating among different investment styles, selecting appropriate investment vehicles (e.g. segregated portfolios or CIS) and whether to use structured products or derivatives. They must ensure that all the investments across the portfolio make sense together and the portfolio of investments is in line with its objectives.

The size and complexity of the multi-asset portfolio determines the range of choices. Simple and relatively small portfolios typically use CIS (i.e. fund of funds), while relatively large portfolios typically use a combination of different investment vehicles. As in many other areas in investments, size does matter and being big is usually an advantage. Size means that portfolios can tap segregated mandates, which are typically less expensive than CIS and customisable, lower fees can be negotiated (due to bargaining power) and transaction costs can be pushed down (due to economies of scale). Large portfolios can use derivatives more flexibly, all else being equal. If the portfolio is too big, however, it may mean that it is cumbersome.

Investment selection is as challenging as security selection. Generating consistent positive net of fees alpha from security selection is difficult and requires skill. Consistently selecting investments that add value requires as much skill as security selection does. The skill set is different, however. Investors who do not have skill would be better off selecting passive investments (although selecting passive investments also requires knowledge and due diligence).

Multi-asset investors need to understand all the asset classes in their portfolios to select investments within each asset class. Multi-asset investors do not need to be experts in each asset class since security selection should be sub-delegated to experts. No individual or firm is good at everything and the available best in class should be employed. This raises the dilemma of using a single or a multi-manager approach, each with its advantages and disadvantages.

Portfolio construction involves the coordination of investment selection across the asset classes in the portfolio. Multi-asset investors, who are responsible for portfolio construction, should have a holistic view of the entire portfolio. With the investment objectives in mind and with an understanding of the interrelationships across different investments, multi-asset investors guide the investment selection within each asset class to ensure that it makes sense across asset classes.

Summary

- Investments should have similar characteristics to those of the indices used to proxy asset classes in SAA. Otherwise, the portfolio may be misaligned with SAA and the investment objectives.

- Active investments are expected to perform differently than passive indices. The total divergence from SAA indices (active risk) should be monitored and controlled.

- Multi-asset investors decide on the split between active and passive investments, allocation among different investment styles, type of investment vehicles, and how derivatives and structured products will be used to control the return and risk profile of multi-asset portfolios.

- While asset allocation determines the majority of the portfolio's long-term risk level, the success of investment selection can drive the portfolio's return level.

- Investment selection requires skill to consistently select investment managers that are consistently successful.

- Multi-asset investors need a broad understanding of all asset classes. Since no single person or firm can be an expert on everything, the security selection in each asset class should be delegated to single asset class experts.

- Portfolio construction coordinates investment selection across asset classes considering the entire portfolio's investment objectives and the interrelationships among investments within different asset classes and across asset classes.

17. INVESTMENT SELECTION PROCESS

Investment selection has three main objectives:

1. Identifying investments that match as closely as possible the desired exposures as per the asset allocation (beta)

2. Identifying investments that potentially add outperformance (alpha)

3. Evaluating whether investments are likely to meet their expected return and risk

Beta exposures align portfolios with their investment strategy so actual portfolios closely reflect the asset allocation, which reflects the investment objectives. Alpha adds to investment returns, either across asset classes (TAA) or within asset classes (investment selection). Finally, investments are like any other product; buyers need to ensure that what they buy fulfils their expectations. *Caveat emptor.*

Quantitative analysis

Investors often tend to rely on past performance to evaluate investments and portfolio managers, but investors who rely only on past performance risk not achieving their investment objectives. History is not a good predictor of future results. Nevertheless, past performance and quantitative analysis of past returns and risks are important factors for evaluating investments and usually a quant screen is the first step in the investment selection process.

Quantitative analysis considers not only past returns, but also risks and assets under management (AUM) with the aim of linking performance with these factors, as well as with market conditions. Calculating risk-adjusted performance better differentiates between performance that was generated by taking risk and performance that was generated by applying investment skill, such as security selection. AUM influences the ability to generate returns (e.g. low AUM may not allow proper diversification of portfolios and high AUM may not allow investing in all opportunities). The link with market conditions explains investments and portfolio managers' past behaviour (e.g. performance during bull and bear markets). Since risk-adjusted performance measures can be manipulated, qualitative judgment and common sense are necessary to understand the nuances of reported numbers.

Quantitative analysis of Fidelity Magellan

Fidelity Magellan is one of the best known active funds. Its portfolio manager between May 1997 and May 1990 was Peter Lynch. Lynch has had phenomenal relative returns by following his particular investment style that is based on the principle of "invest money in what you know". Lynch invested in areas that he understood well and followed common sense and intuition[231]. The fund's historic returns and those of its benchmark, the S&P 500 Index, are a good example for illustrating quantitative analysis.

Figure 17.1 shows the cumulative performance of Fidelity Magellan and the S&P 500 Index from June 1963 to June 2012. Remarkably, the fund has outperformed its benchmark since inception. However, it seems that the pace of outperformance has plateaued, or started to decline, since the early 1990s. The relative performance, or alpha, of the fund since the beginning of the 1990s requires a closer inspection.

Figure 17.1 – cumulative performance of Fidelity Magellan and the S&P 500 Index, June 1963 to June 2012

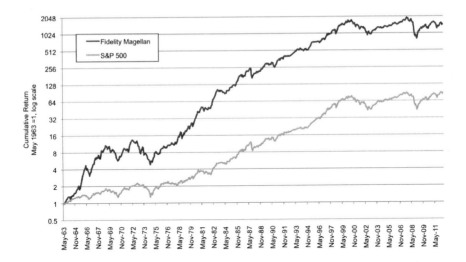

Source: Bloomberg, Fidelity Magellan, S&P 500.

Figure 17.2 shows the cumulative relative performance of the fund since January 1990. Outperformance has turned into underperformance since the beginning of 2004.

Figure 17.2 – cumulative outperformance of Fidelity Magellan, January 1990 to June 2012

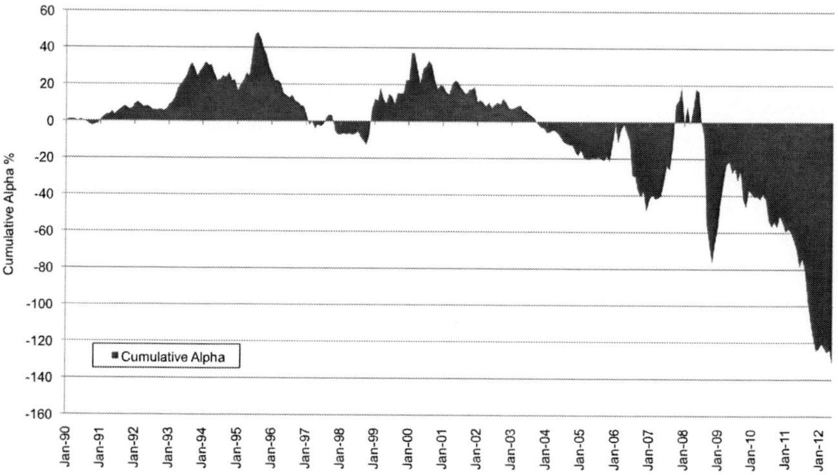

Source: Bloomberg, Fidelity Magellan, S&P 500.

Table 17.1 shows the performance analytics of Fidelity Magellan from June 1963 to June 2012 and from January 2000 to June 2012. The contrast between the analytics over the entire period and over the last 12 years is astonishing. Something has gone wrong.

Table 17.1 – Fidelity Magellan performance analytics, June 1963 to June 2012

Fidelity Magellan Performance Analytics	Jun. 1963 to Jun. 2012		Jan. 2000 to Jun. 2012	
	Fund	**Benchmark**	**Fund**	**Benchmark**
Performance % pa	16.0	9.5	-0.3	0.3
Volatility %	21.7	15.1	18.9	16.2
Sharpe Ratio	0.49	0.28	-0.04	-0.01
Excess Return % pa	6.5	-	-0.6	-
Tracking Error % pa	12.3	-	5.6	-
Information Ratio	0.53	-	-0.10	-
Up-Market Capture[232]	5,317.48	-	120.57	-
Down-Market Capture	100.03	-	102.81	-

Source: Bloomberg, Fidelity Magellan, S&P 500.

Figure 17.3 shows the rolling 36-month annualised tracking error and volatility of the fund and its benchmark. Figure 17.4 shows the rolling beta and correlation with respect of the benchmark. The different shades of the charts' background represent the tenure of the fund's different portfolio managers.

Figure 17.3 – rolling 36-month annualised tracking error and volatility, June 1963 to June 2012

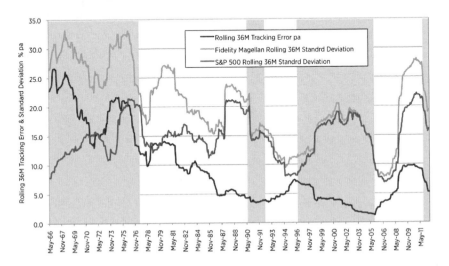

Source: Bloomberg, Fidelity Magellan, S&P 500.

Figure 17.4 – rolling 36-month beta and correlation with respect of the S&P 500 Index, June 1963 to June 2012

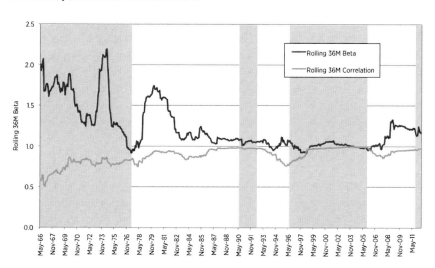

Source: Bloomberg, Fidelity Magellan, S&P 500.

One of the stories of Fidelity Magellan is the different styles of its different portfolio managers. Edward Johnson III managed the fund from its inception in 1963 to May 1977, when Peter Lynch assumed management for the next 13 years. Lynch assumed management of a $20 million fund and left it with AUM of $14 billion. When Lynch stepped down, leaving behind him a legacy, Morris J. Smith managed the fund for two years until July 1992 when, as a practicing Jew, he decided to leave Fidelity for Israel. Each of these portfolio managers was truly active, as indicated by the beta and tracking error, and outperformed. Skilfully taking active risk paid off.

Following Smith, Jeffery N. Vinik took the helm from July 1992 until June 1996. While Vinik's relative performance was not bad in the first few years, he decided to de-risk the fund in 1995, sold technology stocks and purchased bonds due to concerns about a fall in technology stocks. This concern was premature and the fund's relative performance suffered as equities continued to rally.

Robert E. Stansky replaced Vinik in June 1996 and managed the fund until October 2005. As can be seen from the rolling tracking error, he took less and less active risk and closely tracked the benchmark. The term *closet indexer* was used to describe his style. Under Stansky AUM of $100 billion in 2000 fell to $52 billion when he was replaced by Harry W. Lange, who managed the fund until September 2011. Lange's relative performance was disappointing as he underperformed by -2.9% per annum. In September 2011 Lange was replaced by Jeffery F. Feingold.

Figure 17.5 summarises the absolute and relative performance under each manager.

Figure 17.5 – Fidelity Magellan absolute and relative performance under its different portfolio managers, June 1963 to June 2012

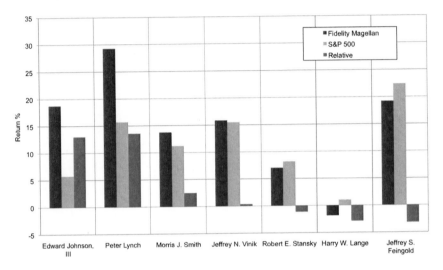

Source: Bloomberg, Fidelity Magellan, S&P 500.

The quantitative analysis shows the different investment styles of the fund's different managers, it shows how performance and risk evolved over time and it shows that nothing lasts forever.

While Lynch was undoubtedly one of the most successful portfolio managers in history, no one can answer the question of how his performance would have been over the last decade. Would he have been able to avoid the pitfall of the technology bubble and the devastating credit crunch? Would he have been able to outperform if managing a behemoth fund of $100 billion? Performance is always a function of skill and luck. A skilful person with luck is a winning combination (better be lucky than smart).

Qualitative analysis

Since quantitative analysis is backward looking and in some cases past performance is unavailable for new investments lacking a track record, investors should seek other matrices for investment evaluation. Combining quantitative and qualitative due diligence for evaluating investments provides a forward-looking element. It is the key to identifying investments that fit the overall portfolio and have a higher probability of success in the future.

Qualitative analysis looks at factors beyond past performance – it informs the evaluator whether investments and portfolio managers are likely to repeat past results going forward. Like many other investment management activities, even an in-depth, thorough and comprehensive analysis is no guarantee for success in selecting investments that will deliver superior results. However, it should increase the probability of success.

Qualitative analysis demands resources. While it is relatively easy to crunch the numbers of past performance, it is more labour intensive to review investments' qualitative aspects. This requires going through materials and factsheets, reading contracts and small print, meeting portfolio managers and considering many different factors. Investors need to be willing to undertake investment selection and be capable of doing so.

Investment evaluation is a dynamic, ongoing process. While the initial evaluation supports the decision of whether to invest, ongoing due diligence is required to support the decision of whether to keep holding investments. Like most other processes in investment management, investment selection needs to be kept up-to-date according to developments.

When investments are made an exit strategy should be formulated. Investors need to know under which circumstances investments are to be sold. A selling price should be agreed such that investments are sold and profits are taken. Investors should limit their greediness and should not risk losing paper or unrealised profits due to falling prices. Selling discipline is critical. It is imperative not to fall in love with investments and not keep holding them without sound forward-looking merits.

Factors to consider in investment selection

When evaluating any investment, investors should consider seven broad categories:

1. Investment profile

2. Risks

3. Liquidity

4. Correlations

5. Legal structure

6. Commercials

7. Product characteristics

This framework ensures that all important factors are considered.

1. Investment profile

Investment profile considers the return and risk profile of investments. It answers the questions of what returns the investment is likely to generate and what investment risk is attached. The potential return and risk profile depends on the asset class to which the investment belongs, the style, sector or segment within the asset class, the investment universe (i.e. permitted securities and instruments that the investment may include) and the investment techniques that the investment may utilise (e.g. long-only, short-selling, derivatives, leverage).

Investments restricted to long-only securities are likely to have a clear, plain-vanilla risk and return profile (mostly defined by a passive index benchmark and the relative risk to the index). Investments that use derivatives, such as options, may have a more complex profile. Investments that utilise leverage may magnify their returns and risks.

Some investments are complex and opaque. If investors cannot understand an investment, cannot identify its role in a portfolio and cannot model how it is going to affect the portfolio's risk and return profile then the investment should probably be avoided. Keeping it simple is sometimes the best strategy.

Actively-managed investments take a risk versus their benchmark. Active risk means that there is potential for outperformance and a risk of underperformance. Portfolio managers may go through long spells of underperformance. *Manager risk* is one of the risks with active management and investors should carefully consider it.

2. Risks

Considering risks should look beyond investment risks at other potential risks.

Operational risk encompasses a wide range of risks, such as system failures, human errors and human misconduct. Operational due diligence is a necessity in particular when evaluating unregulated, managed investments, such as hedge funds, or derivative-based investment products, such as structured products. Bernard Madoff[233] is only one example for the need for, and potential for failure of, operational due diligence. The operational capabilities of portfolio managers should be evaluated, including risk management processes and capabilities.

Counterparty risk is the risk to each party of a contract that the other party will not fulfil the contractual obligations. Many investments, such as certain Exchange Traded Funds (ETFs), use a basket of derivatives, such as swaps, to gain exposure to the desired investments. Investors in a swap-based ETF (as opposed to a full replication ETF, which buys the securities in the index) are exposed to the counterparties of the swaps. ETF providers use different methods to minimise the counterparty risk, such as *collateralisation* of high-quality government bonds and cash to cover any liability, *overcollateralisation* (the value of the collateral is above the value of the liabilities) and diversification of the swaps across different counterparties. The type of the collateral is important. If the counterparty of the underlying swap defaults, the investor in the ETF will receive the collateral. The collateral may be unwanted securities (e.g. illiquid Italian government bonds). Investors therefore should ask for daily disclosure of the collateral.

Principal guaranteed structured products are normally issued by banks. Investors are exposed to the counterparty risk of the bank and its insolvency would mean that the principal is not guaranteed. Lehman Brothers used to issue principal protected products and it became insolvent in 2008; the word *guarantee* should always be taken with a pinch of salt.

Currency forward contracts have counterparty risk for the party who gained on the contract until its maturity since the profit and loss is settled only upon its maturity. One way to mitigate the counterparty risk is using short-dated contracts (one and three months) rather than long-dated ones. Another way is for the parties to agree to use a margin facility and place collateral with a third party on a daily basis for the profits and losses on the forward contract, similar to a futures contract.

Basis risk is the risk of a difference in performance between investments and the underlying index that they track or between derivatives and their underlying. For example, a futures contract on the FTSE 100 Index has a basis risk if the benchmark for UK equities within a multi-asset portfolio is the FTSE All Share Index. This risk arises due to a mismatch between the indices that were used for SAA and/or the composite benchmark of the multi-asset portfolio and the investments within the portfolio. When passive index trackers or futures contracts are evaluated the replication strategy of the trackers should be assessed as well as the tracking error of the trackers or futures contracts with the underlying index.

Another example is when fixed income is represented by government bonds within the multi-asset portfolio composite benchmark while all the available fixed income investments invest in corporate bonds. Investors take unwanted credit risk relative to the benchmark. Over long time periods this may add value due to the credit risk premium. However, during periods of market stress, such as the 2008 credit crunch, credit has massively underperformed government bonds (credit has bounced back and investors who kept holding their credit exposure saw their portfolios recouping loses).

Activities such as *security lending* can reduce the TER of passive investments and improve performance due to a source of revenue for the investment providers, who use some of the revenue to enhance returns. However, there are risks involved in security lending. The investment providers lend securities and should receive and hold collateral in exchange. In case of borrower's insolvency, the collateral should be sufficient to compensate investors for the loss of the lent securities. However, if the value of the collateral is insufficient, investors may suffer a loss.

Different investments have different levels of *transparency*. Some investments disclose their investment techniques and all their holdings. Other investments are like a black box. Investors must feel comfortable before investing in opaque investments since their risks are difficult to assess and the investors need to trust the investment managers.

Some products utilise investment strategies that have limited *capacity*. Capacity constraints are common in investments that have liquidity constraints, such as some hedge fund strategies, portfolios that invest in small capitalisation stocks, and some fixed income strategies such as corporate bonds whose liquidity is unstable. Investments that are beyond their capacity or nearing it may have suboptimal returns or are likely to close to new investments.

3. Liquidity

Liquidity is a combination of the time it takes to sell investments and the cost of selling them. When purchasing investments, investors need to think about whether it will be possible to readily sell them.

Large capitalisation stocks and government bonds of certain countries are among the most liquid investments and normally can be sold quickly without incurring material trading costs. Corporate bonds and small capitalisation emerging market stocks are less liquid. During times of low volume it may be difficult to sell them. Real estate, private equity and certain hedge fund strategies may be very illiquid, selling those takes time and may result in a capital loss due to selling costs (e.g. high transaction costs, exit charges or redemption penalties). Before investing in real estate, for example, investors need to think a few years ahead to ensure that they will be happy with the position since it may be difficult to reduce it.

Some investments may have *lock-in periods,* preventing them from being sold until the expiry of the period, unless penalties are paid. During the 2008 credit crunch some hedge funds had to refuse redemptions and investors could not sell their holdings. In the case of structured products that guarantee principal repayment at maturity investors may lose the guarantee if the product is sold before its maturity. Investments that are not regularly traded on an exchange, such as structured products (excluding Exchange Traded Notes, ETNs, which are exchange traded), do not have an organised secondary market[234] and selling them depends on finding a willing buyer or by going through the product provider if it provides a limited secondary market (e.g. banks that offer structured products typically offer a limited secondary market).

Some investments offer perceived liquidity. Closed-end funds that invest in illiquid securities, such as real estate, may offer daily liquidity. However, due to the illiquid nature of the underlying investments they may trade at a material premium or discount relative to Net Asset Value (NAV), driven by the supply and demand of their shares. This introduces high price volatility as well as a risk of large swings in prices. When investors wish to sell their shares, the share price may swing to a discount. Investing in illiquid investments through a closed-end fund does not create true liquidity.

4. Correlation

Correlation considers the interaction of investments with other investments. Each investment should be considered in portfolio context as part of portfolio construction. Correlations are sometimes difficult to determine, in particular when investments do not have a track record, when returns are not a true reflection of performance (e.g. appraisal based returns) or when the track record is unreliable. Past correlations may have no predictive power since correlations tend to change and structural changes in markets and investments may mean that past behaviour will not be repeated.

When active investments are blended together investors can assess the *correlation of excess returns* as part of the portfolio construction. Different active investments perform differently under different market conditions. Blending alphas that have a low correlation may reduce active risk and deliver smoother returns.

5. Legal structure

The legal structure of investments or the type of vehicles has implications on costs, fees, flexibility, taxes, governance, liquidity and so on. Characteristics that must be considered are whether it is a segregated account or a collective investment scheme, open-end or closed-end fund, and a public or private vehicle. Each legal structure has advantages and disadvantages.

In particular when evaluating private and unregulated investments (in contrast to publicly traded and regulated investments), investors must pay special attention to the transaction's legal aspects and its legal risk. When investment providers are well-established, regulated firms their legal risk is lower (although Lehman Brothers, for example, was a well-established, regulated bank). Investors should go through the legal terms of transactions, in particular private placements, with the help of a legal professional.

Investments within multi-asset portfolios must be eligible. *Eligibility* is determined by the legal structure of the multi-asset portfolio (e.g. a UCITS complaint portfolio has restrictions on eligible investments) and investment constraints. Current laws and regulations, the prospectus and/or the Investment Management Agreement (IMA) of multi-asset portfolios should list the restrictions on investments. Purchasing ineligible investments may result in a breach of regulations (regulatory breach), the prospectus and/or the IMA. Confirming eligibility before the transaction (pre-trade compliance) ensures that portfolios are in line with the investment constraints and avoids compliance issues post-trade.

Some investments are heavily regulated while others are lightly so (e.g. hedge funds). *Regulatory oversight* provides another layer of confidence to investors, but may limit investment flexibility.

6. Commercials

Commercials consider the fees and costs of investments. *Total Expense Ratio* (TER) covers some costs and fees of investments, such as the AMC (*Annual Management Charge*), but may exclude other costs, such as transaction costs. Investors must confirm which costs are covered by the TER and ask for estimates for excluded costs. Rebates may be negotiated to pay back some of the TER on investments. Tax implications should also be considered as part of commercials.

7. Product characteristics

The category of product characteristics is broad and includes factors such as minimum investment requirements and valuation or pricing frequency. Minimum investment has a material impact on small portfolios since either they will not be able to meet the minimum requirement or the investment will make up a large proportion of the portfolio (i.e. concentration risk). Valuation or pricing frequency may have an impact on portfolios that require a certain reporting frequency. Portfolios that need daily pricing typically cannot invest in assets that are not priced on a daily basis.

Turnover[235] measures how frequently securities within a portfolio are bought and sold. Turnover should be considered before purchasing investments since high turnover incurs higher transaction costs and potentially higher taxes than low turnover. Active investments are expected to have higher turnover than passive investments due to more active trading.

Manager selection

The investment selection and manager selection processes share some similar principles. Both aim to consider all aspects for selecting investments. While the investment selection process focuses on the characteristics of the investment or product, the manager selection process focuses on the evaluation of the investment manager. As Bill Gross, the founder of PIMCO[236], put it "finding the best person or the best organization to invest your money is one of the most important financial decisions you'll ever make". Investment selection and manager selection should be combined when evaluating *managed investments* (i.e. investments managed by professional managers).

Active managers need to outperform a benchmark. That is the reason that they are paid fees and the burden of proof is on them to justify the fees. The default is using passive, cost-efficient investments. On average, managers underperform their benchmarks after fees[237]. Beating the benchmark has become even more difficult as more active managers joined the game. As Charles Ellis wrote back in 1975[238] "gifted, determined, ambitious professionals have come into investment management in such large numbers during the past 30 years that it may no longer be feasible for any of them to profit from the errors of all the others sufficiently often and by sufficient magnitude to beat the market averages".

Managers need to generate enough outperformance or alpha to cover the fees and beat the benchmark. For example, a retail fund may have a TER of 1.0% per annum. If the net outperformance target for the active manager is 2.0%, the total return target above benchmark is 3.0% gross of fees. Is there a manager who can consistently beat the benchmark by 3.0% per annum? An amount of $100 discounted by 3.0% per annum over 10 years is $74.4[239]. The reverse is true for the next 10 years, such that active managers need to outperform the benchmark by 25.6% over the next decade to generate 3.0% per annum. The manager thus needs to be very skilled and consistent.

Peter Lynch and Warren Buffett are legendary investors with a multi-year benchmark beating track record. How many Peters and Warrens are out there? Not many. The trick is selecting active managers who have a good time period ahead when they are selected – manager selection is all about selecting managers who are going to outperform, just as security selection is all about selecting securities that are going to outperform an index.

Equity and fixed income valuation techniques, such as discounting future expected cash flows to derive the present value or using ratios like P/E, do not apply to valuation of managed investments and managers. Manager selection requires a different set of tools since it is about selecting people and not securities. The aim is identifying skilled *people* who have the right *philosophy* and *process* with the necessary resources to be able to meet certain investment objectives. Psychology and assessment of human character and talent are important factors in selecting managers.

Comparing managers to their peers may be misleading since industry peer groups are poorly policed, the comparison is often not like with like, and style drifts and size effects, for example, are often not considered. The performance of a manager should be evaluated against appropriate passive benchmarks that follow the same style as that which the manager has employed. If the benchmark is inappropriate, relative performance may be misleading since it may be driven by the manager's style relative to the market, and not by the manager's investment decisions. For example, the performance of a US equity value manager whose performance is compared to the S&P 500 Index may look good or bad when value outperforms or underperforms the general market. This has nothing to do with the manager's security selection skills but rather is due to whether the investment style is in or out of favour.

For portfolios mixing a number of styles, custom benchmarks can be created once the proportion of the different styles is identified. The comparison to a passive index can be complemented by peer group analysis. Often, managers do not beat a passive benchmark and the best approach may be to select the best performers out of a peer group.

Quantitative and style analysis

A manager selection process should use both quantitative and qualitative analysis. This provides both historical and forward-looking perspectives.

The universe of managers that are considered should be as broad as possible. A *quantitative screen* is often used to reduce the number of managers to a manageable long-list based on past performance, assets under management (AUM), style and risk analysis. The quantitative screen can eliminate managers with underperformance over certain time periods (e.g. three and five years, or two out of the last five calendar years), below acceptable minimum AUM (investors normally do not want to hold a large stake in funds and a small AUM may mean that the fund does not have enough assets for diversification and accessing all investments), style mismatch and/or unacceptable risk levels or risk-adjusted performance results.

Style analysis can help independently determine the style of portfolios and verify that managers maintain their style and do not deviate from it (referred to as *style drift*). If a manager's style is not clear there are two approaches for determining it: return-based style analysis and holding-based style analysis.

Return-based style analysis

In *return-based style analysis* (RBSA) a multi-factor model is used to regress the manager's returns with respect of different indices or factors to assess the investment style, as proposed by William Sharpe[240]. RBSA draws from Sharpe's style analysis model, which stipulates that a manager's investment style can be determined by comparing the portfolio's returns with those of a certain number of selected indices. Sharpe is quoted to justify his methodology "if it acts like a duck, assume it's a duck".

RBSA is a statistical technique that identifies what combination of long positions in passive indices would have most closely replicated the actual performance of a portfolio over a specified time period. As managers rarely have a pure style, RBSA finds the combination of style indices that best fit (highest R^2) the portfolio returns. R^2 measures the proportion of variance explained by the model and gives the goodness of fit between portfolio returns and the returns of the style indices. The success of this technique relies heavily on the correct specification of the style indices used in the regression. They must correspond to the portfolio's investment universe and must allow a complete description of the portfolio style. The major advantage of this method is that it is not necessary to know the portfolio's holdings (securities that make up the portfolio and their proportions).

Using Fidelity Magellan as an example, Figure 17.6 shows the results of regressing the 36 monthly returns of the fund with respect of Russell 1000 Value, Russell 1000 Growth, Russell 2000 Value and Russell 2000 Growth indices and rolling the regression to see how the fund's style (value and growth) and size (1000 and 2000) exposures change over time. As expected, a fund with a bias to small cap under the leadership of its first portfolio managers (Edward Johnson III and Peter Lynch) has changed its style to large caps as the fund got closer to its benchmark, the S&P 500 Index.

Figure 17.6 – Fidelity Magellan rolling 36-month regression, January 1979 to June 2012

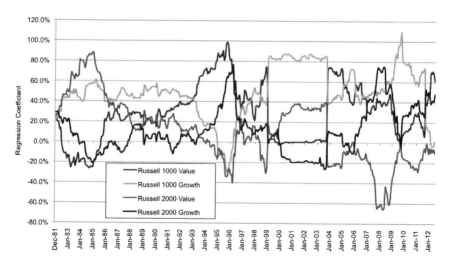

Source: Bloomberg, Fidelity Magellan, Russell 1000 Value, Russell 1000 Growth, Russell 2000 Value, Russell 2000 Growth.

Figure 17.7 shows a limited RBSA using only the four Russell equity indices, US 10-year Treasuries and Treasury Bills. The regression coefficients are constrained to be positive and sum to 100%. The de-risking of the fund as Vinik purchased bonds and sold technology stocks in 1995 is evident as Treasuries and cash explain some of its returns.

Figure 17.7 – Fidelity Magellan return based style analysis, January 1979 to June 2012

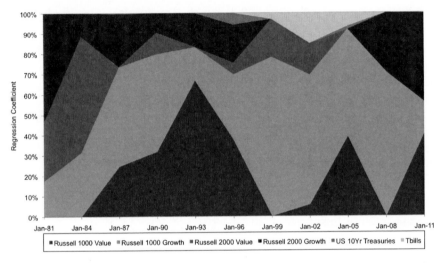

Source: Bloomberg, Fidelity Magellan, Russell 1000 Value, Russell 1000 Growth, Russell 2000 Value, Russell 2000 Growth, USA 10-year Government Bond Total Return, USA Total Return T-Bill.

Figure 17.8 shows regressions of the fund returns on the four Russell indices. The multiple regression uses 36 monthly returns once every 36 months. The results of the regression are translated to style and size scores[241] and are shown on the growth/value large/small cap quarters, representing large cap growth, large cap value, small cap growth and small cap value. The *snail trail* shows how the fund's style and size have changed significantly over time (style drift). All that is needed to conduct RBSA is the portfolio and indices' monthly returns and Microsoft Excel.

Figure 17.8 – Fidelity Magellan style and size snail trail, June 1963 to June 2012

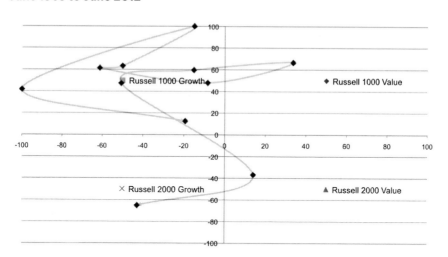

Source: Bloomberg, Fidelity Magellan, Russell 1000 Value, Russell 1000 Growth, Russell 2000 Value, Russell 2000 Growth.

Holding-based style analysis

Holding-based style analysis is a bottom-up approach in which the characteristics of portfolios are derived from the characteristics of the securities that they hold. Holding-based style analysis requires a database with all the securities in the investment universe and their characteristics as well as the holdings in the portfolio. There are a number of off-the-shelf applications[242] that perform holding-based style analysis.

Holding-based style analysis can be used for portfolio construction. When combining more than one sub-portfolio under each asset class, holding-based style analysis can aggregate all the sub-portfolios and show the overall style of the combined portfolio. This allows for controlling risks and exposures of the combination of a number of portfolio managers or sub-portfolios. For example, if all managers are overweight in the same security or a sector, holding-based style analysis can pick this up and investors can decide whether this exposure is desirable. Portfolio construction with the support of holding-based style analysis can combine a core manager with satellite managers to ensure that the managers' styles are complementary and do not overlap. This prevents all the managers' alphas being diversified away or holding all the securities in the benchmark, the result of which would just be an expensive tracker.

An alternative way to determine a manager's style without return or holding-based style analysis is to regress the portfolio's returns against a set of different style indices, each time with a single index. The style of the index with which the portfolio has the highest R^2 indicates the manager's style. This method requires only Microsoft Excel and monthly past returns. The advantage of RBSA over this method is that RBSA identifies the combination of style indices with which the portfolio has the highest R^2 and so it is not restricted to a single style.

Due diligence process

Once the quantitative screen and style analyses are complete, the long-list should be reduced to a short-list of managers who meet the criteria of the manager search. The next step is evaluating the managers using a *qualitative process*. The short-list should be reasonably short (four to eight managers) since from here on the process is labour intensive.

The focus of the qualitative process is on the ability of each manager to add value going forward. The people who are going to manage the portfolio and their personalities should be evaluated. Stable people, with a clear philosophy and a solid skill-based process should give confidence that past performance can be repeated.

Past performance is required to prove that managers know what to do. However, past performance is no guarantee of future results and extrapolating past performance should be avoided. Nevertheless, performance is a key part of the manager evaluation and it should tie in with the other factors in the process. The objective is to distinguish between skill and luck. Skilled managers have a good explanation for the rationale or reasons behind each investment decision. Even if managers missed the investment objectives, good reasons at the time when the investment decision was made can justify disappointing results. Lucky managers usually cannot explain the rationale for their investment decisions.

A due diligence or evaluation process for a manager should consider the following eight factors (eight Ps):

1. Platform

2. Progress

3. People

4. Product

5. Philosophy

6. Process

7. Portfolio

8. Performance

1. Platform

Platform focuses on the type of organisation offering the investment and employing the manager. This has a material impact on the manager's ability to add alpha. Managers should focus on meeting investment objectives and they should have the resources to do so.

One distinguishing factor between types of organisations is sell side versus buy side. *Sell side* (typically large investment banks) is the segment of the investment industry selling investment services to asset management firms; the *buy side* (including asset management firms, pension plans, insurance companies, sovereign wealth funds, endowments and foundations).

The buy side is mainly focused on buying investments (hence buy side), not selling them, although the buy side manages portfolios for clients and sells them as investment products. A Manager of Managers (MoM) or Fund of Funds (FoF) is often on the buy side, buying services from other buy side firms.

The sell side sells products to investors either directly or through the buy side. Most products from the sell side are rule-based (e.g. UCITS compliant, hedge fund replication), as opposed to discretionary. The sell side also provides wealth management services, which should be buy side and mostly based on advisory services to high-net-worth individuals. The buy side is accountable for the performance and risk of portfolios, normally uses discretion and should focus on achieving investment objectives. Each of these two types of organisations offers a wide array of services. The manager evaluator needs to decide which is better fitted to achieve the specific investment objectives.

The *size and reputation* of the organisation matter. Large, well established and regulated organisations should have a history and reputation of offering investments, as well as the resources to support and manage them. Unknown, small organisations should be subjected to enhanced scrutiny.

Large organisations often offer better infrastructure, operations and resources to support managers' investment decisions. Some organisations have a breadth of products and can afford to have central resources to support portfolio managers, such as central research, IT and operations. Operations are the backbone of portfolio management and organisations lacking appropriate operating capabilities may be incapable of delivering investment results.

The investment decision making process in large organisations is often committee driven and portfolio managers may lack flexibility to act quickly. Small boutiques often have more flexible decision making processes and a more entrepreneurial, innovative environment than larger, more mature organisations.

Stability of organisations affects the stability of managers. Stable organisations enable portfolio managers to focus more on managing portfolios and not on politics. Organisations in flux may distract portfolio managers, who may focus on organisational and business changes instead of on managing money. The balance between managing money and being involved in other activities at work is important.

The *client base* of organisations reveals a lot about them. Investors often do not wish to be the largest or sole investor in portfolios. If investors hold a material portion of a portfolio it may have implications on the investors' reporting requirements (e.g. some institutional investors holding more than a certain percentage of a portfolio must include it on their financial statements) and the liquidity of the portfolio (i.e. redeeming a large portion of a portfolio may be a costly, lengthy process and may have an adverse impact on its performance). A large and stable client base provides stability to organisations and portfolio managers may be less concerned about the future of their business and more focused on portfolio management. On the other hand, organisations with an established client base may not be as hungry to generate performance as are small, boutique organisations.

The *incentive structure* of managers affects the ability of organisations to retain them (*key person risk*). A partner in an organisation may be more incentivised than an employee. A well-compensated manager is more likely to be more productive, everything else being equal.

There are advantages and disadvantages to each type of organisation. The main question is whether the type of organisation supports the manager in adding value in line with the investment objectives.

2. Progress

Evaluating the present situation of organisations is assisted by evaluating the progress that they have made over the years. This is similar to assessing the current situation of a company by analysing its balance sheet and assessing its progress over time by analysing its profit and loss account.

Changes in ownership and organisational structure should be considered. For example, organisations that have undergone a merger or acquisition may be struggling to adapt to a new culture. This, and other organisational changes such as a round of redundancies, may be a sign that past results are not going to be repeatable.

The way that organisations have adapted to economic conditions and market changes indicates how they may adapt to change in the future. Some organisations have kept up with change by offering new products and services matching investors' demand while others have lagged, becoming stale. On the other hand, organisations that offer new products too frequently to meet passing fashions may end up too stretched to support all products and lose focus. Organisations must have a clear strategy, which means identifying their core competencies and focusing on them. Organisations that try to be good at everything may end up being not more than average at everything.

If the organisation has been growing, this may change its culture from mean and lean to cumbersome and slow. Some organisations tend to grow during good economic conditions and then shrink when the economy turns south. Hiring and firing employees en masse may be disruptive, although some hiring and firing ensures that new blood runs through the organisation.

Organisations having regulatory issues may have portfolio managers who have no respect for regulations and their focus on portfolio management may be distracted. Repeatable or serious regulatory issues are a red light.

Progress may be positive, with organisations progressing in the right direction, or negative, indicating that past success may not repeat itself. Platform and progress together provide insights to the current situation of the organisation, its history and its likely future direction.

3. People

Arguably, this is the most important factor to consider in manager evaluation. Investment management is all about the people making investment decisions. Even a quantitative, rule-based, black-box portfolio management style is only as good as the people who build the quant models.

The first thing to evaluate in a manager is personality and intelligence. The evaluator needs to look the manager in the eyes and decide whether the manager is a *mensch* (a person of integrity and honour; a good, moral human being) who can be entrusted with money. Unstable people may mean unstable money management.

The *stability* of the team is paramount. Large turnover in a team means that key decision makers do not stay and that there may be something wrong with the team or organisation. Perhaps team members are inadequately compensated or something else pushes people to leave the organisation, such as bad personal relationships or unethical behaviour. High turnover is a warning signal. Very low turnover, on the other hand, may mean that no fresh blood has been through the team and the decision-making process may be stale and archaic. The way that the team works together indicates whether there is a sharing of views and resources. Shared accountability distinguishes between a group, which just cooperates, and a team, which shares accountability. The team's history can indicate whether performance generated in the past is likely to be sustainable.

The compensation structure drives the incentives of team members. Asset-based or performance-based compensation structures have different motivations (i.e. accumulating assets or generating returns), AUM may affect compensation and incentives, and principle-agent issues should be considered. The evaluator is looking for alignment of interests between investment managers and investment objectives.

Key decision makers need to be identified. With only a single decision maker (star manager), a key person risk may be an issue. On the other hand, a final, accountable decision maker is necessary; otherwise investment decisions may turn into consensus decisions of a group or a committee. This may end up with low conviction portfolios, which are based on average views and unlikely to include any contrarian positions. A large team of decision makers usually tends to agree with common views. Carl Icahn said that "when most investors, including the pros, all agree on something, they're usually wrong".

The manager evaluator needs to trust the people, the manager and the investment management team to deliver. They must have skill and talent, or the probability of success is low.

4. Product

Product evaluation covers the characteristics that are related to the product or vehicle itself and are part of the investment selection process. The main characteristics are risks (operational), liquidity, legal structure, commercials and product characteristics.

Some investors require certain vehicle types for regulatory reasons. For example, in a fund of fund (FoF) structure the investing or parent fund (top level fund) may have restrictions on the type of underlying invested or child funds, such as restrictions of a UCITS vehicle on investing in other collective investment schemes (CIS)[243]. UCITS regulations also restrict eligibility of some investments such as direct property and physical commodities. Products investing in those investments cannot be used within a UCITS fund.

Investors may need vehicles to meet tax requirements. In the United Kingdom, off-shore products may need a *reporting status* to be tax efficient for individual investors. The domicile of products may have tax consequences (i.e. on-shore versus off-shore). Non-US persons may need to invest in vehicles that do not accept US persons as investors because of taxation.

The marketability of products can have an impact on their potential investment results. Products that are widely marketed to the retail market may have restricted investment and borrowing powers that products sold only to qualified, sophisticated or institutional investors (such as hedge funds) do not have[244]. It may be advantageous to invest in non-UCITS retail funds (NURS) whose investment powers are less restricted than those of UCITS schemes.

The fees of products are a major consideration. Different products have different fee structures. Lower fees mean higher net investment returns.

The fundamental principle of product evaluation is that the product must fit the requirements of the investor and/or the portfolio.

5. Philosophy

Philosophy is arguably the second most important factor after people in manager evaluation. Philosophy is the belief and vision of the manager on how value is going to be added and which investment strategy is going to outperform within a specific style. These are the fundamental principles that underpin the manager's investment activities with the goal of meeting the investment objectives.

Managers must have a game plan and they must be able to explain it, as well as the drivers for return and risks and the way *value is going to be added*. For example, a value manager believes in purchasing securities that are cheaply priced relative to their fair-value. A growth manager believes in purchasing securities with growth potential that is not included in their current price. Some managers believe that holding securities for the long term adds value, while others believe in short-term, high-frequency trading.

Most of the great investors share common elements in their philosophies about how to beat the market:

- *Be contrarian.* Buy when everyone is selling and sell when everyone is buying.

- *Focus on value.* Buy low and sell high is the fundamental principle of investing. The challenge is to know what is low and what is high.

- *Take a long investment horizon.* It is extremely difficult to predict price direction over the short term since a big chunk of it is noise. The long term is more predictable.

- *Invest in what you understand.* You are accountable for your investment decisions and you need to invest in what you understand.

- *Do your homework.* Average returns do not require a lot of work; just invest in an index. Superior returns require considerable work.

- *Understand the risks.* The secret for long-term superior returns is risk management. Those who survive market falls succeed in the long run.

- *Be dynamic.* Market and economic conditions change. Opportunities and risks come and go. To beat the market you have to be dynamic.

- *Control your emotions.* Behavioural finance is the enemy of the reasonable investor. Resist your behavioural instincts.

- *Learn from the markets.* The markets have many ways to provide information (e.g. dividend yields, bond yields, credit spreads). Listen to the market and learn from it.

- *Always be worried.* Complacency is the enemy of smart investing. Even when everything seems rosy the next crash is around the corner and you must be prepared for it. Ask yourself what can go wrong.

- *Be lucky.* This is not part of anyone's philosophy. I do not have the answer for how to be lucky. However, without luck there is no success.

6. Process

Process is the framework under which investment decisions are made. It is the roadmap and sequence of steps that are required to understand investment objectives, analyse market conditions, reach investment decisions, implement them and review the results. The process provides the structure that links the investment philosophy and strategy with the positions within the portfolio.

The process should be clear and understandable. An opaque process is unlikely to be understood and followed by all members of the investment team. The data sources available to inform the decision making process should be robust. The process should facilitate clear communications among the decision makers and researchers.

The critical point is that the process should be repeatable. A robust and disciplined process increases the probability of repeating past results even if there is a turnover in the investment management team. Sometimes it is more important to understand how investment decisions are reached than to assess the investment decisions themselves.

7. Portfolio

The current position of the portfolio, its portfolio construction and characteristics need to be consistent with its investment objectives and with the manager's philosophy and process. Otherwise, there is a risk of mismatch between the theoretical way that the portfolio should be managed and the practical way that it is managed. Portfolio evaluation asks whether everything comes together and how the manager's views are reflected in the portfolio.

The *risk management* process must be clear, robust and effective. Risk management is critical and investors must feel comfortable that the manager understands risk, can measure it and can manage it.

The *transparency* of managers is part of portfolio evaluation. The evaluator needs to understand the manager and the thought process; otherwise the evaluation may be incomplete. The evaluator cannot understand all the manager's activities, in particular when complex procedures are used (such as sophisticated quantitative models). The evaluator is normally not an expert in the area of the manager's expertise and this is the reason to hire the manager. Nevertheless, the intuition, philosophy and logic behind the manager's thought process and investment techniques should be shared openly by the manager.

8. Performance

The final element in the evaluation process is performance. This is the evaluation's quantitative element. Performance at this stage is different than the initial quantitative screen, since now the objective is to understand the manager's past behaviour during different market conditions. Past performance is not the most important factor in the evaluation. However, there are serious doubts whether a manager who has not been able to deliver performance in the past is going to do so in the future. Why trust someone who failed in the past to succeed in the future?

The main objective of the entire manager selection process is to ascertain whether past performance is repeatable. Performance should be representative and therefore performance over multiple time periods should be considered. Performance needs to be consistent with the manager's philosophy and process to confirm that they have been implemented in practice and have affected portfolio results.

Performance needs to be evaluated relative to portfolio risk. Risk-adjusted performance can reveal whether the manager has benefited by excessive risk taking or luck and not through security selection. This is important when comparing managers with their peers.

Ongoing process

The manager selection process is carried out initially and should then be ongoing. Frequent performance monitoring (monthly) and regular manager contact (quarterly or semi-annually) should be maintained. Once a manager is hired there should be a clear framework under which circumstances the manager would be fired or deselected. *Deselection* should be considered if analysis shows that the manager has drifted from the original investment style (style drift), material changes to the management team have occurred, the investment management process has been influenced by corporate level changes or disruptions, or when there is a persistent, relative underperformance for no discernible reason. Sharp, discreet underperformance should merit a review. However, it should not necessarily lead to deselection if performance is explainable, consistent with the investment process and unlikely to persist.

A *bench* of potential replacement managers is recommended so if a manager needs to be replaced the process is completed as quickly as possible. It is not constructive to keep a manager longer than needed once the decision has been made to deselect the incumbent because of concerns about the manager.

Using an *investment transition* team should be considered to manage the transition between managers, in particular when investments are not accessed through CIS. The portfolio of the incumbent manager normally has some positions in the wish list of the new manager, while other positions need to be sold. *In specie* transfer (i.e. transferring securities) rather than cashing all the positions and then buying new ones may be more cost efficient. During transitions the transaction costs need to be separated from the performance of the new manager so as not to adversely impact it.

Deselecting managers may be a costly process without guarantee that the replacement manager will outperform the incumbent. Good managers who go through a bad patch may recover. Performance should be evaluated over a full economic cycle to give managers sufficient time to deliver and to assess their performance under different market conditions. Investors should not be trigger happy, but patient[245]. Good things come to those who wait.

Style rotation and manager selection

Different investment styles (e.g. value and growth, level of aggressiveness, quality, dividend level, and market capitalisation or size) perform differently during different market conditions. There are plenty of models aiming to add value through *style rotation*. These models are based on discretionary decisions, multi-factor models, quantitative signals, such as momentum and volatility, and so on. The success of these models after transaction costs is arguable although some have been implemented successfully.

One way to implement such strategies is to prepare a bench of managers with different styles and use them according to the style rotation strategies. This strategy may be expensive due to transaction costs and may be disruptive to managers due to frequent and potentially substantial cash flows. Alternatively, the strategy can be implemented using ETFs or futures contracts in a more cost efficient way. Such implementation relies on the success of the style rotation strategy and excludes potential alpha from security selection.

To bridge between the two approaches, a *core-satellite* strategy can be used with the core invested in active managers[246], whose style is neutral or the combination of which is style neutral, while the satellite rotates among different styles using passive vehicles or derivatives. The active managers benefit from stable allocations while the entire portfolio benefits from cost-efficient style rotation.

Investment selection

Investors need to choose the right investments with the right investment managers. This is not a trivial task. There are, however, processes that can be followed to ensure that investors have considered everything that should be considered when choosing investments. Adhering to the process reduces the risk of choosing a wrong investment.

Whether investments are right or wrong depends on the portfolio's investment objectives. Investment objectives should be reflected in the portfolio's benchmark, where the investment strategy is aligned with the investment objectives on one hand, and the benchmark on the other hand. Investments that fit the investment strategy and the benchmark are consequently aligned with the investment objectives. The overall multi-asset portfolio management process ensures that these links are in place. Both the top-down asset allocation and the bottom-up investment selection are aligned with the investment objectives of the investor for the specific portfolio.

Summary

- While past performance is important, investment selection cannot rely on it since history is a poor predictor of future results.

- The qualitative due diligence process looks at investments' forward-looking characteristics.

- The quantitative due diligence process needs to link returns with risk and distinguish between risk taking and skill.

- The combination of quantitative and qualitative analysis aims to differentiate between sustainable skill and unsustainable luck.

- Quantitative due diligence requires more resources and time than qualitative due diligence.

- Investment selection is an ongoing, dynamic process. The initial due diligence supports the buying decision and the ongoing due diligence supports the decision on whether to keep holding investments.

- When making an investment, an exit strategy should be formulated so the investor knows under which circumstances the investment is going to be sold (sell discipline).

- The seven categories to consider when evaluating investments are: investment profile; risks; liquidity; correlations; legal structure; commercials; and product characteristics.

- The principles of the manager selection process can be used to evaluate any investment with the appropriate adjustments.

- On average, managers underperform their benchmarks after fees. Manager selection is a key to the success of active management.

- Valuation techniques used to value equities and bonds cannot be used to evaluate managers. Manager selection is about selecting people, not securities.

- Quantitative screening reduces the universe of managers by analysing past performance, AUM and style. Return-based and holding-based style analysis can be used to identify the manager's style.

- The manager due diligence process should consider the following factors: platform; progress; people; product; philosophy; process; portfolio; and performance.

- Considering these factors should help to determine the likelihood of repeating past performance in the future and distinguishing between skill and luck.

- The manager selection process is initial and ongoing. Managers should be monitored but deselected only for the right reasons.

- Style rotation strategies attempt to change the investment styles in portfolios to benefit from correctly predicting which style is to outperform.

18. ACTIVE VERSUS PASSIVE INVESTMENTS

The active versus passive debate is unresolved. Investors who believe in the capabilities of portfolio managers to add value through security selection tend to invest in active investments. Investors who believe in market efficiency and the underperformance of most managers after fees and expenses[247] tend to prefer passive investments. While theory and probability are stacked against active management it does add an element of excitement. As Friedrich Engels put it, "an ounce of action is worth a ton of theory".

The answer to the active/passive dilemma depends on the skill in picking skilled managers (investors who select outperforming managers add value), the tolerance for underperformance risk (passive investments are bound to underperform by their TER while active investments have outperformance potential and underperformance risk in the magnitude of their relative risk), the choice of how to spend the risk budget (asset allocation versus security selection) and the appetite to pay for active management (active management is more expensive than passive management). Combining passive and active investments is normally the optimal solution for multi-asset portfolios.

To succeed in active management and to outperform a benchmark three fundamental conditions are required:

1. *Dispersion in security prices.* Individual securities must perform differently than the market average. If all securities perform in line with the market average, portfolio return is going to equal that of the market minus fees and transaction costs. Greater dispersion in individual security performance leads to greater variability among prices of securities and to more opportunities for active management. Cross-sectional volatility can be used to measure this dispersion[248].

2. *Skill.* Investment managers must accurately identify which securities will outperform the market (i.e. skill or forecasting ability), have sufficient lead time to act on their insights (before the opportunity disappears) and be able to implement their views. The success or the skill is measured by the *information coefficient* (the correlation between investment decisions and investment results).

3. *Tracking error.* The portfolio constituencies and/or their weights must differ from those of the market as a whole (i.e. active managers need to assume relative risk with respect of the benchmark to add alpha). Zero tracking error means an index tracker.

While managers control the second and third conditions (assuming skill and the portfolio construction process are held constant), the first condition depends on market environment and changes over time.

Active managers exhibit performance cycles. Managers try to outperform by deviating from their benchmark using several levels of investment decisions: market timing (choosing when to enter and exit markets); style (e.g. growth versus value); market capitalisation (e.g. small, mid and large capitalisation); country and sector selection (top-down); and security selection (bottom-up). By understanding and modelling the performance cycles as a function of the level of decisions, multi-asset investors should be able to make tactical changes to the active/passive allocation mix. The allocation should favour more active strategies during the stages of the cycle that are constructive for the active management levels of decisions. Conversely, when the stage of the cycle is unsupportive of active management, more passive investments should be used.

Different factors influence the probability of active management success. Understanding the factors and their impact on active management can help to determine the active/passive mix.

The active/passive allocation depends heavily on *manager skill*[249]. When more skilled managers, in whom there is high conviction, are available the allocation to active management should increase, all else being equal. When available skilled managers are scarce, the allocation to passive management should increase. Selecting skilled managers requires skill and resources. Higher conviction in manager selection skills and available resources to select managers should result in higher allocation to active management. The availability of skilled managers changes over time and so should the allocation to active management.

Numerous practitioners claim there is a connection between *market efficiency* and the potential success of active management. Arguably, as a market is more efficient, the number of mispriced securities and the ability to identify mispriced securities are lower (security prices quickly and accurately price in all information and prices equal fair-values), and hence the active management success rate is lower. As developing markets mature and become more efficient, the scope for active management diminishes and passive investments should get more emphasis.

For example, the efficiency of government bond markets has increased as central banks have become more transparent in recent years. As China becomes more popular with investors, Chinese stocks attract more research, liquidity increases and market efficiency strengthens. As information is shared rapidly in the 21st century and more players are present in the markets, such as hedge funds, certain markets have become more efficient. All these developments make it increasingly challenging for active management to add alpha.

Global emerging market equity is a relatively inefficient asset class. However, while on the face of it this asset class should provide ample opportunities for active management, only a small number of managers are successful in this space. The reason is that such a diverse, global market requires substantial, global resources to be covered properly, in particular since transparency of company information is weaker than in developed economies. Only a small number of managers can research this market and add value through active management.

The debate over the connection between market efficiency and active management is not resolved though. As markets undergo periods of irrationality, there are potential opportunities for active management even in so-called *efficient* markets. Bill Miller[250], one of the most successful active portfolio managers in history, described this as follows: "the market does reflect the available information, as the professors tell us. But just as the funhouse mirrors don't always accurately reflect your weight, the markets don't always accurately reflect that information. Usually they are too pessimistic when it's bad, and too optimistic when it's good".

During rallies in *mega cap stocks*[251], average market return is driven by a relatively small number of large capitalisation stocks. For example, during the 2008 spike in oil prices[252] the performance of the S&P 500 Index was driven by the prices of energy stocks. Managers who underweighted this sector were likely to underperform the market. Since many active managers are underweight mega caps relative to benchmark they may underperform during such rallies.

Narrow *market leadership* means that the returns of a few stocks drive market performance. Returns of most stocks underperform the market average. Wide market leadership means the opposite; most stocks outperform the general market (the returns of few large capitalisation stocks drag the average market return down). Market leadership is related to mega-cap driven markets since mega caps have a larger impact on the return of market capitalisation weighted indices. In narrow market leadership it is more challenging for active managers to beat the benchmark since statistically they have a lower probability of selecting the small number of outperforming stocks.

During rallies of *low quality stocks*, many active managers are likely to underperform the market since most managers invest in higher-quality stocks. For example, in March 2003 equity markets started to rally after recovering from the high-tech bubble burst and the 11 September 2001 attacks. Stocks leading the rally were small capitalisation, high beta and low quality. Many managers lagged their benchmarks since they invested in large-capitalisation, low-beta and high-quality stocks. The underperformance was also driven by the defensive positioning of many managers in the bear market between 2000 and 2003 following the high-tech bubble burst and the difficulty in forecasting the inflection point. In this situation, passive investments were superior, on average.

Declining volatility and credit spreads, increasing correlation among asset classes, and rising *herding and crowded trades* are factors that make the market cycle difficult for active managers. Under these conditions the markets become more *homogenous* and it is more challenging to identify securities that perform differently to the overall market.

Uncertainty means not knowing what is going to happen without the ability to measure the outcomes or assign them probabilities. There is always a degree of uncertainty in financial markets. However, there are times when uncertainty is at extreme levels. When investors just do not know what is going to happen it is better to get closer to benchmark and invest more with passive investments.

During 2010 and 2011 a *risk on, risk off* pattern emerged in markets as investors herded out of risk assets when concerns about the euro sovereign debt crisis emerged and herded back into risk assets when the concerns abated. The resolution of the situation rested with policy makers, not with economic conditions. This uncertain environment (it is difficult to model the will and actions of politicians and governors of central banks) was unsupportive for active management. The choppy market environment was challenging since it was difficult to position portfolios appropriately for any view. One solution was focusing on the long term and taking less risk over the short term by de-risking relative and absolute risk.

Factors such as dispersion of security prices, market efficiency, market leadership and level of uncertainty may affect the probability of active management success. Tracking changes to these factors informs the active/passive split over time.

It is relatively straightforward to track the success of active managers in each market over rolling 12 and 36-month periods, as well as the trend (e.g. over rolling 12-month periods). This should be a proxy for the aggregate influence of the systematic factors. Both the level and trend of active management results should be monitored. Markets where average recent success has been poor and declining are likely to be unsupportive to active management. In these markets the allocation to passive investments should increase. Markets where success has been positive and increasing are more likely to support active management. Past results should be complemented by assessment of the factors that explain and drive them, adding the essential forward-looking forecast.

Cross-sectional volatility

Cross-sectional volatility measures the dispersion of security returns at one point in time (while intertemporal volatility measures the dispersion of returns over time, such as volatility per annum). The formula for calculating cross-sectional volatility is:

$$\sigma_{\text{cross sectional}} = (\Sigma w_i(r_i - r_{\text{avg}})^2)^{0.5}$$

where r_{avg} is the average return across all securities, r_i is the return of security i, and w_i is the weight of security i in the portfolio.

Cross-sectional volatility is a good gauge for the opportunities available to investors to generate active returns (returns in excess of the benchmark). Cross-sectional volatility of security returns is connected to opportunities for alpha generation by investment strategies that emphasise stock selection[253]. The proportion of cross-sectional volatility that is driven by common factors is connected to opportunities for strategies based on common factor movements, such as sector or style rotation or quantitative strategies.

Changes in cross-sectional volatility have direct consequences for investors. Ankrim and Ding[254] found a strong relationship between cross-sectional volatility of asset returns and the dispersion of portfolio managers' performances. A decline in cross-sectional volatility is bad news for skilled managers, but good news for less talented managers. Skilled managers have fewer opportunities to add value through security selection. The performance of less talented managers is likely to be more in line with that of their peers as the performance of skilled managers suffers.

Ankrim and Ding have shown that changes in cross-sectional volatility are driven by a combination of three factors: change in the average volatility of the securities making up the market; change in overall market volatility and change in the security mean dispersion. If security mean dispersion is relatively stable over time, then the change in cross-sectional volatility is mainly attributed to changes in average security volatility and overall market volatility. The result is that cross-sectional volatility will rise with a general increase in security volatility while correlation between securities is held constant, and decrease in cross-sectional correlations while the level of security volatility is held constant. It is therefore possible to track and estimate future cross-sectional volatility based on volatilities of securities and the correlations among them.

Monitoring changes in cross-sectional volatility can be used as one quantitative tool to gauge the potential success of active management. When cross-sectional volatility increases, the allocation to active management should increase, all else being equal, and vice versa when it decreases.

Enhanced indexing

Enhanced indexing is an investment strategy with the objective of generating modest excess returns with low tracking error. The strategy aims to outperform passive index tracking, while not deviating materially from index return, maintaining low turnover and transaction costs and maximising tax-efficiency. Most enhanced indexing investment strategies are quantitative.

Active/passive split in portfolio context

The active/passive split is a key part of the risk budgeting process of multi-asset portfolios. Multi-asset portfolios take two risks relative to benchmark: asset allocation risk (SAA and TAA) and security selection risk. Security selection risk is determined by the aggregate active risks of individual active investments and the split between active and passive investments. Multi-asset investors can control the total risk of portfolios by allocating more or less to underlying active managers. Risk budgeting is a consideration for the active/passive split in portfolio context in addition to the probability of success of active management.

The optimal portfolio construction choice for most investors is combining investments across the full spectrum ranging from passive, through enhanced indexing, to active. This *spectrum strategy*[255] is preferred over one that is all active, all passive or a combination of just highly active and highly passive investments. This is because of diversification of investment styles and active risks. Jack Treynor and Fischer Black concluded in their research[256] that the optimal portfolio is achieved by mixing a benchmark portfolio (passive) with an active portfolio.

The debate

The debate over whether to go active or passive is ongoing. The professional investment industry perhaps has been biased in recommending active management because of its higher fees and turnover that creates brokerage commissions. Passive investments on a grand-scale have become popular since the advent of ETFs in the United States in 1993 and in Europe in 1999. Before ETFs active management was the common choice (except for passive funds) and was most commonly offered to investors by the investment management industry. This has changed and passive investments are now readily available for almost every asset class. Investors have more choices and they need to use them for their benefit.

The objective of active management is generating alpha and it needs to justify its fees. Active management does not always deliver. When it is doubtful whether an active choice is going to generate alpha, passive choice should be the default. When investors are mostly interested in beta exposure and not in alpha, passive is the cost-efficient way to gain access to betas. However, selecting the right manager is an opportunity to generate excess return. Good opportunities should not be passed up lightly. Investing passively requires less effort. However, combining active and passive investments, while requiring more effort, has potential benefits of enhanced performance.

The key to consistently add value to investors is *efficiently* managing portfolios: matching an appropriate investment strategy reflecting the investor's risk profile and investment objectives; investing cash quickly to make it work; rebalancing the asset allocation to maintain its risk/return profile; reducing transaction costs through low turnover and passive investments where alpha is scarce and expensive; minimising taxes; and maintaining a cool head, not allowing behavioural biases to control investment decisions.

Insisting on active management at all times and in each asset class does not serve the interests of investors since active management cannot succeed in all markets under all market conditions. Passive investments are a cost-efficient way to gain exposure to betas. Under certain circumstances beta, and not alpha, is what investors need.

Summary

- To outperform the benchmark active management requires dispersion in performance of securities, skill and tracking error.

- There are several factors influencing the probability of active management success, including manager skill, market efficiency and market leadership.

- Systematic factors can be monitored and the active/passive split should be dynamically managed according to the level of support to active management by market conditions.

- Cross-sectional volatility is a gauge for the opportunities available for active managers in the market. Rising cross-sectional volatility means wider dispersion in security returns, more opportunities for security selection and good news for skilled managers. Declining cross-sectional volatility means the opposite (but good news for unskilled managers since their performance is likely to be more aligned with that of their peers).

- Risk budgeting of multi-asset portfolios is another consideration for the active/passive split.

- Enhanced indexing aims to add modest alpha with low tracking error, lying between passive and active strategies in terms of expected excess returns and relative risk. Most investors will benefit from combining passive investing, enhanced indexing and active investing by diversifying investment styles and active risks.

19. INVESTMENT VEHICLES

Investment vehicles come in different legal structures and types. Each vehicle has advantages and disadvantages and may be appropriate for one investor but not for another. Not all investors can or should access all investment vehicles. As always, the type of investment vehicle should match the investor's objectives and constraints.

Collective Investment Schemes (CIS)

A Collective Investment Scheme (CIS) or *collective* is an investment vehicle pooling the investments of a group of investors to benefit from accumulating sufficient money for proper diversification, economies of scale (e.g. cost sharing) and appointing a professional investment manager.

Small portfolios may not have sufficient assets to properly diversify their holdings as well as to meet the minimums of some investments. When trading costs are spread over more assets, they have a lower impact on each individual investor. Larger portfolios have stronger bargaining power with brokers and can negotiate lower trading commissions. Using professional investment managers should improve the likelihood of having clear investment objectives, a sound investment strategy and correct implementation.

Collectives are also known as *commingled investment schemes*. *Fund* often means a collective, while *mandate* or *account* often means a segregated portfolio.

The legal vehicles and names of collectives differ across countries and regions. Most common collectives include mutual funds in the United States, OEICs (Open Ended Investment Companies) or ICVCs (Investment Company with Variable Capital) in the United Kingdom, SICAVs (société d'investissement à capital variable) in Luxembourg and ETFs (Exchange Traded Funds) globally.

The UCITS (Undertakings for Collective Investment in Transferable Securities) directive is the regulatory framework for many CIS sold across Europe. NURS is a non-UCITS retail scheme, which does not comply with the UCITS regulations. Collectives form a large portion of the professionally managed investments in markets across the world.

Collectives are typically incorporated under company law. The nature of each collective and its investment restrictions is often linked to the regulations and tax rules for the type of vehicle within its jurisdiction.

Typically, collectives include:

- *Investment manager*. Responsible for investment decisions.

- *Fund administrator*. Manages the trading, reconciliations, valuation and unit pricing.

- *Board of directors*[257] or *trustees*. Safeguards the assets and ensures compliance with laws, regulations and rules.

- *Shareholders* or *unit holders*. Invested in the collective and own, or have rights to, the assets and associated income.

- *Distribution company*. Promotes and sells shares/units of the collective.

The Net Asset Value (NAV) is the value of the collective assets less the value of its liabilities. The method for calculating the NAV varies between scheme types and jurisdictions and is subject to relevant regulation.

Collectives are divided into open-end and closed-end funds. An *open-end fund* does not have a limit on the number of shares or units that it can issue. Each share represents partial ownership of the underlying assets that the fund holds. The share price varies in direct proportion to the variation in the value of the fund's NAV. When investors want to invest in the fund by buying more shares, new shares or units are issued to match the prevailing share price. When investors want to sell their shares, the fund buys them back so the assets sold match the prevailing share price. In this way no supply or demand affects the shares and their price continues to directly reflect the value of the underlying assets or NAV. Open-end funds are either *dual priced* or *single priced*. Dual priced funds have a buying price (offer) and a selling price (bid)[258]. The offer price is higher than the bid price and the difference between them is the *bid-offer spread*[259]. Single priced CIS have only one price.

A *closed-end fund* issues a limited number of shares or units. The shares are issued through either an initial public offering (IPO) to the general public or a private placement. The shares are traded on an exchange or directly through the fund manager to create a secondary market subject to supply and demand of the shares. The number of shares is constant, so supply and demand for the shares affects their price. If demand for the shares is high, their price is bid up and they may trade at a premium to NAV. If demand is low, their price is bid down and they may trade at a discount to NAV. Purchasing shares at discount may be an investment opportunity if the discount moves subsequently toward NAV or becomes a premium. Purchasing shares at premium is a risk as the premium can move toward NAV or become a discount. Closed-end funds are called closed-end companies in the United States and *investment trusts* in the United Kingdom.

Further share or unit offerings may be made by closed-end funds if demand is high, although this may affect the share price (i.e. dilute the price of existing shareholders). For listed closed-end funds, the supply and demand forces of the market may amplify a fund's performance because the premium/discount of share prices to NAV can move quickly and materially. This increases the volatility of the fund's returns and funds investing in low volatility assets, such as real estate, can experience equity-like volatility. Closed-end funds may face liquidity issues since purchasing large numbers of shares may move the price, in particular for funds that have low trading volume and low AUM. It may be challenging to build a position in closed-end funds or redeem holdings in them. Liquidity risk and volatility risk of closed-end funds should be carefully considered.

Some collectives, in particular closed-end funds, have the power to borrow money to make further investments (*gearing* or *leverage*). When markets are appreciating this allows the scheme to magnify returns. However, this premise only works if the cost of borrowing is less than the appreciation in invested assets. If the borrowing costs are more than the appreciation in assets then a net loss is achieved. Leverage magnifies positive as well as negative returns. For example, a fund has $1 million of assets and borrows another $0.5 million to invest $1.5 million in the stock market. If the market appreciates by 10%, the fund earns $150,000 or 15% on the assets (150,000/1,000,000), not only the 10% stock market appreciation. However, if the market falls by 10%, the fund loses 15%. Leverage can greatly increase the volatility of returns, both on the upside and downside.

During the 2008 financial crisis many closed-end funds that were invested in real estate utilised high levels of leverage. When the financial crisis struck, real estate prices plunged, investors wanted out, the share prices of the funds sky dived and their liquidity completely dried up. The lessons are to carefully scrutinise leverage, liquidity and closed-end funds.

The availability of collectives varies depending on their target investor base. *Public-availability schemes* are available to most investors within the jurisdiction that they are offered. For example, retail funds are widely available and are therefore subject to heavy regulations, setting certain investment constraints and requiring certain disclosures (in particular risks). The objective of the regulations is to protect retail investors, who are assumed to be unsophisticated, meaning that they do not have the resources and/or skill to research and understand investments. Retail funds are *regulated*.

Limited-availability schemes are limited by regulations to be sold only to experienced and/or sophisticated investors. Since they are not available to the retail market, they are less heavily regulated compared to regulated funds, and hence referred to as *unregulated* funds. Most hedge funds are unregulated. They often have high minimum investment requirements and are restricted to large investors, who are assumed to be sophisticated. High Net Worth individuals and institutional investors have the resources and skill, or they can hire them, to analyse each investment. Such investors do not need the same level of protection by the regulators as retail investors do. They can make informed investment decisions.

Private-availability schemes are limited to the sponsor who set up the fund. For example, a fund of a family office restricted to family members, who can use funds or trusts for tax or estate planning purposes. In the institutional market, there are instances when asset management firms benefit from setting a fund for internal purposes. For example, a TAA stand-alone fund can be used across many portfolios, while the implementation of the TAA positions is done once, saving considerable resources. Private-availability schemes are not publicly quoted and are not sold to investors.

Many funds offer multiple *share classes*. Each share class represents a *pro rata* ownership of all the fund assets. However, the classes typically differ in fees. The differences are supposed to reflect different costs involved in servicing different investor segments. For example, the retail share class may be with an initial commission (*front-end load*). The initial commission may be as high as 5%, meaning that for every $100 paid only $95 is invested for investors. Other share classes may be sold without a front-end load, but with higher annual management fees to compensate for not charging upfront commission. Institutional share classes (I-class) may have a high minimum investment limit and are only available for institutional investors. I-shares are less expensive than retail share classes.

Share classes are also distinguished by *accumulating* and *distributing* shares and *hedged* and *unhedged* shares. Accumulating share classes reinvest cash from interest and dividends while distributing share classes distribute the cash. Distributing share classes are appropriate for investors seeking income. Investors interested in capital growth without income needs should use accumulating share classes, as reinvestment of interest and dividends is a major driver of long-term total returns.

The currency exposure of a hedged share class is hedged to the base currency of the share class (e.g. a fund invested in US equities can offer a pound share classes in which the dollar exposure of the assets is hedged to the pound). The hedging is implemented by the collective's manager, so investors do not need to hedge the currency. The currency exposure of unhedged share classes is not hedged. Investors can control the hedge ratio by combining hedged and unhedged share classes in the desired proportions. The currency of the share class can be different than the base currency of the assets in the collective. For example, a collective investing in UK equities can offer a dollar share class. The dollar is only the accounting currency of the share class. Performance is converted from pounds, the base currency of the assets, to dollars. Investors in the dollar share class still have currency exposure to the pound.

The disadvantages of collectives are:

- Fund management fees (these are often charged directly to the fund's NAV and impact performance).

- Lack of ability to customise investments to the investment objectives.

- Lack of choice (investors can choose which fund to invest in, but they have no control over the choice of individual holdings within the fund; the fund is not customisable).

- Loss of owner rights (such as the company shareholder's right to vote in general meetings) as these rights are delegated to the collective's manager.

Nevertheless, for investors without sufficient assets to properly diversify their portfolios, collectives remain one of the only viable options to achieve diversification and professional management.

Dilution levy and swing price

Dilution levy is a charge that collectives may levy on investors who purchase or sell units to reflect the transaction costs of the subscriptions or redemptions. The objective is to protect the interests of existing unit holders so they are not adversely affected by these transaction costs.

For example, an investor purchases units in a fund that invests in high-yield bonds. The fund needs to purchase bonds to invest the cash (proceeds). Purchasing the bonds involves transaction costs. The fund needs to calculate the transaction costs and add them to the price of the unit. This ensures that the investor who buys the units bares the transaction costs without adversely affecting the other unit holders. Dilution levy also applies when investors want to redeem their units. A dilution levy of 0.5% or more in this case is common. Dilution levy is often used by single priced funds.

Dual priced funds do not charge a dilution levy but rather use a *swing price*. A swing price increases the fund's bid price by the estimated transaction costs, having the same effect as a dilution levy[260].

The magnitude of the dilution levy or swing price depends on the size of the cash flow relative to the fund's AUM and the liquidity of the underlying investments as these two factors determine the transaction costs of purchasing or selling investments. This process ensures that investors in collectives are treated fairly[261]. When investing in collectives, including ETFs, investors should ask about dilution levy or swing price to understand the costs of investing.

UCITS

The Undertakings for Collective Investment in Transferable Securities (UCITS)[262] are a set of European Union Directives. The objective of the original UCITS Directive, adopted in 1985, was to allow for open-end funds investing in transferable securities to be subject to the same regulations in every EU member state.

It was hoped that once such legislative uniformity was established throughout Europe, funds authorised in one member state could be sold to the public in each member state without further authorisation (*passporting*), thereby furthering the EU's goal of a single market for financial services across Europe. The reality differed somewhat from the expectation due primarily to individual marketing rules in each member state that created obstacles to cross-border marketing of UCITS funds with the effect of protecting local asset managers.

The main advantages of UCITS-compliant funds are:

- The funds are liquid, transparent, subject to disclosure requirements and regulated.

- The UCITS framework allows managers access to increased distribution channels, not only in Europe, but also globally (excluding the United States).

- The UCITS regulation aims to ensure diversification, limits leverage, limits shorting and restricts eligible investments, thereby making the funds more appropriate for conservative investors.

These are all advantages for investors, whom the authorities or regulators try to protect. For asset management firms, however, these are constraints on managing money.

The disadvantages of UCITS are:

- Investment restrictions (e.g. direct real estate and commodities are ineligible) and limitations on investment powers and techniques (shorting, leverage, unlimited investment universe and investment flexibility are tools that add value in the right hands but which are limited within UCITS funds).

- The extensive monitoring obligations increase TERs. All the costs of managing funds come from their assets, meaning that investors in funds share these costs.

Investors need to choose between the advantages of increased transparency of regulated CIS versus the increased flexibility of unregulated CIS.

Following the 2008 credit crisis with the failure of many hedge funds, creation of side-pockets and redemption freezing, many investors have become risk averse towards unregulated hedge funds and CIS. With the increasing flexibility of UCITS III, many UCITS-compliant hedge fund strategies started to gain popularity. The phrase *"Newcits"* was coined to describe hedge fund style strategies within the UCITS framework.

These UCITS-compliant hedge fund style funds do not have the full flexibility of unregulated hedge funds (commonly referred to as *Cayman funds* since most hedge funds are registered in the Cayman Islands). UCITS regulations limit the funds to eligible investments and limit the ability to leverage and short (although creative minds use derivatives to leverage and short within the UCITS regulations, as well as to access ineligible asset classes such as commodities). Nevertheless, UCITS style hedge funds offer some of the return and risk profiles of Cayman hedge funds, with the liquidity, regulatory scrutiny and disclosure requirements of the UCITS framework.

Passive investments

The objective of passive investments, such as ETFs and passive funds, is typically tracking the performance of a certain index, a basket of indices or a group of assets such as equities, bonds or commodities. Passive managers use different strategies to achieve this goal, but in general they have a low tracking error target and do not have the discretion to take defensive positions in declining markets. Investors must be prepared to bear the risk of loss and volatility associated with the underlying index or assets. Passive investments are not expected to outperform the index or to protect against the downside in a falling market.

Tracking error refers to the disparity in performance between a passive investment and its underlying index. Tracking error can arise due to factors such as market volatility, the impact of transaction fees and expenses, changes in the composition of the underlying index and the passive manager's replication strategy. Passive investments do not perfectly track the index. *Tracking risk* is a risk to consider in passive investments since the objective is to track the index and not to underperform or outperform it.

ETFs may trade at a discount or premium to their NAV. This price discrepancy is caused by supply and demand factors and may be particularly likely to emerge during periods of high market volatility and uncertainty. This phenomenon may also be observed for ETFs tracking specific markets or sectors that are subject to direct investment restrictions.

ETFs using a *full replication* strategy generally aim to invest in all constituent securities in the same weightings as their benchmark. ETFs adopting a *representative sampling* strategy invest in some but not all of the relevant constituent securities. Multi-factor models and statistical analysis help ETF managers to decide on the most efficient way to replicate the index without purchasing all the constituents and hence reducing transaction costs. Full replication is not a viable option when tracking fixed-income benchmarks, which hold thousands of securities. For ETFs investing directly in the underlying assets rather than through synthetic instruments or derivatives issued by third parties, counterparty risk tends to be low risk. It is, however, a concern when synthetic replication strategies are used.

ETFs utilising a *synthetic replication* strategy use swaps or other derivative instruments to gain exposure to a benchmark. ETF types using synthetic replication can be further categorised into swap-based ETFs and derivative embedded ETFs. Total return swaps allow managers of *swap-based ETFs* to replicate the benchmark performance without purchasing the underlying assets. Swap-based ETFs are exposed to counterparty risk of the other party of the swap and may suffer losses if this party defaults or fails to honour its contractual commitments.

Managers of *derivative embedded ETFs* use other derivative instruments to synthetically replicate the economic benefits of the relevant benchmark. For example, ETF managers can purchase a basket of futures contracts to replicate the index. The derivative instruments can be issued by one or multiple issuers. Derivative embedded ETFs are subject to counterparty risk of the issuers of derivatives[263].

Passive funds versus ETFs

Passive funds and ETFs aim to track an index. Passive funds are less flexible but generally cheaper[264] than ETFs. Passive funds do not offer intraday liquidity and they cannot be shorted while ETFs do offer intraday liquidity and can be shorted.

ETFs offer flexibility and some investors use them instead of futures contracts since they can be traded at small sizes, they do not require special documentation, accounts, rolling over and margins, some ETFs cover markets for which no, or no liquid, futures contracts are available, and some investors who are restricted in using derivatives use ETFs instead. The advantages of futures contracts are that they have lower TERs and cash is not required to cover the full economic exposure (they are not funded positions and only a margin is required). Futures contracts, however, have basis risk and their rolling costs over the long term can surpass the TER of an ETF.

The choice among passive funds, ETFs and futures contracts depends on the investor's needs, access and investment horizon. If no intraday trading and shorting are required, passive funds may be the most cost-efficient choice. If flexibility is required, the investment horizon is long and cash can be committed, ETFs may be the most efficient choice to avoid rolling costs and the risks of futures contracts. Otherwise, futures contracts may be the appropriate choice.

Segregated accounts

Segregated (seg) accounts or mandates are portfolios that are usually managed by an asset management firm for a single client (unless the seg account is unitised and sold to many investors). Seg mandates are not offered to the general public like retail collectives. The investor owns the underlying investments (direct invest), unlike owning a share in a collective, which invests in the underlying investments. Assets in segregated accounts are held separately from the assets of the asset management firm or other investors (hence segregated). The two main reasons for segregating the assets are to clearly separate them so they are not used for wrong purposes (e.g. avoid mixing assets with those of other customers or safeguarding them from illegal activities) and to protect them in case anything happens to the firm, such as bankruptcy.

Segregated accounts are highly flexible and can be tailored to the specific investor requirements. To be able to properly diversify segregated accounts, investors need to invest a considerable amount of money (e.g. a minimum of $50 million). The minimum amount depends on the type of investments. It is lower when investing in large capitalisation stocks of a developed market, higher when investing in corporate bonds and much higher when investing in commercial real estate. Typically, portfolio managers require a certain minimum investment to open a segregated account so it makes commercial sense. Size does matter and not all investors have the choice of accessing segregated accounts. Normally, the fees and costs of seg accounts are expected to be lower than those of equivalent collectives.

Segregated accounts do not have to follow the disclosure and transparency requirements of regulated collectives. This may be an advantage since it enables higher flexibility. On the other hand, this may be a disadvantage since segregated accounts are subject to less regulatory scrutiny. If seg accounts are managed by authorised investment managers, they are expected to professionally manage the assets as required by the authorising authority (SEC in the United States and FSA in the United Kingdom).

Segregated accounts are not subject to a dilution levy or a swing price, as collectives are, since commonly there is only a single investor in the account and other investors do not need protection as they do in collectives. Cash-flow related transaction costs affect the performance of the account based on the execution by its portfolio manager.

While segregated accounts have a few advantages compared to collectives, as always there are disadvantages. If segregated accounts invest in illiquid assets, their liquidity is going to be limited since they do not pool together assets of several investors. For example, if the investor wants to reduce exposure to a segregated account invested in commercial real estate, the portfolio manager needs to sell buildings; a long and expensive process. When a collective invests in real estate and one investor wants to reduce exposure it is likely to be easier, as long as other investors do not sell at the same time and the redeeming investor holds a relatively small proportion of the total assets in the collective.

Another potential disadvantage of segregated accounts relative to collectives is their tax treatment. If investors are not tax exempt or the account is not held within a tax efficient wrapper, they may be taxed on each transaction within the account since they directly own the underlying investments.

Conclusion

The choice of appropriate investment vehicles influences the outcome. Different investment vehicles have different legal structures, fees, investment flexibility and risks. As always, before investing investors need to assess the fit between the choice of investment vehicle and their investment objectives. Investors should understand the investment before investing.

Summary

- The legal structure or type of investment vehicle should be selected to match the investor's investment objective and constraints.

- Collective investment schemes (CIS) pool together the assets of many investors to benefit from diversification, economies of scale (cost sharing) and appointment of professional investment managers.

- The main disadvantage of CIS is the lack of ability to customise investments.

- The price of open-end CIS is closely linked to its Net Asset Value (NAV).

- Closed-end CIS trade at a premium or a discount to NAV. This can introduce high price volatility. Closed-end CIS have limited liquidity.

- CIS that can use leverage should be carefully scrutinised since leverage can materially increase investment risk.

- Dilution levy or swing price are ways to ensure that transaction costs due to subscriptions or redemption in CIS are paid by the investor who is responsible for the cash flows and not by other investors.

- UCITS was created to enable the distribution of funds across Europe.

- UCITS-compliant funds are liquid, transparent and regulated. The requirement for diversification and limitations on shorting, leverage and eligible investments make the funds more appropriate for conservative investors. UCITS funds have limitations on the eligible investment universe and investment techniques with limited flexibility versus unregulated CIS.

- ETFs aim to track an index. The main risks with ETFs are market risk, tracking error and counterparty risk when ETFs use derivatives to gain exposure to index performance instead of full or partial replication.

- Passive funds have less flexibility than ETFs, but they are cheaper.

- Futures contracts may be more cost efficient than ETFs over the short term. Over the long term the rolling costs of futures contracts may surpass the TERs of ETFs.

- Segregated accounts are managed for a single investor. Segregated accounts allow for tailoring to investor's requirements. However, they require a relatively large minimum investment to allow for diversification and for the portfolio manager to agree to manage them.

20. SINGLE-MANAGER VERSUS MULTI-MANAGER

Multi-asset portfolios can use investments managed by either a single manager or multiple managers. A single-manager or in-house portfolio typically has the same investment manager responsible for asset allocation, investment selection and security selection within each asset class.

A multi-manager portfolio (manager of managers or fund of funds), on the other hand, typically[265] follows an *open architecture* approach and has one manager responsible for the overall multi-asset portfolio (asset allocation, investment selection and portfolio construction), but other managers perform the security selection within each asset class. It is a mixture of different personalities and approaches. As always, each approach has advantages and disadvantages.

Choosing between single and multi-manager

When making the choice between single-manager and multi-manager there are a number of factors to consider.

No asset management firm is good at everything. Some firms specialise in equity, others specialise in fixed income and others specialise in alternative investments. Some investment houses believe in top-down asset allocation and others believe in bottom-up security selection. Firms can predominantly use fundamental analysis, quantitative analysis or a combination of both. Some institutions specialise in offering passive investments and others specialise in active investments. A firm with local resources in Asia, for example, would be better positioned to offer Asia-focused investments than firms without a local presence, all else being equal. Combining *best-of-breed* managers in a multi-manager structure allows for *manager specialisation* by picking the specialists in each category. The prerequisite for success is picking the right managers and hence manager selection is key.

Multiple managers means *manager diversification*. This should reduce idiosyncratic risk with any particular manager. According to the fundamental law of active management, through manager diversification the breadth of independent decisions increases and combining uncorrelated information coefficients should increase the information ratio of multi-manager portfolios.

The flip side of diversification is *over-diversification*. When too many managers are used multi-manager portfolios may end up holding most of the securities in the benchmark, creating an expensive index tracker. A portion of the alphas from the different managers is diversified away. A single-manager portfolio can better control the overall diversification and concentrate the portfolio to maintain sufficient tracking error to allow for alpha generation.

Through a multi-manager structure investors can combine different investment styles, such as value and growth, large and small cap, and fundamental and quantitative. Since different styles perform well and poorly under different market conditions, *style diversification* should smooth returns and reduce portfolio volatility. Dynamic style rotation can add alpha.

Multi-manager portfolios may be more appealing to investors and increase the *marketability* of the offering. The unique selling points (USPs) are manager specialisation (best-of-breed, open architecture) and manager diversification. For asset management firms, offering multi-manager portfolios may signal objectivity as the firms are not biased to using solely their in-house capabilities. An open architecture offering may appeal to some investors because of its enhanced objectivity in selecting best capabilities.

Multi-manager structures come at a *cost*. In multi-manager portfolios there are two layers of fees: one at the total portfolio level and a second at each underlying manager level. Multi-manager portfolios require resources for manager selection and ongoing monitoring; these resources cost money. Separate relationships with each manager and Investment Management Agreements (IMAs) are required. These entail relationship management and legal costs. Multi-manager propositions are more expensive than single-manager ones, all else being equal.

Multi-manager portfolios are more *operationally complex*. Investing in external funds or sub-delegating management to external managers increases the complexity of the portfolios.

Risk management of multi-manager portfolios is more complex than that of single-manager portfolios. To manage the total risk of multi-asset portfolios the information on all underlying investments under each asset class needs aggregation. It is easier to obtain information when there is a single manager than when there are multiple portfolios managed by different managers.

With a potential for outperformance, active management comes with a risk of underperformance. There is no guarantee that external managers, as good as they are, will outperform their benchmarks. Managers are typically selected after a spell of outperformance. The question is whether the past track record is sustainable and here is where the manager selection process fits in. Since the costs of a multi-manager proposition are higher than that of a single-manager the hurdle rate for generating positive net of fees returns is higher.

When a manager is replaced the transition must be managed carefully and efficiently because these transitions can be costly, lengthy and harmful to relative performance. *In specie* transitions are not always possible. A transition manager is therefore recommended.

The best solution is usually combining internal and external mangers, as well as passive and active investments. Multi-asset investors should use internal capabilities where it makes sense and outsource investments when internal capabilities are unavailable or not strong enough. Using passive investments has a number of benefits, including reducing costs, controlling total portfolio risk, focusing on active management only where there is high conviction for outperformance and creating a buffer to implement asset allocation changes through the passive investments.

The challenge is that multi-asset portfolio managers, when given the flexibility to choose between internal and external managers, must not be conflicted by commercial reasons to prefer internal managers. The fee and compensation structure must ensure that managers have the incentive to objectively select internal or external managers to benefit the interests of investors.

Manager of Manger versus Fund of Funds

Manager of manager (MoM) structures typically use portfolios whose management is delegated to external managers or sub-advisors. In fund of fund (FoF) structures portfolios purchase shares of collectives managed by external (as well as internal) managers.

There are differences between MoM and FoF. In a MoM it is more difficult and expensive to replace managers since portfolios need to be transitioned from the fired to the hired managers (each time a manager is appointed to manage a portfolio). In a FoF the transition between managers is easier since the share class of one fund is replaced with that of another fund. Managers in a MoM are therefore normally held for a longer term than funds in a FoF. It is easier to change the asset allocation of a FoF than that of a MoM since it is less disruptive to underlying managers.

In a MoM the fees of the underlying managers can typically be negotiated downward. A FoF is typically more expensive than a MoM and should have a higher return objective to overcome the higher fee hurdle. MoM portfolios need a higher AUM than FoF portfolios since assets are shared only by the investors in the MoM while in a FoF the shares of the funds are normally offered to the general public.

MoM portfolios have more flexibility to negotiate investment objectives and constraints with each underlying manager while this flexibility is unavailable in FoF portfolios. The choice depends on investor objectives and the size of the investment (MoM portfolios usually have higher minimums than those of FoF portfolios).

Conclusion

There are numerous choices that investors must make. Single-manager or multi-manager, MoM or FoF are just two of them. Investors need to decide which option is the best to meet their investment objectives. Not all investors have all the choices available to them. Size or bigger AUM means a bigger budget and more choice.

Summary

- Multi-asset portfolios are either single-manager or multi-manager.

- A manager of manager (MoM) portfolio typically uses segregated portfolios and allows for customisation, while a fund of funds (FoF) invests in CIS.

- The factors used to compare a single-manager versus multi-manager include: manager specialisation; manager diversification; over-diversification; style diversification; marketability; costs; operational complexity; risk management; risk of underperformance; and transitions.

- The best solution is probably combining internal and external managers.

- Multi-asset portfolio managers must not be in a conflict of interest between selecting internal and external managers due to commercial reasons.

21. SINGLE ASSET CLASSES

Multi-asset investors need to understand the underlying single asset classes in which multi-asset portfolios invest. While the deep expertise required for security selection in each asset class is typically delegated to single asset class portfolio managers, multi-asset investors need to understand the return and risk characteristics of each asset class, their potential rewards and perils, their interactions with each other and their roles in the overall portfolio. Only with this understanding of each asset class can a multi-asset portfolio be constructed. Often, when multi-asset class portfolio managers discuss their portfolios with clients, an understanding of all asset classes is expected.

Conservative assets and risk assets

It is helpful to divide the universe of asset classes into risk assets and conservative assets. There is no single, clear definition for the two types of assets. However, *risk assets* are assets exhibiting relatively high levels of risk, both in terms of volatility and downside risk, and are expected to generate returns to compensate investors for the risk over time. Risk assets include equities (public and private), high-yield bonds, emerging market debt, commodities and the more aggressive hedge fund strategies. The role of risk assets in portfolios is generating growth and long-term returns. Risk assets are the portfolio's growth engine.

Conservative assets are assets that exhibit relatively low levels of risk and are expected to generate lower returns compared to risk assets. Conservative assets include cash, government bonds, investment grade corporate bonds and the more conservative hedge fund strategies. Conservative assets are expected to perform differently than risk assets. Some conservative assets, such as government bonds, normally benefit when there is general market stress, risk aversion and a flight to quality (or a flight to safety). When risk assets crash, conservative assets are expected to perform better. Conservative assets are expected to generate stable returns or cash flows, providing stability to portfolios. When liabilities are present, another role of conservative assets is hedging liabilities. Government bonds and inflation-linked bonds are commonly used to fulfil this role (as well as swaps and derivatives).

The distinction between risk and conservative assets is unclear in some cases, such as real estate. In other instances conservative assets may turn into risk assets. For example, government bonds of countries such as Italy and Spain during the 2011 European debt crisis or investment grade bonds, such as those of Lehman Brothers, during the 2008 credit crisis. Conservative assets can also be transformed into risk assets using leverage.

Different portfolio roles for asset classes

Each asset class has a role in multi-asset portfolios:

- *Cash*: Stable returns; liquidity to meet short-term expected and unexpected liabilities and quickly invest in opportunities; margin for derivatives; and coverage for derivative positions.

- *Equities*: Long-term portfolio growth and exposure to equity market risk (beta) and equity risk premium. Equities are the most common source for growth in multi-asset portfolios.

- *Government bonds*: Stable nominal returns; income; protection when equity markets are stressed; liability matching; diversification to equity holdings; and exposure to interest rate risk and maturity risk premium.

- *Inflation-linked bonds*: Stable real returns; income; inflation hedge; hedge against long-term liabilities; and investment for retirement.

- *Corporate bonds*: Long-term portfolio growth; exposure to credit risk premium; and income.

- *High-yield bonds*: Exposure to below investment grade credit risk; income; long-term portfolio growth; and a substitute for equities. High-yield is not normally a core holding within a portfolio and normally tapped into opportunistically or tactically.

- *Emerging market debt (EMD)*: Long-term portfolio growth; income; and diversification. Similar to high-yield, EMD is a tactical asset class.

- *Convertible bonds*: Combination of equity-like growth and corporate bond-like capped downside.

- *Real estate*: Diversification; exposure to long-term economic growth; income; liquidity premium; and inflation hedge. One of the main considerations with real estate is illiquidity, high transaction costs and inefficiency of the market.

- *Commodities*: Long-term portfolio growth; diversification; and inflation hedge.

- *Private equity*: Long-term portfolio growth; and liquidity premium.

- *Hedge funds*: Diverse exposure to manager skill and unique investment techniques.

- *Infrastructure*: Diversification; income; and liquidity premium.

The universe of asset classes is expanding. Old asset classes are becoming more accessible (e.g. art, timber) and new asset classes are developed (e.g. leveraged loans, insurance-linked securities and volatility). Multi-asset investors should keep up with the new roles, opportunities and risks that additional asset classes add to portfolios.

Summary

- Conservative assets provide stable returns and risk assets provide long-term growth for portfolios.

- Each asset class has a role within multi-asset portfolios.

Investment selection completes the bottom-up process of populating the top-down asset allocation with appropriate investments. The next section of the book focuses on the steps that lie between asset allocation and investment selection – they are necessary to glue them together to manage multi-asset portfolios.

The multi-asset investment management process, portfolio construction, risk budgeting and implementation are essential for managing portfolios with multiple investments across different asset classes. Currency risk management is relevant for any global portfolio investing in more than a single currency. Derivatives are powerful weapons in the arsenal of multi-asset investors and offer significant efficiencies for multi-asset investing. Model portfolios are a way to disseminate multi-asset views across multiple portfolios.

22. INVESTMENT MANAGEMENT PROCESS

The multi-asset investment management process combines the three pillars of multi-asset investing: SAA, TAA and investment selection, as well as portfolio construction. The challenge is combining long-term asset allocation, short-term adjustments to asset allocation and alpha from security selection across different asset classes.

Not only does each activity have a different investment horizon, but also each activity has different techniques and styles for alpha generation across different asset classes. The ways to add alpha in equities, fixed income, property and alternatives are different. There are numerous choices and some can have a material impact on results. A wrong call on an asset allocation or investment selection decision within a major asset class may topple performance.

An investment management process ensures that the framework for decision making is clear, investment results are repeatable and all aspects of portfolio management, benefits and risk are considered. A robust and disciplined process is a key ingredient to consistent, repeatable results.

The eight steps in the process

The eight steps in the multi-asset portfolio management process are:

1. Investment objectives and constraints

2. Investment strategy

3. Risk budgeting

4. TAA

5. Investment selection

6. Portfolio construction

7. Implementation and rebalancing

8. Review

1. Investment objectives and constraints

The investment management process begins with discussing, clarifying and deciding the investor's investment objectives and constraints for the portfolio. Each investor (or a group of investors) and each portfolio can have different objectives and constraints. The starting point is always the investment objectives.

The role of the financial advisor is helping investors formulate appropriate investment objectives. This may require educating investors, ensuring that they understand the risks and potential rewards of the portfolio. For retail funds one of the objectives of regulators (e.g. SEC, FSA and ESMA[266]) is promoting such education to the mass market where not all investors have access to financial advisors.

Part of the process of setting investment objectives is analysis of the economic backdrop. The economic environment is directly linked to the portfolio's possible results. CMAs for SAA and tactical opportunities depend on the economic situation. Portfolios should be positioned differently depending on valuations, sentiment, interest rate level and the stage in the economic cycle. Investor expectations should be managed based on the current economic backdrop.

Alongside the investment objectives the *investment constraints* should be clarified and defined. The objectives of investment constraints are controlling risks and aligning investments with investors' preferences. Investment constraints limit the potential alpha of skilled portfolio managers. Investors can limit the allocation to each asset class by specifying a range or maximum/minimum for each allocation (e.g. minimum 2% cash to allow for cash flows, tax provisions, liquidity and margin accounts or maximum 50% equities to control overall portfolio risk).

Institutional investors can specify the target allocation to risk assets. The *equity backing ratio* (EBR) method, for example, aims to set the risk level of portfolios by setting the target allocation to equities and property. However, such methods may not capture all risk assets (e.g. emerging market debt and corporate bonds) and all risks (e.g. liquidity and credit risks). Risk classification may be counterintuitive, such as classifying emerging market debt (EMD) as a conservative asset and convertible bonds as a risk asset, while EMD is riskier than convertibles. The objective of truly controlling the portfolio risk level may be missed. It may be better to use volatility targeting or setting a level of risk, such as standard deviation, to control and communicate portfolio risk. By specifying a quantitative risk level, rather than focusing on certain asset classes, the target risk level of multi-asset portfolios captures more risks across more investments.

As part of the investment constraints, investors should decide which asset classes and investment techniques can be used in the portfolio, or in other words define the *investment universe*. Some investors feel comfortable only with the traditional asset classes such as equities, bonds and cash. Other investors agree to include alternative investments such as real estate, private equity, hedge funds, commodities, managed futures and so on. Some investors agree to use derivatives.

The more investment tools that are available for portfolio managers, the better the portfolio that can be constructed. More asset classes mean more diversification opportunities and a wider investment opportunity set. More investment instruments and techniques mean more flexibility and cost efficiency. However, a wider array of asset classes and investment instruments also means more sophistication and expertise are needed to manage the portfolio. Before formulating the portfolio's investment strategy the investment universe and investment techniques should be agreed.

2. Investment strategy

Once the investment objectives, constraints and permitted portfolio management activities are defined, the plan to achieve the investment objectives is formulated. The objectives define what should be achieved, the universe defines which resources and tools are available to achieve the objectives and the investment strategy is the plan of how to achieve the objectives with the available resources and tools.

If the portfolio's investment horizon is long term, the first step in formulating the investment strategy is SAA. SAA is the long-term plan for the portfolio based on CMAs, which are linked to the current economic environment. Since it is more reliable to estimate asset class performance over the long term than the short term, SAA is critical in portfolio positioning. SAA is adjusted to short-term views as part of the TAA process.

If the portfolio's investment horizon is short term, SAA cannot play a part. In this case, the investment strategy should focus on hedging liabilities, minimising risks and being opportunistic (betting on short-term opportunities when they arise). Each investment strategy is different depending on circumstances. The combination of long-term SAA with short-term adjustments forms the investment strategy.

Optimisation is the process of identifying the most efficient asset allocation to target the return objectives within the risk objectives and investment constraints. When the return objective is absolute, SAA optimises the asset allocation in absolute risk space (i.e. maximising the Sharpe ratio) and typically forms the portfolio's long-term composite benchmark. When the return objective is absolute in a sense of targeting a positive return, cash or inflation rate can be the benchmark. When the return objectives are relative to an existing benchmark, SAA optimises the portfolio in relative space (i.e. maximising the information ratio with a tracking error constraint). The tracking error anchors the portfolio to its benchmark and limits the deviations from the benchmark. Portfolios can target an absolute volatility within a range of volatilities with the aim of maximising return for a given volatility. Whatever the return and risk objectives are, the portfolio should have a benchmark to be able to measure investment results.

The results of the optimisation must be overlaid by judgment and common sense. The optimisation is sensitive to CMAs and tends to amplify estimation errors (i.e. allocating more to assets whose return is overstated and/or risk is understated). The ways to address this are through constraining the weights of the asset allocation, using robust methods to estimate CMAs (e.g. bootstrapping), or using robust methodologies to formulate consistent CMAs (e.g. the Black-Litterman model).

The investment objectives and constraints together with the investment strategy should be formalised and documented in an Investment Management Agreement (IMA) or Investment Policy Statement (IPS). Such documents guide the investment decisions and clarify how the portfolio should be managed. Documentation is also instrumental for succession of management.

3. Risk budgeting

Based on the portfolio's risk objectives, the multi-asset investor needs to allocate the risk budget to the three sources of risk and return: SAA, TAA and investment selection. Whether the risk objective is relative to a benchmark (e.g. tracking error) or absolute (e.g. standard deviation) a portion of the total risk must be allocated to each activity. Risk allocation determines the total risk of the portfolio and its potential rewards. Risk budgeting should be dynamic and allocate risks to different activities based on the conviction in each one to add value and the changing magnitude of risk of each activity.

4. TAA

SAA can be supplemented by TAA to adjust the asset allocation to enhance returns as well as to control short-term risks. TAA is optional. However, portfolios should have a capability to quickly alter their asset allocation to be able to effectively manage risks. TAA may be a source of additional alpha. SAA and TAA use different processes with different investment horizons and they can complement each other. If TAA is implemented via a derivative overlay, the effect of asset allocation changes on total risk should be considered to ensure that the portfolio remains within its risk budget. If TAA is implemented via a standalone vehicle, the allocation to the vehicle is determined by the risk budgeting process.

5. Investment selection

Investment selection populates the investment strategy to gain exposure to the different asset classes. This creates a portfolio from the asset allocation. The objectives are creating a portfolio aligned with the investment strategy and enhancing returns through alpha from security selection. Multi-asset investors select underlying securities and/or managers to select securities within each asset class. The choices in investment selection are numerous and range across active or passive, investment styles, manager styles, investment vehicles and so on. The mix of active and passive investments is part of the risk budgeting process and determines the risk budget allocated to security selection. The tracking error of each active underlying portfolio also determines the risk budget allocated to security selection.

6. Portfolio construction

Portfolio construction combines SAA, TAA and investment selection within the risk parameters, aiming to meet the investment objectives. Portfolio construction is responsible for holistically combining different investments under different asset classes in the context of the multi-asset portfolio. Portfolio construction ensures that the investment selection is done with the investment objectives and constraints in mind, taking into account the interrelationships among asset classes and the risk budgeting of the entire portfolio. This ensures that the final portfolio is aligned with the investor's needs and requirements.

7. Implementation and rebalancing

When all the investments are identified, the next step is to ensure that the overall portfolio matches the risk and return objectives. Assessing the risk and expected return before implementation is advisable. Once the portfolio is in line with expectations, the investment choices need to be implemented. Portfolio rebalancing is important to keep the portfolio in line with its investment strategy over time. Investors can use cash flows to reduce the transaction costs of trading underlying investments to rebalance when possible. A disciplined rebalancing process means selling outperforming investments (taking profits) and buying underperforming investments. This is a natural process to sell high and buy low, control risk and enhance returns.

8. Review

The entire process is ongoing and dynamic. Performance should be measured and reviewed regularly to assess whether the portfolio is meeting or on course to meet its objectives, managed within the risk objectives and constraints, and following the investment strategy. The review process should include evaluation of all the different components of the multi-asset portfolio, covering SAA, TAA, investment selection and selected investments. Each of those components should be monitored on an ongoing basis.

The frequency of monitoring should be reasonable. Too frequent monitoring and comparison of managers with benchmarks without allowing them sufficient time to perform may result in damaging changes to investment selections without sound merits. Monitoring the dynamic investment objectives and market conditions ensures that the investment objectives are appropriate and the portfolio is well-positioned to the current economic environment. Dynamic CMAs ensure that the SAA is updated, TAA helps position portfolios in line with market opportunities and risks, and dynamic investment selection aims to match investment choice with the current market environment.

The key is that while the process should be disciplined and descriptive, it also must be dynamic and flexible. Investors need to have a hand on the market pulse and implement changes as and when dictated by changing investment objectives and economic conditions.

Organising the multi-asset team

Multi-asset portfolio management teams need to fulfil various functions to support the investment decision process and management of portfolios. All the functions can either be done within a single team or one team can use different teams, each with its own expertise (SAA, TAA, investment selection). Separation of functions enhances the checks and balances, supporting a proper governance process whereby investment decisions are challenged and the customer interests are better safeguarded. Independent risk and performance functions are essential for robust governance. Ultimately, however, the multi-asset portfolio manager should be accountable for the multi-asset portfolios even when some investment decisions are delegated to others.

Process, process, process

Process is important. It ensures that everything is linked together and that people know what to do. All the different activities should follow the process and consequently the likelihood of meeting investment objectives is higher.

The investment management process must fit the portfolio. The process for a flexible and liquid portfolio is different than that of a cumbersome and illiquid portfolio. When the portfolio is very active, aiming to add performance from different investment opportunities, in the short or long term, the investment management process must allow for quick investment decisions with quick and efficient implementation. The focus would be on TAA and investment selection. Conversely, when the portfolio is slower, aiming to deliver long-term objectives, a different investment process fits. The emphasis should be on SAA, as well as on TAA and investment selection.

After the investment objectives are defined and understood and the size, investment universe and investment techniques are agreed, an appropriate investment process should be formulated based on the specific circumstances and characteristics of each portfolio.

Summary

- The investment management process combines SAA, TAA and investment selection under the four stages of the process: establishing objectives, setting an investment strategy, implementing a solution and reviewing.

- The eight steps in the multi-asset portfolio management process are: investment objectives and constraints; investment strategy; risk budgeting; TAA; investment selection; portfolio construction; implementation and rebalancing; and review.

- Multi-asset portfolio management teams require several functions to manage multi-asset portfolios. One approach is for a single team managing all the functions while an alternative approach is for the team to use other specialist teams for the different functions. The multi-asset portfolio manager should be accountable for all investment decisions.

23. PORTFOLIO CONSTRUCTION

Portfolio construction sits in the middle of the portfolio management process between the top-down asset allocation and bottom-up investment selection. Portfolio construction includes all the steps necessary to construct and manage portfolios, combining SAA, TAA, investment selection, rebalancing and risk management. Portfolio management activities can be separated into formulating investment views and implementing the investment views. Portfolio construction takes the investment views and supplements them where necessary so they are efficiently reflected within portfolios.

The portfolio constructor takes the holistic view of the entire portfolio. While an SAA strategist is focused on long-term asset allocation, a TAA strategist is focused on short-term asset allocation opportunities and risks and a single asset class security picker is focused on one specific asset class, the portfolio constructor needs to have the overall view, fitting together all these components. Portfolio constructors consider the portfolio's return and risk objectives, the interrelationships among different investments across the portfolio and its risk budgeting.

Effective portfolio construction reflects asset allocation views in the portfolio and balances risks and styles across it. Once there is an asset allocation decision to invest in an asset class the portfolio constructor needs to allocate the appropriate amount to the investment selector and instruct what type of investments to select in the asset class. For example, if within equities aggressive investments are selected, the investment selection within fixed income may be defensive to balance risk with equities.

Minimum investment

The amount invested in each asset class or investment should be meaningful to have a material impact on the portfolio and to make it economical to dedicate resources to selecting and monitoring the investment. An investment generating a total return of 10% over a year with an allocation of only 1% within a portfolio contributes 0.1% or 10 basis points to overall portfolio performance. To judge whether this contribution is worthwhile the portfolio's specific circumstances should be considered. However, a more meaningful allocation of 5% would have contributed 0.5% or 50 basis points.

Blending different investment styles

One role of portfolio construction is blending different investments under each asset class. For example, under US equities the choice varies across: investment styles (value and growth); market capitalisation sizes (small, mid and large cap); active management styles (fundamental and quantitative, conservative and aggressive, benchmark hugging and benchmark agnostic, long-only and long-short); degree to which the style is active (passive, enhanced indexing, active); and investment vehicles (segregated, CIS and derivatives).

The portfolio constructer should blend different investment choices to match the portfolio's objectives. When the objective is style neutral, investment styles should be balanced (e.g. 50% value, 50% growth). When the objective is smooth returns, the blend should focus on diversification and investments with low correlation of excess returns. When the objective is low tracking error versus the indices used in SAA, the focus should be on passive investments and active investments with low tracking errors. When the asset allocation is aggressive, selecting defensive investments with low betas can balance it or, conversely, when the asset allocation is defensive, selective aggressive investments with high beta can provide the balance. If the objective is dynamically managing the investment blend to benefit from changing market conditions, the portfolio constructer is fulfilling a role similar to TAA.

Different investment styles perform well or poorly under different market conditions. Forecasting the market conditions and positioning the portfolio accordingly is challenging and adds value only if investors have forecasting ability. As always, lacking forecasting ability the best solution is sticking with the benchmark and minimising changes to avoid transaction costs and noise.

The US equity market has a long history of returns for different investment styles and capitalisation sizes, making it a good example for demonstrating how different investment styles and market caps behave. Figures 23.1 and 23.2 show the performance of the 1,000 largest capitalisation stocks (Russell[267] 1000 Index) in the 3,000 stocks in the Russell universe versus the 2,000 smallest capitalisation stocks (Russell 2000 Index). The Russell 1000 Index represents about 90% of the total market capitalisation of the Russell 3000 Index universe[268]. Large caps have a market cap above $1.8 billion.

Figure 23.1 shows the performance of the Russell 1000 and Russell 2000 indices over distinct annual calendar years since 1990 and Figure 23.2 shows their cumulative performance since January 1979. Large and small cap stocks perform differently, meaning that blending them provides diversification opportunities as well as return enhancement opportunities (although their correlation is relatively high at 0.86).

Generally, the best time to invest in small cap stocks is several months before a recession ends and then move to large cap stocks several months into a recovery. It is, however, difficult to forecast the inflection points and the next stage of the economic cycle. Fundamentally, small cap stocks are less exposed to the global economy than large cap stocks are, because small caps are typically less focused on exporting while some large caps are global conglomerates[269]. Therefore, if the view is positive on the local market but there are concerns with overseas economies (i.e. decoupling), small caps may fair better.

Currency views may have a different impact on large and small companies. A weakening local currency can be good news for large caps, since their exports become more competitively priced and foreign income may increase when measured in local currency. A weakening currency may have no impact on small caps. All these considerations support the allocation decision between large and small caps.

Figure 23.1 – annual returns of large and small caps, January 1990 to June 2012

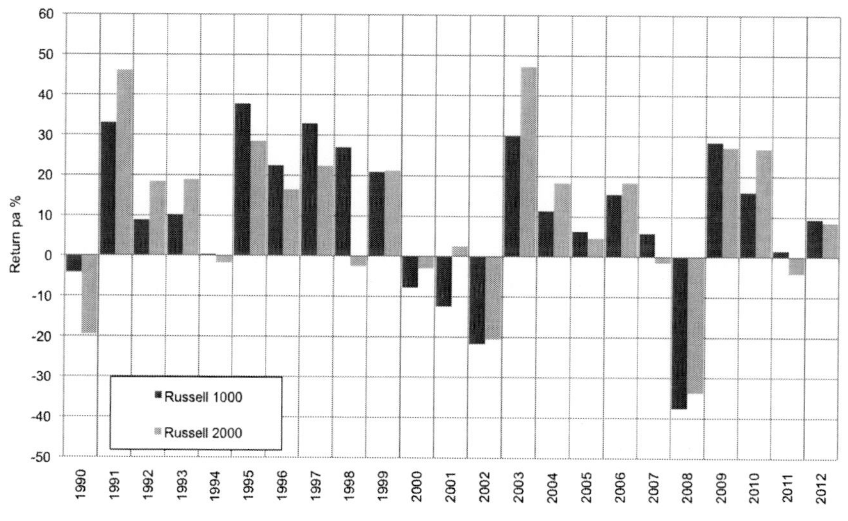

Source: Bloomberg, Russell 1000, Russell 2000.

Figure 23.2 – cumulative return of large and small caps, January 1979 to June 2012

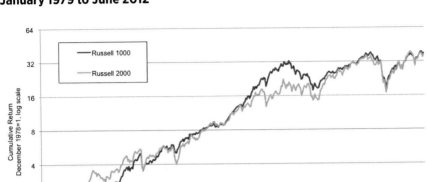

Source: Bloomberg, Russell 1000, Russell 2000.

Figures 23.3 and 23.4 focus on the differences between value and growth. The Russell 3000 Value Index represents value stocks and the Russell 3000 Growth Index represents growth stocks.

Value stocks are considered under-priced by the market. They usually have a low P/E ratio, high dividend yield, low leverage (debt/equity ratio), low price-to-book ratio and low earnings growth expectations.

Growth stocks are expected to experience above average earnings growth. They usually have a high P/E ratio, strong forecasted growth rate, high Return on Equity (ROE) and high Earnings per Share (EPS).

The difference between value and growth is that value investors look for investments with current price below intrinsic value and growth investors look for investments whose price is expected to grow in the future, outpacing priced-in expectations. Growth investors are more focused on future prospects than on current valuations.

Value stocks tend to outperform growth stocks over the long term. However, there are time periods in which growth stocks strongly outperform (e.g. 1991, 1998-1999 and 2009). As value and growth stocks perform differently (correlation 0.85), there are diversification and performance enhancement opportunities.

Figure 23.3 – annual returns of value and growth, January 1990 to June 2012

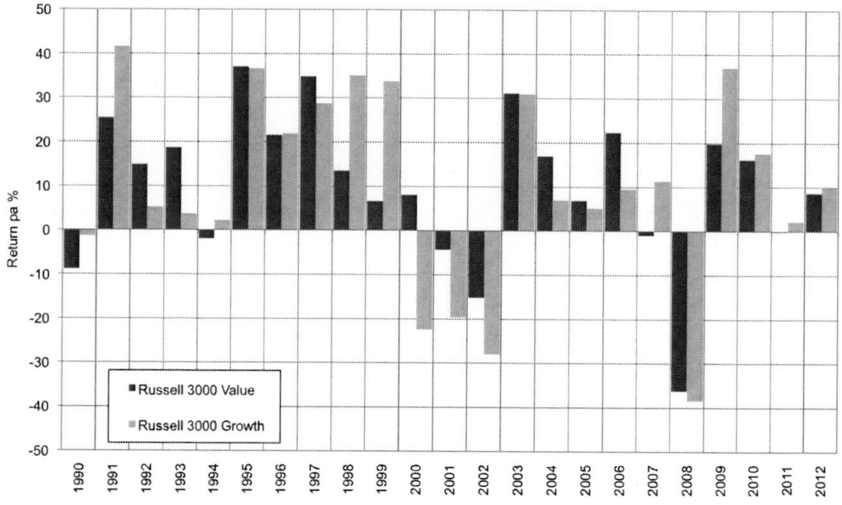

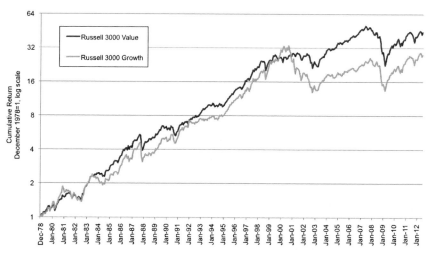

Source: Bloomberg, Russell 3000 Value, Russell 3000 Growth.

Figure 23.4 – cumulative return of value and growth, January 1979 to June 2012

Source: Bloomberg, Russell 3000 Value, Russell 3000 Growth.

Table 23.1 compares the historic volatility and annualised return of the different Russell indices from January 1979 to June 2012.

Table 23.1 – US equity size and style historic return and risk characteristics, January 1979 to June 2012

	Russell 1000	Russell 2000	Russell 1000 Value	Russell 1000 Growth	Russell 2000 Value	Russell 2000 Growth
Performance (% pa)	11.43	11.33	11.89	10.83	13.09	9.17
Volatility (%)	15.71	20.06	21.40	17.67	17.77	23.41
Sharpe ratio	0.39	0.30	0.31	0.31	0.44	0.17

Source: Bloomberg, Russell 1000, Russell 2000,Russell 1000 Value, Russell 1000 Growth, Russell 2000 Value, Russell 2000 Growth.

In 1992 Eugene Fama and Kenneth French published the Fama-French Three Factor Model[270]. The model expands on CAPM by adding size and value factors in addition to CAPM's market risk factor (β). The model assumes that value stocks outperform growth stocks and small cap stocks outperform large cap stocks. By adding these two factors the model aims to evaluate stock prices better than the CAPM does. Small-cap and value are also considered alternative betas or risk factors. By overweighting portfolios to these risk factors outperformance may be generated over the long term (although there are periods in which these factors underperform). FWI indices have a value bias and equally-weighted indices have a small-cap bias relative to market-cap weighted indices.

Core satellite

The core satellite portfolio construction approach separates portfolios into two parts: core and satellite. The core uses passive, inexpensive and liquid investments to gain exposure to *betas*. The satellite uses actively-managed, high-conviction investments to add *alpha*.

Within traditional equity and fixed income investments arguably fewer opportunities exist for active managers to add alpha and investors should not spend time and money seeking alpha in these asset classes. Therefore, the majority of portfolios should be invested in cheap passive investments.

The core aims to track the risk and return characteristics of the SAA, aligning the portfolio with it. The satellite, on the other hand, aims to enhance returns through manager selection, tap less liquid investments to benefit from liquidity premium and include off-benchmark investments.

The allocation between core and satellite depends on how closely the core aligns the portfolio with the risk and return characteristics of SAA. If it is enough to invest 80% of the portfolio in the core to get it sufficiently aligned with SAA (e.g. by measuring the tracking error between the portfolio and a benchmark reflecting SAA), then 20% can be invested in the satellite. However, the risk and return characteristics of the entire portfolio should be assessed to ensure that the satellite does not significantly alter the characteristics of the portfolio from those of SAA with the risk of derailing it from meeting its investment objectives. The assumption of SAA is that the portfolio mirrors the factor characteristics of the SAA's composite benchmark.

The idea behind core satellite is having a balanced access to as many different sources of systematic risk as possible, in a very efficient way, with access to alpha sources where they are needed to add systematic risk (e.g. real estate) or where they can add value (e.g. private equity and hedge funds). Ideally, the structure should be wrapped in a tax efficient vehicle to reduce taxes.

Relationship between risk and return

In economics, it is well-known that optimal profit maximisation is achieved when marginal revenue is equal to marginal cost. In finance, marginal revenue is equivalent to excess return over cash and marginal cost is measured by risk. In an efficient portfolio any small change to asset allocation for the set of current portfolio weights cannot increase excess return over portfolio risk. That is, the current portfolio is optimal and any change introduced to current portfolio weights will lead to a deterioration of efficiency.

Therefore, in line with theory[271], in a well-constructed portfolio the relationship between the *marginal contribution to risk* (MCR) of each investment and its expected contribution to return should be equal. If the ratio between expected return and MCR is higher for one investment than a second one, the allocation to the second investment (with the lower ratio) should be reduced and the allocation to the first investment (with the higher ratio) should be increased. By reducing the allocation to the second investment its MCR decreases and its return to MCR ratio increases, and vice versa with respect to the first investment. When the ratio of return to MCR is equal across all investments, the portfolio is well-balanced and efficient.

This is easier said than done in practice. Limitations in measuring MCR and uncertainty about the estimation of expected returns makes this process sound in theory but often impractical. Nevertheless, it is helpful as a guide for deriving efficient portfolio construction.

Portfolio construction example

The objectives of a UK-based investor are for a moderate portfolio with an absolute risk target (volatility) of approximately 10% within a range of 7% to 13%. Using the CMAs of SAA, a long-term composite benchmark is proposed with the desired volatility, consisting of only the basic asset classes of global equity (with a home bias to UK equities), gilts and cash.

SAA optimisation is conducted with a risk budget of a tracking error between 1.5% and 2.0% relative to the composite benchmark. SAA proposes an efficient asset allocation, including deviations from the benchmark weights, as well as diversification across additional asset classes that are not included in the benchmark (off-benchmark).

The SAA is adjusted to tactical considerations. For example, SAA overweights UK equities due to their higher dividend yield and growth prospects relative to other equity markets. However, while the tactical view is positive on UK equities as well, the overweight is reduced to better spread risk of active positions across the portfolio. SAA materially underweights gilts due to their historically low yields. However, the tactically adjusted SAA increases the weight to gilts since they provide protection against a fall in risk assets.

The allocation to emerging market debt is reduced to more closely align the portfolio's total allocation to risk assets with that of the benchmark. The underweight to Europe excluding UK equities is reduced (i.e. allocation increases) since the short-term view on Europe is constructive as equity valuations in Europe seem attractive. SAA is adjusted for both short and medium-term market views and for portfolio construction and risk management considerations, such as better balancing the risk across active positions and protecting the portfolio against potential downturn in risk assets.

Once the adjusted SAA is set, a TAA overlay is added. The TAA overlay is a basket of long and short positions in markets and is implemented via derivatives where possible or other liquid instruments (ETFs and CIS) where derivatives are unavailable. TAA positions can reverse the adjustments of the SAA. However, TAA has a short-term horizon and these positions can be readily adjusted since they are implemented via liquid instruments (i.e. TAA is a high-frequency, short-term process). The adjusted SAA is implemented via trading underlying investments and has a longer horizon than high-frequency TAA.

The next step in portfolio construction is deciding on the investments under each asset class. For example, the 33% allocation to UK equities under adjusted SAA is populated with a combination of active and passive UK equity investments (e.g. active funds, passive funds, ETFs and individual stocks). The TAA overlay (i.e. adding 2% to UK equities) is implemented by going long a futures contract on the FTSE 100 Index. The portfolio is shown in Table 23.2.

Table 23.2 – illustrative multi-asset portfolio

Asset class	Benchmark	SAA	Adjusted SAA	TAA	Final asset allocation
UK equities	30%	35%	33%	2%	35%
Europe ex-UK equities	6%	4%	5%	-1%	4%
North America equities	15%	12%	13%	1%	14%
Japan equities	3%	2%	2%	1%	3%
Pacific ex-Japan equities	3%	4%	4%	1%	5%
Emerging market equities	3%	4%	4%	1%	5%
Convertible bonds	0%	2%	2%	0%	2%
Gilts	35%	10%	16%	-2%	14%
Inflation-linked gilts	0%	0%	0%	0%	0%
UK corporate bonds	0%	10%	5%	1%	6%
Developed global bonds	0%	2%	2%	-2%	0%
Emerging market debt	0%	3%	2%	-1%	1%
Global high yield	0%	1%	1%	0%	1%
UK property	0%	2%	2%	0%	2%
Europe property	0%	1%	1%	0%	1%
Asia property	0%	1%	1%	0%	1%
Commodities	0%	1%	1%	-1%	0%
Private equity	0%	0%	0%	0%	0%
Hedge funds	0%	4%	4%	0%	4%
Cash	5%	2%	2%	0%	2%
Total	**100%**	**100%**	**100%**	**0%**	**100%**
Expected return	6.0%	6.8%	6.6%	0.2%	6.8%
Expected risk	10.2%	11.1%	10.9%	-	11.6%
Excess return	-	0.8%	0.6%	-	0.8%
Tracking error	-	1.8%	1.5%	-	2.1%
Sharpe ratio	0.58	0.61	0.60	-	0.58
Information ratio	-	0.45	0.41	-	0.39

Model portfolios

Model portfolios or centralised investment propositions (CIPs) are generic portfolios created by asset management firms – they reflect the firm's house views on asset allocation and investment selection. They include different asset allocations matching different levels of risk (risk profiles) for different groups of investors with different risk tolerances. To move from asset allocation models to model portfolios the best investment selection ideas are included under each asset class. Investors may feel that the model portfolio has been customised for their unique risk tolerance. However, the models are used across many investors with broadly similar investment objectives and they are tweaked for larger clients as necessary.

Wealth management firms typically use model portfolios since each client account is managed separately. Fund management houses, selling retail funds, can use model portfolios to easily disseminate the house views across internal fund managers. Discretionary portfolios of wealth managers typically offer FoF for relatively small-sized investors and a combination of segregated portfolios and funds for larger investors. Segregated accounts are used for core assets, such as domestic equities and fixed income, since they make up a large portion of the portfolio (i.e. sufficient size for a segregated account) and can be managed in-house. Funds are used for smaller exposures, tactical allocations and externally managed asset classes.

Portfolio managers or financial advisors should have the flexibility to deviate from the model portfolio to fit it to the specific investor needs and constraints. However, the central house investment strategy should be reflected in all the portfolios with required modifications. Model portfolios are a way to harness the full capabilities of the asset management house for the benefit of each client. The best research ideas and manager selection, for example, are represented in the model portfolios, which are then used as the basis for constructing portfolios for each investor. Individual portfolios look bespoke since they include some adjustments to match investor requirements.

The degree of customisation should match the size of investors' assets. For retail or perhaps affluent markets, customisation should be limited and each investor's portfolio should match the model portfolio – otherwise, the asset management house will not have the sufficient resources to monitor and manage the risks of each bespoke portfolio. High net worth (HNW) and ultra high net worth (UHNW) investors warrant more customisation and deviation from the model portfolios. Model portfolios are a way to scale services across clients.

Financial advisors or bankers should be responsible for relationship management with each investor. Ideally, a dedicated team manages the model portfolios and disseminates them to financial advisors, together with the rationale for changes. This allows financial advisors to focus on relationship management and provide the best investment advice to clients.

Model portfolios should follow SAAs with different risk levels so financial advisors can fit an appropriate strategy for clients according to their risk appetite. Sometimes three different models are offered and sometimes five, starting with the basic distinction between conservative, moderate and aggressive.

Models can be offered in different base currencies, typically dollars, pounds and euro. Some assets, such as global equities, are similar across different base currencies, while fixed income and cash are dissimilar and denominated in the base currency. Therefore, global equities, global bonds, EMD and hedge funds, for example, can be the same across the models, while currency hedging to each base currency differs. However, fixed income and cash for a dollar model should be invested in Treasuries and US T-Bills, for a pound model in gilts and UK T-Bills and for euro in German Bunds and euro money market.

Models in different currencies can have a home bias within global equities. For example, pound or euro-based models can have an allocation of 50% to 70% to UK or European equities within equities, respectively. Dollar-based models can even have a higher home bias since US equities already make up 50% of the market capitalisation of global equities.[272]

Model portfolios are often offered with and without alternative investments (AI). Some investors do not wish to include alternatives in their portfolios and stick only with traditional asset classes. This sacrifices diversification benefits and reduces the opportunity set of their portfolios.

Large investors normally hire a financial advisor who advises them on their investment needs. Smaller investors potentially rely on model portfolios. If they are constructed appropriately following a robust process they are a way to disseminate investment decisions across a large numbers of investors.

Table 23.3 shows three typical asset allocation models, with and without alternative investments.

Table 23.3 – illustrative model portfolios

Without AI	Conservative	Moderate	Aggressive
Equities	20%	50%	75%
Bonds	60%	40%	20%
Cash	20%	10%	5%
Expected return	4.8%	6.1%	7.1%
Expected risk	4.0%	7.5%	11.2%
With AI	**Conservative**	**Moderate**	**Aggressive**
Equities	20%	40%	60%
Bonds	55%	40%	15%
Cash	20%	10%	5%
Alternatives	5%	10%	20%
Expected return	4.9%	6.0%	6.9%
Expected risk	4.0%	6.5%	9.9%

Conclusion

Portfolio construction holistically looks at the entire portfolio and links, from an investment perspective, the different parts together. It also involves activities that are not fulfilled by anyone else. Multi-asset investors decide how everything (SAA, TAA and investment selection) fits together.

Summary

- Portfolio construction sits in the middle between top-down asset allocation and bottom-up investment selection.

- The aims of portfolio construction are: ensuring that portfolio risk and return characteristics reflect those of the investment strategy or policy (SAA); taking a holistic view over the portfolio and instructing the investment selection within each asset class, considering the interrelationships across investments; ensuring that the risks across the portfolio are well balanced and in line with its risk objectives.

- The amount invested in each investment should be material enough to have an impact on the portfolio.

- Portfolio construction blends different investment styles and dynamically manages the blend, benefiting from changing market conditions.

- Core satellite separates the portfolio to a core of passive, inexpensive and liquid investments to gain betas that mirror the composite benchmark used in SAA and a satellite of active, more expensive, less liquid investments that aim to add alpha.

- Portfolios should have a balanced access to as many different sources of systematic risk (betas) as possible, in a very efficient way, with access to alpha sources where they are needed to add systematic risk (e.g. real estate) or where they can add value (e.g. private equity and hedge funds).

- According to theory in a well-balanced, efficient portfolio there is an equal relationship between the marginal contribution to risk of each investment and its expected contribution to return.

- Model portfolios are a way to disseminate the house views on asset allocation and investment selection across the organisation, ensuring that the best investment ideas are reflected in the portfolio of each investor.

- Financial advisors can use model portfolios to construct portfolios, or as a base, and then customise them depending on investor needs.

- Model portfolios should have different levels of risk so investors can be fitted with the right model depending on their risk tolerance.

- Each model portfolio has a base currency. Global equities are similar across models with appropriate changes to currency hedging and home bias. Fixed income and cash differ across models and should be managed to the base currency.

- Model portfolios can be offered with and without alternative investments for investors who wish to exclude alternatives from their portfolios. Excluding alternatives misses diversification benefits and shrinks the opportunity set of the portfolio.

24. IMPLEMENTATION

The objective of portfolio implementation is minimising the *implementation shortfall*, which is the difference between the return of the theoretical target portfolio and that of the implemented portfolio. Implementation shortfall results from differences between target and actual portfolio weights, transaction costs and cash management.

Roger Clarke et al[273] expanded the fundamental law of active management by adding a *transfer coefficient*:

$$IR = TC*IC*BR^{0.5}$$

where IR is information ratio, IC is information coefficient, BR is breadth (these first three variables from the original Grinold's fundamental law of active management) and TC is the transfer coefficient (the added variable).

The transfer coefficient accounts for constraints in portfolio construction. It should capture the ability to represent the investor's views in the portfolio. One way to increase the transfer coefficient is to remove constraints from portfolios as much as possible. Another aspect of the transfer coefficient could be the degree to which investment decisions are efficiently implemented in portfolios. Implementation is one of the drivers of portfolio performance.

Portfolio implementation

Portfolio implementation is executing the investment decisions of SAA, TAA and investment selection by purchasing and selling investments and financial instruments to reach and maintain an actual portfolio, reflecting as much as possible the target portfolio, while considering the costs and practicalities.

One way to implement investment decisions is by purchasing and selling *physical underlying investments*. The core of portfolios is normally made up of physical investments (physicals), which can be a combination of actively and passively managed investments as well as individual securities. The advantages of using physicals are that it is relatively straightforward and it allows benefits to come from active security selection. The disadvantages include relatively high transaction costs, trading physicals may be disruptive to underlying portfolio managers, the investments are funded (i.e. cash commitment is required for the full exposure) and there may be limitations on short selling.

For large portfolios, implementing changes to asset allocation or investment selection through trading underlying investments may take time. Portfolio managers require advance notice to prepare their portfolios for trading to accommodate investment of cash inflow or raising cash to meet cash outflows. Some physical markets are illiquid and implementation needs to be done over a few days. When the trades include high amounts relative to the volume traded on the market, the changes may have a market impact[274].

Portfolios can include ETFs under each asset class that can be used to implement asset allocation changes. The advantages include that most ETFs are liquid, trading them is less disruptive and it is possible to short ETFs. The disadvantages include that ETFs require capital commitment (unlike futures contracts), the TERs of ETFs are normally higher than costs of futures contracts (depending on the holding period; ETFs may be cheaper over the long term), trading ETFs involves transaction costs (normally less so than active portfolios) and using ETFs means that a portion of the portfolio is invested in passive investments (i.e. no access to potential alpha from security selection). The latter is not necessarily a disadvantage and may be a conscious decision to control overall multi-asset portfolio risk, minimise costs and reduce security selection risk.

Implementing asset allocation changes and TAA using *derivatives*, such as futures contracts, is efficient portfolio management (EPM)[275]. Advantages include that most futures contracts are liquid, trading futures is not disruptive to underlying managers, futures contracts can be shorted, transaction costs are relatively low and cash does not need to be committed for the full notional exposure (only cash for margin).

Disadvantages include basis risk, lack of exposure to active security selection, the need to roll the futures at expiry (normally every one or three months), brokerage commissions, futures contracts are unavailable for all asset classes (e.g. convertible bonds), trading futures with large notional may have market impact and futures require setting up accounts and special documentation.

For some asset classes other derivatives can be used, such as CDS for corporate bonds and property total return swaps (PTRS) for property. However, unlike exchange traded derivatives (ETD), these are over-the-counter (OTC) derivatives, which may not be available for use in every portfolio, their liquidity is not as high as that of standardised futures contracts and for some derivatives the basis risk is material (e.g. CDS and PTRS).

The most efficient implementation is usually a combination of all the different methods, depending on availability of financial instruments, holding period, transaction costs and investment objectives. Where futures contracts are unavailable, other financial instruments should be used. When the holding period is long, ETFs or passive funds may be superior to futures contracts since they do not need to be rolled every few months. However, transaction costs (TERs) of holding ETFs are normally higher than those of futures over the short term. If the objective is accessing active security selection, active underlying portfolios should be used instead of ETFs or futures contracts.

Cash management

Cash management is investing cash inflows and raising cash to meet cash outflows. Cash inflows need to be invested to align the portfolio weights with target weights and to control the overall allocation to cash. If the allocation to cash is higher than target and markets rise, the portfolio will suffer a *cash drag* that may adversely impact performance. Conversely, a high allocation to cash in falling markets improves portfolio performance. However, higher cash allocation than target due to implementation is an unintended active position and should be mitigated.

Cash investment is a balance between transaction costs and tracking error due to the divergence between the target and actual allocation to cash. Each cash inflow cannot be practically invested since some asset classes, such as bonds, have minimum trading amounts and frequent investing increases transaction costs. Some portfolios can use a buffer for cash and hold cash outside of the portfolio without affecting performance until the cash amount reaches a certain level and then all the accumulated cash is invested.

When portfolios experience cash outflows, cash needs to be raised by selling investments to meet the outflows, unless enough cash is held to meet them. Portfolios should hold enough cash to meet other regular needs, such as margin requirements when derivatives are held and commitments from investments such as private equity, as well as cash to quickly invest in emerging opportunities. When cash needs to be raised, illiquid assets, such as real estate, cannot be readily sold and the relative allocation to such assets may increase since the relative allocation to other assets decreases as they are sold to raise cash. It is therefore advisable not to allocate the full target allocation to illiquid investments and consider investing in them carefully.

Rebalancing

Portfolio rebalancing is probably one of the most important portfolio management activities since it maintains the risk profile of portfolios over time. As different investments perform differently asset allocation across investments drifts from targets. Rebalancing is selling investments whose allocation is above target and buying investments whose allocation is below target to get the portfolio back in line with target allocations.

Rebalancing is a delicate process, weighing up risk (tracking error) and transaction costs. Rebalancing too frequently involves high transaction costs, whilst rebalancing too infrequently lets the portfolio weights drift from target weights and the tracking error between the actual and target portfolio increases.

Figures 24.1 and 24.2 show the asset allocation of two portfolios starting with target weights of 50% equities and 50% bonds. The first portfolio is rebalanced on a quarterly basis back to target weights and the second portfolio is not rebalanced. As can be seen, without rebalancing the portfolio drifts substantially from its target weights.

Figure 24.1 – 50% equity, 50% bond portfolio with quarterly rebalancing, January 1970 to June 2012

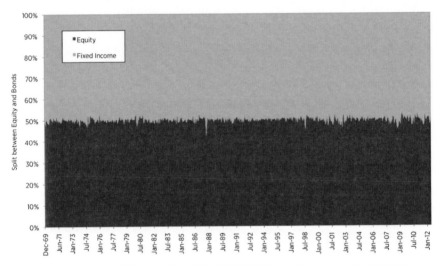

Source: Bloomberg, Global Financial Data, S&P 500, USA 10-year Government Bond Total Return.

Figure 24.2 – 50% equity, 50% bond portfolio without rebalancing, January 1970 to June 2012

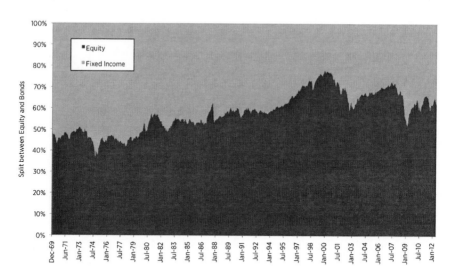

Source: Bloomberg, Global Financial Data, S&P 500, USA 10-year Government Bond Total Return.

Figure 24.3 and Table 24.1 compare the performance and risk characteristics of the two portfolios.

Figure 24.3 – cumulative return, 50% equity, 50% bond portfolio with quarterly rebalancing and without rebalancing, January 1970 to June 2012

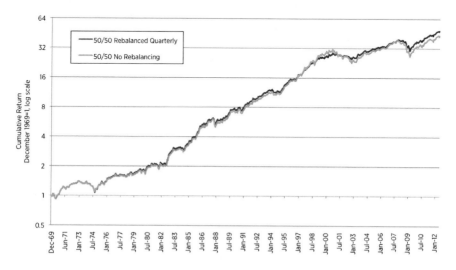

Source: Bloomberg, Global Financial Data, S&P 500, USA 10-year Government Bond Total Return.

Table 24.1 – return and risk characteristics, 50% equity, 50% bond portfolio with quarterly rebalancing and without rebalancing, January 1979 to June 2012

	Quarterly rebalancing	No rebalancing
Performance (% pa)	9.57	9.26
Volatility (%)	9.30	10.25
Max drawdown (%)	-23.11	-31.66

Source: Bloomberg, Global Financial Data, S&P 500, USA 10-year Government Bond Total Return.

The rebalanced portfolio has had modestly higher return and lower risk than those of the non-rebalanced portfolio. One consideration involving performance is whether the transaction costs of rebalancing are higher than the differences in performance (30 basis points per annum). As more illiquid asset classes are included in portfolios the costs of rebalancing increase.

Another consideration involves risk. The risk of the non-rebalanced portfolio changes and after a period of high equity returns the portfolio's asset allocation is tilted toward equities. Equity markets tend to correct after long periods of rising equity prices. This is the point where a well-diversified asset allocation matching the investor's risk profile is most needed. The non-rebalanced portfolio does not have a risk level matching the investor's risk tolerance and the portfolio falls with equity markets.

To reduce some of the transaction costs of rebalancing, cash flows can be used. Cash inflows can be used to buy depreciating assets, instead of selling and buying assets. When cash needs to be raised to meet cash outflows, appreciated assets can be sold to reduce their relative weight.

William Sharpe suggested in a 2010 paper[276] that instead of rebalancing portfolios to target asset allocations, changes in the market capitalisation of asset classes should be considered since they may change the expected returns of asset classes (reverse optimisation) and consequently the portfolio's optimal asset allocation. The goal of this *Adaptive Asset Allocation* policy is developing a rebalancing model that discourages the contrarian nature of traditional rebalancing techniques where investors effectively divest winners to buy recent losers.

Liquidity

One objective of implementation is cost efficiency; minimising the transaction costs of implementing investment decisions. Transaction costs are a function of a number of variables, one of which is liquidity. Some asset classes are relatively illiquid, such as real estate, and the transaction costs of increasing or decreasing their positions may be material. Liquidity is also a function of a few variables, one of which is timing. Trading volumes in markets depend, among other things, on the time period. During months with holidays, such as April (Easter) and December (Christmas), liquidity dries up since investors reduce the amount of trading. During these times changing portfolio positioning involves higher transaction costs than at other times. Global multi-asset portfolios need to consider holidays across the globe, such as Asian, American and European holidays.

One way to overcome liquidity constraints is implementing portfolio changes through liquid futures contracts, although this limits the implementation to the few asset classes for which liquid futures are available. When liquidity returns to markets, the futures can be unwound and physicals can be traded in their place to get the portfolio in line with its target weights.

Conclusion

Implementation determines whether the portfolio that investors think that they have is indeed the one that they do have. While the upside of implementation is to match the investment decisions (i.e. implementation cannot add alpha), the downside is uncapped. A mistake in implementation or operations can derail the entire portfolio and be costly. For large, complex multi-asset portfolios, implementation is a key to success or failure.

Summary

- The objective of implementation is to reduce performance shortfall between the target and actual portfolio due to differences between target and actual portfolio weights, transaction costs and cash management.

- The three ways to implement asset allocation changes are through trading underlying investments, ETFs and derivatives (mainly futures contracts).

- Cash flow management ensures that cash inflows are efficiently invested and cash outflows are met.

- Rebalancing keeps the portfolio's risk profile in line with investment objectives over time.

25. DERIVATIVES

Derivatives are financial instruments whose performance is based or *derived* from the performance or behaviour of the price of underlying assets (*underlying*). The holders of derivatives do not need to hold the underlying. Most financial derivative transactions are cash settled instead of delivering the underlying from the seller to the buyer. Some derivatives, such as options, require a premium payment. Derivatives are often used to manage (hedge) or assume (speculate) risk. The underlying can be interest rates, equity or bond prices, currency rates, commodity prices, credit risk and so on.

Warren Buffett said "I view derivatives as time bombs, both for the parties that deal in them and the economic system... In my view, derivatives are financial weapons of mass destruction". In accordance with this, many investors fear using derivatives. This is a justifiable concern for investors who do not understand derivatives. When used prudently and knowledgably derivatives are useful financial tools to manage risks, transfer risks between parties, and efficiently gain exposure to markets and investments.

Derivatives are either exchange-traded or over-the-counter (OTC). *Exchange-traded derivatives* (ETD) are traded on an exchange, such as Euronext-LIFFE or the CME (Chicago Mercantile Exchange). Each ETD has standardised contract specifications, listing the characteristics of the underlying and the terms of the derivative. Futures contracts and listed options are common types of ETDs. A clearing house is an intermediary between the parties in any ETD transaction. The clearing house is a central counterparty and therefore the counterparty risk is materially reduced. ETDs that trade in high volumes are relatively liquid.

OTC derivatives are usually sold by a bank and can be tailored to the specific requirements of investors. OTC derivatives allow for greater flexibility in terms of expiry date, reference price, notional and underlying compared to ETDs. However, each party in an OTC derivative assumes the counterparty risk of the other party. Simple OTC derivatives are known as *plain vanilla* or vanilla. Complex derivatives are known as *exotic*. Some OTC derivatives are illiquid.

Using derivatives is commonly allowed under *Efficient Portfolio Management* (EPM). Due to the liquidity and relatively low transaction costs of trading some derivatives, using them appropriately is an efficient way to manage some of the exposures and risks in portfolios. Derivatives can be used to synthetically leverage portfolios (e.g. long futures positions do not need the entire exposure to be committed and if cash is not held to cover the economic exposure of futures contracts, the positions are effectively leveraged) and to readily gain short positions by shorting futures contracts or buying put options (without the need to borrow securities for shorting).

Leverage and shorting are two of the risks of using derivatives. Uncovered short positions (i.e. short positions without holding the underlying long position) have a limitless downside potential. Counterparty risk is a common risk, in particular in OTC derivatives. Liquidity risk may be particular issue with exotic OTC derivatives that lack a secondary market.

Some investors are invested in derivatives without realising it. Swap-based ETFs expose investors to derivatives and counterparty risk. Many companies and financial institutions use derivatives. When buying equities or bonds of such companies or institutions, investors indirectly gain exposure to derivatives. Many hedge fund strategies commonly use derivatives as well.

Derivatives contribute to price discovery and market efficiency. Derivatives are liquid and traded in high volumes so they enable arbitrageurs to quickly exploit arbitrage opportunities and eliminate them, moving prices to fair-value.

Futures contracts

Financial futures contracts are legally binding agreements to deliver or take delivery of a specific quantity of a specific asset at a future date at an agreed price. Instead of delivering the underlying, most futures contracts are cash settled (i.e. the difference between the underlying and futures price is paid by the party who owns it to the counterparty). Futures contracts are traded on regulated exchanges with standardised contract sizes and delivery dates.

Both the buyers and sellers of futures contracts must pay collateral (initial margin) for each open contract. The level of margin is determined by the exchange. The initial margin is returned with interest when the position is closed. Positions are marked-to-market on a daily basis by comparing the futures price and the underlying price and crystallising the daily profit and loss each day. If investors lose on a position they must pay the daily loss and if investors have a gain, payment is made to them. These daily payments are known as *variation margin*. The clearing house calls for a margin payment (*margin call*) as and when necessary. Since the clearing house is the counterparty for each futures trade and the profits and losses are crystallised on a daily basis through the operation of the margin, the counterparty and credit risks on futures contracts are minimal.

Futures contracts are available on interest rates, commodities, bonds, single stocks and equity indices. When using futures on equity indices it is important to calculate the *economic exposure* to incorporate the exposure in the asset allocation of multi-asset portfolios. The economic exposure is calculated using the formula:

Economic exposure = Underlying index level X Index multiplier X Number of futures contracts

For example, the index multiplier of a futures contract on the FTSE 100 Index is 10. If the level of the FTSE 100 Index is 5,000, the economic exposure of each futures contract is £50,000. If 100 futures contracts are purchased, the economic exposure is £5 million.

When the exposure to UK equities is gained through futures contracts, corresponding cash should be held to cover the futures position; otherwise the portfolio is leveraged. In this case, £5 million of cash should be held to cover the futures contracts and the allocation to cash in the multi-asset portfolio should be reduced by £5 million since this cash is held to back the futures positions and is not part of the allocation to cash.

When calculating the performance of multi-asset portfolios it is important to include the interest payment on this cash as part of the return of UK equities and not cash. Conversely, when futures contracts are shorted to reduce an exposure to an asset class, the allocation to cash should be increased by the economic exposure. Otherwise, the multi-asset portfolio is under invested.

When futures are used in multi-asset portfolios some of the cash allocation does not represent available cash. About 10% of the £5 million economic exposure above is needed for margin. This should be taken into account when considering available liquidity.

The long futures position in the example above exposes the portfolio to the profit and loss on the underlying index. However, it does not expose the portfolio to the foreign currency (e.g. no exposure to the pound for a dollar portfolio). If the exposure to the FTSE 100 Index should not be currency hedged, cash in pounds should be held in the portfolio to gain the desired currency exposure.

Forward contracts

Forward contracts are similar to futures contracts. However, they are not exchange-traded and are not standardised. Forwards typically do not require the parties to the contract to pay margin and a clearing house does not stand between them. Each party is exposed to the counterparty risk for the entire unrealised gain since daily profits and losses are not settled through the margin facility.

On the other hand, since forward contracts are OTC derivatives they are more flexible for customisation than futures contracts and the parties may agree to include mark-to-market and daily margining. Currency forward contracts are commonly used to hedge currency exposure or to speculate on currencies. The currency forward market is very liquid.

Call and put options

Options give the holder the right but not the obligation to purchase (call) or sell (put) a specified quantity of the underlying at an agreed price (exercise or strike price) on or before a future date (expiry date or maturity) for the payment of a premium.

American options can be exercised at any business day up to and including the expiry day. European options can be exercised only at the expiry day[277].

If the strike price equals the price of the underlying the option is at the money. If the strike price is below (above) the price of the underlying the call (put) option is in the money (the holder can pay less for buying the underlying for a call or receive more for selling it for a put). If the strike price is above (below) the price of the underlying the call (put) option is out of the money (the holder will not pay more for purchasing the underlying for a call or receive less for selling it for a put). Out of the money options may still be valuable if there is still time to expiry and a probability that the option may get into the money.

Options have an asymmetric payoff profile and they can be used to add upside potential without committing all the capital and/or downside protection without sacrificing all the upside potential. This payoff profile costs money in the form of a premium.

Figure 25.1 shows the payoff profile of a call option. The strike price is $20. While the price of the underlying is below $20, the payoff of the option is $0. As the price of the underlying increases above $20, the payoff increases. The upper line shows the payoff and the bottom line shows the profit and loss assuming that a $2 premium was paid. To break even the price of the underlying needs to reach $22 (payoff $22 - $20 = $2 = premium spent).

Figure 25.1 – call option payoff and P&L

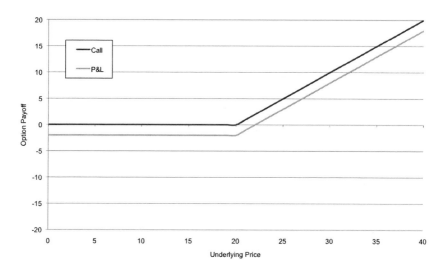

Figure 25.2 shows the payoff profile of a put option. The strike price is $20. While the price of the underlying is above $20, the payoff of the option is $0. As the price of the underlying decreases below $20, the payoff increases. The upper line shows the payoff and the bottom line shows the profit and loss assuming that a $2 premium was paid. To break even the price of the underlying needs to reach $18 (payoff $20 - $18 = $2 = premium spent).

Figure 25.2 – put option payoff and P&L

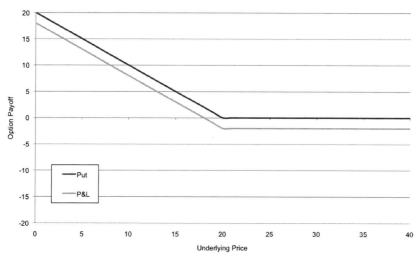

Option combination strategies – such as buying an out of money call and selling a further out of money call to fund some of the premium (bull spread) – limit some of the upside but reduce some of the premium payment. Figure 25.3 shows the payoff of buying a call option with a strike of $20 and selling a call option with a strike of $30. The upside is capped but some of the premium of buying the $20 call is funded through collecting the premium from selling the $30 call.

Figure 25.3 – call option combination payoff and P&L

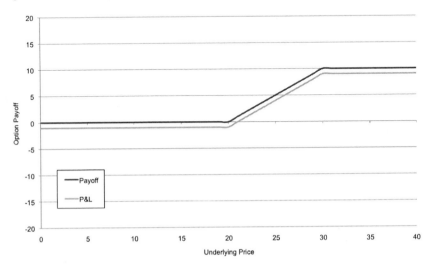

The *intrinsic value* of an option is its value if it was exercised today. The intrinsic value of a call is the price of the underlying minus the strike price. The intrinsic value of a put is the strike price minus the price of the underlying.

The *time value* of an option is the amount by which the option price exceeds its intrinsic value. It is related to the time to maturity and the volatility of the underlying's price. Time value is the risk premium that the seller of the option requires in order to be compensated for selling it.

Figure 25.4 shows the time value of a call option (the upper line). The time value converges with the intrinsic value when the option is deep out of and in the money. The difference between the time value and intrinsic value is highest when the option is at the money.

Figure 25.4 – call option payoff, P&L and intrinsic value calculated by Black and Scholes option pricing model

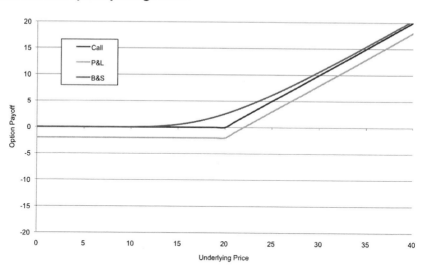

The fair-value of European options can be calculated using the Black and Scholes option pricing model[278]. Other pricing models are used for other options and derivatives (e.g. binomial pricing models).

The five factors that determine the fair-value of an option are:

1. Interest rate

2. Strike

3. Expiry

4. Underlying price

5. Volatility

Volatility is the distribution of the underlying's future price. The higher the volatility the higher the option value since there is a higher probability that the price of the underlying will move the option into the money. This is the only unobservable variable in the option pricing model.

Under the original Black and Scholes model volatility was assumed to be constant. However, volatility depends on the strike price, a phenomenon called *volatility smile*, since volatility increases when the price is further away from the strike and hence charting volatility over strike price looks like a smile. Volatility also depends on the option's maturity. To consider the dependency of volatility on both strike and maturity a *volatility surface* (a three-dimensional graph) is used. More sophisticated option pricing models are based on stochastic models and mean reversion.

Options allow investors to gain exposure to volatility. Since one of the factors driving option price is volatility, investors can use options to go long and short volatility and volatility is one of the factors that needs to be considered when investing in options. Starting from the current option price and the other four factors in the pricing model, it is easy to calculate the *implied volatility* from the price of options.

One way to account for option positions in multi-asset portfolios is by including the premium that was spent on the option in the asset allocation. Cash is spent to pay for the premium to buy an option, which is an asset within the multi-asset portfolio. As the option approaches its expiry the value of the option and its premium approach zero and the profit and loss on the option should be added to the appropriate asset class.

Swaps

Swaps are derivatives in which counterparties exchange a stream of cash flows or benefits of one financial instrument for those of another financial instrument. The benefits depend on the type of financial instruments. For example, in the case of a plain vanilla interest rate swap, fixed interest payments are swapped or exchanged for floating rate interest payments. The two counterparties agree to exchange one stream of cash flows with another stream. These streams are called the legs of the swap. The swap agreement[279] defines the dates when cash flows are to be paid and the way they are calculated. Usually at the time when the contract is initiated at least one of these series of cash flows is determined by an uncertain variable such as an interest rate (e.g. LIBOR), foreign exchange rate, equity price or commodity price. The cash flows are calculated over a notional principal amount, which is usually not exchanged between the counterparties.

Swaps can be used to hedge certain risks such as interest rate risk, inflation and currency risk or to speculate on changes in the expected direction of underlying prices. Since swaps are OTC derivatives they can be customised by the parties.

The most common type of swap is a plain vanilla *interest rate swap*. It exchanges a fixed rate loan with a floating rate loan. The life of the swap can range from two years to over 15 years. For example, party A makes periodic interest payments to party B based on a variable interest rate of LIBOR plus 50 basis points. Party B in return makes periodic interest payments based on a fixed rate of 5.0%. The payments are calculated over the notional amount of $1 million. The variable rate is reset at the beginning of each interest calculation period (e.g. quarter) to the then current LIBOR rate.

Assuming at the first payment date LIBOR is 4.0%, party A needs to pay party B $45,000 and party B needs to pay party A $50,000. The parties will offset the payments and party B will pay party A $5,000. By the next payment date the LIBOR rate jumps to 5.0%. Party A now needs to pay $5,000 to party B. In reality, the actual payments between the parties are lower since the third party to the swap is the bank, which takes a spread. This is the way banks make money from originating swaps.

The flexibility of swaps and their potential long maturity means that interest rate swaps can be used to hedge liabilities when long durations are required and standard bonds with appropriate durations are unavailable.

Other common types of swaps include:

- *Currency swaps.* These involve exchanging principal and fixed rate interest payments on a loan in one currency for principal and fixed rate interest payments on an equal loan in another currency. Currency swaps entail swapping both principal and interest between the parties, with different currencies for the cash flows that the parties exchange.

- *Total return swaps* (TRS). These involve exchanging the total return on one financial instrument with fixed or floating interest payments. For example, a total return equity swap can exchange the total return on the S&P 500 Index with fixed interest payment of 5.0% per annum. Total return property swaps are a way to gain exposure to the property market or property indices without purchasing physical properties.

- *Inflation linked swaps* (ILS), which exchange fixed cash flows with inflation-linked cash flows. ILS are offered with maturities out to 30 years and sometimes out to 50 years. These instruments can be used to hedge inflation risk for long-term investors, such as pension plans.

- *Funded swaps*, which involve exchanging the principal at the outset. Funded swaps are a way to raise cash without selling underlying assets. For example, if a multi-asset portfolio has an allocation to real estate and selling the property is too expensive, a funded total return property swap can be used whereby the total return on the real estate is exchanged with interest payments. The portfolio receives cash up front and periodical interest payments in exchange for the performance of a property index and in effect has shorted the long property position. There is a basis risk, however, between the property index and the actual properties held within the portfolio. This strategy depends on identifying a willing counterparty for the swap as it is an OTC derivative transaction.

Credit Default Swaps (CDS)

Credit default swaps (CDS) are similar to an insurance policy as they oblige the CDS seller to compensate the buyer in the event of a credit event of a bond (as defined in the CDS contract). Generally, the agreement is that when a credit event occurs the buyer of the CDS receives money (usually the face value of the underlying bond) and the seller of the CDS receives the defaulted bond (and with it the right to recover the bond at some later time). The buyer of the CDS does not need to hold the underlying bond. The buyer pays the seller a series of cash flows (CDS fee or spread) in exchange for the obligation to receive a payoff if a credit event occurs. Most CDS are documented using standard forms promulgated by the *International Swaps and Derivatives Association* (ISDA), although some are tailored to meet specific needs.

Corporate credit spreads can be earned in exchange for default risk through investment in CDS. These derivatives provide an unfunded synthetic exposure to similar risks on the same reference entities (i.e. exposure to credit risk). However, owing to a quite volatile CDS basis, the spreads on CDS and the credit spreads on corporate bonds can be significantly different.

CDS prices or spreads are commonly used to gauge the risk level of corporate and sovereign borrowers. As concerns about the solvency of a corporate or a sovereign increase, it will cost more to insure against a default and the CDS spread will expand.

Exotic derivatives

Exotic derivatives have features making them more complex than plain vanilla derivatives. They can derive their prices from a wide range of underlyings, including baskets of financial instruments, natural disasters and the weather.

Financial engineers can create many different desired cash flow payoff profiles using combinations of derivatives. However, the two basic building blocks of derivatives are forwards and options.

Summary

- Derivatives are financial instruments whose performance is derived from the performance or price behaviour of underlying assets.

- Exchange traded derivatives (ETD) are standardised and the role of the clearing house means that counterparty risk is minimised. OTC derivatives are customisable, but the counterparty risk is higher.

- Many investors fear using derivatives. However, when used prudently derivatives are helpful in managing risks, transferring risk between parties and efficiently gaining exposure to markets and investments.

- Derivatives can be used to go long and short investments and synthetically leverage portfolios.

- The risks of derivatives include leverage, shorting, counterparty and liquidity risks (beyond the risks of the underlying assets).

- Financial futures are legally binding agreements to deliver or take delivery of a specific quantity of a specific asset at a future date at an agreed price.

- Through the daily margin facility and the clearing house, the counterparty and credit risks of futures contracts are minimised.

- The economic exposure of futures positions should be included in the asset allocation of multi-asset portfolios with the corresponding reduction in cash when the futures position is long and increase in cash when the futures position is short.

- Forward contracts are similar to futures contracts but they are OTC derivatives. They are not standardised and can be customised. Currency forward contracts are commonly used to manage currency exposure.

- Options give the holder the right but not the obligation to purchase (call) or sell (put) a specified quantity of the underlying at an agreed price (exercise or strike price) on or before a future date (expiry date or maturity) for the payment of a premium.

- Options offer asymmetric payoff profiles and can limit downside risk without sacrificing all the upside potential and/or add upside potential without risking all the capital. The payment of a premium is required for these payoff profiles.

- Options enable investors to go long or short volatility since one of the drivers of their price is the volatility of the underlying's price.

- Swaps are derivatives in which counterparties exchange a stream of cash flows or benefits of one financial instrument for those of another.

- Swaps can be used to hedge certain risks such as interest rate risk, inflation and currency risk or to speculate on changes in the expected direction of underlying prices.

- Due to their flexibility and potential long life, swaps can be used to hedge duration and inflation risks of liabilities with long duration.

- CDS are used to hedge credit risk or to gain exposure to credit risk without the need to hold the underlying corporate bond.

26. CURRENCY

Currency exposure is an integral part of global investments. Each investor and portfolio has a base currency. The base currency of a US based investor is the dollar (USD), that of a UK based investor is the pound (GBP) and for a euro zone investor it is the euro (EUR). Returns of foreign currency denominated investments should be converted to the portfolio's base currency.

Movements in currency can have a large impact on performance of foreign or overseas investments – currency movements can overwhelm the performance of portfolios more than investment selection. Many investors pay considerable attention to investment selection and neglect paying attention to currency risk management. For example, a US investor invests in UK equities, which rise by 10% measured in local currency (pounds). If the dollar depreciates by 15% versus the pound the investor has lost 6.5%[280].

There are instances of investors whose base currency is not a single currency. For example, a British expat living and working in New York City may have current income and expenditures in dollars but long-term retirement liabilities in pounds. This person has an ambiguous base currency. The base currency, which is the accounting currency for calculating portfolio performance, should be a basket of the two currencies.

Some investors have liabilities in multiple currencies. For example, a UK-based global reinsurance company, which sells reinsurance policies to insurance companies in the United Kingdom, United States and the euro zone. The company needs to hold assets in different currencies and manage each one to a different base currency in line with that of the liabilities. However, to account for the assets in the portfolio on the company's balance sheet, the assets need to be converted to pounds.

Currency hedging

Currency risk is a manageable risk. Currency hedging is like making a deposit (long) in the base currency and borrowing (short) in the foreign currency. The short leg of the hedge cancels the long currency exposure of the investment. The performance of the hedged position is similar to that of an investment in the local currency of the investment plus the short-term interest rate on the base currency (the deposit) minus the short-term interest rate on the foreign currency (the borrowing). The short-term interest differential is one of the hedging costs.

Currency hedging can be implemented using currency forward contacts with a maturity of one or three months, rolled over as needed. When using collective investment schemes (CIS), some CIS offer currency hedged share classes that can be used to manage currency risk. Other ways for hedging include currency swaps and options.

The *currency hedge ratio* (the notional value of the currency forward contracts divided by the value of the underlying investment) needs to be determined and should have a range to avoid over hedging. For example, a target currency hedge of 97% within a range of +/- 3% (94% to 100%). Whenever the hedge ratio falls outside of the range due to market movements and/or cash flows, the hedge is rebalanced back to the target hedge ratio. The hedge is imperfect since the hedge ratio changes constantly and a 100% target hedge ratio is impractical since it may easily move to over hedging (i.e. hedging above 100%).

Beyond short-term interest rate differentials, other costs of currency hedging include transaction costs (these are normally low but can be high at times of crisis or for illiquid currencies), cash flows, hedge rebalancing, and opportunity cost when the hedge is implemented on appreciating currencies. When the reason for currency hedging is risk reduction, the opportunity cost should be ignored since the aim is not to profit from a view on currencies.

Optimal currency hedging for long-term investors

Currency hedging is important to long-term investors since unhedged exposure usually (not always) means high absolute volatility of investments. To determine the optimal currency hedging, three factors need to be considered: valuation, volatility and correlation. This is similar to the CMAs of SAA where expected return, volatility and correlation are the three inputs.

Long-term *valuation* is usually the starting point. Exposures to extremely overvalued currencies should be mostly hedged, while exposure to undervalued currencies should be left largely unhedged. The objective of currency hedging should be clarified. If the objective is enhancing portfolio returns, then valuations should be considered as part of the decision on whether to hedge currencies or not. If the objective, however, is reducing portfolio risk, currency hedging should be implemented systematically to certain currencies and asset classes without considering current valuations. When the objective is risk reduction, absolute risk and relative risk should be distinguished. Currency hedging usually reduces absolute risk. However, when the benchmark is unhedged, currency hedging increases relative risk.

Asset *volatility* is the second factor to consider. For relatively low volatility asset classes, such as bonds and cash, high currency hedging ratios are desirable to protect the fixed income stream from currency fluctuations. Not hedging foreign bonds and cash may transform them from a conservative asset in their local currency to a risk asset in foreign currency as their volatility may double or even more than triple.

The third factor to consider is *correlation*. Currency movements that are uncorrelated or negatively correlated with the movements of the underlying asset may offer diversification benefits.

Forecasting currencies

Forecasting currency movements over the short term is notoriously difficult. Forecasting currency movements over the long term, however, has a higher information coefficient. This is similar to easier forecasting of expected equity returns over the next 10 years versus the next few months.

Long-term currency valuations can be assessed using an economic framework based on *purchasing power parity* (PPP)[281], augmented by macro fundamentals such as productivity, terms of trade, interest rate spreads and term spreads[282]. According to PPP an amount of money has the same purchasing power in different countries. The *Big Mac Index* is a popular measure of PPP. A Big Mac should cost the same in different countries, since a Big Mac is a Big Mac.

The prices of the same goods between countries should only reflect exchange rates. This means that the difference in the rate of change in prices or the difference in the inflation rates is equal to the percentage depreciation or appreciation of the exchange rate. A valuation model maps the common long-term trends of macro fundamentals and exchange rates. The deviations between the trends should converge over time. These deviations form a measure for long-term currency misalignments from fair-value and can be used to derive expected currency returns. The hedge ratio is determined based on the magnitude of the overvaluation of a currency relative to its fair-value. A larger overvaluation means a higher hedge ratio.

Currency hedging of foreign bonds

International bonds diversify yield curve risk in portfolios and expand their investment opportunity set. However, investing in foreign bonds involves currency risk.

There is no strong case for systematically hedging currency risk of volatile assets (other than to implement currency views). However, the impact of currency hedging on conservative assets is material. The volatility of currency when investing in unhedged foreign bonds, low volatility hedge funds and cash, for example, may be higher than that of the assets themselves.

Figures 26.1 and 26.2 show the monthly returns of US government bonds measured in local currency (dollars) and measured in pounds (from the perspective of a UK based investor who does not hedge the currency risk of the US bonds). The charts demonstrate the increased volatility of US government bonds when currency risk is included.

Figure 26.1 – monthly returns of US government bonds measured in dollars, January 2000 to June 2012

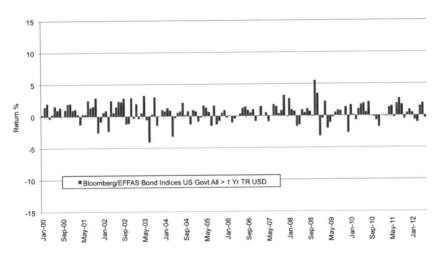

Source: Bloomberg, Bloomberg/EFFAS Bond Indices US Govt All >1 Yr.

Figure 26.2 – monthly returns of US government bonds measured in pounds, January 2000 to June 2012

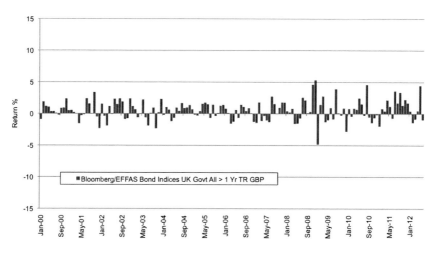

Source: Bloomberg, Bloomberg/EFFAS Bond Indices US Govt All >1 Yr.

Figures 26.3 and 26.4 show the monthly returns of US cash measured in dollars and in pounds. US cash in its local currency has close to zero volatility. US cash in pounds is a risk asset with a volatility of 9%. Returns on foreign cash vividly demonstrate currency risk.

Figure 26.3 – monthly returns of US cash (1-month LIBOR) measured in dollars, January 2000 to June 2012

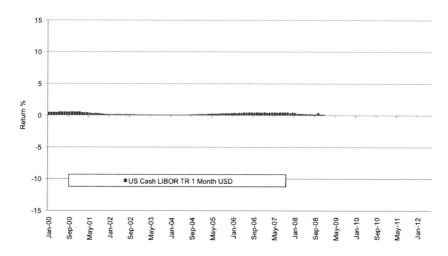

Source: Bloomberg, US Cash LBIOR TR 1 Month.

Figure 26.4– monthly returns of US cash (1-month LIBOR) measured in pounds, January 2000 to June 2012

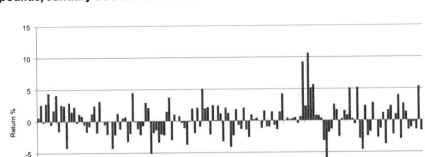

Source: Bloomberg, US Cash LBIOR TR 1 Month.

The conclusion is that for foreign bonds and cash the hedge ratio should be high. The correlation between bond returns and currency movements is low or negative. If it is negative then by hedging the currency exposure of foreign bonds diversification benefits are lost. If the correlation is positive, the diversification benefits are lower. In any case, the effect on volatility of not hedging foreign bonds outweighs the benefits of diversification and the currency risk of foreign bonds should be hedged to minimise risk[283]. If there is no forecasting skill of currencies, a useful rule of thumb is to always hedge all the currency exposure of conservative assets, such as bonds, cash and certain hedge fund strategies.

Currency hedging of equities

For risk assets, such as equities, the risk reduction properties of currency hedging are not straightforward.

Figures 26.5 and 26.6 show the monthly returns of the S&P 500 Index measured in local currency and pounds. The charts demonstrate that the volatility of unhedged and hedged equity return is similar. Currency hedging does not have a material impact on already volatile returns.

Figure 26.5 – monthly returns of US equities measured in dollars, January 2000 to June 2012

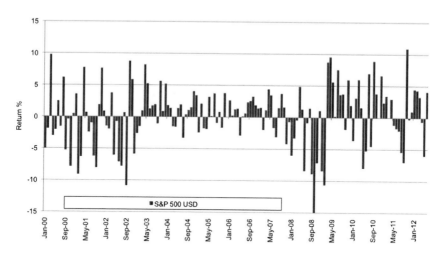

Source: Bloomberg, S&P 500.

Figure 26.6 – monthly returns of US equities measured in pounds, January 2000 to June 2012

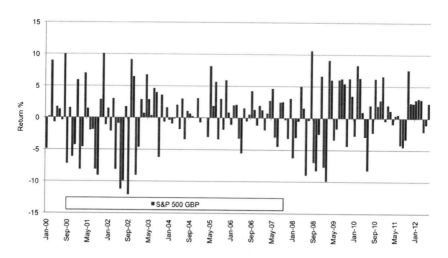

Source: Bloomberg, S&P 500.

Unhedged equity volatility can sometimes be lower than that of hedged foreign equity, depending on the correlation between currency movements and underlying equity returns. Hedging may result in losing diversification benefits. The increased risk due to reduced diversification should be balanced with the reduced risk due to reduced currency volatility. Correlations are not stationary and change over time. The diversification effects of currencies therefore change and the currency hedging decision should be dynamic to take into account changes in correlations (as well as changes in forecasts of currency fair-value and returns).

Currency hedging usually reduces absolute risk but increases relative risk when the benchmark is unhedged. Global equity benchmarks are normally unhedged and currency hedging is a relative risk position.

The conclusion is that because equity returns are already volatile and the absolute risk reduction impact of currency hedging is immaterial relative to the risk level of equities, equity currency hedging should be discretionary to implement views on currencies, not employed systematically to reduce absolute risk.

Table 26.1 shows that from January 2000 to June 2012 the performance of US equities in local currency (dollars) and converted to pounds was almost identical. The volatility of US government bonds and cash, however, was materially higher when converted to pounds. During this time period the increased currency risk just increased volatility without adding returns.

Table 26.1 – risk characteristics of US government bonds, equities and cash measured in dollars and pounds, January 2000 to June 2012

	US government bonds		S&P 500 Index		US 1-month LIBOR	
Currency	USD	GBP	USD	GBP	USD	GBP
Volatility (%)	4.94	5.33	16.23	16.43	0.63	9.17
Performance (% pa)	6.41	6.46	1.26	1.50	2.66	2.90

Source: Bloomberg, Bloomberg/EFFAS Bond Indices US Govt All >1 Yr, US Cash LBIOR TR 1 Month, S&P 500.

Figure 26.7 shows the rollercoaster of the GBP/USD spot exchange rate. This ride ended where it started at about $1.60 per £1.

Figure 26.7 – GBP/USD exchange rate, January 2000 to June 2012

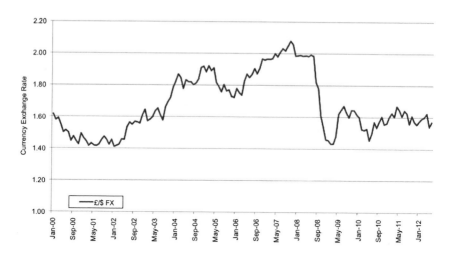

Source: Bloomberg.

Currency hedging of illiquid investments

Currency hedging of illiquid investments may require a source of liquidity from elsewhere in the portfolio since the hedged illiquid investments cannot be readily sold to rebalance the hedge ratio. One example is hedging direct property. If the hedged currency appreciates, cash from other asset classes has to be raised to cover losses on the hedge as property cannot be sold quickly.

Alpha currency overlay

An alpha currency overlay is a basket of long and short positions in currency derivatives (normally currency forward contracts). The difference between an alpha currency overlay and a currency hedging overlay is that the alpha overlay tries to add alpha to the portfolio (not to reduce currency risk) and it can go long currencies (not only short as with a currency hedging overlay). Alpha currency programmes can be accessed through CIS or stand-alone portfolios whose objective is adding alpha through currency trading. However, a CIS is funded while an overlay does not need the full cash commitment and hence it is more capital efficient.

Carry trade

A carry trade is an investment strategy in which investors borrow (short) in a low-yielding currency and use the funds to invest (long) in a high-yielding currency. The objective is benefiting from differences in interest rates between the currencies. Leverage is often used to enhance potential returns. The risk is depreciation of the borrowed currency relative to the invested currency.

For example, a yen carry trade has been popular due to the very low interest rates in Japan. A trader borrows one million yen from a Japanese bank, converts the funds into dollars and buys a US bond for the equivalent amount. Assuming the bond pays 4.5% and the Japanese interest rate is set at close to 0%, the trader expects to make a profit of 4.5% as long as the exchange rate between the dollar and the yen does not change against the trader (i.e. as long as the yen does not appreciate versus the dollar). If the exchange rate stays the same the trader expects to make a profit of 4.5%. The potential gains can be leveraged. If the trader uses a leverage factor of 10:1, then the expected profit increases to 45%.

The carry trade is a risky strategy because of the uncertainty of exchange rates. In the example above, if the dollar were to fall in value relative to the yen then the trader would run the risk of losing money. These transactions generally involve high leverage, so a small movement in exchange rates can result in huge losses unless the position is hedged appropriately.

Conclusion

Currency is often a forgotten asset class. All global multi-asset portfolios are exposed to currencies. Currency risk is manageable, thanks to derivatives, and investors have a choice as currency risk also has potential gains. Investors need to decide when and where to take this risk. It is extremely difficult to predict currencies over the short term. Arguably, it is easier to predict currencies over the long term. However, there are hedging decisions that investors need to make.

Summary

- Currency exposure and risk are part of any global portfolio.

- Each portfolio and investor has a base currency. All returns and risks should be measured and managed in the base currency.

- Currency risk is a manageable risk, normally via currency forward contracts. Currency hedging is like making a deposit in the base currency and borrowing in the foreign currency. One cost of hedging is the short-term interest rate in the base currency minus the short-term interest rate in the foreign currency.

- The objective of currency hedging should be risk reduction and/or benefiting from currency views.

- The three factors that should be considered when determining the hedge ratio (the notional value of the currency forward contracts dividend by the value of the underlying investment) are valuation, volatility and correlation.

- It is difficult to forecast currencies over the short term. It is arguably easier to forecast currency movements over the long term based on purchasing power parity (PPP) and other fundamental factors.

- The volatility of unhedged foreign bonds is much higher than that of hedged bonds. Currency risk of foreign bonds should be hedged.

- The volatility of equities is high whether currency is hedged or not. Currency risk of equities should be discretionarily hedged to incorporate views on currencies.

- Hedging currency of global equities normally reduces absolute risk but increases relative risk since the global equity benchmark is normally unhedged.

- Hedging the currency of illiquid investment is challenging since the underlying investment cannot be easily sold to recover losses on the hedge and the losses should be funded from elsewhere in the portfolio.

- Alpha currency overlay is a basket of short and long positions on currencies with the objective of adding alpha (not only hedging currency risk) and with the ability to go long currencies (not only to short currencies like a currency hedge overlay).

- The carry trade is an investment strategy of borrowing in a low interest rate currency and investing in a high interest rate currency. The risk in the strategy is currency movements (appreciation of the borrowed currency).

27. RISK BUDGETING

Risk budgeting is the process of allocating the total portfolio risk (*risk budget*) to the different sources of risk and return. In multi-asset portfolios these sources are SAA, TAA and investment selection. Multi-asset risk budgeting is not trivial since there are many variables to consider (the risks and interactions of asset allocation and investments) with different investment horizons (long term for SAA and short term for TAA and investment selection). The risk budgeting exercise may need to combine absolute and relative risks when multi-asset portfolios have an absolute risk target while they are invested in underlying investments with relative risk targets.

The risk budget is typically displayed as a total tracking error for the multi-asset portfolio, within a range. For example, a target tracking error of 4% within a range of 1% to 7%. The range is needed since it is impossible to manage portfolios to a target tracking error as it changes due to changes in the volatility of markets, investments and benchmarks. Investors should apply discretion to increase or decrease the tracking error based on the view of whether to take more or less risk depending on available opportunities and risks. The risk budget aims to limit that discretion to anchor the portfolio to its benchmark or investment policy so deviations from the benchmark are limited, depending on the risk objective. That is, risk budget controls the permitted risk of the portfolio relative to the risk target as per the investment policy.

Multi-asset investors need to decide how to divide the total risk budget across the different sources of risk and return. The tracking error allocated to SAA constrains SAA optimisation and determines the magnitude of the deviations of SAA weights from those of benchmark (when SAA does not equal the benchmark). The tracking error allocated to TAA determines the magnitude of the TAA positions relative to SAA. The risk budget of investment selection determines the split between active and passive investments and the aggregated tracking error of active underlying investments. The risk budgeting process is dynamic since market conditions, volatility, correlations and investment decisions across all levels (SAA, TAA and underlying investments) constantly change.

Quantitative approach

A quantitative approach to multi-asset risk budgeting is to progressively change the tracking error budget to SAA, TAA and investment selection considering the expected alpha and tracking errors of underlying investments, correlations among alphas (excess returns), correlations among SAA (betas) and investments' alphas, and so on. The objective of this iterative process is identifying a portfolio with the highest information ratio given the required outperformance target. The process is similar to asset allocation optimisation in relative space. However, the optimisation does not only involve asset classes, but also the investments under each asset class.

The information ratio is normally highest for the lowest tracking error, so maximising only the information ratio probably results in a portfolio very close to the benchmark (an expensive tracker). In a similar way to mean-variance optimisation, the exercise should maximise expected excess return for a given level of risk, or minimise risk for a given level of expected excess return.

The output of the quantitative approach is as accurate as the inputs. Investors need to make many assumptions about different asset classes and investments, the interrelationships among all the variables and combine investments and processes (SAA and TAA) with different investment horizons. Since the inputs are based on many subjective assumptions, the result may not be the desired one; it is very sensitive to the assumptions and may be counterintuitive.

Practical approach

A more practical approach to risk budgeting is achieved by dividing the process into four stages:

1. *Decide on SAA tracking error.* This is based on how propitious SAA is currently. The process focuses on a target information ratio considering the required and expected relative performance from SAA. The investor optimises several asset allocations with different tracking errors (e.g. 0.5%, 1.0%, 1.5% and so on), chooses an SAA satisfying the required excess return and for which taking additional relative risk does not add material excess return. The CMAs of different asset classes and the slope of the efficient frontier can be used as a guide for this stage.

2. *Decide on TAA tracking error.* The risk budgeting to SAA and TAA can be combined as a total risk budget to asset allocation. This is a simple way to address the different investment horizons of SAA and TAA. Alternatively, TAA can have a separate risk budget with a range and the TAA manager may use discretion to decide on how much of the risk budget to use depending on the available opportunities for TAA to add value.

3. *Decide on investment selection tracking error.* The investor needs to consider the expected excess performance of underlying investments, based on the manager's due diligence process, as well as whether the market environment is supportive of active management (e.g. cross sectional volatility, market efficiency and opportunities for active managers in each market). The risk budgeting decision is the split between active and passive investments in each asset class. If there is high conviction in active management, more should be allocated to it. Conversely, more should be allocated to passive investments when the conviction in active management is low. Larger allocation to active management increases the risk of investment selection and larger allocation to passive investment reduces this risk. The risk budget allocated to investment selection also depends on the tracking error of each active investment and the correlations among their excess returns.

4. *Calculate the expected total tracking error, information ratio and outperformance of the entire portfolio.* This final step is important since it ensures that the total portfolio is in line with its risk budget. If the total risk level of the portfolio does not match the requirements and expectations, steps one to three should be repeated to change the portfolio's overall risk level. The risk report of the entire portfolio should provide risk decomposition to asset allocation and security selection to ensure that the desired risk budget allocation is indeed reflected in the portfolio.

This is an iterative process of trial and error until the desired result is achieved. While perhaps not grounded in sophisticated mathematics, optimisation and finance theory, it does enable the desired result to be reached.

When deciding on changes to portfolios due to risk budgeting, the transaction costs of the changes need to be considered. When the transaction costs are material the potential benefits of risk allocation should be weighed against the definite loss of return due to transaction costs.

The slope of the efficient frontier

The slope of the efficient frontier is the Sharpe ratio of the asset allocation and it is determined by the amount of additional return gained per increase of risk. The slope of the efficient frontier is a function of change in return over change in risk. The expected return of a diversified asset allocation is a function of the expected returns of the underlying asset classes. The expected risk is a function of the risks and correlations of the underlying asset classes (the correlations also determine the curvature of the frontier). As the expected returns of asset classes are higher and/or the risks and correlations are lower, the slope of the efficient frontier is steeper.

When asset classes have attractive valuations, expected returns are high (e.g. corporate bonds after the 2008 credit crunch or equities after the 2000 high-tech bubble burst). When there is a large dispersion in returns of different asset classes, their correlations are low, with more diversification benefits. These are the times when there are attractive opportunities for asset allocation and allocating more of the risk budget to asset allocation is more advantageous. Since the conviction in formulating long-term expected returns is higher than over the short term, when SAA can add more value, more risk should be allocated to it. This is the reason that the first step in the risk budgeting approach is to decide how much risk to allocate to SAA.

When there are opportunities in SAA, the total risk of multi-asset portfolios should be higher, all else being equal. The slope of the efficient frontier, relative to historical slopes, can be used as a tool to decide on the total risk level of portfolios within the allowable range.

The efficient frontier's slope indicates the expected risk premium. Risk premium is the compensation that investors expect for taking risk. When the risk premium is high, taking more risk is worthwhile. When the risk premium is low, taking more risk is not well compensated. When the slope of the efficient frontier is steep and for every additional unit of risk the markets are expected to handsomely compensate investors, more risk should be taken.

Conclusion

Portfolios have a budget of risk to spend on markets. Multi-asset portfolios consist of different processes and investments. Multi-asset investors need to decide how to best allocate the total risk to the different sources of risk and returns. Risk is a scarce resource and giving more risk to investments with attractive expected returns and/or skilled decision makers enhances returns.

Summary

- Risk budgeting of multi-asset portfolios needs to allocate the total risk to the three sources of risk and return: SAA, TAA and investment selection.

- Often the multi-asset risk budget needs to consider different asset classes with different risks, the interrelationships among them, their different horizons, as well as absolute and relative risks.

- Risk budget controls the portfolio's permitted risk relative to the target risk in the investment policy.

- Risk budget: allocates tracking error to SAA to determine the deviations of its weights from those of the benchmark; allocates tracking error to TAA to determine the deviation of its weights from those of SAA; and determines the split between active and passive investments and the aggregated tracking errors of active investments to determine security selection risk.

- A quantitative approach to multi-asset risk budgeting is optimising a portfolio including SAA, TAA and investment selection to find the highest information ratio for a given level of target excess return. However, this method is based on numerous subjective assumptions.

- A practical approach to multi-asset risk budgeting breaks the process into four stages: decide on SAA tracking error based on how propitious SAA is; decide on TAA tracking error; decide on the split between active and passive based on conviction in active management; and combine all the components and calculate total portfolio risk. If total portfolio risk is not at the desired level, repeat steps one to three.

- The efficient frontier's slope guides the amount of risk to allocate to SAA. The slope indicates the risk premium that markets are expected to compensate investors for assuming risks. When the slope is steep there are attractive valuations of asset classes (i.e. high expected returns) and/or risks and correlation are low (i.e. there are more opportunities across asset classes). This is the time to take more asset allocation risk.

Armed with the understanding, tools and techniques for SAA, TAA, investment selection and portfolio construction the multi-asset portfolio can be managed. The next section focuses on risk management.

28. RISK MANAGEMENT

Managing risk is the core of managing investments[284]. The guiding principles of multi-asset investing are that certain risks are compensated over the long term, others are not and should be minimised, and that diversification across imperfectly correlated risk sources, both beta and alpha, reduces overall risk.

Risk is the driver of performance and without risk there is no performance. Absolute performance needs absolute risk and relative performance needs relative risk. Managing risk must be a core competency of any investor. Effective risk management is critical for the long-term survival of portfolios and investment management firms. The primary objective of any investor should be to minimise the *risk of ruin*.

Risk management is the means to reduce the likelihood of an event where the investment objectives are missed, as well as the magnitude and duration of such an event. Asset allocation is the main method for setting long-term risk. However, the flaws of SAA modelling expose investors to model risk. In addition, the path or journey matters. Few investors have vision to focus on the long term and not lose their nerve when short-term performance is disappointing. Investors are path dependent. SAA takes a long-term view and should be changed to address short-term concerns.

Most of the time, over the long term, taking risk is rewarded. Risk assets should outperform conservative assets. However, the success and failure of risk management are measured when risk assets fall and when event risks materialise. During market stress (when markets go *belly up* or *pear shaped*) investors tend to sell risk positions as their value tends to fall. Proper risk management determines which portfolios are prepared for such events. It is almost impossible to predict event risks, but portfolios should be positioned to survive them.

One key for long-term outperformance is mitigating the dangers of market falls. To outperform the market over the long term it is more important to substantially outperform during market crashes than modestly outperform when markets rise, as this compounds to long-term outperformance.

Risk management and *risk measurement* are two separate but related activities. Risk measurement is necessary to support risk management. Risk measurement is focused on quantifying and communicating risk. Risk management is making tactical and strategic decisions to control risks that should be controlled and exploit risky opportunities that should be exploited for a gain. Investment management is all about taking risks to generate returns and controlling unwanted risks. Successful investment management effectively manages all risks by controlling the downside and exploiting the upside. Risk management is informed by risk measurement but requires experience, intuition and common sense in addition to the quantitative measures. The quantitative measures support informed judgment.

Risk is the uncertainty or randomness measured by the *distribution of future returns*. The riskiness of a distribution depends on investor preferences. There is no uniform ranking of risk for all distributions and investors; the ranking depends on investor preferences. Risk is the possibility of a return being different from what is expected or anticipated. In this sense, there is no distinction between different types of risk. Market risk, credit risk and operational risk can each derail realised return from expected return.

Since risk is a distribution of future returns, it is multifaceted and cannot be defined by a single metric or a number. The full distribution needs to be considered. Risk measures summarise the distribution of returns. However, as with any summary, it does not comprehensively cover everything. The common tendency to reduce risk to a single number demonstrates the difficulty investors have when thinking about uncertainty.

Risk measurement

The essence of risk measurement is to provide a realistic view of what could happen to the assets in a portfolio in the future. It is impossible to predict the specific future outcome, but rather the idea is to provide an informed judgment on the range or distribution of possible outcomes. Quantitative risk measurement aims to calculate and communicate an estimate of the possible future returns. Knowing the *distribution of future returns* and the *sources of risk* that generate the distribution is the fundamental objective of risk measurement. The three goals of risk measurement are to: identify known risks faced by the portfolio; expose, quantify and communicate those risks; and try to understand and identify unknown or unanticipated risks. As Donald Rumsfeld put it "there are known knowns; there are things we know that we know. There are known unknowns; that is to say there are things that, we now know we don't know. But there are also unknown unknowns – there are things we do not know we don't know."

The first step in risk management is to know the risks to which the portfolio is exposed (i.e. measuring risks). Quantitative methods of risk measurement use current portfolio holdings and by using their characteristics (i.e. risks, returns and correlations) estimate the portfolio risks and quantify them. The quantitative methods should inform a qualitative view. Investors need to know the major risks in their portfolios and the risk measurement process should inform of the details of the risks. Investors who do not understand the risks in their portfolios and cannot *feel* how portfolios should behave under certain scenarios may be managing portfolios that are too complex.

Risk measures, such as volatility and VaR, provide a sense of the distribution of returns and together with decomposition of risk they help investors to understand the sources of risk. Investors need to understand the sources of risk and which actions can be used to reduce or remove unwanted risks.

Sensitivity analysis

Sensitivity analysis is a relatively straightforward way to measure the sensitivity of portfolios to changes in one or two variables at the same time[285]. For example, if the expected risk of SAA is calculated using CMAs, a range of volatilities for equities can be used and the total risk of SAA can be easily calculated under each one.

The analysis shows how the portfolio's expected risk is affected by changes to one variable. The assumed volatility of equities and bonds can be changed, the risk of the portfolio can be calculated under each level and the results can be presented in a two-dimensional table. Sensitivity analysis is helpful both to check the effect of changing a variable on portfolios and the effect of changing an assumption on the model's ability to evaluate model risk.

Figure 28.1 shows a portfolio's sensitivity to equity volatility. The portfolio's volatility is calculated for different levels of equity volatility.

Figure 28.1 – sensitivity analysis of 20% equities, 50% bonds, 20% cash and 10% alternative investments portfolio to changes to assumed equity volatility (1% to 29%)

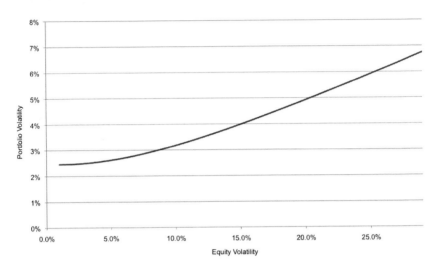

Scenario analysis

Scenario analysis is similar to stress testing. Different economic scenarios are predicted, each one is assigned a probability and market conditions are forecasted under each one. The expected risk, return and impact on the portfolio are calculated. The idea is that the portfolio should perform reasonably well under probable scenarios and planned actions should be prepared for unlikely scenarios (risk scenarios), but scenarios with large potential impact. The portfolio cannot outperform under each scenario and still meet its investment objectives under the central scenario. However, preparation is recommended so quick action can be taken – if there are unacceptable risks they should be mitigated.

All-weather portfolios are constructed to perform well under both favourable and unfavourable economic and market conditions. Developing a mutually exclusive and collectively exhaustive (MECE) set of scenarios, constructing a portfolio that should perform well under each one and using leverage to enhance the likely modest returns of the portfolio across the different scenarios can be used to create an all-weather portfolio. The portfolio needs to use a variety of asset classes and investment techniques, such as hedging, to deliver a positive return under different market conditions. Achieving this goal requires tight and robust risk management.

Multi-factor risk models

One of the most common ways to measure risk exposures is through multi-factor models that use a multivariate linear regression to measure the sensitivities or loadings of portfolios to different factors. Multi-factor models use factors clearly representing different sources of risk. For example, equity risks can be represented by equity indices across geographic regions, investment styles and market capitalisations. Interest rate risk can be represented by return differences between medium and short-term government bonds. Credit risk can be represented by return difference between high-yield and government bond indices with the same duration.

The goal is to identify all the risks to which the portfolio is exposed so investors can eliminate or mitigate all risks except those which are in line with investment objectives. Investors need to decide on the potential reward from each risk. The risk premium associated with each factor can be estimated by comparing returns of investments with high exposure to each factor and those with no or low exposure. Investors can then decide on constructing a portfolio with appropriate risk attributes that are expected to be compensated.

Backtesting and backtested analytics

One of easiest ways to measure portfolio risk, when no sophisticated risk management systems are available except for Microsoft Excel, is using backtested analytics.

The first step is sourcing the monthly total returns of the investments in the portfolio, their benchmarks and the portfolio composite benchmark. Using monthly returns has a few advantages. A monthly basis is a typical reporting period for most investments and monthly returns are available for less liquid investments, such as hedge funds. Weekly and daily returns may not be available for each investment. The objective is to calculate risk over meaningful time periods (36 or 60 months) and monthly returns are appropriate. The disadvantages of monthly returns are that they do not account for intra-month activities and sufficient history is required to calculate meaningful statistics (a minimum of 36 observations or three years).

In order to get a history of all investments when actual investment history is unavailable, the history is backfilled with appropriate benchmark returns. In some cases an appropriate benchmark is difficult to identify and a proxy should be used. When the choice of benchmark is ambiguous, a regression analysis can be used to identify the most appropriate benchmark (by the highest R^2 or beta) or to use a combination of benchmarks using multiple regression analysis. When the multi-asset portfolio includes directly invested securities (e.g. US equities) the total allocation to those can be represented as a sub-portfolio with its appropriate benchmark (e.g. if 10% of the portfolio directly holds US equities, they should be represented as a 10% allocation to a US equity sub-portfolio with its own benchmark). At the end of the first step a database of monthly returns is created with monthly investment returns, their benchmark returns and the multi-asset portfolio composite benchmark returns.

The second step is using current weights to each investment and the current total composite benchmark weights to calculate the backtested return series for the portfolio (r_p), underlying investments' benchmarks (r_{ib}) and total portfolio composite benchmark (r_b). These return series are easily calculated with Microsoft Excel's SUMPRODUCT formula by multiplying the current weights to each investment with the corresponding monthly returns of each investment or its benchmark.

The third step is to calculate the covariance matrix of the investments in the portfolio. The covariance matrix is used to decompose risk. The fourth step is to calculate the risk statistics for the three return series.

From the backtested return series it is easy to calculate different performance risk measures. For example, standard deviation and maximum drawdowns can be calculated for each return series. The tracking error of the portfolio versus its composite benchmark is the standard deviation of (r_p - r_b). Tracking error can be broken down to asset allocation by calculating the standard deviation of (r_{ib} - r_b) and security selection by calculating the standard deviation of (r_p - r_{ib}).

Risk decomposition

Marginal contribution to risk (MCR) or decomposition of risk is one of the most useful tools in risk analysis. The calculations of MCR require matrix operations. Matrix operations are convenient when dealing with data of portfolios and benchmarks. It is easy to use Microsoft Excel for matrix operations (or array formulas)[286].

Assume a simple three-asset portfolio and a composite benchmark with the characteristics shown in Table 28.1.

Table 28.1 – three-asset portfolio and benchmark

Asset	Benchmark W_B	Portfolio W_P	Active W_A	Volatility	Correlation matrix		
					Equities	Bonds	Cash
Equities	60%	65%	5%	15%	1.00	-0.10	-0.20
Bonds	30%	25%	-5%	5%	-0.10	1.00	0.00
Cash	10%	10%	0%	1%	-0.20	0.00	1.00

The first stage in most risk analytics is to derive the covariance matrix of assets. There are different ways to estimate the volatilities and correlations of asset classes. A simple approach is using historic returns to estimate these parameters. Assuming that the values in the table are the estimates of volatility and correlation, the covariance matrix is populated using the formula:

$$\sigma_{i,j} = \rho_{i,j}\sigma_i\sigma_j$$

where $\sigma_{i,j}$ is the covariance between investments i and j, $\rho_{i,j}$ is the correlation between investments i and j, and σ_i and σ_j are the volatilities of investments i and j, respectively. The covariance matrix (V) looks like Table 28.2.

Table 28.2 – three-asset covariance matrix

Asset	Equities	Bonds	Cash
		Covariance matrix (V)	
Equities	0.0225	-0.0008	-0.0003
Bonds	-0.0008	0.0025	0.0000
Cash	-0.0003	0.0000	0.0001

The standard deviation of the benchmark is calculated using the formula:

$$\sigma_B = (W'_B V W_B)^{0.5}$$

where W_B is the vector of benchmark weights, W'_B is the transposed vector of benchmark weights and V is the covariance matrix.

The formula in Microsoft Excel[287] is:

```
SQRT(MMULT(MMULT(TRANSPOSE(W),V),W)
```

Calculating the portfolio's standard deviation uses the same formula, except W_B is replaced by W_P. The tracking error of the portfolio relative to its benchmark also uses the same formula, except W_B is replaced by W_A, the vector of active positions (W_P-W_B).

Using the formulas above the benchmark volatility is 8.96%, the portfolio volatility is 9.69% and the tracking error is 0.81%.

MCR is the rate of change in risk with respect to a small change in the size of a position. That is, by how much portfolio/benchmark risk changes for a small increase in the weight of each investment. Mathematically MCR is the first derivative of the risk measure with respect of the individual position.

The formula to calculate MCR of tracking error is:

$$MCRi = W_{(A,i)}W'_A V/TE$$

where MCRi is MCR for asset i and TE is the tracking error of the portfolio.

The same formula is used to calculate the MCR of the portfolio or the benchmark's absolute risk, except W_A is replaced by W_P or W_B and tracking error (TE) is replaced by the volatility of the portfolio or the benchmark, respectively.

In Microsoft Excel using the format of the tables above[288], the formula is:

TRANSPOSE(TRANSPOSE(W)*MMULT(TRANSPOSE(W),V)/TE)

The MCR can be expressed as percentage by dividing each MCR by the relevant volatility or tracking error. The results of the calculations are as shown in Table 28.3.

Table 28.3 – marginal contribution to risk

Asset	MCR tracking error		MCR volatility benchmark		MCR volatility portfolio	
Equities	0.71%	87.74%	8.87%	99.09%	9.67%	99.83%
Bonds	0.10%	12.26%	0.10%	1.12%	0.04%	0.37%
Cash	0.00%	0.00%	-0.02%	-0.21%	-0.02%	-0.20%
Total	0.81%	100.00%	8.96%	100.00%	9.69%	100.00%

Through MCR analysis the portfolio's absolute and relative risks are decomposed to their sources. It is easy to observe that the equity overweight is the source of the vast majority (almost 88%) of tracking error. The allocation to equities is the source of the vast majority of absolute risk in the benchmark and more so in the portfolio. The exposure to cash reduces risk. This is due to the low volatility of cash and its negative correlation with equities.

Asset allocation versus risk allocation

Risk decomposition demonstrates the difference between asset allocation (capital allocation) and risk allocation. In the portfolio above the benchmark asset allocation is 60% equities, 30% bonds and 10% cash. The risk (standard deviation) allocation is, however, 99.09% equities, 1.12% bonds and -0.21% cash. While the asset allocation seems diversified and balanced, the risk allocation is completely overwhelmed by equities (as demonstrated by the two pie charts in Figures 28.2 and 28.3). One of the objectives of risk management and risk budgeting is to properly diversify the asset allocation across risks.

Figure 28.2 – asset allocation (capital allocation)

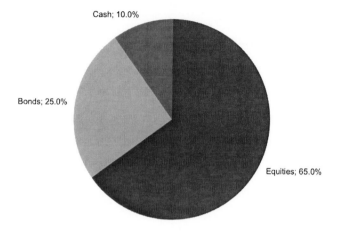

Figure 28.3 – risk allocation

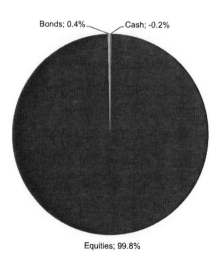

The way to address the risk concentration in apparently balanced portfolios is to move away from asset allocation to risk allocation. The building blocks of risk allocation are not asset classes, but rather risk factors. Each investment is mapped to its risk factors using multi-factor models. Investments are then combined together into *multi-factor portfolios* (instead of multi-asset portfolios) to achieve the desired diversification across risks. The risk premiums of risk factors are used to calculate the estimated portfolio return, rather than asset class expected returns.

Risk parity[289] is an alternative approach to portfolio management, focusing on allocation of risk rather than allocation of capital. The objective is to create portfolios in which each investment has an equal contribution to overall portfolio risk. Edward Qian concludes that a 60/40 equity/bond portfolio will suffer tremendous losses when equity markets have severe losses since a direct relationship exists between loss contribution to a portfolio from its underlying components and their risk contribution counterparts[290]. That is, investments with a high contribution to portfolio risk (volatility) will have a high contribution to downside risk or losses. One way to construct truly diversified portfolios with significant downside protection is to balance the risk contribution (hence loss contribution) from risk assets and conservative assets.

Adjusting VaR and standard deviation to fat tail risk

Fat tail risk is not captured by standard deviation, which assumes a normal distribution of returns. However, volatility can be adjusted to higher moments (skewness and kurtosis) quite simply.

VaR can be adjusted for skewness and kurtosis analytically by the *Cornish-Fisher approximation*[291] using the formula:

$$z_c = z + (z^2 - 1)S/6 + (z^3 - 3z)K/24 - (2z^3 - 5z)S^2/36$$

where z is the critical value for the VaR confidence level (z is -1.96 at 95% and -2.33 at 99% confidence level), S is skewness, K is excess kurtosis (kurtosis minus 3) and Z_c is the adjusted critical value.

The adjusted VaR is calculated using the formula:

$$\text{Adjusted VaR} = \mu - z_c \sigma$$

Standard deviation can be adjusted using the same methodology by the formula:

$$\text{Adjusted } \sigma = z_c \sigma / z$$

where adjusted σ is the standard deviation adjusted for fat tail risk and σ is the unadjusted standard deviation. z_c/z is the multiplier by which to adjust the standard deviation for skewness and kurtosis.

From the Cornish-Fisher formula it is intuitive that excess kurtosis and negative skewness increases the adjusted standard deviation.

Skewness and kurtosis are not robust statistics since they are highly dependent on the measurement period. A bootstrapping technique can be utilised to estimate more robust statistics.

Table 28.4 shows the annualised standard deviations, skewness, excess kurtosis, Z_c, adjustment factor (z_c/z) and adjusted standard deviation for different asset classes. As the skewness is more negative and the excess kurtosis more positive the adjustment of standard deviation is larger. Adjusted volatility can be used in optimisation to better capture fat tail risk of different asset classes and address the non-normality of investments' distributions.

Table 28.4 – Cornish-Fisher approximation adjustment for fat-tail risk, January 1994 to June 2012

	Macro hedge funds	US treasury bonds	Equity long/ short	Global equities	UK property	Emerging market debt	Relative value hedge funds
Volatility (%)	6.64	4.73	9.47	15.72	3.95	14.28	4.35
Skewness	0.20	-0.10	-0.22	-0.73	-2.27	-2.12	-2.85
Kurtosis	1.02	0.99	1.93	1.45	8.56	12.58	15.89
Zc (Z - 1.96)	-1.93	-2.07	-2.19	-2.33	-2.87	-3.17	-3.21
Multiplier	0.98	1.06	1.12	1.19	1.46	1.62	1.64
Adjusted (s %)	6.53	5.01	10.59	18.66	5.79	23.12	7.13

Source: Bloomberg, HFRI Macro, HFRI Equity Hedge, Bloomberg/EFFAS Bond Indices US Govt All > 1 Yr, MSCI World, UK IPD TR All Property (measured in £), JPM Emerging Markets Bond Index Plus EMBI+ Composite.

Autocorrelation

Prices of directly held real estate are subject to smoothing through the process of appraisals and infrequent valuations. Real estate prices are not quoted on exchanges as are prices of public equities. The valuations are linked to the most recent valuation as a starting point. This can lead to real estate volatility appearing to be lower than it may actually be.

Some hedge fund strategies are subject to similar issues. The effect is that for some hedge fund strategies reported risk measures, such as standard deviation and beta, may be underestimated and risk adjusted performance measures, such as Sharpe ratio, may be overestimated. This may lead to misjudgment of the risk characteristics of those hedge fund strategies.

If investors rely solely on reported standard deviations, which may be underestimated, they may over allocate to hedge funds or real estate and thereby the expected risk adjusted return of portfolios may be misleading.

One common statistical property that hedge fund and direct property returns exhibit is *serial correlation* (autocorrelation) in returns or *trending*. Trending causes risk estimates to be lower than they should be.

Serial correlation is defined as the correlation of a variable with itself over successive time intervals. This means that there is a significant positive or negative correlation in returns over time and historical performance can appear to be smoother than it really is.

Academic studies have shown a number of potential sources for serial correlation in hedge fund returns such as: market inefficiencies; time-varying expected returns; time-varying leverage; and incentive fees with high water marks. However, one study[292] has shown that the most likely explanation for this phenomenon in some hedge fund strategies is the illiquidity of underlying investments (i.e. investments in securities that are not actively traded and for which prices are not always readily available).

Some hedge fund managers have difficulties in obtaining up-to-date valuations of their positions in illiquid and complex over-the-counter securities. When confronted with this problem, hedge funds are obliged to use either the last reported transaction price (*stale price*) or an estimate of the current market price. Either process can easily create unavoidable lags in the evolution of the net asset value of the hedge fund.

An analysis of HFRI hedge fund style indices shows that the hedge fund styles exhibiting the most significant serial correlation are convertible arbitrage, relative value and event driven. These styles include some of the most illiquid traded securities and financial instruments[293]. On the other hand, the hedge fund styles exhibiting the lowest serial correlation are macro and equity hedge[294]. These styles invest in liquid financial instruments such as equities, government bonds, currencies and futures contracts.

The pattern of returns of many hedge funds also exhibits other statistical properties, such as a bias towards extreme returns (negative skewness and positive excess kurtosis), indicating that the distribution of returns is not normal. This, together with the serial correlation in returns, means that standard mean-variance optimisation techniques are too restrictive for portfolio construction when hedge funds are included.

A relatively simple methodology to unsmooth a return series was developed for real estate at the beginning of the 1990s[295]. Due to smoothing in appraisals and infrequent valuations of properties, the returns of direct property investment exhibit autocorrelation. The approach employed has been to *unsmooth* the observed returns to create a new set of returns, which are more volatile and whose characteristics are believed to more accurately capture the characteristics of the underlying property values. To unsmooth the observed returns there are three steps.

First, calculate the *autocorrelation coefficient of the first order* (ρ_1) of the return series. This is easily done by calculating the correlation of the observed returns with the 1-period lagged returns (i.e. correlation of r_t and r_{t-1}). The correlation is the first order autocorrelation coefficient.

Second, calculate a new monthly return series using the formula[296]:

$$r_t = [r^*_t - \rho_1\, r^*_{t-1}]/[1 - \rho_1]$$

where r_t is the true (or adjusted) return at time t and r^*_t is the observed return at time t.

The newly constructed series has been unsmoothed and adjusted for the serial correlation of the first degree of the original series.

Third, the new series can be used to calculate the standard deviation and beta of the investment, as well as its correlation with other assets. These unsmoothed statistics reflect more closely the true economic properties of investments. The standard deviation of the unsmoothed series increases when the first order autocorrelation coefficient is positive (while a negative coefficient, which is not expected, results in lower standard deviation).

Figure 28.4 compares a cumulative return of the original historic monthly *smoothed* return series with a recreated *unsmoothed* return series of HFRI Fixed Income Convertible Arbitrage Index. The chart shows the differences in the smoothness of the two return series.

Figure 28.4 – observed and unsmoothed cumulative return of fixed income convertible arbitrage, January 1990 to June 2012

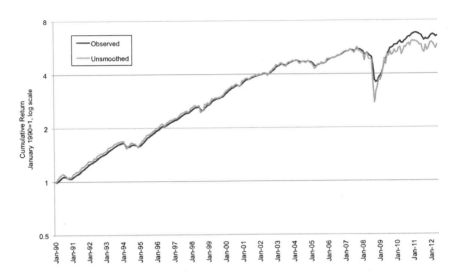

Source: Bloomberg, HFRI RV Fixed Income Convertible Arbitrage.

Figures 28.5 and 28.6 show the original and adjusted monthly returns. The volatility has increased in the second chart through unsmoothing the returns.

Figure 28.5 – observed monthly returns of fixed income convertible arbitrage, January 2000 to June 2012

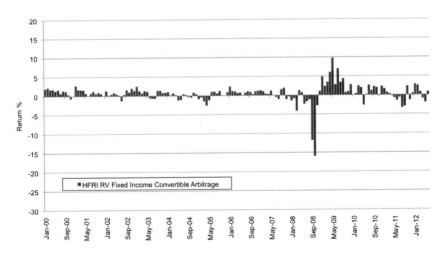

Source: Bloomberg, HFRI RV Fixed Income Convertible Arbitrage.

Figure 28.6 – unsmoothed monthly returns of fixed income convertible arbitrage, January 2000 to June 2012

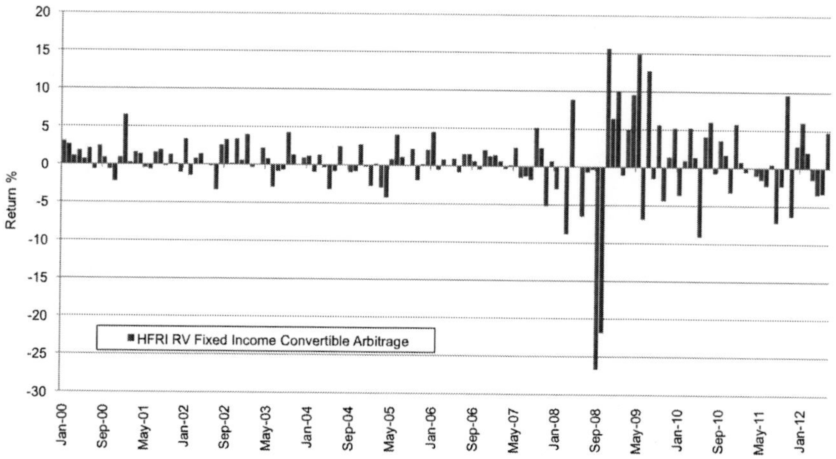

Source: Bloomberg, HFRI RV Fixed Income Convertible Arbitrage.

Table 28.5 shows the results of unsmoothing the return series of those HFRI indices that display statistically significant serial correlation.

Table 28.5 – observed and unsmoothed return and risk characteristics of hedge fund strategies and global equities, January 1990 to June 2012

	HFRI Fund Weighted Composite	HFRI Equity Hedge	HFRI Macro	HFRI Event Driven	HFRI Relative Value	HFRI FI Convertible Arbitrage	MSCI World Index
ρ_1	0.30	0.24	0.16	0.38	0.44	0.58	0.09
StDev							
Observed (%)	7.10	9.30	7.60	4.40	4.40	6.70	15.70
Unsmoothed (%)	9.60	11.90	9.00	7.20	7.20	13.10	17.20
Performance							
Observed (%)	11.20	12.90	12.50	11.90	10.20	8.70	5.20
Unsmoothed (%)	11.00	12.70	12.40	11.70	10.00	8.20	5.00
Sharpe ratio							
Observed (%)	1.11	1.02	1.20	1.24	1.53	0.79	0.12
Unsmoothed (%)	0.79	0.78	1.00	0.81	0.92	0.36	0.09

Source: Bloomberg, HFRI Fund Weighted Composite, HFRI Equity Hedge, HFRI Macro, HFRI Event Driven, HFRI Relative Value, HFRI RB Fixed Income Convertible Arbitrage, MSCI World.

It is evident from the table that for series that exhibit significant serial correlation the adjustment for standard deviation is noticeable when compared to series with weaker serial correlation. For example, for the Convertible Arbitrage Index, which exhibits the most significant autocorrelation, the observed annualised standard deviation is 6.7% while the unsmoothed annualised standard deviation is 13.1%.

An alternative approach[297] to adjust for autocorrelation is using quarterly rather than monthly returns. Standard deviation of series exhibiting positive monthly autocorrelation should increase under this method.

Some commonly used risk data, such as maximum drawdown, should be unaffected by serial correlation. When constructing hedge fund portfolios both quantitative and qualitative analyses need to be used. When looking at quantitative data, risk data that are unaffected by serial correlation should be used as well as the adjusted data for volatility and correlation.

Risk management tools – mind your money

When there is a risk that investors do not want to take, one technique is *trading* positions. For example, if equity markets are extremely unpredictable and investors do not want to take equity risk, selling equities is a way to control it. *Diversifying* portfolios across asset classes, such as government bonds, can protect portfolios from equity market falls. Proper diversification reduces some risks (idiosyncratic risks). When investments are illiquid (e.g. small cap stocks) or selling physical holdings is too expensive, derivative markets may provide efficient solutions. This may introduce other risks, such as basis risk.

If investors are uncomfortable with equity exposure, shorting futures contracts is a way to *hedge* equity risk. If investors are worried about equity markets diving but still want to benefit from a potential rally, buying put options can eliminate some downside equity risk but keep some upside potential. This *insurance* may not be cheap and a premium will have to be paid for it.

Risk management tools hence fall into four categories:

1.   *Trading.* The first risk management technique is taking action or trading positions within portfolios. If the risk level in portfolios is too high (or too low), or portfolios are exposed to unwanted risks, investors can change the portfolio composition to adjust the risk level. For example, reducing the exposure to equities and increasing the exposure to cash reduces the volatility and the exposure to equity markets. Reducing the exposure to corporate bonds and increasing the exposure to government bonds reduces credit risk (it can, however, increase interest rate risk or exposure to sovereign risk). The ability to trade portfolios depends on the liquidity of positions. Large, illiquid portfolios may not be able to trade quickly enough or trading may be costly. For example, selling a large position in an illiquid

corporate bond may involve a haircut (such as 60 cents on the dollar) or bids at a reasonable price may not be accepted. Under these circumstances, hedging or insurance may be more efficient.

2. *Diversification.* Diversification is a method of reducing idiosyncratic (non-systematic) risk in portfolios. Systematic risk, however, cannot be diversified away. Holding investments that tend to perform well during market stress, such as government bonds, managed futures and long volatility, adds a layer of protection.

3. *Hedging.* Hedging is a risk management technique whereby a long position that exposes portfolios to unwanted risks is removed using a short position with high correlation to the long position. Therefore, losses on the long position are offset by gains on the short position, and vice versa. The extent of the offset or the effectiveness of the hedge depends on the correlation and exposure between the long and short positions. For example, a portfolio that is long US equities can hedge the positions by shorting a futures contract on the S&P 500 Index. The hedge is imperfect since the portfolio is long a basket of equities and the hedge is a position on the S&P 500 Index. Differences in performance between the equity basket and the S&P 500 Index mean that the hedge is imperfect. The difference in performance between the equity basket and the futures contract is *basis risk*. Another imperfection of the hedge is that the exposure of the long position needs to match the exposure of the hedge. The hedge needs to be rebalanced if market movements change the value of the long and short positions at different rates. The hedge ratio (ratio between market value of the hedge over market value of the hedged assets) is not 100%. Hedging caps downside risk as well as upside potential of the long position. A hedge is relatively cheap when using liquid derivatives or ETFs (that can be shorted as well).

4. *Insurance.* Insurance means purchasing protection on risky positions. For example, a portfolio with a long basket of US equities can protect the downside risk by purchasing a put option on the S&P 500 Index. The downside risk is limited to the exercise price of the option plus the premium paid. Insurance, unlike hedging, costs upfront money (a premium). Unlike hedging, insurance does not cap the upside potential. To reduce the premium cost investors can sell or write out of the money put options. This, however, caps the upside potential.

Delta hedging

An essential aspect of option trading is controlling unwanted risks. For most traders, the unwanted risk is usually directional price movement or delta risk. One motivation for controlling some or all of the delta exposure is if the purpose of the trade, for example, is to gain exposure to changes in volatility rather than price.

Delta hedging is the practice of buying or selling options and/or the underlying asset in order to reduce the net delta in an open position. For example, assume an investor has the view that implied volatility in call options on the S&P 500 Index was overpriced and the desired trade is to short that volatility. The call option is at the money and has a delta of about 50. If the investor shorts two of those calls, the net delta would be about -100. In order to delta-hedge the position, the investor buys 100 shares of an S&P 500 tracker at the current price. If all the positions are entered at once (buying the shares and selling the calls) the combined position is *delta neutral*.

All options have some gamma (the delta of options changes in response to changes in the price of the underlying) and so the initial hedge is only the first step. As the underlying moves around over time, the net delta of the position will change as well. The obvious response to any changes would be to adjust the hedge continuously, buying and selling the underlying asset tick-by-tick in order to stay completely neutral at all times. However, that is impractical for several reasons:

- Transaction costs would eat up any profits

- Contract sizes may prevent sufficiently granular hedges

- The discrete nature of market prices means a continuous hedge is impossible

Hedging continuously represents one extreme approach. The other extreme is never hedging or doing so infrequently. The key to *dynamic hedging* is to navigate the two extremes, avoiding undue delta exposure while keeping transaction costs as low as possible.

Conclusion

Risk management is at the centre of everything in life. You are one of the risk managers of the family. Too much risk may mean disaster. To increase the chances of survival, risk management is a must.

Summary

- Without risk there is no performance. Therefore, risk management is at the core of multi-asset investing.

- Successful risk management distinguishes between portfolios and investment management firms that survive and those which do not.

- Risk measurement is focused on quantifying and communicating risk. Risk management is making tactical and strategic decisions to control risks that should be controlled and exploit risky opportunities that should be exploited for a gain.

- Sensitivity analysis tests the impact of changes in one or more variables on portfolios. Scenario analysis tests the impact of different economic conditions on portfolios.

- Multi-factor risk models break the risk of the portfolio into exposures to different risk factors. Each portfolio is a bundle of risk factors and multi-factor models can unbundle the portfolios and quantify their risk exposures.

- Backtesting risk analytics are a simple way to quantify portfolio risks without any sophisticated risk measurement system and with a limited amount of data (monthly investment and benchmark returns).

- Risk decomposition shows the contribution to risk from each position in multi-asset portfolios. Breaking down risk to asset allocation and security selection is particularly relevant to multi-asset portfolios.

- Asset allocation may be very different than risk allocation. Risk decomposition can reveal the risk allocation.

- Standard deviation is an appropriate measure when returns are normally or close to normally distributed. When returns are not normally distributed, volatility should be adjusted for fat tail risk. The Cornish-Fisher approximation can be used to make this adjustment.

- Autocorrelation is common for asset classes for which returns are based on valuations (smoothened) and true volatility is understated. Unsmoothing returns produces a better estimate of true volatility.

- Risk management uses four techniques to manage risks within portfolios: trading; diversification; hedging; and insurance.

The next chapter covers investment strategies and is the last in Part 3 of the book, implementing a solution. The chapter provides a wide range of investment strategies to tackle different market and economic conditions and investment objectives. The strategies demonstrate how to use many of the concepts and ideas covered so far.

29. INVESTMENT STRATEGIES

Investment strategy is the plan – the set of rules, principles and processes – that guide the asset allocation and investment selection of a portfolio to reflect its investment objectives and constraints. A strategy is about making choices, deciding what to do and what not to do. Investment strategy is about balancing potential performance and potential risks.

The Holy Grail of investment strategy is performing well when markets rally and avoiding falls when markets crash (being conservative when markets fall and aggressive when markets rise). Unfortunately, the reality of investments is that only a small number of highly skilled investors are able to achieve this and they charge a very high fee for this service. For the rest of us, it is a balancing act of accepting downside risk and sacrificing upside potential. Most investment strategies aim to balance these two contradicting forces, reaching a compromise.

This chapter reviews some general investment strategies that are appropriate for different circumstances, market conditions or specific investment objectives. The strategies in this chapter provide examples of how to link investment objectives, market conditions and investment strategies. The examples are general and as always the strategy must be tailored to the investor's specific circumstances and objectives.

General principles

Investment strategy starts with the required expected return, a projection of future needs for cash, in the form of both income and capital. Investors need to project annual withdrawals from their portfolios and evaluate what happens if cash outflows cannot be achieved. This is the first assessment of risk. Starting from willingness to take risk is wrong since it is greatly affected by recent events and mood. For example, most individual investors would be much more risk averse after or during a bear market, such as in 2002 or 2008.

When the required return is known, the required risk level can be calculated using the assumed relationship between risk and return. For example, using CMAs the expected risk and return of an asset allocation is calculated. Investors need to decide whether the risk level is acceptable, both objectively (ability to take risk) and subjectively (willingness to take risk). If the risk level is acceptable, the required return can be achieved. If the risk level is unacceptable, the required return must be adjusted until the risk level is acceptable. Investors need to reach a balance between return and risk. The trade-off between risk and return can be reflected in asset allocation, investment selection and incorporation of risk management techniques to control some unwanted risks. Once the required return and accepted risk are determined, an investment policy can be formulated.

Asset allocation is clearly important. However, investment selection is as important as asset allocation (depending on the circumstances). The academic debate shows that there is no definitive answer on the importance of asset allocation relative to investment selection so no risk should be taken and proper attention should be paid to both activities.

Diversification reduces risk, expands the investment opportunity set, and balances correct and incorrect market decisions (investors are humans and will make incorrect calls). However, including too many asset classes in portfolios may be wrong for several reasons, such as:

- Diminishing benefits of diversification

- Increasing correlation of additional assets within the portfolio

- Over diversification and reduction in tracking error (benchmark hugging)

- Increasing complexity in modelling esoteric asset classes

- Increasing transaction costs of portfolio rebalancing

- The need to use more illiquid investments

The number of portfolio managers in a multi-manager portfolio should be limited as well; otherwise the portfolio may be an expensive tracker as all manager alphas are diversified away. As the number of managers increases more resources must be spent to monitor them. It is better to have a more focused portfolio with fewer managers with meaningful allocations. Multi-asset portfolios strike a balance between simplicity and complexity.

These are some of the general principles of investment strategy of any multi-asset portfolio. The investment strategy should be tailored to the specific objectives and circumstances and combine asset allocation with investment selection.

Types of multi-asset portfolios

Multi-asset portfolios can be divided into three broad categories. The first category includes portfolios that aim to outperform a benchmark. The benchmark is either a composite benchmark that is set by SAA to match the portfolio's long-term return and risk profile or a peer group sector. The portfolio has relative return and risk objectives in respect of the benchmark.

The second category is risk targeting portfolios. These portfolios have a range of accepted absolute risk (usually based on investors' attitude to risk or ATR) and the aim is to generate the highest possible return within the risk range.

The third category includes flexible portfolios. The portfolio manager decides on the risk level of the portfolio and its composition. These are typically absolute return or target return portfolios, aiming to generate cash or inflation plus returns over a certain investment horizon. Absolute return portfolios cover either long/short portfolios (normally these can be classified as hedge funds) or long only portfolios. Diversified Growth Funds (DGF) are an example of multi-asset portfolios with an absolute return objective and the aim of providing a diversified solution, combining dynamic asset allocation and investment selection, potentially with equity-like returns and lower volatility than that of equities.

Short-term investment strategies

Short-term investors should hold mostly cash and while their main objective is probably beating Treasury bills, their desire is for absolute, positive return. They have no long-term liabilities to hedge as part of the investment objectives. The safe-haven asset class is cash since inflation risk is low over the short term and there is no duration risk relative to long-term liabilities.

The investment strategy should change as a function of the level of interest rates. When short-term interest rates are high more risk can be taken since cash return is high (providing a cushion) and bonds, if held to maturity, deliver higher yields, as well as the potential for capital gains if interest rates fall. When short-term interest rates are low, investors have a lower cushion since cash return is not enough to protect the portfolio from a negative return of even a moderate allocation to risk assets.

Figure 29.1 shows the probability of meeting a 5% target return over one year for different levels of cash return for a portfolio of 20% equity, 50% bonds, 20% cash and 10% alternative investments. As the interest-rate level increases, so does the probability of reaching the target.

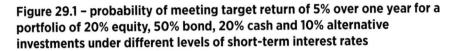

Figure 29.1 – probability of meeting target return of 5% over one year for a portfolio of 20% equity, 50% bond, 20% cash and 10% alternative investments under different levels of short-term interest rates

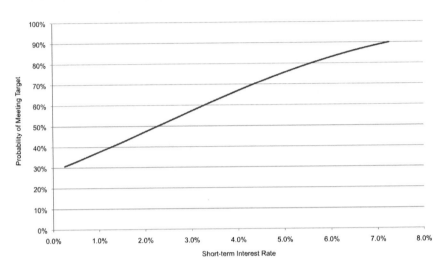

Short-term investors should normally invest only in traditional, liquid investments. Holding illiquid investments is risky since selling them at the end of the investment horizon may be costly. Many illiquid investments need a long investment horizon to deliver their returns (such as private equity) and the high transaction costs of some investments (such as property) make sense only if the holding period is long so costs are spread over many years.

The strategy for short-term investors is holding cash and bonds with maturities matching cash outflows. Deviations from cash and bonds should be considered carefully. Taking equity risk, for example, may result in losses with insufficient time to recoup them. Equities are for long-term investors.

Over the short term it makes sense to use a *buy and hold* investment strategy. Buy and hold, as the name suggests, is buying positions and then holding them without actively changing them. One reason is that to be successful active management requires breadth (as per the fundamental law of active management) and over the short term there is insufficient time to make enough active investment decisions. The information ratio of an active strategy over the short term is likely to be low. Another reason for buy and hold is that it is more difficult to predict markets over the short run and the information coefficient may be low.

The short-term strategy should be based more on systematic rules than on discretion. A *rule-based strategy* implements changes based on predetermined events. For example, the asset allocation may be rebalanced if the allocation to an asset class drifts more than 5% from initial target allocation. Discretion, on the other hand, requires investors to evaluate the situation and make an investment decision. Owing to the short horizon, there is unlikely to be sufficient time to correct mistakes in discretion so regret risk is high.

SAA does not work over the short term. SAA is based on CMAs, whose investment horizon is normally 5 to 10 years. Predicting CMAs over the next year is more tactical and inappropriate for SAA. The asset allocation over short term requires more judgment, as opposed to a systematic approach such as that of SAA. SAA is based on forecasting the average return per year while SAA is going to be there for many years, so the average works. When the horizon is one year, average annual return over one observation is statistically insignificant and highly uncertain.

What is short or long term? As Albert Einstein said "it is all relative". Short term is relative to long term and they are relative to each investor's unique circumstances and perspective. For an endowment with a perpetual investment horizon 20 years is short term. For a 50-year-old individual investor building a retirement portfolio, 20 years is not such a short term. For a portfolio manager whose performance is frequently measured versus a benchmark, 20 years is very long term. The standard for defining horizons in capital markets is that short term is considered to be less than a year and long term is more than a year. As John Maynard Keynes put it "in the long run we are all dead".

Long-term investment strategies

Long-term investors have more flexibility than short-term investors. They have time to adjust the investment strategy and to adapt themselves, for example by postponing retirement or reducing expenditures, based on the progress toward achieving the investment goals. A pension plan has time to increase contributions or postpone the retirement age (although this may require legislation changes or negotiations with labour unions). An endowment has time to seek more contributions and bequests. More time is valuable and it means more flexibility.

Long-term investors may have liabilities and inflation is a risk over the long term. Cash is therefore not a safe-haven since it does not protect against inflation and it has a duration mismatch with long-term liabilities. Government or inflation-linked bonds with durations matching that of liabilities are the safe-haven assets. Cash is not risk-free over the long term.

The benchmark for long-term investors should be the investment objectives. The success of the investment strategy is measured relative to meeting the investment objectives.

Long-term investors have different objectives to short-term investors. Investors differ based on their type. Individuals target a minimum standard of living and endowments target a minimum spending rate. The ability to generate income or cash flows from portfolios is the objective. Long-term investors should model income needs (actuaries do this for insurance companies and pension schemes). Endowments need to balance the interests of current and future generations and most of their wealth accumulation comes from contributions, not investment performance.

Private wealth is the most volatile and difficult to forecast. Families spend wealth and there are fewer opportunities for intergenerational wealth accumulation compared with institutional investors. Wealth is spent, consumed and donated, taxes and fees are paid and some invest in private ventures that do not come out well. Had private wealth been just invested for the long term it would have grown to significant highs. For example, $1 million invested in the S&P 500 Index on 1 January 1926 and left alone would have grown to over $3 billion today. The investment horizon and plans for private investors can change suddenly due to changing plans of individual family members.

Institutional investors are more stable. Insurance companies and pension plans have investment strategies that are linked to regulations (although change in regulation can change the investment horizon and planning). Endowments have a mission and they do not change it often and without a good reason. Institutional investors are very different from private ones and can have a more stable, long-term investment strategy. Each investor needs a customised investment strategy that may change over time.

The long-term investment strategy should be dynamic and linked to current market conditions and the investment objectives. All the principles of multi-asset investing apply to long-term strategies.

Momentum versus contrarian

Momentum strategies invest in investments when they trend upward with the aim of benefiting from their momentum (*make the trend your friend*). As the prices rise, more investors purchase the asset and its price continues to rise. The risk, of course, is the inflection point. What goes up must come down. Investments that rise may be a bubble, or just inflated, and may fall. Prices reflect the discounted future prospects of assets. As prices rise, usually based on historic news and current high expectations, there is more room for disappointment and a drop in prices.

Contrarian strategies invest in investments that have fallen in value with the view that they are undervalued or going to revert back to the mean (mean reversion). Another way to think about contrarian strategy is investing contrary to the common view. If all investors and *experts* say invest in X, then short X or invest in Y. Go contrary to the herd. The risk with a contrarian strategy is that out-of-favour investments may stay so for a long time and in favour investments have a positive momentum until it reverses.

To generate above average or superior returns investors must invest in non-consensus views. Investing with the consensus generates market returns. Only investors who have the insight to form non-consensus views that are correct can beat the market[298]. Generating alpha therefore requires contrarian strategies.

Strategies to reduce fat tail risk

Hedging the left, fat tail of the distribution of portfolio returns becomes popular after market crashes. The techniques for fat tail risk hedging have become more sophisticated over the years. Fat tail hedging or protection strategies usually involve purchasing insurance in the form of options – insurance costs money. These strategies should perform well when markets crash and protect some of the portfolio downside. However, when markets go sideways or upwards, these strategies may cost dearly and cause portfolios to lose performance.

When markets have been trending upward, implied volatility is subdued and purchasing insurance is relatively cheap. However, optimism dominates and investors are less risk averse than on average. This is the time to purchase fat tail insurance since it is relatively cheap and as market prices are higher, bubbly conditions develop and the crash or correction is getting closer. However, most investors are focused on generating returns rather than controlling risks and forget about downside risk and insurance. After the crash, implied volatility is high, investors are risk averse and pessimism dominates. Then investors tend to purchase insurance when it is most expensive, market prices are already low and risk levels are subdued.

One obvious way to protect the downside is to change the portfolio's asset allocation to a more conservative one just before a crash. The advantage is the (perceived) simplicity of the strategy. The disadvantages are the transaction costs of trading (these can be addressed by trading derivatives instead of underlying positions), the opportunity cost of missing performance of a more aggressive asset allocation and the extreme difficulty in correctly predicting the future. Hoping to switch from an aggressive to conservative strategy just before a market crash and back to aggressive before a market recovery is naïve. Few can make such market timing calls. Getting it wrong (staying invested aggressively in the crash and missing the recovery with a conservative strategy) can be costly.

Figure 29.2 shows the performance of S&P 500 Index from January 2000 to June 2012. The index returned a meagre 1.3% per annum over this time period. Missing the five worst months would have returned 6.4% per annum. Missing the five best months, however, would have returned -2.5% per annum. In this example, the benefits of missing the worst months exceed the loss of missing the best months. However, the example clearly demonstrates the consequences of timing the market correctly and incorrectly. The example also demonstrates the power of mitigating losses when markets fall.

Figure 29.2 – S&P 500 total return, missing worst and best five months, January 2000 to June 2012

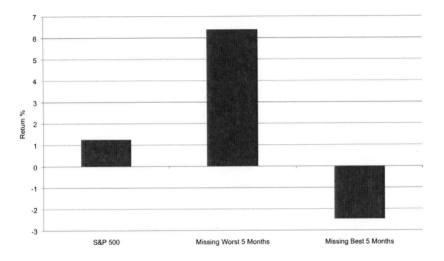

Source: Bloomberg, S&P 500.

An alternative to switching the entire asset allocation is maintaining positions in asset classes that should provide a natural protection when equity and risk assets crash. For example, long duration government bonds, safe-haven currencies (dollar, yen, Swiss franc) and gold are some investments that typically benefit from a flight to quality.

Figure 29.3 shows the average monthly performance of the S&P 500 Index ranked by deciles from January 1992 to June 2012 and the corresponding performance of US Treasury bonds. As can be seen, US Treasury bonds with maturities over one year have performed better on average during the worst equity market returns than during strong equity market performance. A flight to quality explains this.

Figure 29.3 – S&P 500 and US Treasury returns ranked by S&P 500 deciles, January 1992 to June 2012

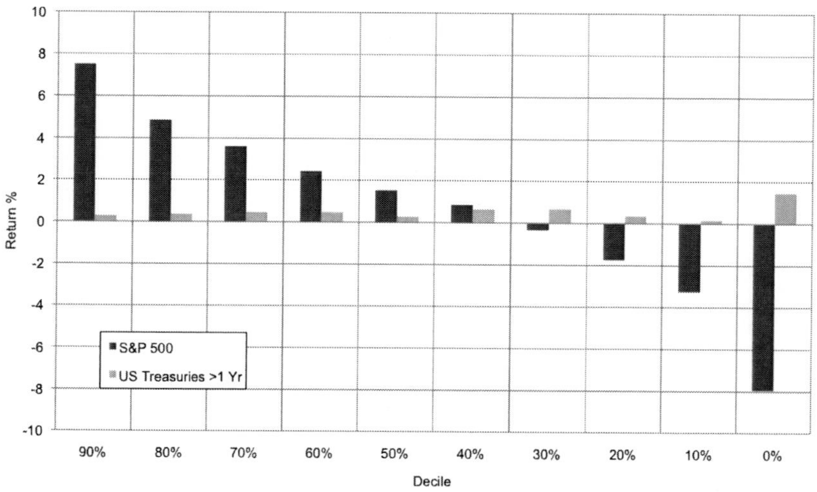

Source: Bloomberg, S&P 500.

Insuring the downside can be readily implemented by purchasing out-of-the money put options on markets that may fall. It is more efficient to purchase put options on equity markets forming a well representative sample of the equity markets to which the portfolio is exposed. Put options can be chosen based on their underlying markets, the correlation between underlyings and portfolio holdings, the liquidity of the options and their price. Purchasing put options costs money (a premium). Some of the premium can be funded through selling further out-of-the-money put options (as Figure 29.4 illustrates). This strategy maintains some upside but limits the downside protection to reduce the cost of the protection.

Figure 29.4 – put option combination payoff and P&L

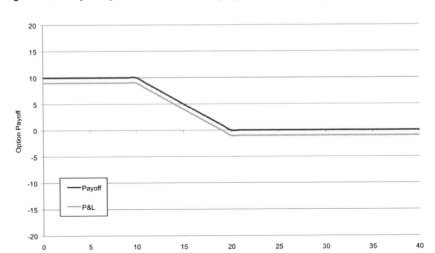

Instead of purchasing put options on equity markets, VIX call options or VIX futures contracts can be used. The VIX tends to rise quickly when equity markets fall (as Figure 29.5 illustrates) as implied volatility of traded options increases. Implied volatility reflects forward-looking market expectations and the VIX should remain at a high level as long as the market expects high volatility and equity market weakness ahead. Unlike a call option on equities, which is a risk-on trade, a call option on the VIX is a risk-off trade since a rise in the VIX is associated with a fall in equity markets. One downside of this strategy is that it can be very expensive. VIX protection strategies must be dynamic since after the VIX jumps up when equity markets fall it tends to fall back again when calm returns to markets. Therefore, the strategy must take profits after the VIX rises, otherwise all profits will be lost.

Figure 29.5 – S&P 500 and VIX returns ranked by S&P 500 deciles, January 1992 to June 2012

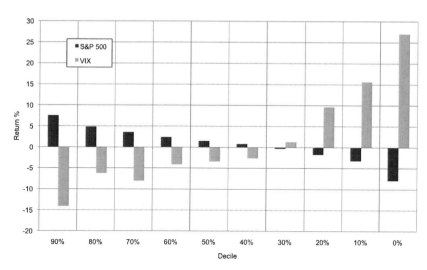

Source: Bloomberg.

Using managed futures is another protection technique as they can reduce excess kurtosis and shift negative skewness to the right. The return distribution of managed futures is typically skewed to the right. Adding an allocation to managed futures to portfolios can change their return profile.

Figure 29.6 shows the average monthly returns of the S&P 500 Index from January 1994 to June 2012 ranked by deciles alongside the performance of the Dow Jones Credit Suisse Managed Futures Hedge Fund Index. Managed futures have performed the best when the equity market performed the worst.

Figure 29.6 – S&P 500 and managed futures returns ranked by S&P 500 deciles, January 1994 to June 2012

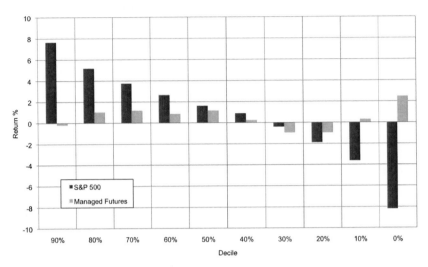

Source: Bloomberg, S&P, Dow Jones Credit Suisse.

Table 29.1 shows the worst[299] time periods of equity market performance since January 1994, alongside the returns of managed futures and US Treasury bonds. In most cases, managed futures have provided downside protection, albeit there were some episodes when the equity market crashed and managed futures delivered negative returns (e.g. the market correction of May 2011).

Table 29.1 – worst S&P 500 returns and corresponding returns of US Treasuries and managed futures, January 1994 to June 2012

Start month	End Month	S&P 500 %	Managed Futures %	US Treasury Bonds %
Feb-1994	Mar-1994	-6.96	3.83	-4.17
Jul-1996		-4.42	0.10	0.17
Mar-1997		-4.11	-0.95	-0.98
Aug-1997		-5.60	-7.27	-1.07
Jul-1998	Aug-1998	-15.37	8.72	3.22
Jul-1999	Sep-1999	-6.24	0.75	0.58
Jan-2000	Feb-2000	-6.82	-2.09	1.72
Apr-2000	May-2000	-5.00	-1.71	-0.07
Sep-2000	Nov-2000	-13.12	3.90	3.00
Feb-2001	Mar-2001	-14.88	5.04	1.44
Jun-2001	Sep-2001	-16.75	5.53	5.85
Apr-2002	Jul-2002	-20.15	17.40	7.01
Sep-2002		-10.87	4.11	2.84
Dec-2002	Feb-2003	-8.84	11.83	4.11
Jun-2007	Jul-2007	-4.71	-1.91	1.75
Nov-2007	Feb-2009	-50.94	16.73	13.70
May-2010	Jun-2010	-12.80	-3.63	3.76
Aug-2010		-4.51	4.87	2.14
May-2011	Sep-2011	-16.26	-4.15	7.82
Average		**-12.02**	**3.22**	**2.78**
Median		**-8.84**	**3.83**	**2.14**

Source: Bloomberg, S&P, Dow Jones Credit Suisse.

The charts in Figure 29.7 show the return distributions of US equities, US Treasury bonds and managed futures. Table 29.2 summarises risk, return and distribution attributes of the three investments, as well as those of asset allocations combining them. Managed futures and government bonds have been excellent diversifiers to equities and they help reduce the negative skew of the return distribution and lower its kurtosis. Less negative skew and lower kurtosis is what investors should seek in order to achieve an investment strategy with lower downside and higher upside.

Figure 29.7 – distribution of monthly returns and normal distribution of S&P 500, US Treasuries and managed futures, January 1994 to June 2012

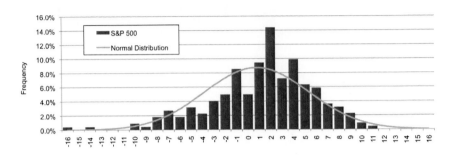

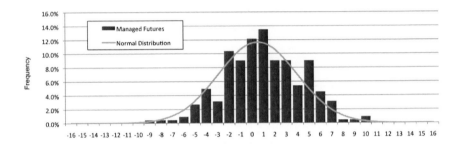

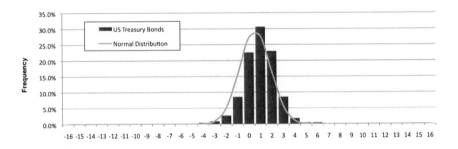

Source: Bloomberg, S&P, Dow Jones Credit Suisse.

Table 29.2 – performance and risk characteristics of S&P 500, US Treasuries and managed futures and portfolios combining them, January 1994 to June 2012

	S&P 500	Managed Futures	US Treasury Bonds	90% Equity 10% MF	90% Equity 10% Bonds	80% Equity 10% MF 10% Bonds
Performance (% pa)	8.01	5.75	6.17	7.99	7.97	7.92
Volatility (%)	15.64	11.69	4.73	14.00	14.00	12.38
Skewness	-0.65	0.03	-0.10	-0.59	-0.65	-0.58
Kurtosis	0.92	-0.02	0.99	0.63	0.92	0.60
Sharpe Ratio	0.31	0.23	0.65	0.35	0.35	0.39

Source: Bloomberg, S&P, Dow Jones Credit Suisse.

Insured asset allocation

Insured asset allocation is commonly called *dynamic asset allocation*. Dynamic asset allocation changes the asset allocation to alter the portfolio risk exposure in a predetermined way (rule-based and systematic as opposed to discretionary). However, this name is misleading since all asset allocation strategies should be dynamic; not only this one.

The premise behind insured allocation is that investors' risk tolerance depends on portfolio value. If the portfolio value falls below a certain level (*floor value*) investors' risk tolerance falls to zero, and a larger portion of the portfolio should be invested in conservative assets. As the portfolio value rises above the floor, the investors' risk tolerance increases and a larger portion of the portfolio should be invested in risk assets. Insured asset allocation dynamically changes the portfolio allocation between risk and conservative assets based on portfolio value relative to the floor (replicating a put option). Insured portfolios tend to follow the momentum and invest more in asset classes that perform well.

Constant Proportion Portfolio Insurance (CPPI) is a common strategy for insured asset allocation. The formula determining the amount invested in risk assets is:

$\$ \text{ in risk assets} = m * (\text{assets} - \text{floor})$

where m is the risk asset investment multiplier, assets is the value of total assets held in the portfolio and floor is the minimum allowable portfolio value.

Assets minus floor is the *cushion* or funds that can be invested in risk assets. The risk asset multiplier, m, has a value greater than one. The floor has an initial positive value and it grows or fluctuates over time. A constant proportion of the cushion (m) is invested in risk assets. When the cushion equals zero the portfolio stops investing in risk assets. If the portfolio value falls below the floor the portfolio is locked in cash and remains invested in cash (cash lock-in risk), unless the investor re-launches the portfolio with a new investment strategy.

The multiplier (m) determines the maximum risk asset movement that is needed to lock the strategy in cash. For example, a multiplier of 5 means that the strategy should work as long as the risky position does not move by more than 20% between rebalances. The multiplier can dynamically change inversely with market volatility to add another layer of protection against locking the strategy in cash.

For example, assume a portfolio with a total asset value of $100, a minimum floor of $75 and m of 2. The initial allocation to risk assets is $50 (2*(100 - 75)). If risk assets fall 10% their value in the portfolio is $45. The portfolio now consists of $45 risk assets and $50 conservative assets, with a total value of $95. The new investment in risk assets is going to be $40 (2*(95 - 75)). The portfolio has sold risk assets when they fell. After rebalancing the portfolio has $40 in risk assets and $55 in conservative assets.

Black Monday occurred on 19 October 1987 when equity markets around the world crashed. The Dow Jones Industrial Average (DJIA) fell 22.6%, the largest one day percentage fall for this index. The most popular explanation for the crash is sales by program traders. Portfolio insurance strategies, such as CPPI, sold equities as equity markets started to fall. This was a vicious circle; as more equities were sold, the further equity markets fell.

Black Monday demonstrated the vulnerability of CPPI strategies. When markets fall too much too quickly, CPPI strategies do not have sufficient time to sell dropping assets and move the investment to the safe assets. Under these circumstances, CPPI is not able to protect portfolios from falling below the floor. *Gap* is defined as the value of risk assets relative to the cushion. To protect the CPPI structure from a sudden fall in risk assets, investors can take a gap risk insurance policy. The insurance will pay the CPPI in case risk assets fall by a certain percentage.

Cash lock-in risk means that once the floor is breached the portfolio is fully invested in conservative assets and cannot reinvest in risk assets. One way to reduce this risk is diversification. For a CPPI structure that uses only equity and cash, risk is high. However, instead of investing only in equities, CPPI can use a diversified multi-asset portfolio. By determining the appropriate level of risk in the multi-asset portfolio, the CPPI structure can minimise gap and cash lock-in risk. Such an offering based on a multi-asset portfolio with CPPI protection is often called a *protected multi-asset portfolio*.

Figure 29.8 compares a backtested CPPI strategy with the S&P 500 Index over the period January 2000 to June 2012. Over this time the CPPI strategy generates a similar return to the equity market with much lower drawdowns.

Figure 29.8 – cumulative performance of backtested CPPI strategy on 50% US equities and 50% US Treasury bonds and S&P 500, January 2000 to June 2012

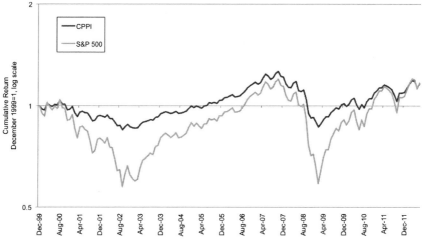

Source: Bloomberg, Global Financial Data, S&P.

Absolute return

Absolute return portfolios have an objective of delivering positive returns. The reference benchmark is cash or inflation and the portfolio has a target return over the benchmark. The portfolio manager is expected to hedge downside risk when markets are falling.

The absolute return objective is difficult to achieve. On the one hand, if the target is cash plus 4% (a target of 4% is common since it represents the equity risk premium) the portfolio must take material risks to be able to meet its return objective. On the other hand, if the objective is to avoid negative returns the portfolio must protect the downside by buying protection (expensive) or switching the portfolio to a conservative strategy before the market falls (needs foresight). Generating high returns while protecting the downside is the ultimate quest of active management.

When short-term interest rates are high it is easier to achieve positive nominal returns since cash provides a safe return. However, when short-term interest rates are high it usually means that inflation is high or increasing so cash may not provide a positive real return. If the absolute return target is cash plus 4% and the short-term interest rate is 4%, the total target return is 8%. This is an equity-like target return and equity-like risk usually needs to be assumed to achieve the target.

Most absolute return portfolios should use derivatives. This is likely to be the only way to purchase downside protection and/or to be able to de-risk and re-risk the portfolio quickly and cost efficiently to position it to market developments. Some absolute return portfolios also use leverage since they are positioned to perform positively under different scenarios and under some scenarios the expected returns are consequently modest. Therefore, leverage is required to augment returns.

Successful absolute return strategies must be managed by managers who have forecasting skills and correctly apply discretion. There are no common rule-based strategies for achieving relatively high positive returns with minimal downside risk (some quant hedge funds may have such strategies). Consistently successful absolute return strategies are rare and usually expensive (since skilled managers know it and demand a payment for their skill).

Volatility targeting portfolios

Volatility targeting or risk controlled multi-asset portfolios are managed within a range of volatilities. Instead of targeting a certain return above a benchmark or an absolute return, the portfolios are managed to target volatility and aim to maximise returns for that level of risk. The portfolios are unconstrained (e.g. by a tracking error to a benchmark) and should match the investor's risk appetite. If properly managed, the portfolios remain within the volatility band, keeping in line with the investor's risk tolerance even if market conditions change.

One of the challenges with managing volatility targeting portfolios is keeping the volatility within the range. As the volatility of financial markets changes, portfolio volatility may change without any action from the investor. Investors need to rebalance the portfolio to keep the volatility within range.

A second challenge is how to measure volatility. Ex ante measures can be very sensitive to temporary changes in market volatility and require frequent portfolio rebalancing, leading to high turnover and transaction costs. Using the VIX as a measure of volatility causes the portfolio to rebalance frequently, selling after markets fall and buying after they have risen (selling low and buying high). Rebalancing based on temporary changes to volatility does not serve the investor's interests. An alternative is measuring volatility over a long time frame, using ex post volatility or a combination of ex post with ex ante to guide volatility within the range.

The range of volatility is important. Portfolios should have a range since it is impossible to maintain target volatility without flexibility. Investors should have the flexibility to take more or less risk based on their market views. Changing portfolio volatility should be part of the SAA and TAA decisions. When investors expect markets to fall, when uncertainty is at high levels and/or when volatility is at high levels, they may decide to reduce portfolio volatility, and vice versa when the outlook is positive.

The volatility range itself can change as well if it is based on the volatility of market indices (such as a combination of equities, bonds and cash). When the volatility range changes so should the portfolio benchmark since it needs to target approximately the mid-range of the volatility band.

Target-date funds

The asset allocation of target-date or *lifecycle funds* gradually and dynamically changes from aggressive to conservative as investors approach retirement. The *glide path* of the asset allocation sets the way the asset allocation changes. When investors are relatively young, with a long investment horizon and employment, the ability and willingness to take risk are higher (although some young investors have less willingness to take risk since investing is new to them and they may have less ability to take risk since their wealth is relatively low). For such investors a portfolio with a high allocation to risk assets is appropriate. As investors approach retirement, the ability and willingness to take risk diminishes and the portfolio should invest more in conservative assets. When investors reach retirement, the portfolio should buy them an annuity to provide income.

Each target-date fund has a maturity, such as 2050. The 2050 fund is appropriate for investors who plan to retire at or around that year. The main advantages of target-date funds are their simplicity and asset allocation management. Most investors do not have the expertise or time to manage their personal pension scheme. Target date-funds aim to provide a simple, buy and hold solution that investors can purchase and hold until their retirement. The risk of the funds is supposed to be managed and fit the risk tolerance of investors until retirement. These funds are an investment solution for defined contribution pension schemes.

One major risk of target-date funds is inflation. Over a long investment horizon the main objective should be maintaining the purchasing power of investments. A second major risk of target-date funds is that the investor's savings for retirement are entrusted with one fund and one fund manager. Inappropriate management of the fund may be devastating for the investor.

Portable alpha

Portable alpha refers to a process of isolating the return of investments from market risk (beta) or separating alpha and beta. Isolating the alpha is usually accomplished by removing the beta exposure by shorting a derivative.

For example, a portfolio manager manages an equity portfolio whose benchmark is the S&P 500 Index. The manager is very successful at picking stocks and outperforms the benchmark by 5% during a time when the benchmark fell by 10%. The manager added 5% alpha, but the portfolio still fell by 5%. To make this 5% of alpha portable, the manager could have shorted S&P 500 Index futures contracts at the beginning of the year. This would have given a return of 5% – the manager's isolated alpha without the beta exposure to the S&P 500 Index.

To use this portable alpha, investors can gain exposure to the S&P 500 Index via a cheap index tracker, borrow against the portfolio, invest in the active manager and reduce the beta risk of the manager by shorting S&P 500 Index futures contracts. The investor would have effectively gained cheap exposure to the S&P 500 Index and transported the manager's alpha into the portfolio. Alternatively, the investor may not buy the S&P 500 Index tracker and just import the manager's alpha.

In multi-asset portfolios the allocation to alpha depends on the allocation to beta. Asset allocation sets the proportion allocated to each asset class. When the allocation to an asset class is small because of SAA, the opportunities to allocate to active alpha-generating strategies within this asset class are limited. Using portable alpha, alpha sources can be imported to portfolios independently of the beta exposure.

Most active strategies deliver both alpha and beta exposure (i.e. beta exposure to the benchmark plus alpha from active risk). Market neutral hedge fund strategies, for example, aim to deliver pure alpha without any beta exposure. Often, multi-asset investors wish to gain exposure only to alpha without the beta and this can be achieved using portable alpha techniques. It is also often criticised that active managers charge fees not only for alpha, for which fees are paid, but also for the beta exposure, which could be cheaply achieved through passive exposures. Portable alpha enables the isolation of alpha and the fee negotiation with the manager to focus only on alpha (e.g. by focusing on performance fees linked to pure alpha).

The main risks with portable alpha are that managers may underperform (negative alpha), resulting in a loss. If this happens when the market rises, a loss will be incurred on the short derivative position as well.

Solutions for concentrated stock positions

Executives and entrepreneurs often find themselves having concentrated positions in a single stock. Executives accumulate holdings in their company's stock over the years as part of their compensation package and successful entrepreneurs whose company went public have large exposure to their company's stock. Often these positions cannot be sold due to restrictions on sales or because these individuals do not want to send a negative signal to the market by selling their holdings. The undiversified positions are risky, not only because of the high equity concentration, but also because of the idiosyncratic exposure to the stock of a single company, which is also linked to the investor's employment or business.

A potential solution is a *collar*, buying an out-of-the-money put option on the stock and at the same time selling an out-of-the-money call option on the stock. The two transactions do not require spending cash since selling the call funds buying the put. The downside is protected while the upside is capped. The new position can be used to borrow cash on margin since it is suitable collateral as it has limited downside. The cash can then be used to invest in a well-diversified multi-asset portfolio.

Bond ladder

A bond ladder is a portfolio of bonds with each security maturing at a different date with regular intervals (e.g. maturities of 2, 3, 4, 5 and 6 years). This structure minimises interest rate risk and increases liquidity. When a bond matures, the proceeds are invested in a new bond. The advantage of a bond ladder is that investors do not need to sell bonds before maturity and incur capital losses if bond prices depreciate.

Dollar cost averaging

Dollar cost averaging, which is applicable to any currency, not only the dollar, is an investment strategy of investing equal monetary amounts over regular time intervals. This means that more shares are purchased when prices go down and fewer shares are purchased when prices go up. The idea is to reduce the total average cost per share of the investment.

Barbell

A barbell investment strategy is investing in high risk, high octane investments and at the same time in low risk, protective investments. This is a wonderful strategy when uncertainty is at high levels. The asset allocation may be overall neutral equities versus the benchmark, for example, but overweight emerging markets within equity to maintain upside potential. Gilts can be held in line with the benchmark weight for protection, but concurrently with an overweight to credit within fixed income. Global bonds can be underweight but an allocation to emerging market debt within global bonds is held for benefiting from a potential rally in risk assets.

These positions have an upside potential and a downside protection. The downside protection is relative to benchmark, not in absolute terms relative to cash. This is not an absolute return strategy but rather a relative return strategy that should reduce the tracking error and prepare the portfolio for a dichotomy or binary world. It is going to be good or bad, but we do not know which. The portfolio must be prepared to perform reasonably well under both scenarios.

Substitute asset classes

High-yield bonds can be used as a substitute for equities. Both are risk assets. High-yield bonds should perform well in recoveries when corporate balance sheets are improving. Equities can still lag and high-yield bond spreads can narrow more quickly than equities rally. Over the long term, however, equities have a higher expected return than high-yield bonds. The expected return of high-yield is that of investment grade corporate bonds plus a below investment grade credit premium.

Over the short term the spreads on high-yield can overshoot reasonable default rates (i.e. risk is mispriced and spreads are higher than actual risk). The market may overact to economic developments, under-price high-yields (offering very high spreads) and create investment opportunities. This may be behavioural finance overcoming standard finance and irrational, emotional markets prevailing.

Figure 29.9 shows how global high-yield bonds perform on average during different returns of global equities (ranked by deciles of MSCI World Index).

Figure 29.9 – MSCI World and global high-yield bonds returns ranked by MSCI World deciles, January 1990 to June 2012

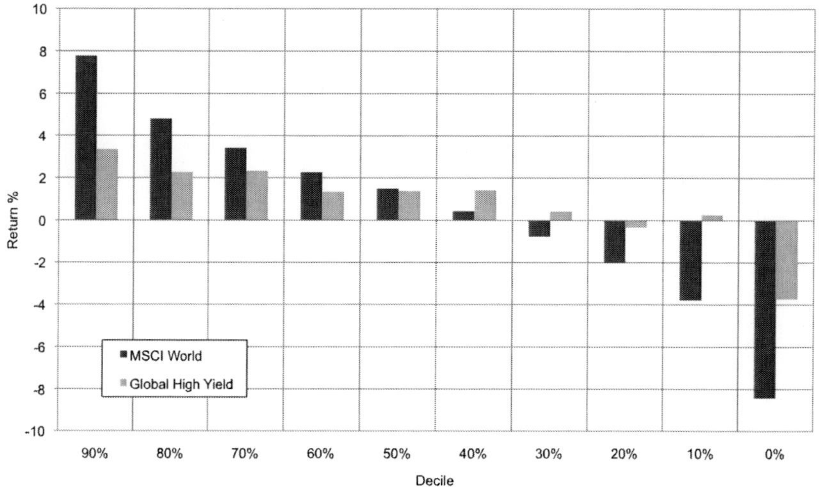

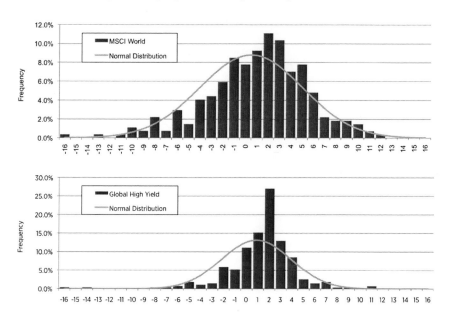

Source: Bloomberg, MSCI, Barclays Capital.

The charts in Figure 29.10 compare the return distribution of global high-yield bonds and global equities.

Figure 29.10 – distribution of monthly returns and normal distribution of MSCI World and global high-yield bonds, January 1990 to June 2012

Source: Bloomberg, MSCI, Barclays Capital.

Table 29.3 shows how global high-yield bonds performed during the periods of worst performance of global equities since January 1990. Table 29.4 shows the return and risk characteristics of the two asset classes.

Table 29.3 – worst MSCI World returns % and returns of global high-yield bonds %, January 1990 to June 2012

Start month	End month	MSCI World	Global High Yield
Jan-1990	Apr-1990	-16.11	-1.81
Aug-1990	Sep1-990	-19.28	-12.57
Jun-1991		-6.36	2.96
Nov-1991		-4.55	0.52
Jan-1992	Mar-1992	-8.63	7.39
Sep-1992	Oct-1992	-4.00	-0.40
Nov-1993		-5.81	0.20
Feb-1994	Mar-1994	-5.85	-8.35
Nov-1994		-4.50	-0.52
Aug-1997		-6.81	-0.67
Oct-1997		-5.39	-4.38
Aug-1998		-13.45	-14.68
Jan-2000		-5.77	-0.54
Apr-2000	May-2000	-6.54	-2.31
Sep-2000	Nov-2000	-12.28	-6.58
Feb-2001	Mar-2001	-14.44	-1.96
May-2001	Sep-2001	-17.97	-4.35
Jun-2002	Mar-2003	-21.33	8.00
Mar-2005	Apr-2005	-3.97	-3.30
Nov-2007	Feb-2009	-53.58	-26.67
Jan-2010		-4.11	1.10
May-2010	Jun-2010	-12.50	-3.38
May-2011	Sep-2011	-19.41	-8.46
Apr-2012	May-2012	-9.53	-2.39
Average		-11.77	-3.46
Mean		**-7.72**	**-2.13**

Source: Bloomberg, MSCI, Barclays Capital.

Table 29.4 – performance and risk characteristics of MSCI World and global high-yield bonds, January 1990 to June 2012

	MSCI World	Global High Yield
Performance (% pa)	4.96	10.23
Volatility (%)	15.70	10.53
Skewness	-0.61	-1.50
Kurtosis	1.17	9.01
Beta	1.00	0.45
Correlation with MSCI World	1.00	0.67
Sharpe Ratio	0.10	0.65

Source: Bloomberg, MSCI, Barclays Capital.

High-yield portfolios

Some multi-asset portfolios have investment objectives of generating high income. A typical objective can be to generate 110% of the dividend yield of the S&P 500 Index or to generate a certain level of income per annum. During time periods of high interest rates, meeting the income objective is relatively easier than during periods of low interest rates.

Dimson, Marsh and Staunton studied the effect of dividend yield on UK equity returns over the 110 year period from 1900 to 2010[300]. According to their study, investment in a low-yield strategy would have returned 8.0% per annum over the period. An investment in high-yield stocks would have returned 10.9% per annum. Across 21 countries the average high-yield premium is 4.4% per year. Since the beginning of 2000 the average yield premium was 9.1% per annum.

The yield premium, however, is considered as a value premium. Value stocks are stocks that have attractive valuations as measured by P/E ratio and dividend yield. Growth stocks pay low or no dividends. While higher risk would seem an obvious explanation, the research of Dimson el al indicates that portfolios of higher yielding stocks and countries have actually proved less risky than equivalent investments in lower yielding growth stocks. It seems, therefore, that a high-yield equity strategy does pay off for long-term investors.

Liability Driven Investments (LDI)

The simplest way to manage multi-asset portfolios against liabilities of a defined pension fund is to split it into two parts: a liability matching part and a growth part. Fixed income and derivatives (e.g. interest rate swaps) should be used for the liability matching part. The objective is to reduce shortfall risk or tracking error versus liabilities. The growth part should have an objective of expected return to close down a funding shortfall (most commonly) or to increase a surplus (only lucky pensions). The growth part should be a well-diversified, multi-asset portfolio matching the return and risk objectives of the trustees of the pension scheme.

Actively-managed passive investments

Actively managing passive investments, or betas, is an investment strategy of utilising passive investments, such as passive funds, ETFs and futures, and actively managing them within a portfolio, with the aim of adding value through SAA and TAA. The advantages are simplicity, relatively low cost and no risk of underperformance due to active security selection. The philosophy is that SAA is the main determinant of portfolio risk and there is higher conviction in SAA and TAA than security selection. The disadvantage is that the strategy does not have exposure to potential alpha from security selection. A plus version may include passive investments for all asset classes that can be accessed through passive investments and active investments for asset classes that cannot be accessed via passive investments, such as real estate. In addition, the portfolio manager may have flexibility to use active investments when deemed appropriate. This allows more asset classes to be utilised than in the all-passive version.

Inflation

A low level of inflation is a natural and healthy condition for the economy. However, high inflation or hyperinflation is unhealthy and has adverse effects on many asset classes. As always, the investment strategy needs to be adaptive, dynamic and change as economic conditions change. When inflation is high, real assets should benefit. The four real assets are commodities, inflation-linked bonds, real estate and infrastructure. Commodities and inflation-linked bonds are liquid and can be added to portfolios quickly to hedge inflation (or held strategically as diversifiers). Real estate and infrastructure are illiquid and adding them to portfolios is costly and they are appropriate only for portfolios with a long-term horizon.

Figure 29.11 shows the correlation between equities, government bonds, property, commodities, inflation-linked bonds and infrastructure and US inflation between January 2000[301] and June 2012. Real asset classes have a positive correlation with inflation. The correlation between real estate and inflation may be misleading since both real estate and inflation have experienced an uptrend over the measuring period. Government bonds have a negative correlation with inflation, showing that their price drops when inflation rises.

Figure 29.11 – correlation between inflation and different asset classes, all returns in dollars except for IPD in pounds, January 2000 to June 2012

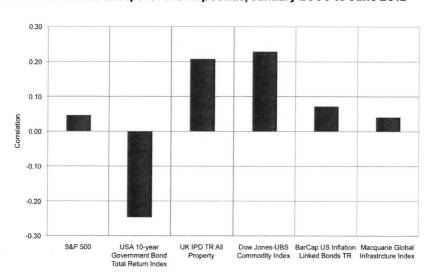

Source: Bloomberg, S&P, Global Financial Data, IPD, Dow Jones UBS, Barclays Capital, Macquarie.

Stagflation

Stagflation is a period of high and increasing inflation with simultaneous contracting economic growth or a recession. Under a *normal* economic cycle, during recession inflation should ease. However, stagflation is probably the worst economic condition as it combines both a recession and inflation. The investment strategy during stagflation is adjusting the portfolio to the economic conditions and investing in asset classes that should fare better than others.

Real estate is an asset class that should perform well because the cost of borrowing is still low (before central banks increase it to combat inflation), the real value of mortgages falls because of inflation and the prices of real estate should increase to keep up with inflation. The risks are aggressive tightening of monetary policy by central banks causing variable borrowing costs to increase, recession dampening demand for property and the present value of property falling due to an increasing discount factor.

Commodities are another asset class that should perform well during stagflation. During the 1970s stagflation equities lost most of their real value due to falling equity markets and inflation. However, commodities were one of the best performing asset classes. For example, the oil price increased (although this may have been the cause of the stagflation, not only its result). Gold and precious metals should perform well because of inflation and because investors seek asset classes that perform well and gold is probably one of them.

Cash can be a good investment during stagflation. If central banks raise interest rates, short duration money market investments should benefit. Cash should at least outperform equities, which struggle, and bonds, which are an awful investment during stagflation because the real value of cash flows depreciates due to inflation and the price of bonds may fall due to increasing interest rates. The question is whether cash return is higher than inflation. If it is, cash is indeed a good investment. If it is not, then cash will not maintain its purchasing power.

Inflation-linked bonds may be a good investment. However, if inflation is already high, linkers are going to be expensive. If inflation is expected to continue rising, linkers will provide a hedge against it.

Deflation

Deflation is an economic condition where inflation is negative. The Japanese economy has been in deflation since the early 1990s. Deflation may lead an economy into a depression or a liquidity trap, whereby interest rates are close to zero and central banks lose their ability to stimulate the economy through monetary tools. Japan is an example of a *liquidity trap*[302]. Investment strategy needs to adapt to economic conditions and portfolios should be invested in asset classes that should fare better than others during deflation.

Cash could be a good route to take (again). With negative inflation, cash real value increases, albeit with close to zero short-term interest rate cash return is low. Long-duration government bonds should perform well. With negative inflation, interest rates are expected to decrease and stay down. This should support the prices of bonds and decreasing interest rates should benefit long duration bonds the most. Other asset classes such as equities, commodities, credit and real estate are all expected to struggle during deflation and when there is a risk of the economy sliding into a depression.

Rotating investment strategy

Investors can devise a number of investment strategies, each appropriate for different economic conditions. When such economic conditions develop, portfolios can quickly shift to the new strategy. A rotating strategy requires preparation.

Investment strategies for rational and irrational markets

During financial crisis correlations among asset classes increase (investors flock out of risk assets, which fall together) and markets become irrational. A *convergent strategy* should be used during periods of rationality and a *divergent strategy* during periods of irrationality. Convergent thinking occurs when people gather information and experiences from a variety of sources to solve a problem. The result is one answer, which hopefully is correct. Divergent thinking occurs when people start with a stimulus and instead of looking for one answer they generate many ideas and possible solutions. A number of solutions may be better than one answer.

Divergent investment strategies include managed futures and global macro hedge funds. These strategies should provide diversification benefits and more diversification at time of crisis when the correlation of other asset classes increases. Convergent strategies focus on fundamental data, evaluate the intrinsic value of securities, go long or short depending on whether the investor thinks securities are under/overvalued and hope for the price to rationally converge to the intrinsic value. This works if the investor is correct and markets are rational.

Divergent strategies aim to profit when the market ignores fundamentals and behaves *irrationally*. They try to identify a serial correlation in prices to exploit trends and momentum that reflects changing market themes and investor sentiment. Through holding long positions in derivatives whose prices are affected by volatility (such as options), managed futures and global macro are long volatility – volatility spikes up at a time of financial crisis or market crashes and provides protection when markets fall.

Conclusion

Investment strategies are different ways to manage portfolios, with the aim of meeting investment objectives over both the short term and long term. The strategy of multi-asset investing is a field of its own. Successful multi-asset investors know when and how to use appropriate investment strategies.

Summary

- Investment strategy is the plan, a set of rules, principles and processes that guide the asset allocation and investment selection of a portfolio to reflect its investment objectives and constraints.

- The Holy Grail of investment strategy is to be conservative when markets fall and aggressive when markets rise.

- Investment strategy should start with required expected return. The risk level should match the return and if the risk level is unacceptable, the required return should change. When the risk/return balance is reasonable, an investment strategy can be formulated.

- Both asset allocation and investment selection are critical for success.

- Adding more investments does not necessarily add value.

- Investment strategy must be tailored to the specific investment objectives and constraints.

- Investors with a short-term horizon should mostly hold cash and bonds with maturities matching cash outflows. Deviations from safe haven assets should be carefully considered. Buy and hold, rule-based strategies without SAA are appropriate.

- Investors with a long-term horizon have time to adjust the investment strategy and adapt themselves according to the progress toward achieving the investment objectives. Cash is not a safe haven since inflation is a risk and liabilities typically have long durations.

- Momentum strategy invests in assets that trend upwards, risking missing the inflection point. Contrarian strategy invests in assets that are out of favour, with the risk that they will stay out of favour for a long time.

- Strategies to reduce fat tail risk include switching asset allocation to a more conservative one; purchasing assets that provide protection (e.g. long duration government bonds); purchasing put options (insurance) or purchasing call options or futures on the VIX; and holdings asset with attributes that change the return distribution (e.g. managed futures).

- Constant Proportion Portfolio Insurance (CPPI) is an insured asset allocation strategy aiming to protect the portfolio from falling below a predetermined floor value.

- Absolute return strategies balance a high target return (e.g. 4% above cash) with the objective of positive return. The strategy needs to take risk to be able to achieve the target return while protecting the downside to achieve the positive return. Such a strategy needs skill and discretion.

- A volatility targeting investment strategy aims to achieve the highest possible return for a given level of risk, while maintaining its risk level over time.

- Target-date funds employ an investment strategy that changes its asset allocation from aggressive to conservative as the maturity of the fund approaches. These funds are designed as a retirement solution for investors in defined contribution pension schemes.

- Portable alpha is a strategy where a manger's alpha is isolated by going long the manager's fund and removing the beta exposure (e.g. through shorting a futures contract). Alpha can be imported to a portfolio even when the beta exposure to the asset class is low. Active managers can be hired to deliver pure alpha without beta exposure.

- A collar is one solution for concentrated stock positions. By buying a put and shorting a call on the stock the combination makes suitable collateral to borrow against it on margin and diversify the position.

- A bond ladder keeps a constant maturity of a bond portfolio to reduce interest rate risk.

- Dollar cost averaging is a strategy to build a position over time and average the cost and entry price.

- A barbell strategy combines conservative positions with aggressive positions so the portfolio performs reasonably well when markets fall and rally.

- Substituting asset classes enables switching certain risk assets with lower risk assets that while having a lower upside also have a lower downside risk.

- High-yield portfolios aim to deliver high income and can be a substitute for bonds when interest rates are low.

- LDI manages the assets in line with liabilities. The relevant risks are shortfall risk and tracking error against liabilities.

- A portfolio of actively-managed passive investments aims to deliver alpha through SAA and TAA, while keeping costs at a minimum and eliminating the underperformance risk of security selection (as well as the alpha potential from security selection).

- Inflation, stagflation and deflation are three economic conditions that require different investment strategies since different asset classes will perform well and poorly during these conditions.

The number of investment strategies is endless and new investment strategies are invented as financial innovation continues in the face of new economic conditions that continue to emerge. The list of investment strategies is not exhaustive. However, it should provide some ideas on different common investment strategies.

This concludes Part 3 of book, implementing an investment solution. The three main activities under this part were TAA, investment selection and the management of the entire multi-asset portfolio.

It is done. The portfolio is alive. Now the focus turns to results. Performance is the ultimate result of investing. Everything is done with one ultimate objective – generating performance.

PART 4

REVIEWING

Part 4 moves to the final stage of the multi-asset portfolio investment management process: reviewing. It focuses on evaluating and understanding the performance of multi-asset portfolios.

30. PORTFOLIO REVIEW

Multi-asset portfolio management is a perpetual task. After the investment objectives are established, the investment strategy is formulated and the investment solution is implemented. The final stage is reviewing the results, risk, portfolio positioning and economic conditions. Armed with all that information investors need to go back to the first stage of the process and evaluate whether the investment objectives are still valid and whether the portfolio is on track to meet them. The process is an endless loop.

This part of the book focuses on performance attribution of multi-asset portfolios. Multi-asset performance attribution is often a challenge to produce and interpret. As the portfolio becomes more complex the performance attribution is even more challenging.

Multi-dimensional performance attribution breaks down the performance not only into the traditional asset allocation and security selection effects but also into the SAA and implementation differential effects. When multi-currency and currency hedging are included, the attribution becomes more complex.

The other side of performance review is risk review. The performance and risk review should go hand in hand. Performance should be linked to risk so investors understand how risks taken were compensated. Investors need to ensure that the performance and risks are in line with expectations and in line with the way portfolios are managed and positioned. There should be no surprises since investors should know how portfolios should perform and what the risks are. If they are surprised, the investors may not have had a handle on the way portfolios are managed.

Risk management is part of both portfolio management and portfolio review and it was covered in Part 3 of the book as part of the third stage of the investment management process, implementing a solution. As performance attribution breaks down the performance into its different components, risk decomposition should break risk into its different components.

The performance and risk functions in an asset management firm should be independent of the portfolio management function. Independent oversight of performance and risk is appropriate governance since it ensures that portfolio managers cannot bias or cook the performance numbers and that portfolios are managed within their risk parameters.

Summary

- The fourth and final stage of the multi-asset portfolio management process is reviewing.

- Reviewing includes performance attribution and risk review.

- Reviewing helps investors understand the risk and performance drivers of portfolios.

- Performance and risk functions should be independent of the portfolio management function for good governance and oversight.

31. PERFORMANCE ATTRIBUTION

Performance attribution is the process of interpreting portfolio performance and explaining the sources of returns. Investors need to understand how returns were achieved to evaluate success or failure. Performance attribution decomposes returns into asset allocation, investment selection and the interaction between them. For multi-asset, global, multi-manager portfolios, performance attribution is much more challenging and complex than for single asset class portfolios.

Return decomposition analysis (performance attribution)

The goal of return decomposition analysis or performance attribution is decomposing the difference between total portfolio return and total benchmark return (relative performance or active management effect). The *active management effect* is subdivided into three effects:

1. Allocation effect

2. Selection effect

3. Interaction effect[303]

Allocation effect measures the value added through asset allocation. A positive allocation effect occurs when portfolios are overweight asset classes that outperform the total portfolio benchmark or underweight asset classes that underperform the total benchmark. A negative allocation effect occurs when portfolios are overweight asset classes that underperform the total benchmark or underweight asset classes that outperform the total benchmark. The formula for calculating the allocation effect is:

$$\text{AA Effect} = (w_{pi} - w_{bi}) * (r_{bi} - r_b)$$

where w_{pi} is portfolio weight to asset i, w_{bi} is benchmark weight to asset i, r_{bi} is benchmark return of asset i, and r_b is total portfolio benchmark return.

Security selection effect measures the value added through security selection in each asset class relative to its benchmark (i.e. the asset class' benchmark). The relative performance is weighted by the benchmark allocation to the asset class. The formula for calculating the selection effect is:

$$\text{SS Effect} = w_{bi} * (r_{pi} - r_{bi})$$

where w_{bi} is benchmark weight to asset class i, r_{pi} is portfolio return of asset class i, and r_{bi} is benchmark return of asset class i.

Interaction effect measures the combined impact of selection and allocation decisions within each asset class. For example, if an investor had superior security selection and overweighted that particular asset class, the interaction effect is positive. If an investor had superior selection, but underweighted that asset class, the interaction effect is negative. In this case, the investor did not take advantage of the superior selection by overweighting that asset class.

Since many investors consider the interaction effect to be part of the selection or allocation effect, it is often combined with either of these effects. The formula for calculating the interaction effect is:

$$IE = (w_{pi} - w_{bi}) * (r_{pi} - r_{bi})$$

where w_{pi} is portfolio weight to asset class i, w_{bi} is benchmark weight to asset class i, r_{pi} is portfolio return of asset class i, and r_{bi} is benchmark return of asset class i.

The three effects together make the total active management effect.

Active management effect = allocation effect + selection effect + interaction effect

An example can illustrate the methodology. Assume a multi-asset portfolio investing in UK equities, among other asset classes. The benchmark of UK equities is the FTSE All Share Index and the benchmark of the multi-asset portfolio is a composite benchmark.

FTSE All Share Index return = 9% = r_{bi}

Composite benchmark allocation to UK equities = 7% = w_{bi}

UK equity portfolio return = 8% = r_{pi}

Portfolio allocation to UK equities = 15% = w_{pi}

Total composite benchmark return = 7% = r_b

AA Effect = $(w_{pi} - w_{bi}) * (r_{bi} - r_b)$ = (15% − 7%)*(9%−7%) = 16bp

SS Effect = $w_{bi} * (r_{pi} - r_{bi})$ = 7%*(8% − 9%) = −7bp

IE = $(w_{pi} - w_{bi}) * (r_{pi} - r_{bi})$ = (15% − 7%)*(8% − 9%)= −8bp

Active management effect = 16bp − 7bp − 8bp = +1bp

In this example, the total management effect is positive. Asset allocation was positive as the investor overweighted UK equities by 8% and UK equities (as measured by their benchmark, the FTSE All Share Index) outperformed the multi-asset portfolio's composite benchmark. This was a good asset allocation call.

However, within UK equities the investor underperformed the benchmark of UK equities by -1% and the security selection effect was negative. The interaction effect is the combination of the asset allocation overweight to an asset class where security selection was negative and the interaction effect was negative. The positive asset allocation effect was more than enough to outweigh the negative security and interaction effects.

Table 31.1 shows an illustrative example of a performance attribution of a multi-asset portfolio.

Table 31.1 - performance attribution

Asset class	Weight (%)			Performance (%)			Attribution (bp)		
	Portfolio	Benchmark	Relative	Portfolio	Benchmark	Relative	SS	AA	IE
UK equities	35	30	5	3	4	-1	-30	6	-5
Europe ex. UK equities	4	6	-2	2.5	3	-0.5	-3	-1	1
North America equities	14	15	-1	5	5	0	0	-2	0
Japan Equities	3	3	0	-2	-1	-1	-3	0	0
Pacific ex. Japan equities	5	3	2	3	7	-4	-12	9	-8
Emerging market equities	5	3	2	4	8	-4	-12	11	-8
Convertible bonds	2	0	2	2	2	0	0	-2	0
Government bonds	14	35	-21	1	0.5	0.5	18	47	-11
Corporate bonds	6	0	6	2	1.5	0.5	0	-8	3
Developed global bonds	0	0	0	1	1	0	0	0	0
Emerging market debt	1	0	1	2	3	-1	0	0	-1
Global high-yield	1	0	1	3	2.5	0.5	0	0	1
UK property	2	0	2	0.5	1	-0.5	0	-4	-1
Europe property	1	0	1	-0.5	0.5	-1	0	-2	-1
Asia property	1	0	1	1.5	1.5	0	0	-1	0
Commodities	0	0	0	1.5	2	-0.5	0	0	0
Private equity	0	0	0	4	3	1	0	0	0
Hedge funds	4	0	4	2	1	1	0	-7	4
Cash	2	5	-3	0.5	0.5	0	0	7	0
TOTAL	100	100	0	2.6	2.75	-0.15	-43	54	-26

The portfolio underperformed its benchmark by 15 basis points. Security selection was negative with the main areas of weakness being the UK, Pacific ex. Japan and emerging market equities, while government bonds outperformed their benchmark. Asset allocation was positive, in particular the decision to underweight government bonds, which underperformed the portfolio's total composite benchmark. The interaction effect was negative, in particular underweighting the outperforming government bonds.

Performance contribution

Performance contribution measures how much an investment contributes to a portfolio's overall performance. Contribution is the weight to an investment times its return. In the example above, the allocation to UK equities is 35% and their return was 3%. Hence the contribution is 35% * 3% = 105 basis points.

Multi-dimensional performance attribution

When a portfolio benchmark is a peer group or when the composite benchmark is different than SAA, performance attribution can be further broken down to the SAA effect and the implementation differential effect.

The *SAA effect* measures the attribution to SAA. It isolates the performance due to different allocation weights between SAA and the benchmark. The *implementation differential effect* measures the attribution due to the deviations between target portfolio weights and actual portfolio weights, or in other words the attribution from deviations between policy and implementation. This effect measures the effectiveness of portfolio implementation.

$$\text{SAA Effect} = (w_{SAAi} - w_{bi}) * (r_{bi} - r_b)$$

where w_{SAAi} are the SAA target weights.

$$\text{Implementation Differential Effect} = (w_{pi} - w_{SAAi}) * (r_{bi} - r_b)$$

The asset allocation effect includes SAA, TAA and the implementation differential. The multi-dimensional performance attribution breaks down the asset allocation effect into its different components.

The challenge when portfolios are benchmarked against peer group sectors is that the peer group performance is comprised of active portfolios. Performance attribution cannot calculate the performance of active asset classes in line with the peer group since the breakdown is normally unavailable (e.g. the performance of active UK equity managers within a multi-asset peer group is not always available). Hence, performance attribution needs to estimate the performance of each asset class in the peer group using passive indices. This causes a distortion between the total peer group performance and the estimated performance using passive indices. Performance attribution of portfolios benchmarked against peer groups is therefore distorted and the relative performance is only a crude estimate.

In a similar way to hedge fund indices, peer groups suffer from survivorship bias. When portfolios are compared to the median return within a peer group, in particular over long time periods (three years and above), the median calculation includes only peers that have survived over the measuring period, biasing the median upwards. Investors need to be aware of this when benchmarking portfolios to peers.

Global, multi-asset, multi-currency, multi-manager

The decomposition methodology works when all the necessary inputs are available. However, multi-manager portfolios may have a mismatch between the benchmarks of each asset class and the composite benchmark. For example, equities can be represented within the composite benchmark by the MSCI World Index while the underlying US equity portfolios are benchmarked against the Russell 1000 Value Index, Russell 1000 Growth Index, Russell 2000 Value Index and Russell 2000 Growth Index.

The multi-manager investor is responsible for asset allocation decisions among investment styles and sizes (value versus growth and large versus SMID). These asset allocation calls are within an asset class (US equities) and not across asset classes. However, the classic performance decomposition methodology includes these asset allocation decisions under security selection and not under asset allocation. If the multi-asset investor uses currency hedging the decomposition methodology cannot show separately the currency hedging effect. A different attribution methodology is needed.

To decompose the portfolio returns, four return series have to be defined:

r_p = portfolio returns, using portfolio monthly returns. If it is a multi-manager portfolio, portfolio returns are the weighted actual returns of the underlying portfolios.

r_{mb} = composite manager benchmark, using the monthly returns of the weighted benchmarks of the underlying portfolio managers using the portfolio weights. For example, a portfolio with an allocation of 15% UK equities whose benchmark is FTSE All Share Index, which returned 9%, includes 15% * 9% representing the benchmark return of UK equities in the composite manager benchmark.

r_{mbfx} = composite manager benchmark with currency hedging decisions. The relevant benchmarks are hedged in line with the currency hedging decision of the multi-asset investor.

r_b = portfolio benchmark, using the monthly returns of the total portfolio benchmark.

The decomposition then uses the following formulas:

Asset Allocation = $r_{mb} - r_b$

Security Selection = $r_p - r_{mb}$

Total Relative Return = $r_p - r_b$

Currency Hedging = $r_{mbfx} - r_{mb}$

Total Relative Return = Asset Allocation + Security Selection = $(r_{mb} - r_b) + (r_p - r_{mb}) = r_p - r_b$.

The currency hedging effect is not part of the total relative return, but rather a sub-segment. The relative return of each underlying portfolio can be easily evaluated by comparing each portfolio return with its benchmark.

Futures

Multi-asset portfolios should use futures. They are liquid and cost efficient. The issue with performance attribution of futures is that futures are unfunded. Investors do not need to spend all the cash to gain the exposure, only the margin, which can be only 10% of the notional exposure. The portfolio needs to hold cash to cover the notional exposure of the long futures positions so it is not geared or leveraged. The interest on the covering cash is attributed to the cash of the multi-asset portfolio, not to the underlying of the futures (e.g. the interest on cash backing a long UK FTSE 100 Index futures position is included under cash and not under UK equities). At times of high interest rates and when the futures positions are held for a long time, this can be material. The interest on the cash backing the futures should be attributed to the underlying asset class and removed from cash.

Many performance attributers add the profit and loss (P&L) of the futures as a *contribution* to the performance attribution. This method does not take into account the multi-asset portfolio benchmark. Going long UK equities via futures, when the multi-asset portfolio benchmark falls -5% and UK equities fall only -2%, may be shown as a negative asset allocation effect since the contribution (P&L) of the futures is negative. Overweight UK equities was a good decision (UK equities outperformed the multi-asset portfolio benchmark by +3% and the overweight added value) but going long UK equities lost money (-2%). The P&L of the futures can thus distort the attribution of overweighting UK equities.

Geometric versus arithmetic relative returns

The difference between portfolio and benchmark return is known as excess return or relative performance. There are two ways to calculate excess return: arithmetic and geometric. *Arithmetic excess return* is the profit or loss relative to benchmark expressed as a percentage:

$r_A = r_p - r_b$

where r_A is arithmetic excess return, r_p is portfolio return and r_b is benchmark return.

Geometric excess return, r_G, is the profit or loss relative to benchmark expressed as a percentage of the final value of the benchmark return:

$r_G = (1+r_p)/(1+r_b) - 1$

Both versions are commonly used. Geometric excess return is more common in the United Kingdom and Europe, while arithmetic excess return is more common in the United States.

The main arguments for using arithmetic excess return are its ease of use and simplicity. The three main arguments for using geometric excess return[304] are proportionality, convertibility and compoundability.

- *Proportionality.* Geometric excess return demonstrates the proportional increase in size of the portfolio versus the benchmark. For example:

$P_0 = £1$ million

$P_T = £500K$

$r_p = -50\%$

$B_0 = £1$ million

$B_T = £250K$

$r_b = -75\%$

$r_A = -50\% - (-75\%) = +25\%$

$r_G = (1 - 0.5)/(1 - 0.75) - 1 = 100\%$

- *Convertibility*. Geometric excess returns are convertible across currencies. When converting portfolio and benchmark returns in different currencies the arithmetic excess return changes. Since the portfolio and benchmark have been compounded by the same currency return, the added value remains the same when using geometric excess return. This explains why geometric excess return is more common outside the United States, where the dollar is typically the single currency.

- *Compoundability*. Geometric excess return is compounded over time. *Time-weighted returns* are calculated by chain-linking each performance period within the overall measuring period. For example, assume portfolio return of 7% each quarter and benchmark return of 5%:

$$r_p = (1.07)^4 = 31.1\%$$

$$r_b = (1.05)^4 = 21.6\%$$

$$r_A = 31.1 - 21.6 = 9.15\%$$

This does not match the arithmetic process of adding relative returns since 2% + 2% + 2% + 2% = 10% and not 9.15%.

Each quarter the geometric excess return of 1.9% can be chain-linked over the four quarters to get 7.8%:

$$r_G \text{ compounded is } (1.019)^*(1.019)^*(1.019)^*(1.019) - 1 = 7.8\%$$

$$r_G = ((1 + 31.1/100)/(1 + 21.6/100) - 1)^*100 = 7.8\%$$

The geometric excess return can be compounded.

Investors are mainly interested in portfolio value at the end of the measuring period and by how much the portfolio has grown relative to what its growth would have been had it been invested in its benchmark. In rising markets arithmetic excess return is greater than the geometric and vice versa in falling markets.

Conclusion

The only way to judge a portfolio is performance. Performance includes return and risk. Performance checks whether the portfolio is on track to meet its objectives and whether it does what it says on the tin.

Summary

- Performance attribution explains the sources of returns in portfolios.

- Classic performance attribution breaks the relative performance of portfolios into allocation effect, selection effect and interaction effect.

- Performance contribution is the allocation to investment times its return.

- Multi-dimensional performance attribution further breaks down the allocation effect into the SAA effect and the implementation differential effect.

- When portfolios are benchmarked against peer group sectors, performance attribution needs to use passive indices to estimate the performance of each asset class. Therefore, there is a distortion between the official benchmark performance and its estimate.

- Global multi-asset, multi-manager, multi-currency portfolios need a different performance attribution methodology to capture the different investment decisions.

- When using futures contracts that are backed with cash the interest rate on the cash should be moved from cash in the portfolio to the underlying asset class of the futures position.

- Mixing contribution and attribution when accounting for futures positions can be misleading and can distort the performance attribution.

- Geometric excess return versus arithmetic has advantages, although it is not as simple as the arithmetic.

This concludes Part 4 of the book and the final stage of the multi-asset portfolio management process.

Conclusions

Multi-asset investing encompasses all the stages and techniques of modern portfolio management. The starting point is always the investment objectives. Investors must understand what return they want to achieve and what return they can realistically achieve. Because forecasting the future precisely is impossible, and requires a mix of standard finance and psychology, investors must understand risk. Risk is the probability of not achieving the expected return. Potential outcomes have a distribution, not a single deterministic result.

Armed with clear objectives, investors need to formulate a plan, an investment strategy. Time is the investor's friend; the longer the investment horizon the higher the chances of meeting objectives. SAA is used to set the long-term asset allocation. SAA should combine as many asset classes as possible, including alternatives, to blend uncorrelated betas (cost effective sources of risk premiums). However, dynamic asset allocation is the key, in particular in our risky world. Dynamic SAA and TAA complement each other and guide the portfolio through perils and opportunities.

Investment selection is as important as asset allocation and can be a source of scarce alpha. Investors should be stingy. Cutting costs increases returns. Expensive active investments should be used when they make sense and combined with passive investments.

Disciplined portfolio construction puts it all together, with the portfolio constructor accountable for the entire endeavour. Risk management keeps the portfolio on track and helps it survive the risks of the journey. Portfolio management is a never ending story and reviewing the objectives completes the circle of multi-asset investing.

This book aims to cover all the steps of constructing and managing multi-asset portfolios. However, this does not conclude the required knowledge for multi-asset investing. Multi-asset investors need to understand the underlying building blocks of multi-asset investing, the single asset classes and investment types. My next book, *Multi-Asset Investing II: A practical guide to asset classes*, will aim to help investors do this.

Bibliography

Amenc, Noel, Lionel Martellini, Jean-Christophe Meyfredi, Volker Ziemann, 'Performance of Passive Hedge Fund Replication Strategies', EDHEC Risk and Asset Management Research Centre (September 2009).

Ankrim, Ernest, Zhuanxin Ding, 'Cross-Sectional Volatility and Return Dispersion', *The Financial Analysts Journal* 58 (2002).

Arnott, Robert, Peter Bernstein, 2002, 'What Risk Premium is Normal', *Journal of Portfolio Management* (10 January 2002).

Arnott, Robert, Clifford Asness, 2003, 'Surprise! Higher Dividends = Higher Earnings Growth', *The Financial Analysts Journal* (January-February 2003).

Arnott, Robert, Jason Hsu, John West, *The Fundamental Index: A Better Way to Invest* (Wiley, 2008).

Bacon, Carl, 2002, 'Excess Returns – Arithmetic or Geometric?', *Journal of Performance Measurement* (Spring 2002).

Barras, Laurent, Olivier Scaillet, Russ Wermers, 'False Discoveries in Mutual Fund Performance: Measuring Luck in Estimated Alphas', *Journal of Finance* 65 (2010).

Bjørland, Hilde, Håvard Hungnss, 'The Importance of Interest Rates for Forecasting the Exchange Rate', Statistics Norway Research Department (2003).

Black, Fischer, Myron Scholes, 'The Pricing of Options and Corporate Liabilities', *Journal of Political Economy* (1973).

Black, Fischer, Robert Litterman, 'Global Asset Allocation with Equities, Bonds, and Currencies', Fixed Income Research, Goldman, Sachs & Company (1991).

Black, Fischer, Robert Litterman, 'Global Portfolio Optimization', *The Financial Analysts Journal* (September 1992).

Bradely, Efron, Robert Tibshirani, *An Introduction to the Bootstrap* (Chapman and Hall/CRC, 1994).

Brinson, Gary, Nimrod Fachler, 'Measuring Non-US Equity Portfolio Performance', *Journal of Portfolio Management* (Spring 1985).

Brinson, Gary, Randolph Hood, Gilbert Beebower, 'Determinants of Portfolio Performance', *The Financial Analysts Journal* (July-August 1986).

Brinson, Gary, Brian Singer, Gilbert Beebower, 'Determinants of Portfolio Performance II: An Update', *The Financial Analysts Journal* 47 (1991).

Brooks, Chris, Harry Kat, 'The Statistical Properties of Hedge Fund Index Returns and Their Implications for Investors', *The Journal of Alternative Investments* (Fall 2002).

Burton, Malkiel, *A Random Walk Down Wall Street: The Time-tested Strategy for Successful Investing* (W. W. Norton & Company, 1973).

Busse, Jeffrey, Amit Goyal, Sunil Wahal, 'Performance and Persistence in Institutional Investment Management', *Journal of Finance* 65 (2010).

Campbell, John, Robert Shiller, 'Valuation Ratios and the Long-Run Stock Market Outlook: An Update' (2001).

Campbell, John, Samuel Thompson, 'Predicting Excess Returns Out-of-Sample: Can Anything Beat the Historical Average?', *Review of Financial Studies* 21 (2007).

Campbell, John, Karine Serfaty-de Medeiros, Luis Viceira, 'Global Currency Hedging', *The Journal of Finance* (February 2010).

Chen, Nai-Fu, Richard Roll, Stephen Ross, 'Economic Forces and the Stock Market', *Journal of Business* 59 (1986).

Chhabra, Ashvin, 'Beyond Markowitz: A Comprehensive Wealth Allocation Framework for Individual Investors', *The Journal of Wealth Management* 7 (2005).

Chinn, Menzi, Guy Meredith, 'Testing Uncovered Interest Rate Parity at Short and Long Horizons During the Post-Bretton Woods Era', The National Bureau of Economic Research (NBER) (2005).

Chopra, Vijay, William Ziemba, 'The Effect of Errors in Means, Variances and Covariances on Optimal Portfolio Choice', *Journal of Portfolio Management* (Winter 1993).

Clarke, Roger, Harindra de Silva, Steven Thorley, 'Portfolio Constraints and the Fundamental Law of Active Management', *The Financial Analysts Journal* 58 (2002).

Cornish, A. and Fisher, R., 'Moments and cumulants in the specification of distributions', *Review of the International Statistical Institute* (1937).

Dimson, Elroy, Andrew Jackson, 'High Frequency Performance Monitoring', *The Journal of Portfolio Management* (Fall 2001).

Dimson, Elroy, Paul Marsh, Mike Staunton, 'Triumph of the Optimists: 101 Years of Global Investment Returns' (2002).

Dimson, Elroy, Paul Marsh, Mike Staunton, 'The Worldwide Equity Premium: A Smaller Puzzle' (2006).

Dimson, Elroy, Paul Marsh, Mike Staunton, 'Keeping faith with stocks', Credit Suisse Research Institute (2009).

Dimson, Elroy, Paul Marsh, Mike Staunton, 'Looking to the long term', Credit Suisse Research Institute 2009.

Dimson, Elroy, Paul Marsh, Mike Staunton, 'Fear of falling', *Credit Suisse Global Investment Returns Yearbook 2011.*

Dimson, Elroy, Paul March, Mike Staunton, 'The Quest for Yield', *Credit Suisse Global Investment Returns Yearbook 2011.*

Ellis, Charles, 'The Loser's Game', *The Financial Analysts Journal* 31 (1975).

Ellis, Joseph, 'Ahead of the Curve: A Commonsense Guide to Forecasting Business and Market Cycles' (Harvard Business School Press, 2005).

Elton, Edwin, Martin Gruber, 'Risk Reduction and Portfolio Size: An Analytic Solution', *Journal of Business* 50 (1977).

Elton, Edwin, Martin Gruber, 'Differential Information and Timing Ability', *Journal of Banking and Finance* (1991).

Fama, Eugene, 'Random Walks in Stock Market Prices', *The Financial Analysts Journal* 21 (1965).

Fama, Eugene, 'Efficient Capital Markets: A Review of Theory and Empirical Work', *Journal of Finance* 25 (1970).

Fama, Eugene, Kenneth French, 'The Cross-Section of Expected Sock Returns', *Journal of Finance* 47 (1992).

Fama, Eugene, Kenneth French, 'Common Risk Factors in the Returns on Stocks and Bonds', *Journal of Financial Economics* 33 (1993).

Fama, Eugene, Kenneth French, 'The Equity Premium', *Journal of Finance* 57 (2002).

Fisher, Philip, *Common Stocks and Uncommon Profits* (Harper & Bros, 1958).

Fung, William, David Hsieh, 'Hedge Fund Benchmarks: A Risk Based Approach', *The Financial Analysts Journal* 60 (2004).

Galbraith, John, *A Short History of Financial Euphoria* (Penguin, 1994).

Geltner, David, 'Smoothing in Appraisal-Based Returns', *Journal of Real Estate Finance and Economics* 4 (1991).

Geltner, David, 'Estimating Market Values from Appraised Values without Assuming an Efficient Market', *Journal of Real Estate Research* 8 (1993).

Getmansky, Mila, Andrew Lo, Igor Makarov, 'An Econometric Model of Serial Correlation and Illiquidity in Hedge Fund Returns', *Journal of Financial Economics* 74 (2004).

Goetzmann, William, Roger Ibbotson, 'History of the Equity Risk Premium', Yale ICF Working Paper No. 05-04 (2005).

Gold, Richard, 'Why the Efficient Frontier for Real Estate is "Fuzzy" ', *The Journal of Real Estate Portfolio Management* 1 (1995).

Gordon, Myron, 'Dividends, Earnings and Stock Prices', *Review of Economics and Statistics* (The MIT Press, 1959).

Graham, Benjamin, David Todd, *Security Analysis* (McGraw-Hill, 1934).

Graham, Benjamin, *The Intelligent Investor* (1949).

Grinold, Richard, 'The Fundamental Law of Active Management', *The Journal of Portfolio Management* 15 (1989).

Hasanhodzic, Jasmina, Andrew Lo, 'Can Hedge-Fund Returns be Replicated?: The Linear Case', *Journal of Investment Management* 5 (2007).

Heston, Steven, Geert Rouwenhorst, 'Does Industrial Structure Explain the benefits of International Diversification?', *Journal of Financial Economics* 36 (1994).

Ibbotson, Roger, Paul Kaplan, 'Does Asset Allocation Policy Explain 40, 90 or 100 Percent of Performance?', *The Financial Analysts Journal* (January-February 2000).

Ibbotson, Roger, Peng Chen, 'Long-Run Stock Returns: Participating in the Real Economy', *The Financial Analysts Journal* (2003).

Ibbotson, Roger, Peng Chen, Kevix Zhu, 'The ABCs of Hedge Funds: Alpha, Betas and Costs', *Financial Analysts Journal* 67 (2011).

Idzorek, Thomas, 'A Step-by-step Guide to the Black-Litterman Model' (2005).

Jaeger, Robert, Michael Rausch, Margaret Foley, 'Multi-Horizon Investing: A New Paradigm for Endowments and Other Long-Term Investors', *Journal of Wealth Management* (Summer 2010).

Jensen, Michael, 'The Performance of Mutual Funds in the Period 1945-1964', *Journal of Finance* 60 (1968).

Jorion, Philippe, 'Portfolio Optimization with Constraints on Tracking Error', University of California at Irvine (2000).

Kahneman, Daniel, Amos Tversky, 'Prospect Theory: An Analysis of Decision under Risk', *Econometrica* 47:2 (March 1979).

Kahneman, Daniel, Mark Riepe, 'Aspects of Investor Psychology', *The Journal of Portfolio Management* 24 (1998).

Knight, Frank, *Risk, Uncertainty and Profit* (1921).

Kostovetsky, Leonard, 'Index Mutual Funds and Exchange-Traded Funds', *The Journal of Portfolio Management* (Summer 2003).

Litterman, Bob, *Modern Investment Management: An Equilibrium Approach* (Wiley, 2003).

Lo, Andrew, Harry Mamaysky, Jiang Wang, 2000, 'Foundations of Technical Analysis: Computational Algorithms, Statistical Inference, and Empirical Implementation', *Journal of Finance* 55.

Lo, Andrew, Craig MacKinlay, *A Non-random Walk Down Walk Street*, (Princeton University Press, 2001).

Lo, Andrew, 'The Adaptive Markets Hypothesis: Market Efficiency from an Evolutionary Perspective', *Journal of Portfolio Management* (2004).

Lowenstein, Roger, *When Genius Failed: The Rise and Fall of Long-Term Capital Management* (Random House, 2001).

Lynch, Peter, *One Up on Wall Street* (Simon & Schuster, 2000).

Mandelbrot, Benoit, 'The Variation of Certain Speculative Prices', *The Journal of Business* 36 (1963).

Markowitz, Harry, 'Portfolio Selection', *The Journal of Finance* 7 (1952).

Marks, Howard, *The Most Important Thing: Uncommon Sense for the Thoughtful Investor* (Columbia University Press, 2001).

Merton, Robert, 'Lifetime Portfolio Selection under Uncertainty: The Continuous Time Case', *Review of Economics and Statistics* 51 (1969).

Merton, Robert, 'An Analytic Derivation of the Efficient Portfolio Frontier', *Journal of Financial and Quantitative Analysis* 7 (September 1972).

Michaud, Richard, *Efficient Asset Management* (Oxford University Press, 1998).

Modigliani, Franco, Merton Miller, 'The Cost of Capital, Corporation Finance and the Theory of Investment', *American Economic Review* 48 (1958).

Qian, Edward, 'On the Financial Interpretation of Risk Contribution: Risk Budgets Do Add Up', *Journal of Investment Management* 4 (2006).

Qian, Edward, 'Risk Parity and Diversification', *The Journal of Investing* 20 (2011).

Reinhart, Carmen, Kenneth Rogoff, 'This Time is Different: A Panoramic View of Eight Centuries of Financial Crises' (2008).

Roll, Richard, 'A Critique of the Asset Pricing Theory's Tests', *Journal of Financial Economics* 4 (1977).

Roll, Richard, 'A Mean-Variance Analysis of Tracking Error', *The Journal of Portfolio Management* (1992).

Ross, Stephen, 'The Economic Theory of Agency: The Principal's Problem', *American Economic Review* 2 (1973).

Ross, Stephen, 'The Arbitrage Theory of Capital Asset Pricing', *Journal of Economic Theory* 13 (1976).

Roy, Arthur, 'Safety First and the Holding of Assets', *Econometrica* (July 1952).

Samuelson, Paul, 'Proof that Property Anticipated Prices Fluctuate Randomly', *Industrial Management Review* 6 (1965).

Scherer, Bernd, *Portfolio Construction and Risk Budgeting* (Risk Books, 2007).

Shiller, Robert, *Irrational Exuberance* (Princeton University Press, 2005).

Schneewies, Thomas, 'Dealing with Myths of Managed Futures', *The Journal of Alternative Investments* (Summer 1998).

Senechal, Edouard, 'The Challenges of Declining Cross-Sectional Volatility', *Barra Horizon* (Autumn 2004).

Sharpe, William, 'A Simplified Model for Portfolio Analysis', *Management Science* 9 (1963).

Sharpe, William, 'Capital asset prices: A theory of market equilibrium under conditions of risk', *Journal of Finance* 19 (1964).

Sharpe, William, 'Mutual Fund Performance', *Journal of Business* 39 (1966).

Sharpe, William, 'Imputing Expected Security Returns from Portfolio Composition', *Journal of Financial and Quantitative Analysis* 9:3 (1974).

Sharpe, William, *Investments* (Prentice Hall, 1985).

Sharpe, William, 'Integrated Asset Allocation', *The Financial Analysts Journal* (September-October 1987).

Sharpe, William, 'Determining a Fund's Effective Asset Mix', *Investment Management Review* (December 1988).

Sharpe, William, 'The Arithmetic of Active Management', *The Financial Analysts Journal* 47 (1991).

Sharpe, William, 'Asset Allocation: Management Style and Performance Measurement', *The Journal of Portfolio Management* (Winter 1992).

Sharpe, William, 'Adaptive Asset Allocation Policies', *The Financial Analysts Journal* 66 (2010).

Shefrin, Hersh, Meir Statman, 'The Disposition to Sell Winners Too Early and Ride Losers Too Long: Theory and Evidence', *Journal of Finance* 40 (1985).

Sorensen, Eric, Keith Miller, Vele Samak, 'Allocating between Active and Passive Management', *The Financial Analysts Journal* 54 (1998).

Stanyer, Peter, 'Guide to Investment Strategy: How to Understand Markets, Risk, Reward and Behaviour', *The Economist* (2006).

Statman, Meir, 'Behavioral Finance Versus Standard Finance', AIMR Conference Proceedings (1995).

Statman, Meir, 'Behaviorial Finance: Past Battles and Future Engagements', *Association for Investment Management and Research* (November-December 1999).

Swensen, David, *Pioneering Portfolio Management: An Unconventional Approach to Institutional Investment* (Free Press, 2000).

Swensen, David, *Unconventional Success: A Fundamental Approach to Personal Investment* (Free Press, 2005).

Taleb, Nicholas Nassim, *Fooled by Randomness: The Hidden Role of Chance in Life and in the Markets* (Texere, 2004).

Taleb, Nicholas Nassim, *The Black Swan: The Impact of the Highly Improbable* (Penguin, 2008).

Tobin, James, 'Liquidity Preferences as Behavior Toward Risk', *The Review of Economic Studies* (February 1958).

Tobin, James, 'A General Equilibrium Approach to Monetary Theory', *Journal of Money Credit and Banking* 1 (1969).

Tobin, James, 'What is Permanent Endowment Income?', *The American Economic Review* 64 (1974).

Tokat, Yesim, Nelson Wicas, Francis Kinniry, 'The Asset allocation Debate: A Review and Reconociliation', *FPA Journal* (2006).

Treynor, Jack, Fisher Black, 'How to Use Security Analysis to Improve Portfolio Selection', *Journal of Business* 46 (1973).

Tversky, Amos, Daniel Kahneman, 'Judgment under Uncertainty: Heuristics and Biases', *Science, New Series* 185 (1974).

Xiong, James, Roger Ibbotson, Thomas Idzorek, Peng Chen, 'The Equal Importance of Asset Allocation and Active Management', *The Financial Analysts Journal* 66 (2010).

ENDNOTES

Preface

[1] Sir Isaac Newton said on simplicity: "nature is pleased with simplicity. And nature is no dummy".

Introduction

[2] A portfolio is a collection of investments held by an asset management firm, individual investor or institutional investor.

[3] United States, United Kingdom and Germany, respectively.

[4] Individuals with a long investment horizon and an appropriate risk appetite may soundly invest their pension plan only in equities.

[5] Defined benefit (DB) is a retirement plan where employee benefits are based on a formula using factors such as salary history and duration of employment (i.e. final salary pension scheme). Investment risk is borne by the company and portfolio management is under its control. Defined contribution (DC) is a retirement plan where the company contributes regular payments. However, the employee is responsible for portfolio management, bares investment risk and benefits are a function of the plan's asset value at retirement.

[6] A composite benchmark combines multiple market indices, each representing each asset class within the portfolio with appropriate weights. For example, a composite benchmark can be 50% S&P 500, 40% US Treasury Bond index and 10% US Treasury Bills index (cash).

[7] An investment opportunity set is all the investments that the investor can make at a given point in time. The opportunity set is largely determined by the investments that the investor can afford to make and the scope of allowable investments within the portfolio.

[8] *Harvard College v. Amory*, 9 Pick. (26 Mass.) 446 (1830).

[9] Uniform Prudent Investor Act.

[10] **www.fsa.gov.uk**

[11] Merriam-Webster's online dictionary.

[12] Sappurisa Sutta.

1. Return objectives

[13] Return on invested money is similar to Return on Capital Employed (ROCE). ROCE compares earnings with capital invested in the company by dividing net profit before tax by capital employed.

[14] 10% over three years equal to 3.23% per annum as $(1 + 10\%)^{(1/3)} - 1 = 3.23\%$.

[15] The principle that investment gains should be spent equally between current and future generation is referred to as intergenerational equity.

[16] James Tobin, 'What is Permanent Endowment Income?', *The American Economic Review* 64 (1974).

[17] Total return benchmarks normally include 'TR' or the words 'Total Return' in their name.

[18] The US equity market has moved sideways over the last decade. It has finished close to where it started. Without dividends the return of the S&P 500 would have been negative.

[19] LIBOR is London Interbank Borrowing Rate. This is an international, commercial rate at which banks lend money to each other. It forms a reference rate for a range of borrowing, benchmarks and derivatives. There are LIBOR rates in different currencies and different time periods. LIBOR is the offer rate and LIBID is the bid rate. The offer rate is used for client borrowing (the rate at which the bank offers to lend money) and the bid rate is used for client deposits. LIBOR fluctuates with supply and demand throughout the day. In order to have an official daily rate, every day at 11:00am the British Bankers' Association (BBA) produces the daily LIBOR fix.

[20] Long-only is a portfolio that cannot short investments. Shorting is borrowing a security and selling it with the hope that if its price fall it will cost less when it is paid back. The investor profits from a short when the price of the security falls. Going long is buying an investment and profiting when its price increases.

[21] Financials is a sector containing firms that provide financial services to commercial and retail customers. The sector includes banks, investment funds and insurance companies.

[22] Purchasing power is the amount of goods and services that can be purchased with a unit of currency.

[23] $82 = 100/(1 + 2\%)^{10}$.

[24] US Treasury bonds have enjoyed a strong rally over the last four decades.

[25] -95 basis points to be precise: $(1 + 4\%)/(1 + 5\%) - 1 = -0.95\%$. Fisher parity links inflation, nominal and real interest rates by the formula $1 + r_i = (1 + r_r)(1 + E(i))$, where r_i is nominal interest rate, r_r is real interest rate and $E(i)$ is expected inflation rate.

[26] Cash has struggled to beat inflation over the last decade in a low interest environment.

[27] Portfolio managers who work for companies that are also brokers are more incentivised to churn portfolios since their companies benefit from brokerage fees.

[28] Passive portfolios also have turnover in line with the changes in the index, which they aim to replicate.

[29] Stephen Ross, 'The Economic Theory of Agency: The Principal's Problem', *American Economic Review* 2 (1973).

[30] One of the basic principles in finance is the law of one price. Identical assets or risks should sell at the same price. Arbitrage is when two identical assets have different prices. Arbitrageurs can buy (long) the under-priced asset and sell (short) the overpriced asset for a riskless profit.

[31] The term 'US Person' is used in different US laws and regulations with different meanings. Under the definition of section 7701(a)(30) of the Internal Revenue Code a US Person includes a citizen or resident of the United States; a domestic partnership or corporation; and certain estates and trusts.

[32] $7\% = 10\%*(1 - 30\%)$.

[33] Offshore banking uses banks located outside the country of the investor's residence, typically in a low tax jurisdiction (tax haven) with the advantages of enhanced privacy, low or no taxation and protection against local financial or political instability.

2. Benchmarks

[34] Edwin Elton and Martin Gruber, 'Differential Information and Timing Ability', *Journal of Banking and Finance* (1991).

[35] Start with a benchmark value of $100. The benchmark has $50 equities and $50 bonds. The end values are $45 = 50*(1 - 10%) equities and $52.5 = 50*(1 + 5%) bonds. The end benchmark value is $97.5 = 45 + 52.5. New rebased benchmark weights are 46% = 45/97.5 equities and 54% = 52.5/97.5 bonds.

[36] CFA Institute.

[37] The Dow Jones Credit Suisse Fixed Income Arbitrage Hedge Fund index lost -11.75% over the 3-month period August to October 1998.

[38] Roger Lowenstein, *When Genius Failed: The Rise and Fall of Long-Term Capital Management* (Random House, October 2001).

[39] William Fung and David Hsieh, 'Hedge Fund Benchmarks: A Risk Based Approach', *The Financial Analysts Journal* 60 (2004).

[40] Roger Ibbotson, Peng Chen, Kevix Zhu, 'The ABCs of Hedge Funds: Alpha, Betas and Costs', *The Financial Analysts Journal* 67 (2011).

[41] Hedge Fund Research Index.

[42] A common way to address a one-day lag in pricing is to calculate the monthly performance of the portfolio from the NAVs of the 1st of the month to the 1st of the next month, instead of from the last trading day of the previous month to the last trading day of the current month.

[43] Arithmetic return = $\Sigma r_t / n$, where r_t is the return at time t, and n is the number of returns (Microsoft Excel formula AVERAGE). Arithmetic return is higher than geometric return. For example, a portfolio returns -10% in one period and then +20% in the second period. The arithmetic average return is 5% = (-10% + 20%)/2. The geometric average return is 3.9% = $[(1 - 10\%)*(1 + 20\%)]^{(1/2)} - 1$. Arithmetic return is the first moment of a distribution and standard deviation is its second moment. Arithmetic average should be used to estimate or express the return over a single time period. Geometric or compounded return describes the accumulation of portfolio value over time.

3. Risk objectives

[44] The only ways to generate returns without taking risk are through either holding cash or investing in true arbitrage opportunities.

[45] 'Knightian uncertainty' is named after Frank Knight who distinguished risk and uncertainty is his paper of 1921 'Risk, Uncertainty and Profit'.

[46] Richard Roll, 'A Mean-Variance Analysis of Tracking Error", *The Journal of Portfolio Management* (1992). Philippe Jorion, 'Portfolio Optimization with Constraints on Tracking Error', University of California at Irvine (2000).

[47] $\sigma = [\Sigma(r_n - \mu)^2/n]^{0.5}$ where σ is the standard deviation, r_n is the n return, μ is the average return and n is the number of returns. Microsoft Excel function STDEV.

[48] In probability theory, the normal distribution (Gaussian distribution) is a continuous probability distribution that has a bell-shape probability density function. The distribution is defined by its first two moments: mean (location of the peak) and variance (or standard deviation, which is the square root of the variance). The normal distribution is an outcome of the Central Limit Theorem (CLT), which states that under certain conditions the sum of a large number of random variables is distributed approximately normally.

[49] This is an approximation that assumes that returns are independent across time. This is reasonably realistic but may be incorrect.

[50] The return/risk ratio has increased from 2 to 9.2 going from an investment horizon of one year to 10 years. 9.2/2 = 4.6, which is larger than the square root of 10 (3.46). The reason is that return has been compounded, not only multiplied by time (10).

[51] More precisely 9.8% = 1.96*5%.

[52] Microsoft Excel formula AVERAGE.

[53] Microsoft Excel formula STDEV.

[54] Microsoft Excel formula SKEW.

[55] Microsoft Excel formula KURT.

[56] One technique for adjusting standard deviation for fat tails is the Cornish-Fisher approximation, which is covered in the chapter on risk management.

[57] NORMSDIST is the Microsoft Excel function that returns the standard normal cumulative distribution function. The distribution has a mean of zero and a standard deviation of one. Excel uses this function in place of a table of standard normal curve areas.

[58] $(\mu-x)/\sigma$ is the z-score of x.

[59] Geometric return is calculated by adding one to each periodic return, multiplying these values together, taking the nth root of the product (n is the number of returns) and subtracting one. Geometric Return = $\Pi(1 + r_n)^{(1/n)} - 1$. Investments compound at geometric returns. Geometric return is approximately equal to the arithmetic return less 50% of the variance of returns.

[60] LN is the formula that returns the natural logarithm of a number in Microsoft Excel.

[61] NORMSINV is a Microsoft Excel function that returns the inverse of the standard normal cumulative distribution. The distribution has a mean of zero and a standard deviation of one.

[62] In descriptive statistics, summary statistics are used to summarise a set of observations to communicate the population or entire sample as simply as possible. Statisticians commonly try to describe the observations in measure of location or central tendency (e.g. mean), dispersion (e.g. standard deviation), the shape of the distribution (e.g. skewness and kurtosis) and statistical dependence (e.g. correlation). When summary statics are used some information about the distribution is not used and lost.

[63] In statistics, a result is statistically significant if it is unlikely to have occurred by chance. As the number of observations or returns used to arrive at the result increases, it is more statistically significant.

[64] Peak to trough return. In Microsoft Excel, if column A contains portfolio levels starting in cell A1, dragging down the formula A1/MAX(A1:A1)-1 in cell B1 relative to the corresponding cells in column A calculates the drawdowns of the portfolio.

[65] The chapter on risk management covers more risk measurement and management techniques.

[66] In the United States the Federal Reserve Board's Open Market Committee (FOMC) sets the federal funds rate. In the United Kingdom the Bank of England (BOE) sets the base rate. In Europe the European Central Bank (ECB) sets the key interest rates for the Eurozone.

[67] 4.5% = (1 + 10%)*(1 - 5%) - 1.

[68] OPEC is the Organisation for Petroleum Exporting Countries.

[69] Credit Default Swap (CDS) is an agreement that the seller of the CDS will compensate the buyer in the event of a loan default or credit event. The buyer of the CDS pays the seller a series of payments (the CDS fee or spread) in exchange for receiving a payoff in the case of a credit event. Effectively, CDS is similar to an insurance against a credit event.

[70] Margin buying is purchasing securities using cash borrowed from a broker, using other securities as collateral. The difference between the value of the collateral and that of the loan has to stay above a minimum margin requirement to protect the

broker from a fall in the value of the collateral. When the value of collateral falls below the minimum margin requirement, the broker or exchange issues a margin call to the investor, who must increase the collateral or close the position.

[71] Market impact is the effect that a market participant has when buying or selling an investment. It is the extent to which the buying or selling moves the price against the buyer or seller, i.e. upward when buying and downward when selling.

[72] Basel Committee of Banking Supervision.

[73] Jérôme Kerviel was a rogue trader who caused Société Générale, the French bank, to lose €4.9 billion in January 2008 due to fraudulent, unauthorised trading.

[74] A graphical expression of interest rates over time, the yield curve is also known as the term structure of interest rates. There are different types of yield curves, such as par curve, zero coupon curve, swap curve, forward curve and so on. Par curve uses the gross redemption yield on government bonds. The shape of the yield curve could be upward sloping (as the maturity is longer, the interest rates are higher and investors are compensated for the longer maturity), downward sloping (as the maturity is longer, the interest rates are lower and it normally indicates reducing inflationary pressures) and flat yield curve (usually indicating a stable inflationary environment).

[75] YTM is the internal rate of return (IRR) earned by investors who buy the bond today at its prevailing market price, assuming that the bond will be held to maturity and all coupons and principal payments will be made on schedule. YTM is the discount factor that equates all cash flows to current price.

[76] Macaulay Duration is calculated using the formula $D_m = \Sigma(C_t/(1 + y)^t/P)t$. C_t is cash flow at time t, y is the bond yield-to-maturity, P is the current bond price and t is the time to maturity. Microsoft Excel has a formula DURATION to calculate Macaulay duration. Modified Duration is $D = D_m/(1 + y)$. Alternatively, $D = (P_{down} - P_{up})/2\Delta y P_0$. P_{down} and P_{up} are the bond prices for small changes downward and upward in yield, Δy is the change in yield, and P_0 is the current bond price.

[77] $C = (P_{up} + P_{down} - 2P_0)/(P_0{}^*\Delta y^2)$.

[78] The concept of good and bad volatility is discussed in Peter Stanyer, 'Guide to Investment Strategy: How to Understand Markets, Risk, Reward and Behaviour', *The Economist* (2006).

4. Rational or irrational markets

[79] Eugene Fama, 'Efficient Capital Markets: A Review of Theory and Empirical Work', *Journal of Finance* 25 (1970).

[80] Burton Malkiel, *A Random Walk Down Wall Street: The Time-tested Strategy for Successful Investing* (W. W. Norton & Company, 2007).

[81] Eugene Fama, 'Random Walks in Stock Market Prices', *The Financial Analysts Journal* 21 (1965).

[82] The random walk hypothesis is not a consensus. A different view is presented in Andrew Lo, Craig MacKinlay, *A Non-random Walk Down Walk Street* (Princeton University Press, 2001).

[83] Paul Samuelson was an American economist and the first American to win the Nobel Memorial Prize in Economic Sciences.

[84] Paul Samuelson, 'Proof that Property Anticipated Prices Fluctuate Randomly', *Industrial Management Review* 6 (1965).

[85] William Sharpe, "A Simplified Model for Portfolio Analysis", *Management Science* 9 (1963). William Sharpe, 'Capital Asset Prices – A Theory of Market Equilibrium Under Conditions of Risk', *Journal of Finance* 19 (1964).

[86] Franco Modigliani, Merton Miller, 'The Cost of Capital, Corporation Finance and the Theory of Investment', *American Economic Review* 48 (1958).

[87] Daniel Kahneman and Amos Tversky, 'Prospect Theory: An Analysis of Decision under Risk', *Econometrica* 47:2 (March 1979).

[88] Franco Modigliani and Merton Miller, 'The Cost of Capital, Corporation Finance and the Theory of Investment', *American Economic Review* 48 (1958).

[89] Hersh Shefrin and Meir Statman, 'The Disposition to Sell Winners Too Early and Ride Losers Too Long: Theory and Evidence', *Journal of Finance* 40 (1985).

[90] Amos Tversky and Daniel Kahneman, 'Judgment under Uncertainty: Heuristics and Biases', *Science, New Series* 185 (1974).

[91] Daniel Kahneman received the 2002 Noble Memorial Prize in Economic Sciences for "having integrated insights from psychological research into economic science, especially concerning human judgment and decision-making under uncertainty" (**www.nobelprize.org**).

[92] Daniel Kahneman and Mark Riepe, 'Aspects of Investor Psychology', *The Journal of Portfolio Management* 24 (1998).

[93] The posterior probability of a random event or an uncertain proposition is the conditional probability that is assigned after the relevant evidence is taken into account. Prior probability is the probability before the data is taken into account.

[94] Nicholas Nassim Taleb, *Fooled by Randomness: The Hidden Role of Chance in Life and in the Markets* (2004).

[95] Nicholas Nassim Taleb, *The Black Swan: The Impact of the Highly Improbable* (2008).

[96] Elroy Dimson and Andrew Jackson, 'High Frequency Performance Monitoring', *The Journal of Portfolio Management* (Fall 2001).

[97] Andrew Lo, 'The Adaptive Markets Hypothesis: Market Efficiency from an Evolutionary Perspective', *Journal of Portfolio Management* (2004).

[98] Heuristics refer to experience-based techniques for problem solving, learning and discovery. Where an exhaustive search is impractical, heuristic methods are used to speed up the process of finding a satisfactory solution. Examples include using a rule of thumb, an educated guess, an intuitive judgment or common sense.

[99] Daniel Kahneman and Mark Riepe, 'Aspects of Investor Psychology', *The Journal of Portfolio Management* 24 (1998).

5. The relationship between reward and risk

[100] William Sharpe, 'Capital asset prices: A theory of market equilibrium under conditions of risk', *Journal of Finance* 19 (1964). Jack Treynor, John Lintner and Jan Mossin have also developed the model independently.

[101] The Prize in Economics 1990, press release.

[102] $7.2\% = 4\% + 1.2{*}(8\% - 4\%)$

[103] In Microsoft Excel the function SLOPE returns the beta.

[104] Richard Roll, 'A Critique of the Asset Pricing Theory's Tests', *Journal of Financial Economics* 4 (1977).

[105] Eugene Fama and Kenneth French, 'Common Risk Factors in the Returns on Stocks and Bonds', *Journal of Financial Economics* 33 (1993).

[106] Stephen Ross, 'The arbitrage theory of capital asset pricing', *Journal of Economic Theory* 13 (1976).

[107] Nai-Fu Chen, Richard Roll, Stephen Ross, 'Economic Forces and the Stock Market', *Journal of Business* 59 (1986).

[108] William Sharpe, 'Mutual Fund Performance', *Journal of Business* 39 (1966).

[109] Portfolio managers may be tricksy.

[110] An alternative to the Sharpe ratio is Roy's safety-first criterion. The safety-first ratio is calculated as [E(r) - Threshold Return]/Var(r) where E(r) is the expected return; Threshold Return is the investor's required return and Var(r) is the volatility (variance, σ^2) of returns. The optimal decision is choosing a portfolio with the highest safety-first ratio. When returns are normally distributed the safety-first ratio is very similar to Sharpe ratio. Arthur Roy, 'Safety First and the Holding of Assets', *Econometrica* (July 1952).

[111] The Sortino ratio uses return over target return (originally known as the minimum acceptable return or MAR) in the numerator and a downside risk measure (square root of the target semi-variance) in the denominator.

[112] The omega ratio is the probability of a gain over the probability of a loss.

[113] The Calmar ratio is return over maximum drawdown.

6. Investment constraints

[114] In the United States a short-term holding period is one year or less. Short-term capital gains are taxed at the ordinary income tax rate. The long-term holding period is more than one year. Long-term capital gains are taxed at the discounted long-term capital gains rate, which could be 0% to 15% depending on the investor's marginal tax rate.

[115] Association of British Insurers (**www.abi.org.uk**).

8. Historical performance of asset classes

[116] Geometric Annualised Return = $\Pi(1 + r_t)^{(k/n)} - 1$ or in Microsoft Excel PRODUCT(1+rt1:rtn)^(k/n)-1. rt is the periodical return, n is the number of periodical returns and k is the number of periodical returns per year (i.e. 252 for daily returns, 12 for monthly returns and 4 for quarterly returns). When the length of the periodical returns is less than a year, annualising the returns may be misleading.

[117] The proportion of extreme negative returns decreases dramatically when the years of the Great Depression and World War II (1920s, 1930s and 1940s) are omitted.

[118] John Galbraith, *A Short History of Financial Euphoria* (Penguin, 1994).

[119] *Lady Windermere's Fan*, Act III (1892).

[120] Robert Shiller, *Irrational Exuberance*, Princeton University Press (2000)

[121] The Bretton Woods system of monetary management established the rules for commercial and financial relations among the world's major industrial states in the mid-20th century. It obliged each country to adopt a policy that maintained the exchange rate by tying its currency to the dollar. On 15 August 1971 the United States unilaterally terminated convertibility of the dollar to gold and the system ended as the dollar became a *fiat currency*.

[122] The Nixon Shock was a series of measures taken by US president Richard Nixon in 1971 including unilaterally cancelling the direct convertibility of the dollar to gold that essentially ended the existing Bretton Woods system.

[123] The Smithsonian Agreement was a December 1971 agreement that adjusted the fixed exchange rates established at the Bretton Woods Conference of 1944. Although the other currencies were still pegged to the dollar until 1973, the main difference from the previous regime was the abolition of the dollar's convertibility into gold guaranteed by the US Treasury, making the dollar effectively a fiat currency

[124] Carmen Reinhart and Kenneth Rogoff, 'This Time is Different: A Panoramic View of Eight Centuries of Financial Crises' (2008).

9. Combining asset classes

[125] Performance '% pa' is annualised (per annum) geometric average return.

10. Diversification

[126] The function CORREL is Microsoft Excel. $\rho_{x,y} = \text{Covariance}(x,y)/\sigma_x\sigma_y$. Covariance$(x,y) = \Sigma(x_i - \mu_x)(y_i - \mu_y)/N$.

[127] Harry Markowitz, 'Portfolio Selection', *The Journal of Finance* 7 (1952).

[128] Edwin Elton and Martin Gruber, 'Risk Reduction and Portfolio Size: An Analytic Solution', *Journal of Business* 50 (1977).

[129] James Tobin, 'Liquidity Preferences as Behavior Toward Risk', *The Review of Economic Studies* (February 1958).

[130] Equity sectors include consumer discretionary, consumer staples, energy, financials, health care, industrials, information technology, materials, telecommunication services and utilities.

[131] Steven Heston and Geert Rouwenhorst, 'Does Industrial Structure Explain the benefits of International Diversification?', *Journal of Financial Economics* 36 (1994).

[132] Gary Brinson, Randolph Hood, Gilbert Beebower, 'Determinants of Portfolio Performance', *The Financial Analysts Journal* (July-August 1986).

[133] Gary Brinson, Brian Singer, Gilbert Beebower, 'Determinants of Portfolio Performance II: An Update', *The Financial Analysts Journal* 47 (1991).

[134] Roger Ibbotson, Paul Kaplan, 'Does Asset Allocation Policy Explain 40, 90 or 100 Percent of Performance?', *The Financial Analysts Journal* (January/February 2000).

[135] William Sharpe, 'The Arithmetic of Active Management', *The Financial Analysts Journal* 47 (1991).

[136] Yesim Tokat, Nelson Wicas, Francis Kinniry, 'The Asset allocation Debate: A Review and Reconciliation', *FPA Journal* (2006).

[137] James Xiong, Roger Ibbotson, Thomas Idzorek, Peng Chen, 'The Equal Importance of Asset Allocation and Active Management', *The Financial Analysts Journal* 66 (2010).

[138] David Swensen, *Pioneering Portfolio Management: An Unconventional Approach to Institutional Investment* (Free Press, 2000).

[139] David Swensen, *Unconventional Success: A Fundamental Approach to Personal Investment* (Free Press, 2005).

[140] The Yale Endowment, 2009 (**www.yale.edu**).

[141] For a similar idea see Ashvin Chhabra, 'Beyond Markowitz: A Comprehensive Wealth Allocation Framework for Individual Investors', *The Journal of Wealth Management* 7 (2005).

[142] Robert Jaeger, Michael Rausch, Margaret Foley, 'Multi-Horizon Investing: A New Paradigm for Endowments and Other Long-Term Investors', *Journal of Wealth Management* (Summer 2010).

[143] Philip Fisher, *Common Stocks and Uncommon Profits* (Harper & Bros, 1958).

11. Capital Market Assumptions

[144] R^2 of a linear regression is the square of the correlation coefficient between the observed and modelled (predicted) data values. The statistic gives information about the goodness of fit of the model. It is a statistical measure of how well the regression line approximates the real data points.

[145] William Goetzmann, Roger Ibbotson, 'History of the Equity Risk Premium', Yale ICF Working Paper No. 05-04 (2005).

[146] Eugene Fama, Kenneth French, 'The Equity Premium', *Journal of Finance* 57 (2002).

[147] Elroy Dimson, Paul Marsh, Mike Staunton, 'Triumph of the Optimists: 101 Years of Global Investment Returns' (2002).

[148] Elroy Dimson, Paul Marsh, Mike Staunton, 'The Worldwide Equity Premium: A Smaller Puzzle' (2006).

[149] Elroy Dimson, Paul Marsh, Mike Staunton, 'Keeping faith with stocks', Credit Suisse Research Institute (2009).

[150] Roger Ibbotson, Peng Chen, 'Long-Run Stock Returns: Participating in the Real Economy', *The Financial Analysts Journal* (2003).

[151] Robert Arnott, Jason Hsu, John West, *The Fundamental Index: A Better Way to Invest* (Wiley, 2008).

[152] Elroy Dimson, Paul Marsh, Mike Staunton, 'Looking to the long term', Credit Suisse Research Institute (2009).

[153] US Federal Reserve Bank (Fed) for dollar, Bank of England (BoE) for pound and European Central Bank (ECB) for euro.

[154] Treasury Bills have a maturity below one year; Treasury notes have maturities between one and 10 years; and Treasury bonds have maturities above 10 years.

[155] Government bond yields reflect inflation expectations. When inflation expectations are low or high, bond yields are low or high, respectively, to compensate investors for inflation risk.

[156] Elroy Dimson, Paul Marsh, Mike Staunton, 'Looking to the long term', Credit Suisse Research Institute (2009).

[157] Real yield of an inflation-linked bond is its yield-to-maturity. The real yield is the growth rate of purchasing power earned by holding the bond to maturity.

[158] Elroy Dimson, Paul Marsh, Mike Staunton, 'Keeping faith with stocks', Credit Suisse Research Institute (2009).

[159] Roger Ibbotson and Peng Chen also found that P/E increases accounted for only a small portion of the total return of equity. Roger Ibbotson, Peng Chen, 'Long-Run Stock Returns: Participating in the Real Economy', *The Financial Analysts Journal* (2003).

[160] Elroy Dimson, Paul Marsh, Mike Staunton, 'Keeping faith with stocks', Credit Suisse Research Institute (2009).

[161] John Campbell, Samuel Thompson, 'Predicting Excess Returns Out-of-Sample: Can Anything Beat the Historical Average?', *Review of Financial Studies* 21 (2007).

[162] Myron Gordon, 'Dividends, Earnings and Stock Prices', *Review of Economics and Statistics*, The MIT Press (1959).

[163] Elroy Dimson, Paul Marsh, Mike Staunton, 'Keeping faith with stocks', Credit Suisse Research Institute (2009).

[164] Robert Arnott, Peter Bernstein, 'What Risk Premium is Normal', *Journal of Portfolio Management* 10 (January 2002).

[165] OECD is the Organisation for Economic Cooperation and Development. IMF is the International Monetary Fund.

[166] John Campbell, Robert Shiller, 'Valuation Ratios and the Long-Run Stock Market Outlook: An Update' (2001).

[167] Assumptions used for calculating expected returns are an inflation rate of 2.5% until January 1997 and a breakeven inflation rate from 10-year TIPS since then; end of month dividend yields and P/E ratios; a long-term GDP growth rate of 3.2%; lag of 2.0%; and a long-term P/E ratio of 16.8.

[168] Dividend yield of major indices are available on Bloomberg.

[169] Economic statistics of different countries are available at **stats.oecd.org**.

[170] Annualised P/E effect for next 10 years = $(16.8/15.7)^{(1/10)} - 1 = 0.7\%$.

[171] As of the end of June 2012 the 10-year Treasury yield was 1.67% and the US 10-year inflation-linked bond yield was -0.46%, giving a breakeven inflation rate of 1.67 - 0.46%) = 2.13%.

[172] Elroy Dimson, Paul Marsh, Mike Staunton, 'Looking to the long term', *Credit Suisse Global Investment Returns Yearbook 2009*, Credit Suisse Research Institute (2009).

[173] Yield-curve roll down is the return component associated with a bond's duration as it diminishes over time, along with the lower yield usually required for a shorter bond (assuming an upward sloping yield curve).

[174] Elroy Dimson, Paul Marsh, Mike Staunton, 'The quest for yield', *Credit Suisse Global Investment Returns Yearbook 2011*.

[175] Methodologies for unsmoothing autocorrelated returns and adjusting for fat tails are covered in the chapter on risk management.

[176] Bootstrapping is covered in the chapter on optimisation.

[177] Robert Arnott, Clifford Asness, 'Surprise! Higher Dividends = Higher Earnings Growth, *The Financial Analysts Journal* (2003).

[178] The Consumer Price Index (CPI) measures changes in the price level of consumer goods and services purchased by households. The Retail Price Index (RPI) measures change in the cost of a basket of retail goods and services in the United Kingdom.

[179] As of the end of June 2012. Source: Global financial data, Moody's Corporate AAA Yield.

[180] The Black-Litterman model is explained in the chapter on optimisation.

[181] Using monthly returns of UBS Convertible Bond index and S&P 500 Index from January 1999 to June 2012 and Microsoft Excel function SLOPE.

12. Optimisation

[182] Typical quantitative optimisation techniques include linear or nonlinear programming, quadratic programming or mixed integer programming.

[183] Robert Merton, 'An Analytic Derivation of the Efficient Portfolio Frontier', *Journal of Financial and Quantitative Analysis* 7 (September 1972).

[184] The asset allocation with a standard deviation of 4% is 8% equities, 68% bonds, 2% cash and 22% alternative investments, giving an expected return of 5.5% and Sharpe ratio of 1.12 (assuming risk-free return of 1%).

[185] Richard Gold, 'Why the Efficient Frontier for Real Estate is "Fuzzy" ', *The Journal of Real Estate Portfolio Management* 1 (1995).

[186] Under the assumption of quadratic utility mean-variance analysis is optimal.

[187] To show the required return the utility function is algebraically rearranged to $r_p = U + \sigma^2/\lambda$.

[188] $\sigma_G = (LN(1 + (\sigma_A/(1 + \mu_A))^2))^{0.5}$. $\mu_G = LN(1 + \mu_A) - (\sigma_G)^2/2$. Probability of exceeding x% over n years $= 1-NORMSDIST((LN(1+x)-\mu_G)/(\sigma_G/(n^{0.5})))$.

[189] Supranational is an international organisation or union whereby member states transcend national boundaries or interest to share in the decision-making and vote on issues pertaining to the wider grouping. The European Union and the World Trade Organisation are examples of supranationals.

[190] ARCH is Autoregressive Conditional Heteroskedasticity and GARCH is Generalised Autoregressive Conditional Heteroskedasticity.

[191] Benoit Mandelbrot, 'The Variation of Certain Speculative Prices', *The Journal of Business* 36 (1963).

[192] For example, -10% per annum in first five years and 30% per annum in last five years is equivalent to 8% per annum over 10 years.

[193] Vijay Chopra, William Ziemba, 'The Effect of Errors in Means, Variances and Covariances on Optimal Portfolio Choice', *Journal of Portfolio Management* (Winter 1993).

[194] Efron Bradely, Robert Tibshirani, *An Introduction to the Bootstrap* (1993).

[195] Michaud, Richard, *Efficient Asset Management* (Oxford University Press 1998).

[196] This is one of the reasons that using dividend yields and P/E ratios as the basis for formulating long-term equity expected returns rather than applying a constant equity risk premium to the 10-year government bond yield is more robust. It better links expected returns to the stage of the economic cycle.

[197] Fischer Black, Robert Litterman, 'Global Portfolio Optimization', *The Financial Analysts Journal* (September 1992).

[198] Bayesian probability interprets the concept of probability as a degree of plausibility of a proposition based on the given state of knowledge.

[199] In Bayesian probability, a prior probability distribution (called the prior) is the probability distribution expressing uncertainty about an uncertain quantity p before the *data* (e.g. the investor's views) is taken into account.

[200] Marginal contribution to risk (MCR) measures how much additional risk would be added to a portfolio if an additional 1% were to be invested in the investment for which MCR is measured.

[201] Market capitalisation data is available at the Word dataBank (**databank.worldbank.org**).

[202] William Sharpe, 'Imputing Expected Security Returns from Portfolio Composition', *Journal of Financial and Quantitative Analysis* 9 (1974).

[203] William Sharpe, 'Adaptive Asset Allocation Policies', *The Financial Analysts Journal* 66 (2010).

[204] William Sharpe, 'Investments' (1985).

[205] Fischer Black, Robert Litterman, 'Global Asset Allocation with Equities, Bonds, and Currencies', *Fixed Income Research*, Goldman Sachs & Company (1991).

[206] A diagonal matrix has values only in its diagonal and its other cells have values of zero.

207 If 36 monthly observations are used to calculate the covariance matrix $\tau = 1/(36 - 1) = 0.0286$. If 60 monthly observations are used $\tau = 1/(60 - 1) = 0.017$.

208 Charlotta Mankert, 'The Black-Litterman Model: Mathematical and Behavioural Finance Approaches Towards its Use in Practice', Sweden, Royal Institute of Technology School of Industrial Engineering and Management (2006).

209 In probability theory, according to the Central Limit Theorem (CLT) the sum of many independent and identically distributed (i.i.d.) random variables (or alternatively random variables with specific types of dependence) tends to be distributed according to one of a small set of attractor distributions. When the variance of the i.i.d. variables is finite, the attractor distribution is the normal distribution. CLT states that, under certain conditions, the mean of sufficiently large number of independent random variables, each with finite mean and variance, will be approximately normally distributed.

210 For a full review of the technical aspects of the Black-Litterman model refer to Thomas Idzorek, 'A Step-by-step Guide to the Black-Litterman Model' (2005).

13. Tactical Asset Allocation

211 William Sharpe, 'Integrated Asset Allocation', *The Financial Analysts Journal* (September-October 1987).

212 Richard Grinold, 'The Fundamental Law of Active Management', *The Journal of Portfolio Management* 15 (1989).

213 Cash equitisation is gaining instant market exposure. It is commonly achieved through futures contracts or ETFs. For example, if an investor wants to gain exposure to the equity market before selecting an active fund, equitisation can be used to maintain market exposure until the decision is made and implemented. This way, the portfolio is not out of the market.

14. Forecasting

214 Andrew Lo, Harry Mamaysky, Jiang Wang, 'Foundations of Technical Analysis: Computational Algorithms, Statistical Inference, and Empirical Implementation', *Journal of Finance* 55 (2000).

215 GDP is Gross Domestic Product. GDP is the market value of all officially recognised final goods and services produced within a country in a given period. GDP per capita is often considered an indicator of a country's standard of living.

[216] Harry Markowitz, 'Portfolio Selection', *The Journal of Finance* 7 (1952).

[217] Robert Merton, 'Lifetime Portfolio Selection under Uncertainty: The Continuous Time Case', *Review of Economics and Statistics* 51 (1969).

[218] Fischer Black, Myron Scholes, 'The Pricing of Options and Corporate Liabilities', *Journal of Political Economy* (1973).

[219] The Gross Domestic Product (GDP) of the United States has grown on average by 3.25% per annum between 1947 and 2011.

[220] Joseph Ellis, 'Ahead of the Curve: A Commonsense Guide to Forecasting Business and Market Cycles' (2005).

15. Economic cycle

[221] The chart was created using the output of the sine function (Microsoft Excel SIN function) for values between zero and two times pi (3.1416).

[222] The invisible hand is a term in economics used to describe the self-regulating nature of the marketplace. It is a metaphor first coined by Adam Smith.

[223] Leading indicators are measureable economic factors that change before the economy starts a particular pattern or trend. Leading indicators are used to predict changes in the economy, but are not always accurate. Bond yields, for example, are leading indicators because they reflect how traders anticipate and speculate upon trends in the economy. Lagging indicators are measureable economic factors that change after the economy has already begun to follow a particular pattern or trend. Unemployment, corporate profits, labour costs and interest rates are examples of lagging indicators.

[224] Bureau of Economic Analysis (**www.bea.gov**). The website of the Bureau is a source of free economic data.

[225] PMI is produced by the Institute for Supply Management within the Unites States (**www.ism.ws**) and the Markit Group outside the United States.

[226] The ISM Manufacturing Index is based on surveys of more than 300 manufacturing firms by the Institute of Supply Management.

[227] The New Residential Construction Report is issued by the US Census Bureau jointly with the US Department of Housing and Urban Development (HUD).

[228] The Citigroup Economic Surprise indices are objective and quantitative measures of economic news. They are defined as weighted historical standard deviations of data surprises (actual releases versus Bloomberg survey median). A positive reading

of the index suggests that economic releases have on balance beaten consensus. The indices are calculated daily in a rolling three-month window. The weights of economic indicators are derived from relative high-frequency spot FX impacts of 1 standard deviation data surprises. The indices also employ a time decay function to replicate the limited memory of markets.

16. Investment selection

[229] Benjamin Graham is considered the father of fundamental equity security analysis and value investing. He authored, together with David Dodd, the famous book *Security Analysis* (1934) and Graham authored the book *The Intelligent Investor* (1949) on value investing. Graham's most famous pupil was Warren Buffett.

[230] Managed investments are professionally managed portfolios of assets.

17. Investment selection process

[231] Peter Lynch, *One Up on Wall Street* (2000).

[232] Up-Market Capture measures the portfolio's relative performance during periods when the benchmark has risen. The measure is calculated by dividing the portfolio's returns by the benchmark's returns during up-market. Down-Market Capture measures the same but during down-markets. The array formula in Microsoft Excel for up-market capture is

$$PRODUCT(IF(r_b>0,(1+(r_p)/100),1))-1)/(PRODUCT(IF(r_b>0,(1+(r_b)/100),1))-1.$$

[233] Bernard Madoff pleaded guilty to 11 federal felonies in March 2009 and admitted to turning his wealth management business into a massive Ponzi scheme that defrauded thousands of investors of billions of dollars. Madoff said he had begun the Ponzi scheme in the early 1990s. However, federal investigators believe that the fraud began as early as the 1970s, and those charged with recovering the missing money believe the investment operation may never have been legitimate. The amount missing from client accounts, including fabricated gains, was almost $65 billion. The court-appointed trustee estimated actual losses to investors of $18 billion. On 29 June 2009 he was sentenced to 150 years in prison, the maximum allowed.

[234] In a secondary market investors purchase securities or assets from other investors, rather than from issuing companies. The national exchanges, such as the New York Stock Exchange and the NASDAQ, are secondary markets. In any secondary market trade, the cash proceeds go to an investor rather than to the underlying company/entity directly. A newly issued IPO will be considered a primary market

trade when the shares are first purchased by investors directly from the underwriting investment bank; after that any shares traded will be on the secondary market, between investors themselves. In the primary market prices are often set beforehand, whereas in the secondary market only forces like supply and demand determine the price of the security.

[235] Annual fund turnover = [(Purchase of securities + Sales of securities) - (Subscription of units + Redemption of units)]/[Average fund value over 12 months].

[236] Pacific Investment Management Company LLC (PIMCO) is an investment firm, headquartered in Newport Beach, California, and is the world's largest bond investor.

[237] William Sharpe, 'The Arithmetic of Active Management', *The Financial Analysts Journal* 47 (1991).

[238] Charles Ellis, 'The Loser's Game', *The Financial Analysts Journal* 31 (1975).

[239] $100/(1 + 3.0\%)^{10} = 74.4$.

[240] William Sharpe, 'Determining a Fund's Effective Asset Mix', *Investment Management Review* (December 1988) and William Sharpe, 'Asset Allocation: Management Style and Performance Measurement', *The Journal of Portfolio Management* (Winter 1992).

[241] Style score is calculated by $(\beta_{RU10VA}+\beta_{RU10GR})-(\beta_{RU20VA}+\beta_{RU20GR})$ and is represented by the x-axis (-100 is 100% growth and +100 is 100% value). Size score is calculated by $(\beta_{RU10GR}+\beta_{RU20GR})-(\beta_{RU10VA}+\beta_{RU20VA})$ and is represented by the y-axis (-100 is 100% small cap and +100 is 100% large cap).

[242] Such as BarraOne and Style Research.

[243] UCITS regulations have restrictions on the maximum exposure to any one CIS, maximum aggregated exposure to non-UCITS CIS and investment in CIS that can itself invest in other CIS without certain limitations.

[244] In the United Kingdom, Qualified Investor Schemes (QIF) are authorised investment funds (AIF, collective investment schemes authorised and regulated by the Financial Services Authority, FSA) with wider investment and borrowing powers than either UCITS or NURS funds and can be marketed only to qualified investors as defined by the FSA within the Collective Investment Scheme Source Book (COLL handbook), which can be found at **www.fsa.org.uk**.

[245] Patience is a good virtue. However, when necessary, investors should act quickly.

[246] Typically, a core-satellite strategy holds passive investment in its core and active investments in its satellite.

18. Active versus passive investments

[247] Michael Jensen, 'The Performance of Mutual Funds in the Period 1945-1964', *Journal of Finance* 60 (1968). Following Jensen's study numerous other studies have reached a similar conclusion that the average actively-managed fund does not capture alpha net of fees and expenses. Two recent studies include Laurent Barras, Olivier Scaillet, Russ Wermers, 'False Discoveries in Mutual Fund Performance: Measuring Luck in Estimated Alphas', *Journal of Finance* (2010) and Jeffrey Busse, Amit Goyal, Sunil Wahal, 'Performance and Persistence in Institutional Investment Management', *Journal of Finance* 65 (2010).

[248] Edouard Senechal, 'The Challenges of Declining Cross-Sectional Volatility', *Barra Horizon* (Autumn 2004).

[249] Eric Sorensen, Keith Miller, Vele Samak, 'Allocating between Active and Passive Management', *The Financial Analysts Journal* 54 (1998).

[250] Bill Miller is Chairman and CIO of Legg Mason. Miller was the portfolio manager of Legg Mason Capital Management Value Trust. Under his management the Trust outperformed its benchmark, the S&P 500 Index, over 15 consecutive years from 1991 to 2005. The Trust underperformed its benchmark over five out of six years during the period 2006 to 2011. Miller ceased co-managing the Trust in 2011.

[251] Mega caps are the biggest companies in the investment universe as measured by market capitalisation. Some mega caps include Apple, Exxon Mobil, Microsoft, PetroChina, Wal-Mart, IBM, Royal Butch Shell, AT&T, General Electric and China Mobile.

[252] On 3 July 2008 crude oil price hit an all-time record of $145.29 per barrel on the NYMEX, New York Mercantile Exchange.

[253] Edouard Senechal, 'The Challenges of Declining Cross-Sectional Volatility', *Barra Horizon* (Autumn 2004).

[254] Ernest Ankrim, Zhuanxin Ding, 'Cross-Sectional Volatility and Return Dispersion', *Financial Analysts Journal* 58 (2002).

[255] Bob Litterman, 'Modern Investment Management: An Equilibrium Approach' (2003).

[256] Jack Treynor, Fisher Black, 'How to Use Security Analysis to Improve Portfolio Selection', *Journal of Business* 46 (1973).

19. Investment vehicles

[257] The board of directors of an OEIC is usually headed by the authorised corporate director (*ACD*), an FSA authorised firm that assumes control over the board. The *depository* is a firm, usually a bank, authorised by the FSA and independent of the ICVC and the board, holding legal title to the ICVC investments and is responsible for their safe custody.

[258] Dual priced CIS create a price for creation and cancellation of units/shares. The creation price is different to the offer and the cancellation price is different to the bid. Additional created units are placed in the *manager box* for future purchases. When there are material redemptions units are sold from the manager box to protect existing investors from trading costs. Adjusting the bid/offer closer to cancellation/creation prices allows manager to protect existing investors in changing market conditions.

[259] Fund return can be calculated offer-to-bid or bid-to-bid. Offer-to-bid is net of initial sales charge. Bid-to-bid is gross of initial sales charge.

[260] Swing prices can affect return and risk calculations. Returns are calculated based on swung prices. If the initial or end prices have been swung, it will affect performance (hence it is affected both by trading activity in the fund and performance of the fund's investments) and volatility.

[261] The treating customers fairly (TCF) initiative is central to the delivery of the retail regulatory agenda of the Financial Services Authority (FSA) in the United Kingdom.

[262] The European Commission provides information on UCITS (**ec.europa.eu/internal_market/investment**).

[263] Over-the-counter derivatives are subject to counterparty risk. Exchange traded derivatives minimise counterparty risk through the clearing house and the margin facility.

[264] Leonard Kostovetsky, 'Index Mutual Funds and Exchange-Traded Funds', *The Journal of Portfolio Management* (Summer 2003).

20. Single-manager versus multi-manager

[265] A fettered fund-of-fund portfolio is restricted to investing in the internal funds managed by the same fund management group. An unfettered fund-of-fund portfolio can invest in external funds and possibly in internal funds as well.

22. Investment Management Process

[266] ESMA is the European Securities and Markets Authority (**www.esma.europa.eu**).

23. Portfolio Construction

[267] **www.russell.com/indexes**

[268] The Russell 3000 index measures the performance of the largest 3000 US companies representing approximately 98% of the investable US equity market.

[269] The top 10 holding in the Russell 1000 index are Apple, Exxon Mobil, IBM, Microsoft, Chevron, General Electric, Procter & Gamble, AT&T, Johnson & Johnson and Pfizer.

[270] Eugene Fama, Kenneth French, 'The Cross-Section of Expected Sock Returns', *Journal of Finance* 47 (1992).

[271] Bernd Scherer, *Portfolio Construction and Risk Budgeting* (Risk Books, 2007).

[272] US investors tend to view equities as three asset classes: US equities, EAFE equities (Europe, Australasia and Far East or developed non-US equities) and emerging markets.

[273] Roger Clarke, Harindra de Silva, Steven Thorley, 'Portfolio Constraints and the Fundamental Law of Active Management', *The Financial Analysts Journal* 58 (2002).

[274] Market impact is the effect that market participants have when buying or selling assets. When buying asset price may move upward and when selling it may move downward against the buyer or seller. For large investors (e.g. financial institutions), market impact needs to be considered before implementing investment decisions. If the moved amount is large relative to the turnover or volume of the asset, then the market impact may be several percentage points and should to be assessed alongside other transaction costs.

24. Implementation

[275] According to the FSA, Efficient Portfolio Management is investment techniques and instruments that are economically appropriate in that they are realised in a cost effective way and they are entered into for one or more of the following specific aims: reduction of risk; reduction of cost; generation of additional capital or income for the scheme with a risk level which is consistent with the risk profile of the scheme

and the risk diversification rules laid down in COLL (Collective Investment Schemes sourcebook).

[276] William Sharpe, 'Adaptive Asset Allocation Policies', *The Financial Analysts Journal* (May-June 2010).

25. Derivatives

[277] A Bermuda option can be exercised only on selected dates. An Asian option is linked to the average rate or price of the underlying over a time period.

[278] Fischer Black, Myron Scholes, 'The Pricing of Options and Corporate Liabilities', *Journal of Political Economy* (1973).

[279] Commonly, standardised ISDA (International Swaps and Derivatives Association) contracts are used to enter into swap transactions.

26. Currency

[280] $(1 + 10\%)*(1 - 15\%) - 1 = -6.5\%$

[281] According to PPP the amount of money across countries should have the same purchasing power and prices of goods across countries should only reflect exchange rates. According to the law of one price, in the absence of transaction costs and trade barriers identical goods should have the same price in different markets when the price is expressed in the same currency.

[282] Hilde Bjørland, Håvard Hungnss, 'The Importance of Interest Rates for Forecasting the Exchange Rate', Statistics Norway Research Department (2003) and Menzi Chinn, Guy Meredith, 'Testing Uncovered Interest Rate Parity at Short and Long Horizons During the Post-Bretton Woods Era', The National Bureau of Economic Research (NBER) (2005).

[283] John Campbell, Karine Serfaty-de Medeiros, Luis Viceira 'Global Currency Hedging', *The Journal of Finance* February (2010).

28. Risk management

[284] Risk management could have been included in Part 4 of the book, reviewing, or Part 2, implementing a solution. Risk should be managed as part of the portfolio management activities (first line of defence) and is therefore part of the solution. Risk

should also be reviewed to ensure that portfolio risk is in line with expectations (second line of defence). The reason to include it in this part of the book is that risk management is a critical part of portfolio management and it would be a mistake to leave it only for the review stage of the process.

[285] A third variable is possible but it makes the analysis three dimensional.

[286] To enter a matrix or array function in Microsoft Excel the buttons Ctrl-Shift-Enter must be pressed together.

[287] Remember to press Ctrl-Shift-Enter when entering this formula in Microsoft Excel.

[288] When entering the formula all the cells in the column with the MCRs for each investment should be selected and then Ctrl-Shift-Enter should be pressed together.

[289] Edward Qian, 'Risk Parity and Diversification', *The Journal of Investing* 20 (2011).

[290] Edward Qian, 'On the Financial Interpretation of Risk Contribution: Risk Budgets Do Add Up', *Journal of Investment Management* 4 (2006).

[291] Cornish and Fisher, 'Moments and cumulants in the specification of distributions', *Review of the International Statistical Institute* (1937).

[292] Mila Getmansky, Andrew Lo, Igor Makarov, 'An Econometric Model of Serial Correlation and Illiquidity in Hedge Fund Returns', *Journal of Financial Economics* 74 (2004).

[293] Additionally, some hedge funds include direct loans to companies for which no direct market price may be available.

[294] The first degree autocorrelation coefficients of these two hedge fund indices are not significantly different than zero at 95% confidence level.

[295] David Geltner, 'Smoothing in Appraisal-Based Returns', *Journal of Real Estate Finance and Economics* 4 (1991) and David Geltner, 'Estimating Market Values from Appraised Values without Assuming an Efficient Market', *Journal of Real Estate Research* 8 (1993).

[296] Chris Brooks, Harry Kat, 'The Statistical Properties of Hedge Fund Index Returns and Their Implications for Investors', *The Journal of Alternative Investments* (Fall 2002).

[297] Chris Brooks, Harry Kat, 'The Statistical Properties of Hedge Fund Index Returns and Their Implications for Investors', *The Journal of Alternative Investments* (Fall 2002).

29. Investment strategies

[298] Howard Marks, *The Most Important Thing: Uncommon Sense for the Thoughtful Investor* (Columbia University Press, 2001).

[299] Return worse than -4.0%.

[300] Elroy Dimson, Paul March, Mike Staunton, 'The Quest for Yield', *Credit Suisse Global Investment Returns Yearbook 2011*.

[301] The correlation between infrastructure and inflation is since July 2000. Infrastructure is represented by an index of listed infrastructure, not directly invested infrastructure.

[302] The liquidity trap of Japan refers only to near zero interest rates, not to the liquidity trap as defined in Keynesian economics.

31. Performance attribution

[303] Gary Brinson, Nimrod Fachler, 'Measuring Non-US Equity Portfolio Performance', *Journal of Portfolio Management* (Spring 1985).

[304] Carl Bacon, 'Excess Returns – Arithmetic or Geometric?', *Journal of Performance Measurement* (Spring 2002).

INDEX